MUSIC
IN THE
ELEMENTARY
SCHOOL

Robert Evans Nye

School of Music
University of Oregon

Vernice Trousdale Nye

College of Education
University of Oregon

4th Edition

MUSIC IN THE ELEMENTARY SCHOOL

Prentice-Hall, Inc., Englewood Cliffs, New Jersey 07632

Library of Congress Cataloging in Publication Data

NYE, ROBERT EVANS.
    Music in the elementary school.

    Includes bibliography and index.
    1. School music Instruction and study United States.
I. Nye, Vernice Trousdale, joint author. II. Title.
MT3.U5N94   1977   372.8'7   76-43982
ISBN 0-13-608117-7

MUSIC IN THE ELEMENTARY SCHOOL, 4th edition

Robert Evans Nye / Vernice Trousdale Nye

Printed in the United States of America

10 9 8 7 6 5 4 3 2 1

PRENTICE-HALL INTERNATIONAL, INC., *London*
PRENTICE-HALL OF AUSTRALIA PTY. LIMITED, *Sydney*
PRENTICE-HALL OF CANADA, LTD., *Toronto*
PRENTICE-HALL OF INDIA PRIVATE LIMITED, *New Delhi*
PRENTICE-HALL OF JAPAN, INC., *Tokyo*
PRENTICE-HALL OF SOUTHEAST ASIA PTE. LTD., *Singapore*
WHITEHALL BOOKS LIMITED, *Wellington, New Zealand*

Contents

3 Learning, 19

4 Individualized Instruction in Music, 43

5 Planning and Organizing to Teach Music, 56

6 Evaluation, **104**

**LEARNING
MUSIC BY
MOVEMENT
AND
RHYTHM**

II

7 Movement, Rhythm, and Dance, **115**

8 Percussion Instruments, **128**

9 Learning Music Concepts, **142**

Preface

This fourth edition of *Music in the Elementary School* is designed as a text and resource book for the elementary education major, the music major, the student teacher, and the teacher-in-service. It is a comprehensive book from which college teachers and their students can select activities and problems that are pertinent to their needs. For example, students can be assigned selected activities in the methods class, continue to use the book during student teaching, and, still later, in professional teaching.

The authors consider music education to be a part of education rather than an isolated art. The various thought processes, individualization of instruction, levels of accomplishment, discovery, inquiry, the conceptual approach, and other aspects of educational thought and theory become components of music teaching. The learning sequence—from data to concepts to generalizations—is explained and exemplified, and the classroom becomes a laboratory for learning music. Thus, how children learn, selecting content for teaching, and the choosing of strategies come into focus rather than an easy prescribed routine which is unrealistic in competent day-to-day professional teaching.

The grade level approach has become less tenable because of the stress on the importance of teaching at the level of understanding of each child and the growing trend to organize children in non-graded groups. This edition reflects the tendency toward increasing individualization of instruction. However, frequent references to grade or age levels provide assistance for those who maintain the grade level organization.

The reader will find a new organization of the book and some new chapters. There are now six Parts: Educational Foundations, Learning Music by Movement and Rhythm, Learning Music by Improvisation and Composition, Learning Music by Singing and Playing, Analyzing Music, and For Further Study. These titles reflect the belief that music is learned by means of four basic activities with which musical concepts are directly related: movement, making music, creating music, and analyzing music. New chapters are "History and Philosophy," which provides some background for the subject, "Individualized Instruction in Music," "A New Pathway to Music," which is concerned with improvisation and composition, "Analysis," which has the purpose of broadening the concept of listening experiences, and "References for Further Study," which attempts to protect the reader from superficial treatment of large subjects by referring to basic sources.

A balance of teaching strategies is recommended, and teachers are advised to keep in mind that music should be taught as an experience to be lived rather than as a subject to be learned.

The education and teaching experience of one of the authors has been primarily within the field of music; that of the other has been primarily within the field of education. They hope that their collaboration will reinforce the concept of music as an essential part of elementary education.

The authors acknowledge the valuable assistance of Thomas Regelski and Allen Richardson, who provided suggestions and encouragement for the writing of this revision.

R.E.N.
V.T.N.

MUSIC
IN THE
ELEMENTARY
SCHOOL

The best teacher will not be confined to any particular previously laid out plan, but will from the different methods make out one of his own; not indeed one that is stereotyped and unalterable, but one that he may modify and adapt to the varying wants and circumstances of his different classes.

LOWELL MASON
1792–1872

EDUCATIONAL FOUNDATIONS OF MUSIC TEACHING

I

History and Philosophy

Historical Aspects of Music Education Music education in the United States has an interesting history that places it in a unique position among the branches of music study. It is an expression of the needs of the people rather than a product of an artistic elite. Its roots are in the singing school of the early days of the nation when Lowell Mason, William Billings and others responded to the desire of communities that church singing be improved by organized instruction in music fundamentals and note reading.[1]

Some classroom teachers included music as part of the school day from the earliest times, but efforts to accept music officially might have been delayed further had not Lowell Mason volunteered to teach music gratis in one school and to provide the instructional materials at his own expense. His great success resulted in being officially authorized in August, 1838, to teach and supervise music in the Boston schools. By 1841 about one half of the students in the upper two grades of Boston's grammar schools were receiving regular music instruction. These students were at today's junior high or middle school level. In 1854 Mason claimed that there existed "a

[1] The earliest known singing school was in 1712.

multitude of young persons . . . who are much better able to appreciate and to perform music than were their fathers; and experience proves that large classes of young persons, capable of reading music with much accuracy, may easily be gathered together in almost any part of New England, or indeed, of the United States."

Among Mason's teaching principles were the following, condensed by the authors:

1. Since students learn by seeing and hearing, and because what they learn should be an evident and logical deduction from well established facts, a teacher guides the pupils to learn by their own powers of reasoning.

2. Educational steps are placed in a logical order that coincides with the natural development of the child, who learns a thing step by step when the necessary skills and background are acquired.

3. The teacher does not depend fully upon books, rules, or formulas, and thus will not teach by merely telling. The teacher depends upon present proof making its appeal to the mind of the pupil.

4. The primary values of music instruction will be social and moral.

5. There will be a strict but loving guidance of the pupil; music should be pleasant and agreeable; the pupil will be actively thinking and learning things constantly; gratification will come from the attainment of knowledge.

Mason's much quoted motto for teachers was:

THINGS BEFORE SIGNS;
PRINCIPLES BEFORE RULES;
PRACTICE BEFORE THEORY.

Elementary school music began to be offered officially in some cities in the 1850s, but it was not until 1864 that music instruction was approved and financed in Boston's primary grades. Luther Whiting Mason joined the Boston music staff, specializing in elementary school music and becoming its dominant figure in that century, being called upon to assist the music programs of Japan.

**Music
Methods**

In 1834 the Boston Academy of Music formed a class for instruction in the methods of teaching music, a short summer lecture course held for a few days in August. Each succeeding year enrollment increased until there were 200 persons from all parts of the nation being instructed in how to improve their teaching in singing schools and public schools. As early as 1836 some of these students organized their free time to discuss other matters of concern to music education, church music, and performing groups. Lowell Mason encouraged them, and in 1840 helped to form the National Music Convention to satisfy this demand. Because in those days colleges and universities did not offer course work in music education, other music conventions were organized throughout the country. These conventions were brief, usually from three to five days in length. Their value and popularity created a demand for the *musical normal institutes* held in summers for two to three months duration, forerunners of the present-day summer session. George Root organized the first institute in New York City in 1853. These continued into the 1920s, when teachers' colleges began offering summer courses in their music education departments. The most important figure in innovative elementary school music of that day was Mrs. Satis Coleman, Teachers College, Columbia University, who antedated the approach of Carl Orff to some degree.

Music education became an integral part of the teacher education program of the nation, and the four year degree in it, first introduced at the Oberlin Conservatory, became possible in the teachers colleges of the 1920s. Thus, music education can be traced from the singing school, music convention, and musical normal institute to the teachers college. To repeat: the roots of music education are in the needs of the common man; this is in contrast to other branches of music study, the roots of which can be traced to clerical origins or to aristocratic societies which produced a cultural elite.

About the time the teachers' college appeared to have made a permanent place for itself on the American scene, a countermovement began in state legislatures that almost obliterated that institution. The history of this movement is not entirely clear, but some observers claim that it was a result of the vast majority of legislators having earned "subject matter" degrees and their belief that teachers colleges were unnecessary because, "If one knows his subject, that is all he needs to know to be able to teach it." Thus, education, and music education along with it, became departments in liberal arts colleges and universities, institutions that originally offered only subject matter with no vocational objectives. In a teachers college the course work in all areas is related to the vocational goal as much as possible. This is not common practice in liberal arts institutions, thus music education, along with the rest of education, was and is to this day affected by this dislocation from the teachers college environment.

In the liberal arts environment, elementary music education often suffered due to a confusion of the word "elementary" with "simple" by faculty and administrators who lacked knowledge of education. There were many examples of college teachers being assigned by such administrators to teach elementary school music in the erroneous belief that because it was "simple," anyone who knew music was qualified to teach it. Fortunately, much less of this situation exists today, although it has yet to be completely eradicated. This is only one of the many problems created when education was placed under the control of people who often had little understanding of or sympathy with education. Even today, some music departments fail to recognize what is inherent in the term "music education": that education is the noun and music the adjective.

A fortunate circumstance, the work in music education of two European composers of stature, Zoltán Kodály and Carl Orff, has tended to increase understanding of and respect for elementary music education in the United States. Another healthy influence has been the interest of private music teachers in applying methods adapted from music education to their studio teaching. Still another positive tendency has come from the almost universal realization that the large majority of music graduates will become teachers, if not in public schools, in private studios and in institutions of higher learning. This has resulted in a closer bond between all areas of music because of the importance of teaching to the large majority of students.

**Aims of
Instruction**

In the early days of music education in the United States there were two primary aims of instruction, to read music and to sing acceptably. Later, performance, both vocal and instrumental, was added to these. Teachers assumed that by this contact with music, understanding of music and improved social and ethical behavior were somehow absorbed in ways that defied explanation. At any rate, performance became the major criterion of music programs. Still later, appreciation and understanding of music subject matter were assigned positions of importance among the goals of instruction. The attempts to realize these new goals usually resulted in learning mere facts about music rather than acquiring the ability to analyze music. A more recent aim has been to achieve musical responsiveness through the study of music by using as tools the concepts that comprise music as an academic discipline. Achieving this is aided by the development of instructional and performance objectives in the cognitive, affective, and psychomotor domains. The teacher should be cognizant that some affective evidence is difficult or impossible to acquire. Music is an *affective* art, based upon feelings that cannot be accurately verbalized. Nevertheless, music involves *cognitive* (intellectual) and *psychomotor* (physical) experiences and is learned through the integration of these three learning "domains," since no one domain functions in isolation.

The general goal of the teacher of music is to create a learning environment that will not only develop the talents of the musically gifted but will develop aesthetic musical responsiveness in all students.

A Philosophy of Music Education

Bennett Reimer, who proposes an aesthetic approach to teaching music, states that the arts are vital to humanity because they meet two basic human needs: self-understanding and the need for significance.[2] People use the arts as means to explore reality.

To have an aesthetic experience the learner first has musical perception, and follows this with a musical reaction. This is similar to an earlier teaching idea: musical experience first, the study of what was experienced second, and third, the musical experience repeated, with richer meaning to the learner. This makes musical experience paramount, and the study portion of the method becomes subservient to the event of the first importance

[2] Bennett Reimer, *A Philosophy of Music Education* (Englewood Cliffs, N.J.: Prentice-Hall, Inc., 1970).

—the musical experience itself. Thus, musical experience is the end, and the study of music a means to that end.

Reimer emphasizes exploration as the primary avenue to music study; it is basic to an aesthetic approach or method. In order for students to perceive music (to have a musical perception), they must be analytical listeners on their level of development as they participate in all musical activities. To be an analytical listener a person must be equipped with certain tools, and these are concepts of rhythm, dynamics, tempo, melody, harmony, texture, tone quality, and form. Again, these are tools developed and used by students in their exploration of music; they are *not* ends in themselves.

The definition of perception is a broad one that goes far beyond simple recognition. It includes behaviors such as discriminating, discerning, discovering, recalling, relating, comparing, anticipating, and distinguishing.[3] It may be that there is no higher level of perceiving than that involving a musical composition. The musical reaction that follows perception consists of subjective responses such as feeling, being absorbed, being moved, and empathizing. Reimer lists four "means" behaviors that are aesthetic only to the extent they influence perception and reaction: producing music (singing, playing, composing, conducting), analyzing music (examining, classifying, comparing, contrasting, differentiating, and others), evaluating music (judging, rating, criticizing, justifying, ranking), and valuing music (liking, identifying with, admiring, cherishing). The authors would add degrees of disliking to the valuing list. Acceptance of the above rationale is not intended to deny the need for learning about the cultural heritage and for experiencing music as a socializing influence.

Various organizations and conferences have, since about 1960, made serious attempts to redefine the role of music in education. As early as 1959 the American Association of School Administrators adopted the following resolution:

> It is important that pupils, as a part of general education, learn to appreciate, to understand, to create, and to criticize with discrimination those products of the mind, the voice, the hand, and the body which give dignity to the person and exalt the spirit of man.

The National Association of Secondary School Principals added in 1962:

> Schools push for excellence in all subjects. At the same time, the mass media outside the school all too frequently focuses students' attention on shallow, mediocre models of the good life. Students exercise value standards as they make independent intellectual judgments about artistic quality in all of these experiences. . . . Students need to learn how to exercise social responsibility in making personal and group decisions about the arts.[4]

---

[3] Bennett Reimer, "Aesthetic Behaviors in Music," in *Toward an Aesthetic Education* (Reston, Va.: Music Educators National Conference, 1971), p. 76.

[4] National Association of Secondary School Principals, *The Arts in the Contemporary School* (Washington, D.C.: The Association, 1962), pp. 4–5.

In response to these statements and the declarations of the Yale Seminar (1963) and the Tanglewood Symposium (1968), there has been brought into being a curriculum based upon the concepts comprising the structure of music as an academic discipline—those concerned with tempo, dynamics, rhythm (duration), pitch (melody, harmony), texture, tone quality, and form.

The position of the preschool and elementary school has been enhanced by research findings that state ages three through eleven as the optimum time for developing attitudes, interests, and skills. In these years, the musical experience should deal with broad areas rather than with activities such as singing, music reading, and listening taught in relative isolation. These broad areas are composing, performing, and analyzing music with conceptual learning an integral part of each area. Music is now "sound based," as it should be. While method is a necessary way to organize instruction, the most important single factor is the teacher. A competent teacher can succeed with any feasible method.

When music functions as it should in the classroom, children will enjoy music and have aesthetic experiences with it. Enjoyment will result from children's involvement in the processes of planning, producing, analyzing, and evaluating musical experiences which grow out of realistic personal and environmental problems that have significance in their lives.

References

BIRGE, EDWARD B., *History of Public School Music in the United States.* Philadelphia: Oliver Ditson Company, 1937. Reprinted by the Music Educators National Conference, Reston, Va., 1967. An interesting account of the early years of American music education.

GONZO, CARROLL, "Aesthetic Experience: A Coming of Age in Music Education," *Music Educators Journal,* December 1971, p. 34.

LARSON, RICHARD, "Behaviors and Values: Creating a Synthesis," *Music Educators Journal,* October 1973, p. 40.

MEAD, MARGARET, "Music is a Human Need," *Music Educators Journal,* October 1972, p. 54.

REIMER, BENNETT, *A Philosophy of Music Education.* Englewood Cliffs, N.J.: Prentice-Hall, Inc., 1970.

———, "Putting Aesthetic Education to Work," *Music Educators Journal,* September 1972, p. 28.

RICH, ARTHUR L., *Lowell Mason, the Father of Singing Among the Children.* Chapel Hill, N.C.: The University of North Carolina Press, 1946.

TELLSTROM, A. THEODORE, *Music in American Education Past and Present.* New York: Holt, Rinehart and Winston, Inc., 1971.

A Learning Environment for Music

Organizational Plans

Teachers must be prepared to work in several different types of school organizations. The design that has become customary is the 6-3-3 plan, referring to years in the elementary, junior high, and high schools. A more recent pattern is a 4-4-4 organization: primary, middle, and high school. Some schools include kindergarten with the primary school, resulting in a 5-4-4 arrangement. An objection to these new patterns is that the mixture of ten-to-fourteen-year-olds seems to be illogical in terms of their differing stages of physical, social, and mental development. Some educators answer this objection with their assumption that the ten-and-eleven-year-olds of today are far more mature physically and socially than those of that age group earlier in this century, and that the placing of the ninth graders in the high school will free the middle school, which includes the other two junior high years, from a former domination by the senior high school.

Alternative schools are organized to meet the demands of the community, segments of the community, and some educators. They indicate dissatisfaction with the established system of education. By means of these schools, special needs are met, and the educational program is assumed to be more relevant to the learner. Such schools range from traditional schools in which the "basics" are emphasized, to experimental schools of many types. They can include the entire school, some age levels within the school, or only one group of students. An attractive example was the IMPACT project [1] in which the arts formed the core of the elementary school curriculum and the other subjects were planned in accordance with this concept.

Open education is a plan in which children are to be free to explore, make observations, reflect, and test their ideas. The school day is integrated, not segmented, and learners can pursue a problem of their choice in depth, unhampered by traditional subject barriers. Some group instruction takes place, but the focus is on the individual learner and the freedom to learn.

The *self-contained classroom* is a type of curricular organization in which a group of students is in contact with one teacher for a major portion of the school day. It is in contrast to the *departmental* organization which divides the day into as many time periods as there are subjects, with each subject taught by a different teacher who specializes in it. Historically, there are three different concepts of the self-contained classroom: (1) all subjects taught by one teacher (with occasional assistance), (2) all subjects except music, art, and physical education taught by one teacher, and (3) all subjects in the primary school taught by one teacher, with varying degrees of departmentalization in the middle school. In relation to this it may be of interest to teachers of music that art, music, and physical education were introduced into the curriculum as special subjects, taught by specialists, and they are identified in educational history as the traditionally specialized subjects. Even so, history also reveals several reversals of opinion that have at times assigned basic responsibility for music teaching to classroom teachers.

In some situations the organizational plan of the school may be derived from restrictions demanded by building space rather than from any educational theory. The amount of time allocated to music teaching is often determined by the type of organization employed within a school or within a class. The organization also influences the space needed, the learning materials and equipment, and the number and qualifications of personnel.

In order for children to become involved in the excitement and process of learning, they must have access to a learning environment that makes it possible for them to explore their interests and problems.

---

[1] *Arts Impact: Curriculum for Change—A Summary Report* (University Park, Pa.: The Arts IMPACT Evaluation Team, 1973). Gene C. Wenner, et al., "IMPACT," *Music Educators Journal* (January 1973).

The Physical Environment

Learning is difficult when attempted in impure air, uncomfortable temperatures, and improper lighting. The busy teacher who is in the same classroom all day will sometimes fail to notice insufficient ventilation, unhealthy temperatures, and faulty lighting because of gradual changes as the day progresses. Classroom committees can be established to give children experience in assuming responsibility and to relieve the teacher of part of this routine task.

The arrangement of the furniture influences the type of learning that can take place. Seating of the entire class should be appropriately arranged to make it possible for students to take part in discussion as well as in individual and group work, and to provide opportunity for listening effectively and courteously to any class member who is speaking, singing, or playing an instrument. Chairs and desks should be selected for the varying sizes of children so that each child can be comfortably seated.

The varied activities in music make moveable furniture a necessity. Seating (or temporary standing) will be changed at times for singing in large and small groups, playing instruments, creative interpretations, rhythmic responses, individualized instruction, and dance. Special seating may be needed if some of the children have difficulty hearing or seeing. The manner in which children move from one activity to another is established by clear instruction from the teacher and by teacher-pupil planning. The teacher's well-formulated questions stimulate the children to plan and take responsibility for this part of classroom routine. Ways of leaving and entering a music room, going to and from a music room or assembly room, and moving books, instruments, and other materials are additional aspects of organization and routine.

In listening-analysis activities the mood of a recorded composition can be heightened by drawing shades, turning lights on or dimming them, by employing color or placing objects in a way to reinforce the aural effect.

When instruments and equipment are selected, the teacher chooses those that produce excellent tone quality, are durable, attractive, and easy to store, and are suitable for the age group. When songs are selected, the teacher looks for simplicity and variety in the melody, repeated parts that assist rapid learning, content interesting to the age group, proper range for the voices, appropriate length for the maturity level, rhythmic appeal, and a suitable, attractive accompaniment. The song is examined to find what teaching purpose it can serve. Is the song worth learning? Is it a worthy art, folk, or popular song? Does it contribute to the realization of the stated objectives?

Every school should provide each student from age seven and up with copies of two of the music textbooks (basal series) and access to a variety

11

of supplementary books and materials. Recordings and teacher's books accompanying the textbooks should also be available. Each building should contain a learning resource center or library that provides not only books about music but recordings, video tape equipment, films, filmstrips, transparencies, and programed and self-instructional materials. The MENC [2] lists the following instruments expected to be in every basically equipped classroom: various drums of high and low pitches, six pairs of rhythm sticks, sandblocks, woodblocks, maracas, claves, cymbals, finger cymbals, tambourines, triangles, cowbell, five sets of melody bells, one set of resonator bells, jingle bells, jingle clogs, gong, slide whistle, four soprano recorders, assorted xylophone-type instruments, four Autoharps, one ukulele, and one guitar. Besides these there should be easy access to an overhead projector, screen, film projector, record player, two tape recorders, and a metronome.

A system of distributing materials and collecting them should be planned with and executed by the children, who should know where and how to store them. For example, if small plastic wind instruments are used, each should be labeled with the child's name and be placed in containers to keep them clean. For sanitary reasons children should not exchange instruments, but if this is necessary, a disinfectant for plastic must be used; the instruments must be cleaned periodically with disinfectant applied with a small brush or cotton swab.

Criteria must be established, preferably with the children, for proper use of the room in viewing films and television, listening to radio programs, and using the music learning center or stations. A classified card file of recordings should be part of the teacher's equipment. Teachers who are prepared, and who have made provision for proper directions and routine, usually exude a feeling of confidence and security that is reflected in the behavior of the child. Children sense insecurity in teachers and they are disturbed by it.

The physical environment necessary for individualized instruction is one in which the customary rows of desks are absent. Instead, children work at tables, on the floor, at wall displays, at chalkboards and charts, and at learning stations. Hallways, closets, booths, and alcoves are used to provide space for many types of activities. There is a variety of borrowed, inexpensive, and free materials and objects with which children experiment. The usual music equipment is present: melody instruments, music books and books related to music, percussion instruments, chording instruments, recordings, pictures, puzzles and games, and flash cards. The sound center recommended by the Manhattanville Music Curriculum Program will probably be included, and there might be a science-of-sound center, a multimedia center, an electronic music center, and an instrument construction center. Care is taken that students are not confused by an

[2] Music Educators National Conference, *The School Music Program: Description and Standards* (Reston, Va.: The Conference, 1974).

overly rich environment; teachers need to arrange one that challenges and interests but does not overwhelm. When students work at individual projects they may need equipment such as radios, phonographs, tape recorders of varied complexity, tape players, teaching machines, television sets, film and filmstrip projectors, and perhaps an electronic piano and a synthesizer. While programed materials are in conflict with the creative and discovery approach, they may be suited to the learning style of some children. Furthermore, programed instruction has values for every student in the area of music skills, and for reinforcing the learning of both skills and concepts. The crucial issue is how well these materials assist in the realization of the identified objectives. See Chapter Four, *Individualized Instruction in Music.*

In the elementary classroom a music learning center can be located out of traffic lines and in a place in the room which is relatively secluded, yet accessible. It may be in a booth off the main classroom or it may consist of one large table or several smaller ones upon which can be placed materials such as books, bells and other small instruments, music to play on the instruments, recordings, a record player with headsets, a viewer, filmstrips and a filmstrip projector, a tape recorder, various sound-producing materials, and machines for experimentation. The center could include bulletin boards on which can be mounted information about community musical events, composers, recommended radio and television programs, musical achievements of students, charts, musical symbols, cartoons, jackets from books about music and from recordings, newspaper and magazine clippings, notation of unnamed familiar songs which can be identified by studying this notation, favorite songs, rhythm patterns, and pictures relating to musical subjects. However, the bulletin board must be arranged attractively and changed frequently if it is to accomplish its mission of attracting maximum interest. Soft mallets for the bells and headsets with the record player can eliminate or reduce interference with other activities in the room. By teacher-pupil planning, criteria for the use of the music materials and equipment are established. These criteria should also include when and how children are to work in the music learning center.

Expanding the Classroom

Music teachers of today use cultural resources in the community to enrich learning. The expansion of the learning environment makes it necessary for the teacher to become familiar with all areas and facilities of the school plant and community which can be useful for music instruction. When students explore the musical resources of the community, and when parents and other community resource people contribute to the music program, the physical boundaries for music learning are thereby expanded.

Scheduling and Time Allotment

The MENC-recommended time allotment for each child in grades K–3 varies from 100 to 150 minutes per week on a daily schedule. The time allotment for each child in grades 4–6 varies from 150 to 200 minutes per week on a daily schedule. Instrumental music classes meet from 100 to 150 minutes weekly for two or three days of the week.

At the present time there is widespread experimentation with scheduling music study. A music teacher may have large blocks of unscheduled time in order to be available to individual students and small groups who need assistance in whatever type of music activity they have contracted. Sometimes activities are scheduled on an hourly basis for intermediate grades that individualize instruction; for example, guitar lessons at 9 o'clock, elementary chorus at 10 o'clock, and analyzing music at 11 o'clock. Conventional types of scheduling may approximate daily periods of at least twenty minutes for primary grades and periods of thirty minutes for at least three times a week for intermediate grades. When compared to MENC standards, this time allotment for primary grades is minimal and that for intermediate grades substandard.

Classroom teachers who teach their own music are free to alter the music schedule from day to day and week to week as long as their programs are accomplishing what they should in terms of the objectives.

There is danger in music specialists being overscheduled to the point where they lack time to assist and plan with classroom teachers and children. This can happen in situations where the classroom teachers are involved in teaching music as well as in situations where specialists are theoretically solely responsible for it. Music learning takes place in many situations other than in the music period, and regardless of how much or how little teaching responsibility a specialist may be assigned, the importance of the classroom teacher in creating an overall learning environment results in that person being an indispensible figure in the total music program.

Managing the Classroom

A teacher's knowledge and skill in music are of value only in terms of organizing and managing the music activities so that they strike a balance between the routine and the creative, between stability and change. Efficient routine is necessary to avoid overlooking detail; the main reason for taking care of detail is to provide more pupil-teacher time and energy for creative and problem-solving types of learning and teaching. A teacher needs to know procedures that should and should not be routinized. The children should understand the value of these procedures, exactly how they are to be done, and then evaluate the degree of efficiency resulting from them. While overroutinization can stifle creativity, a proper amount of routine saves time and assists the orderly sequence of events in the music period. Experienced teachers have found the following ideas to be helpful.

A chord played on piano or Autoharp, or a tone played on the bells can be a signal for a change of activity. Such means for giving directions are more conducive to pleasant feelings than the teacher's voice directing children to do something. When a teacher makes advance preparations for a lesson by doing such routine things as assembling materials, writing on the chalkboard the titles and page numbers of songs, words to rote songs, notation for class study, the order of activities, and other directions, general efficiency is promoted. Through pupil discussion, evaluation, and modification of the order and directions of activities indicated, children are involved and see meaning and purpose in the sequence of activities. The teacher should make certain that every child can see and hear what is spoken, sung, played, danced, or dramatized.

Grouping

In the effort to make provision for individual differences and the ways children learn, teachers group students in order to accommodate varied interests, abilities, and rates and styles of learning in music. The groups work in designated areas of the room, in the hall, the library, in conference rooms or other nearby areas. The activities with which the groups are engaged could include: composing music; planning accompaniments; evaluating different interpretations; practicing difficult sections of music; learning songs from recordings; or any number of things. While grouping can be done at any level, it can be more effectively employed at the intermediate level. When children have not participated in group work, the teacher should begin by organizing one small group while the remainder of the students work as a class or as individuals. The teacher then *gradually* organizes additional groups until the time comes when most or all of the class can be involved in this manner.

In groups:

concepts can be clarified, hypotheses stated, generalizations formed and evaluated. Feelings of belonging, security, acceptance, respect, and mutual trust can be developed. . . . A constructive and experimental approach to learning can be nurtured, and the excitement of discovery and sharing of ideas with the group can increase the depth and breadth of children's learning. There are limitations as well as values of group work that teachers should know. *First,* group work should be limited to some purpose that members of the group can share. *Second,* group work should be limited to activities in which the children possess or can be taught the skills needed to develop the activities. . . . *Third,* group work should be limited to activities in which cooperative action is required to achieve stated purposes. If an activity can be completed by an individual, or by several individuals working independently, there is no need to organize a working group. *Fourth,* group work should be limited to activities in which effective working relationships can be maintained. If interpersonal conflicts and differences in points of view cannot be reconciled, progress cannot be made by forcing individuals to work in a group. *Fifth,* group work should be limited to situations in which the diverse talents of children can be put to use. If each child is required to do the same thing in an activity, individual differences will be neglected and unique contributions will not be obtained from each child.[3]

[3] John U. Michaelis, *Social Studies for Children in a Democracy,* 5th ed. (Englewood Cliffs, N.J.: Prentice-Hall, Inc., 1972), pp. 332–33. Reprinted by permission of Prentice-Hall, Inc., the copyright owner.

The Baltimore Public Schools contributed an outline of the grouping process which the authors have expanded:

1. *In the total class group* the teacher:

Introduces a music concept or skill.

Introduces one or more problems related to the concept or skill.

Clarifies and plans with the children the problem to be solved by each small group.

Identifies and groups children who can work well together.

Locates materials to be used by each group.

Designates the area of operation for each group.

Establishes time limits.

Plans with the children ways for them to work effectively in the groups.

Identifies the signal for returning to the large class group to share small group and individual accomplishments when appropriate.

2. *In the small group* the students:

Clarify their purpose.

Decide upon a tentative plan.

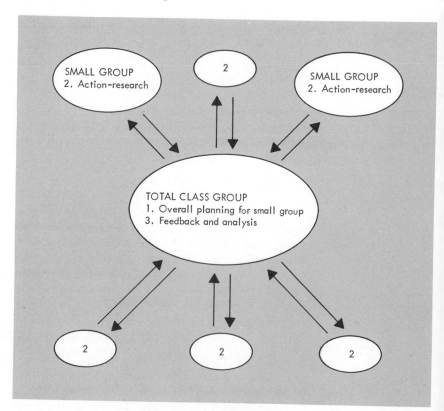

A Grouping Model

Identify the responsibilities of each individual.

Do research and processing.

Interpret and summarize their findings.

Make value judgments.

Decide if and how they will share their findings with the larger class group.

3. *In the total class group* the members of the small groups:

Report to and/or perform for the total group.

Answer questions asked by classmates.

Receive suggestions from peers and teachers as to ways to improve.

Record data from small groups and analyze and interpret the information; draw conclusions.

Evaluate in terms of their purpose.

The teacher circulates among the groups, giving assistance. Close supervision is usually necessary for productive learning to take place. Some groups need only a minimum amount of supervision whereas others need considerable guidance. The teacher's role is to offer suggestions, ask questions, commend children for good work, be a coinquirer and resource person when needed. If the teacher finds that some children lack skills to complete a task, skills groups may be organized to help them master these skills as tools before they return to the original small group. Not all children must work in groups simultaneously.

The Psychological Environment

Children must become involved in working with both peers and adults in a positive and accepting atmosphere. The environment must be organized to provide time for children to inquire into the various elements of music. In order to do this, they will need to be taught the cognitive skills of how to explore, experiment, compare, contrast, hypothesize, interpret, generalize, analyze, synthesize, evaluate, and apply acquired knowledge to the exploration and solution of new and related musical problems. For learning to occur, children need to know that they have the respect, acceptance, encouragement, and support of both their peers and their teachers. Children are thus encouraged to accept uncertainty about knowledge—to gather, process, and evaluate supportive data from various sources. Positive reinforcement is needed to encourage children to persist until they have explored a problem to its fullest. In music classes some types of learning may not be comprehended if lecturing and discussion predominate, since the skills of musical performance and many understandings about musical sounds are acquired only by participating in and listening to music.

References

KLOTMAN, ROBERT H., ed., *Scheduling Music Classes.* Reston, Va.: Music Educators National Conference, 1968.

MUSIC EDUCATORS NATIONAL CONFERENCE, *The School Music Program: Description and Standards.* Reston, Va.: The Conference, 1974.

Learning

3

A child needs the opportunity to participate spontaneously, enthusiastically, and completely, in the various aspects of music. No other life experience can bring more thrills and enjoyment, or feelings of individual worth and self-completeness, than experiences in some or all areas of music. With the many occasions it provides for self-involvement and personally initiated activities, music is an effective way for individuals to become acquainted with their unique musical abilities, their ways of solving musical problems, and their ways of expressing themselves creatively. Self-respect, acceptance, and respect by peers may result from satisfying musical accomplishments.

Teaching and learning are different operations. Teaching consists of actions intended to induce learning, and learning consists of acquiring knowledges, skills, and feelings by means of perceptions and concepts resulting from the stimulation of the senses. Because the two are different, it is possible for learning to take place without teaching. In the school environment it is assumed that learning occurs as a result of interactions between teacher and learner, although this may or may not be entirely true. Teachers and learners engage in types of verbal and nonverbal cognitive operations such as defining, examining, translating, designating, interpreting, applying, demonstrating, analyzing, classifying, synthesizing, and evaluating; psychomotor skills such as musical performance and body movement in relation to musical stimuli; and affective reactions of nonverbal nature that indicate feelings, intentions, and ideas. Concepts of teaching and learning are affected by whether one considers learning as a large group, small group, or individual affair.

Knowing the Children

Seeking and obtaining understanding of how children learn is a prerequisite to becoming a competent teacher. Children learn in any situation as complete personalities. They are the product of everything that has happened to them in the past and of everything that is presently happening to them. Prior experiences of children must be analyzed before one can plan programs for optimum development.

When teachers do not know and understand children, they fail to find ways to span the gap between the learner and the subject matter of music. The problem of the teacher's knowing the subject but failing to know the child is a very old one. It has affected all levels of learning. To most teachers "it is obvious that concerns for the child and for the subject matter are met only as the characteristics of both are known, prized and preserved. The problem that has plagued teachers and curriculum formulators for ages is how to do just that—plan a course of study based on knowledge of children *and* subject matter." [1]

Research in child development emphasizes the importance of building positive self-concepts within children which provide a basis for learning and performance in all areas of music. As a result of children's physical, cognitive, and affective characteristics, how adults respond to and interact with them, and their views of others and of themselves, they are conditioned and/or motivated to express themselves either positively or negatively. The way children perceive themselves is not necessarily the way others view them. Their own self-image is paramount since it determines how and what they think, say, and do about music.

As a basis for diagnosing children's levels of maturity and their instructional level in music, some teachers rely on the characteristics of children as presented by developmental psychologists such as Gesell. These characteristics, stated in terms of the "typical" student at a specific age, usually disregard individual differences. Despite this, a point of reference for the teacher is essential. When teachers use developmental characteristics, they employ them only as tentative guides for designing

---

[1] James Raths, "Mutuality of Effective Functioning and School Experience," in *Learning and Mental Health: 1966 Yearbook* (Washington, D.C.: Association for Supervision and Curriculum Development), p. 9.

programs, objectives, learning experiences and teaching procedures, for determining levels of competency, and as a means for identifying which children are performing at or above a level generally expected of a particular age.

Weaknesses of the norm characteristics established by some developmental psychologists include lack of due consideration of the influence of the type of teaching strategies, the children's background of musical experiences, and the impact of family living conditions and environment upon the child's learning. All children mature physically, socially, and emotionally at different rates; some six-year-olds are as mature physically and intellectually as some seven- or eight-year-olds, with boys usually one year behind the girls in maturity throughout the elementary school years. Thus it is impossible for teachers to assist individuals in reaching their highest potential in music if they teach children as if their age or grade determined their level of musical performance. This is why moves toward individualized instruction, nongraded classrooms, and informal education have become necessary.

The grade-level-age-characteristic approach is outdated in view of what has been proved by leading psychologists in learning theory. That venerable approach has long been educationally indefensible. Educators recognize that there are stages of development that every child passes through in the journey toward maturity, but they are also aware that children vary noticeably in the ways and time it takes them to complete these stages. Thus, evidence accumulates that negates the grade-level school organization and brings into focus programs based upon each child's rate and style of learning. Furthermore, this evidence casts serious doubt on the validity of educational books and programs based upon a rigid age and grade approach.

Piaget's Stages of Cognitive Development

Jean Piaget, a Swiss developmental psychologist, has advanced a realistic sequence of the intellectual (cognitive) development of children. Though some of his theories need to be further researched and substantiated, his stages of cognitive growth provide teachers with a meaningful guide to the growth of children's cognitive abilities.

These stages are age-related, not age-determined. There is a possibility that children who function at the preoperational level will reason about a musical problem in a specific manner, and that children who function at the concrete or formal operations level will use very different thought processes. Piaget has presented the characteristics of thought at different stages.

According to him there are rather definite stages of the development of intelligence, each carrying with it the embryonic elements of behavior or intelligence required in the succeeding stage. Unless these embryonic elements are encouraged to grow they can contribute little or nothing to the next stage. The various stages or levels of development have a fixed order, but their time of appearance varies with the physical development, experience background, and society or culture of which the individual is a product. Piaget's four stages are as follows:

Sensorimotor or Preverbal Stage—Birth to 2 Years During this span of time children engage in numerous interactions with objects, situations, and people in their immediate environment through use of the senses: they listen, look, smell, taste, touch, grasp, feel of textures, pound, manipulate, suck, and experiment with objects. Thus their evolving mental development and structures are altered to accomodate the new data. At this stage infants' thinking centers around use of their sensory and psychomotor behaviors. They are usually unable to use representational thought processes and of necessity must act out what is contained in their minds. The sensorimotor stage is prior to language development.

Preoperational Stage—Ages 2–7 During the preoperational years the child must span the gap between the sensorimotor activities of the infant and the internal mental activities of the school-aged child. Language and mental images are gradually substituted for the sensorimotor activities of infancy. Instead of grasping, things are requested. The mother is thought of even though she is not visible. Make-believe play and dramatic movement are very important because through them the children are assimilating symbolically the experiences, roles, and ideas of their immediate environment. Simultaneously, assimilation is being balanced by accommodation, which is the primary function of imitation. Through imitation young children are able to accommodate different experiences, thus expanding their concepts.

This phase of development is designated as preoperational because most children are unable to engage in thought that involves operations on data. Characteristics of most children at this level are their inability to combine parts into a whole, to arrange parts in different ways, and to reverse operations or processes. Some children can begin to classify objects with obviously common attributes. They also begin to place things in a series. Mental pictures or symbolic representations are being formed; children usually function intuitively, not logically, based on their immediate experience and perception. Symbols are used to represent objects, and labels and names are acquired for experiences, a type of concept formation.

Concrete Operations Stage—Ages 7–11 The term *concrete operations* means that children can now operate in thought on concrete objects or their representations. They can serialize, extend, subdivide, differentiate, or combine existing structures into new relationships or groupings. They now think logically about things rather than accepting surface appearances.

As children accumulate and assimilate knowledge and data from their actions, and accommodate or adjust their mental structures to the new data and knowledge, thinking processes are altered. Even though most children at this stage of cognition can usually employ logic, their thinking has its basis in the concrete rather than the abstract. The mental ability necessary for the combining of various elements is developed usually toward the end of this stage. The combining of operations is used to discover the concept of a hierarchy. Learners discover that they can combine parts of a whole in many different ways and still not alter the total. They learn to classify, order, number, use concepts of space and time, conservation and reversability, and to discriminate in increasing degrees of exactness.

Stage of Formal Operations—Ages 11–12 to Adulthood This period of cognition usually appears in early adolescence. Children can now reason on the basis of hypothesis and the abstract, not just on the basis of objects or the concrete. They construct new operations, attain new structures and grouping of structures, and develop relationships between and among ideas. In other words, learners are operating on operations, which means they are capable not only of thinking about concrete things and situations but can think about and analyze the thoughts of others and they can identify variables in problems and analyze them critically. Level four is the highest level of intellectual thought.

Obviously, children must develop mental processes in order to be able to assimilate, to accommodate, to act, to think, and to reorganize and reclassify information. For instance, until young children have learned to control pitch, at least to some degree, with their singing voices, they cannot sing a recognizable tune or learn a new one. The *spiral* concept of the curriculum is considered to be a series of encounters with ideas or situations in which the children successively accommodate themselves.

Piaget states that the principal goal of education is to create men who are capable of doing new things—men who are creative, inventive, and discoverers; not simply repeating what other generations have done. The second goal of education is to form minds which can be critical, can verify, and not accept everything they are offered. The great danger today is of slogans, collective opinions, ready-made trends of thought. We have to be able to resist individually, to criticize, to distinguish between what is proved and what is not. So we need pupils who are active, who learn early to find out by themselves, partly by their own spontaneous activity and partly through material teachers make available to them; who learn early to distinguish between what is verifiable and what is simply the first idea to come to them.[2]

New Concepts of Child Development

Changes in our view of the world bring with them changes in our view of the child and of man. Contrary to Piaget's sequence of four stages, today's psychologists are emphasizing the fact that all aspects of development are neither fixed nor necessarily orderly. The concept that development is modifiable is extremely important. Educators once believed that a child at age six would behave in a "six" way, and a child at seven in a

[2] Richard Ripple and Verne Rockcastle, eds., *Piaget Rediscovered* (Ithaca, N.Y.: School of Education, Cornell University, 1964), p. 5.

"seven" way, and if children did not behave in these specified ways, they were designated as either retarded or gifted. Research indicates that this belief is unsubstantiated. Children grow and learn at different rates and use different styles of learning at each age level. Attitudes toward learning and the rate and amount learned usually result from the types and quality of physical, intellectual, and social stimulation received. Children's learning is further influenced by the amount of positive and emotional support they receive as well as what innate characteristics they inherit.

The concepts of both grade levels and age levels in terms of what children are able to accomplish have been undergoing revision. Individual differences among children are far greater than had once been thought, and it is known that some children can accomplish feats believed possible only of older children some years ago. There have been changes on the intellectual level. Under certain conditions young children can intellectualize at a level thought to be impossible until recently. Children are maturing earlier and educators are learning that even physical characteristics of age groups have undergone change.

What, then, is the value of child development charts where a norm is "established" for various groups of children? Despite the exceptions, they are still useful as general guides for teachers. By knowing general norms, a teacher can judge whether or not a class of a certain age is performing on that level, or if its *mental* age is higher or lower than the norm would indicate. Child development consists of mental, social, emotional, and physical growth. Any child can be above or below the norm for any one of these characteristics. Knowing this, teachers can plan for children's education on the level where they are, and this implies extensive individualization of instruction.

The list of general norms stated below are descriptions of development; they are not limitations or prescriptions and can be expanded and altered. They describe general similarities in patterns of physical, mental, social, and emotional growth at certain stages of development. The following chart of general norms may serve as a basis for analyzing a child's level of growth and maturity and as one type of guide for diagnosing, analyzing, and organizing music curricula and daily lesson plans. What are the advantages and disadvantages that may result from using general norms as presented below?

General Norms

NURSERY SCHOOL AND KINDERGARTEN
(ages 4 and 5)

Steady rate of growth; growth in height is increasing more rapidly.

active; right or left handedness is established.

Large muscles better developed than small muscles; constantly physically

Size of head disproportionately large; child is top heavy and falls often.

Teeth and body structures are growing and changing; vigorous action results in fatigue.

Uses all of the body in physical activities; lacks discriminate use or fine coordination of various parts of the body.

Voices are small; pitch is often underdeveloped.

Attention span is relatively short, depending on the interest and the activity; most children are very active, affectionate, and aggressive.

Language development is limited; speech skills are underdeveloped, but both language and speech are improving rapidly.

Some children are shy and are limited in ways of expressing ideas and feelings.

Often self-centered; wants to be involved and motivated; cares little what peers think; is very individualistic; emotions are intense, with brief extremes of happiness, anger, hate.

They often have a limited understanding of ownership.

Sex roles are not clearly defined.

The harmonic sense is rudimentary.

Enjoys the security of repetitious activity.

Desires to be accepted by adults; needs warmth and security from them; enjoys individual attention.

Beginning to develop independence; tries to help self; gradually depends less upon adults.

The beginning of cooperative play in relatively small groups; much of learning is nonverbal.

Very inquisitive about surroundings; is eager to learn and to respond; is very alert; learns through manipulating concrete objects and reenacting real situations.

Interested in the "here and now," "what and what for," and in realizing immediate goals.

Live in a world of make-believe and imagination; the child is imitative.

Creative, spontaneous, and uninhibited.

They work alone or in very small groups.

EARLY PRIMARY
(ages 6 and 7)

Many children are still unable to sing in tune; most voices are light and high in quality and pitch, but some are low; there are usually many different ranges present. The overlapping of ranges at the beginning of the school year will permit about five or six consecutive scale pitches to be sung by the large majority of the class, usually from middle C to the G or A above.

Rapid rate of growth for six-year-olds; children want warm, personal attention.

Large muscles are more developed than small muscles; children tend to move with the entire body as a unit; a lengthening of the limbs.

Until age six eye-hand coordination is poorly developed.

At age seven the heart grows rapidly; muscular development is uneven; motor skills are steadily developing; eye-hand coordination improves; attention span increases.

Missing front teeth of some six- and most seven-year-olds make perfect pronunciation and diction difficult.

Six-year-olds are extremely active and constantly on the move; they have a relatively short attention span; they are easily fatigued; at age seven children alternate between active and quiet behavior.

Eager and anxious to learn.

The harmonic sense is largely undeveloped.

Children are highly competitive; they fight with words rather than with fists; many six-year-olds are often aggressive, egotistical, and often uncooperative.

Children are highly imaginative and enjoy imitating; they are interested in and are curious about their surrounding environment; they enjoy sounds and sound effects.

Rudimentary understanding of time, space, and money values.

Learn through use of concrete materials, in terms of experience background, and through participation under wise supervision; limited utilization of the abstract.

Children need encouragement, acceptance, and support from adults.

At age seven group activities are increasing in popularity; there is some evidence that interests of boys and girls are diverging.

At age seven the concept of the right and wrong ways of doing things is beginning to emerge.

MIDDLE ELEMENTARY
(ages 8 and 9)

Heart is developing more slowly and causes periods of fatigue.

The attention span is expanded.

Permanent teeth of some are still appearing.

Slow, steady physical growth; girls are more mature than boys; this age group has better coordination, is conscious of detail, and is able to devote attention to activities that require control of small muscles of body, hands, feet, and eyes; children are more interested in detailed and intricate work.

Vocal cords and lungs are developing rapidly; more control of voice and of breathing; the singing voice of the nine-year-old is better in quality, range, and dependability.

The harmonic sense is not well developed for eight-year-olds, but a growing number of nine-year-olds possess it.

Interest in musical and game activities requiring use of small muscles is expanding even though intricate muscular coordination continues to be difficult and taxing.

Communication skills are more highly developed, including reading skills and a larger vocabulary.

Need for encouragement, acceptance, and praise from adults; sensitive to criticism.

Peers become important; children are better able to cooperate and work in groups; interest in gangs of the same sex and secret codes is strong, particularly at age nine; this is a time of joining groups; eight-year-olds are usually interested in cowboys, rough and ready play, and they are prone to accidents.

The age of hero worship and love for folklore begins to emerge at about age nine; children need sound and sensitive adult models; children are interested in patriotism.

Interested in how instruments are made and how they produce sounds.

Interest in other cultures and in the expanding world environment.

Become more interested and involved in more difficult movement and creative dramatics.

Children enjoy ridiculous humor and the humor of everyday situations; a growing appreciation of imaginary adventure.

They are rather indiscriminately interested in anything new to them, particularly the eight-year-olds; they are eager to expand their knowledge.

An increasing number of individual differences and abilities appear; a wide range of reading abilities is evident.

Rapid development in independence and in work-study habits.

These children need guidance and experience in evaluation of their individual performances and of the performances of others; greater ability in self-evaluation.

Nine-year-olds are very conscious of what is right and wrong; they desire to do things correctly; they seek help on specific skills and on mastering information.

Continue to learn best through use of varied and concrete materials and through active participation under wise supervision.

Understand concepts of simple fractions, time, and money.

LATER ELEMENTARY
(ages 10 and 11)

A pause in physical growth for some to be followed by a period of rapid growth; girls usually mature more rapidly than boys; rapid growth implies an awkward stage.

The harmonic sense develops rapidly; the diaphragm is developing and expanding; some sixth-grade boys will develop the initial stage of the changing voice.

Seeks approval of the peer group; needs to "belong;" is inclined to be overcritical of self and others; is often prejudiced.

The ability to work both independently and with others is more highly developed; the ability to follow leadership of others is present.

Preadolescents often become extremely critical, unpredictable, and defiant.

Vision is comparable to that of adults.

Children have increased energy; they are interested in activity.

A wide range of individual ability.

Interests of boys and girls usually divergent.

Secondary sex characteristics may be present.

Teasing and hostility between boys and girls.

Listless at times, but highly active generally.

Resentment of any kind of attention or activity that appears to cause an individual to lose status with the group; seek to conform to standards exemplified by child leaders in the group and by the majority of peers.

There is desire for the approval and understanding of adults even though they seek to become more independent of them.

They are often silly and giggle unnecessarily; they are often loud, rough, and like to joke.

Attracted to adults who possess humor and warmth, and who are constructive, mature, and positive in their approach.

Interested in music concerned with adventure, mystery, humor, work, transportation, inventions, outer space, home and family life.

Wants to know why as well as how; is inquisitive about scientific reasons that support facts, situations, and theories.

Interest in an increased understanding of an expanding environment including time and number concepts; more complete understanding of the contributions of past achievements to present-day culture. Interest in different types of music and music of different cultures.

Become more critical of musical performance.

Possess the background for understanding and enjoying fantasy.

Sustained and intense interest in activities that hold meaning and purpose.

Inquiry and Problem Solving

Some believe that creative inquiry is synonymous with the conceptual approach. When children solve musical problems by creating music of their own, they find a need to learn about tone qualities, repetition, contrast, balance, unity, variety, tension, release, dynamics, tempo, rhythm, melody, harmony, and notation. When they evaluate their compositions, they often find ways to improve and refine them. In these ways they discover a need for knowledge that has immediate application. The process results in thinking in new and different ways. It provides the motivation for children to learn more effectively than with approaches that stress acquisition of facts because they are working to develop ideas and they are learning things relevant to their interests.

The creative process is necessary for self-fulfillment. It seems that children respond to learning whenever they can become personally involved in this process, regardless of aptitude or socioeconomic background. To be creative is to think in uncharted ways; it could be termed learning through discovery.

It is commonly said that children need to be "free" in order to create, and this has led to much misunderstanding. Some have mistakenly believed that children must not be restricted. In the first place, there must be certain teacher- and self-designed restrictions to make it possible to have a classroom situation in which creativity can flourish. At the beginning of the process, to give children the confidence that they can produce their own music, many music teachers restrict these children to using only a few tones of the pentatonic scale on metalophones and xylophones. This restriction frees them to create because they are protected from the complexities of the complete major scale with its leading tones. Conformity to basic rules, such as how and when to play instruments, the care and storage of equipment, the distribution of various music materials and their collection, and taking turns in class discussion, are necessary routine matters. Such things get in the way only when they become ends in themselves instead of being functional.

For many years creative problem solving has been recognized as an effective way of learning. The sequential steps in the problem solving process are listed below but are not always employed sequentially in approaching the solution of problems.

1. Identifying and stating the problem.
2. Determining types of data sources needed.
3. Collecting data.
4. Processing pertinent data.
5. Making hypotheses and inferences.
6. Forming conclusions and generalizations and applying these to the solution of new problems.

An example of this might be the case of Johnnie, who in fifth grade is learning to play the trumpet. He notices that in music of the eighteenth century the trumpet plays only chord-line melodies or repeated note parts, and this is a problem worth investigating because he likes to play diatonic tunes as well as bugle-type music. His problem is "Why do the trumpets play only chord-line parts in this music?" Johnnie and his classmates collect data by listening to more music. They find that later on in the nineteenth century the trumpets are assigned scale-line melodies by the composers. Their hypotheses about this include:

> The composers of the eighteenth and early nineteenth centuries did not want the trumpet to play melodies that were step-wise in construction.
>
> The trumpet players did not like to play anything that did not have bugle-call or repeated-note characteristics.
>
> Nobody had thought of the trumpet as an instrument that should play scale-line parts.
>
> The players did not know the fingering, so could not play scale-line parts.

At this point they decide that they have insufficient data to test any of these theories, so it is necessary to collect more data. They go to the library to seek help. The librarian guides them to books on instruments. What they find leads them to agree that none of their theories is correct, because the reason the trumpet did not play scale-line melodies was that it was mechanically unable to do so; the valve had not yet been invented. The problem had been solved, but led to more questions about other instruments and their history. The concepts the children worked with led them to a generalization, "Present-day musical instruments have evolved from earlier forms; a series of inventions which expanded the capabilities of instruments gradually gave the composers more pitches and tone qualities with which to work." In this process their concept of music through the ages and into the future was expanded, and they gained another way to think about instrumental music and its human relationships. Their expanding generalization about the evolution of instruments and expansion of tone qualities was later guided by the teacher to include consideration of the electronic music of today and the strong possibilities of new tonal resources being added to music as far into the future as the children could imagine. It is vital to the learning process that validated concepts and generalizations are applied to new and related situations in this way in order that learnings be extended and tested by experimenting with these musical generalizations through some type of performance.

Learning to Think Musically

Percepts and Concepts

Music is an aural art, and the stimuli that bring forth musical responses are musical structures varying from a single sound source to highly complex sources. When musical perception takes place, the learner's mind becomes aware of aspects, organizations, and relationships of the music being experienced; a percept is the mental residue of this sense perception. Repeated and related percepts can result in concepts, and concepts in turn influence new and old perception.

Musical responses can be either observable (overt) or unobservable (covert), the latter taking place within the mind. Overt responses can be any form of performance such as moving, singing, playing, writing, and conducting. Covert responses include sensations, feelings, and thoughts. Percepts, when combined, become the musical concepts of the learner; obviously these concepts are outgrowths of the child's personal experiences and percepts, and are discovered and processed by the learner. Because each person's experiences and mental processes are different from those of any other person, and because the same is true of musical experiences and physiological and mental inheritance, concepts therefore differ from person to person. Concepts are very complex and are continually being developed and modified. They cannot be communicated verbally with precision because the one who attempts the communication is speaking from a personal interpretation of the relevant concepts. Verbal communication of music concepts can improve to the extent that those exchanging information happen to hold approximately the same version of the concepts. Many of the covert responses cannot be verbally communicated.

To think conceptually one progresses from the level of perception of objects, events, and situations to making associations, to formulating concepts, to grouping two or more concepts to form a generalization, to applying the generalization in solving related problems. In thinking inductively the learner begins with a problem, collects and analyzes his data, and then formulates concepts from the data which in turn are combined and summarized as generalizations.

When young children examine a bell set, they feel it, may attempt to taste it, look at its shiny smooth surface, eventually discover that it can produce sound and experiment with this characteristic; they may form a mental image (percept) of a bell set which is stored in their minds and retrieved when they need it. Later, when they relate this percept to other types of keyboard instruments, they have made an association based on the common elements of the appearance of the keyboard and the fact that it can produce pitches on the different instruments. Through this series of experiences children gain the concept of keyboard instruments. This concept continues to expand as they acquire progressively more experiences with it, and it becomes a part of their thinking process. For example, when children first see a celesta, they will want to find out what new manner of keyboard instrument it is, what it is used for in the orchestra, how the sound is produced, and why it sounds different from other keyboard instruments they know. The ability to do this results from the acquisition of a concept that is useful when learners are confronted with a problem concerning keyboard instruments. The more known about the construction of these instruments, what produces the sound, and what makes the tone qualities differ, the greater will be the ability to think conceptually and act in terms of keyboard instruments.

The lesson for the teacher implied from the above is that children should be assisted to have accurate and clear perception of any aspect of music under study because they cannot develop precise associations and meanings unless they can differentiate between the characteristics of what is being studied—in this instance, the bell set. The teacher seeks ways to set up purposes in the minds of children and assists them in their observations, discussions, and in summarizing or evaluating the outcomes of their experiences. Children's finding should be listed, interpreted, grouped, labeled, analyzed, and related whenever possible. This entire process may be initiated with questions such as "What is it?" "How do people use it?" "Is it like any other instrument?" "How is it different from other instruments?" Vocabulary is introduced and used in order for pupil discussion to take place.

Some musical concepts are highly abstract, such as the interdependence of the various elements of music. The inception of this concept takes place when children find that recognizable melody cannot take place without some form of rhythm. This concept is gradually acquired through experiences with a number of melodies and rhythms. For instance, "Happy Birthday to You" and "The Star-Spangled Banner" are completely different melodies, but there is a rhythm pattern common to both. The child should discover that the first parts of these two songs have identical rhythm and that "Joy to the World" utilizes the major scale in its beginning measures, but it is the rhythm that clearly distinguishes it from the way the major scale is commonly played. The children can try to invent a melody without rhythm to find that rhythmic feeling may be reduced but cannot be eliminated. Out of these experiences grows the generalization that the interdependence of pitch and rhythm produces melody. Later on, harmony and other musical elements will expand the generalization of the interdependence of these elements in producing various types of music, and the children will use this principle in creating their own music.

Unless the teacher plans the lesson in such a way that the children know what they are listening for in melody and rhythm, they might conclude that they are simply singing a song or clapping a rhythm because the teacher told them to do it. The teacher must bring the focus of the lesson clearly to the attention of the children. This is done by planning some type of activity that reveals to the teacher what the children already know about the content of the lesson, or one which connects with the children's past experiences. Then the focusing of the lesson may be brought about through questioning or class discussion of the problem before it, and writing important points on the chalkboard. In class discussions there should be references to past experience, to possible future activities, and the problem should be defined and clarified. Unless the purpose for the activity is made clear in the thinking of the students, little learning results.

"Musical understanding may be approached fundamentally by grasping combinations of sounds and the succession of patterns by which these sounds become interrelated. Isolated tones become meaningful when associated with other tones. Problems in the perception of rhythm, harmonic progression, texture, and formal design require similar modes of studied relationships. Habits of concentrated attention to stimulate memory and frequent comparisons to motivate critical attitudes are then essential to the task of coordinating the intellect with sense perception." [3]

The Structure of the Subject

The current philosophy of learning emphasizes that beneficial and purposeful learning can be attained and used if it is acquired through a program that is organized around the basic structure of a subject. Therefore attention is being directed to the function and use of structure in the teaching and learning of music. Exploration and identification of appropriate learning experiences are involved in these concerns which will make it possible for children to acquire knowledge of the structure of a subject.

"To learn structure is to learn how things are related. . . . In order for persons to be able to recognize the applicability or inapplicability of an idea to a new situation and to broaden their learning thereby, they must have clearly in mind the general nature of the phenomenon with which they are dealing." [4] In other words, the child must understand the subject of music, which includes all of its related parts that comprise its structure. The teacher must be concerned with the relevance of the con-

[3] Abraham A. Schwadron, *Aesthetics: Dimensions for Music Education* (Washington, D.C.: Music Educators National Conference, 1967), p. 95.

[4] Jerome Bruner, *The Process of Education* (Cambridge Mass.: Harvard University Press, 1960), p. 7.

tent of the structure to the child's interest and abilities and select those parts appropriate for study by children who vary in maturity and musical capacity. Structure is "organizing concepts, which formulate the way we think things are related. . . . Concepts are used to provide the children with a systematic method of attack on areas where they seek new knowledge." [5] When these concepts and generalizations have been selected and translated, experiences that allow children to discover them are then planned. To enable children to discover and learn the structure of music it is necessary that concepts be explored in sequential order. Research indicates that in many situations music teachers have neglected to organize a pertinent and logical sequence of experiences for developing concepts. Relationships of the different levels of knowledge are lost when this occurs.

Advantages and Disadvantages of Structure

A program organized in a logical, sequential format provides continuity of experiences. Often, especially in the preprimary and primary grades, the music program is a random assortment of unrelated activities. Even though children are exposed to a variety of experiences they may not perceive the structure of music or its methods of inquiry. In a sequentially-developed program, children should explore and develop concepts commensurate with their maturity levels. This consideration prevents teachers from operating at a conceptual level which is too difficult for the majority of children. When children learn the component parts of music in relation to a meaningful structure (main ideas), musical content is more readily understood and the details remembered for longer periods of time. As children employ structure they can use it in their future research and organization of knowledge, thus making it possible for them to transfer knowledge from one learning experience to another.

Weakness in a conceptually structured music program lies within its failure to provide time for the inclusion of current musical events and problems that evolve within any school or home environment. Attention to these relevant problems may interrupt the closely structured and sequenced activities, thus disturbing the continuity of the program. Some teachers place too much emphasis on structure and continuity, leaving little time for children to experiment and explore music on their own. In competent teaching this does not occur; structure, content, and creative processes are combined into a meaningful pattern.

For students to understand the structure of music they must learn to process information at the data, concept, and generalization levels, since these three levels of information comprise the structure. If students are to process data and to grow in conceptualization, they must learn to use different levels and types of thought processes. In assisting children in their development and use of varied levels of thought, the teacher assists them in using different levels and types of questions. Developing thought processes and questioning strategies follow.

[5] Bruce R. Joyce, *Strategies for Elementary Social Education* (Chicago: Science Research Associates, Inc., 1972), p. 27.

In developing cognitive thought processes, the teacher begins by providing learners with data-collecting experiences by means of which concepts can be derived. Degrees of expansion and complexities of these concepts yield an increasing mental ability to interpret and to make generalizations. From there the process moves on to a higher level in which learners have practice in analyzing and synthesizing data, evaluating and judging as required by the experience or problem, and then they have an opportunity to make application of this knowledge in solving new problems. It is important that in music learning, thinking abilities which call for the use of music skills as well as music knowledge be activated.

In formulating questions and using them to teach cognitive understandings and competencies, one will find that there are many different models. However, because these models contain similar elements, they are frequently more alike than different. The models that will be discussed here are those of Taba, and Bloom and Krathwohl.

Taba's
Cognitive
Tasks

I. CONCEPT FORMATION (collecting and organizing data)   In general, the sequence by which cognition takes place in the mind of the learner may be guided by Taba's three Cognitive Tasks and the sequenced questions listed under each task below. Concept formation is basic to other cognitive processes and is the necessary foundation for formulating generalizations.

A. Identifying and enumerating through use of the ear, eye, and body various musical characteristics, elements, objects, and events such as pitch, rhythm, instruments, and concerts. What did you hear? See? Feel? (Identify. List. Examine. Compare.)

B. Grouping in accordance with common qualities, uses, or other characteristics. For example, types of chords, even and uneven meters, types of phrases, and classifications of instruments. How can we group these most logically? If we don't know, what can we do or where can we go to find out?

C. Discriminating between the features of these and abstracting common characteristics or elements, like the instances of 4/4, 5/4, 6/8, and 7/8 meters being different, yet containing the same note values or possibly using the same tempos. How are they alike? What names should we give to these categories?

II. INTERPRETING DATA AND GENERALIZING   After data have been assembled and ordered, and after an understanding of the relevant concepts has been achieved, it is possible to relate concepts and use them to form **34** generalizations. Notice the types of questions that follow:

A. Examining the same aspect of music in several different compositions.
Example: What are the outstanding rhythm patterns in each of these songs?

B. Comparing the same aspect of music in several different compositions.
Example: Contrast these rhythm patterns; how are they the same; how are they different?

C. Generalizing.
Example: This type of song tends to have a characteristic rhythm pattern.

D. Explaining.
Example: The characteristic rhythm pattern is the result of each song's relationship to the same national dance.

III. APPLICATION OF DATA, CONCEPTS, AND GENERALIZATIONS   Concepts, subconcepts, and generalizations can be used to:

A. Compare objects, performances, activities, or phenomena.
Example: How can we use the concept of a stage work in comparing a stage play with an opera? A ballet with a musical comedy?

B. Predict possibilities.
Example: What do you think would happen if there were no woodwinds in symphony orchestras? If there were no percussion section? What would happen if there were no symbols to depict accidentals in music?

C. Supporting predictions.
Example: Why do you believe the woodwinds are needed in symphony orchestras? What evidence can you give to prove that the percussion section is important? How do you know that it would not sound *better* if all accidentals were abandoned?

D. Verifying.
Example: How can we find out if instrumental music in Asia includes woodwinds? Are drums in African music more or less important than drums in our music? Where can we find evidence to solve these problems?

All types of thinking are contained in each of Taba's steps—data translating, interpreting, inferring, applying, analyzing, synthesizing, and evaluating. One of the common errors teachers make is asking questions in an artificial structured order. Children's learning is not that neatly structured, thus teachers should note that strict adherence to the sequential listing of Taba's three cognitive tasks as presented above should not always be practiced. The emphasis should be placed on the "product" or type of answer and thinking evidenced from the question asked. Sometimes data level questions can cause the highest type of thinking to occur in the mind of the learner.

Presented below is a chart adapted from Jarolimek and Bacon [6] which illustrates the use of questioning strategies in developing cognitive process skills employing the Taba model.

Questioning Strategies Involving Cognitive Process Skills

Task	Procedures	Illustrative Questions
I. Concept Attainment and Augmentation	Teachers can help children learn to form or augment concepts through asking questions which require children to: (a) summarize their observations; (b) help identify common properties (attributes) for grouping; and (c) label or define the grouping.	(a) *Observation* 1. What did you hear? See? Feel? Find? (b) *Grouping or Classifying* 1. What belongs together? On what criterion? (c) *Labeling or Defining* 1. What would you call these groups? 2. What belongs under each heading? 3. How would you name or label this?
II. Generalizing and Making Inferences from Data	Teachers can help children in forming generalizations and making inferences from data by asking questions which require children to: (a) compare and contrast data from different samples (differentiation); (b) interpret the meaning of certain data; (c) make reasonable inferences based on the data itself; and (d) develop a generalization.	(a) *Comparing and Contrasting (Differentiating)* 1. What did you hear? See? Feel? Find? 2. What things are the same? Different? 3. How can you distinguish among things partly the same and partly different? (b) *Interpreting Data* 1. What does this mean? 2. How does it relate to other things? (c) *Making Inferences* 1. What can you infer from this? Imply? 2. What do the data suggest? (d) *Developing Generalizations* 1. What can you conclude?

[6] John Jarolimek and Philip Bacon, codirectors, *A Behavioral Approach to the Teaching of Social Studies.* Monograph, Tri-University Project in Elementary Education, Social Studies-Science (Seattle: University of Washington Press, May, 1968).

Task	Procedures	Illustrative Questions

III. Application of Knowledge	Teachers can help children in learning to apply knowledge by asking questions which require them to make application of facts and generalizations by:
	(a) exploring
	(b) focusing
	(c) interpreting data (extending ideas and perceiving relationships)
	(d) summarizing, concluding, or generalizing
	(e) verifying (verifying predictions, hypotheses, and inferences)
		(a) *Exploring*
		  1. What will happen if we omit all rests when we perform this music?
		(b) *Focusing*
		  1. Why do you think that the first hypothesis could or would happen?
		(c) *Interpreting*
		  1. How could this change the ———?
		  2. What would be the consequences?
		(d) *Summarizing, Concluding, or Generalizing*
		  1. What can we say in general about our hypothesis (guess prediction)?
		(e) *Verifying*
		  1. Let's test (try out, perform) to find if it is possible that this will really happen.

The Bloom-Krathwohl Taxonomy [7]

Questions The term *question* can be used to mean any intellectual stimulus that calls for a response. Questions, problems, and tasks have always had a prominent place in pedagogy, but today they are planned to encourage various forms of thinking rather than being used in random ways. The *Taxonomy* is a system of classification that is organized sequentially; its purpose is to provide definitions and examples of the major categories of cognitive thinking. Teachers use these categories, with their examples, to design and analyze questions so that their students may engage in specified types of thinking. Questions are formed in relation to the knowledge the students possess.

The *Taxonomy* categories are sequential and cumulative; each level of thinking includes elements of all of the lower categories. For example, memory is basic to each, and to reach the highest category, evaluation, the mind utilizes a sequence that begins with memory, then adds translation, interpretation, application, analysis, synthesis, in that order to achieve evaluation.[8]

[7] Benjamin Bloom, and David R. Krathwohl, *Taxonomy of Educational Objectives; Handbook I: The Cognitive Domain* (New York: David McKay Company, Inc., 1956).

[8] Norris M. Sanders, *Classroom Questions: What Kinds?* (New York: Harper & Row Publishers, 1966), p. 10.

Memory is basic to all forms of thought. There can be simple and complex questions in every category which can be useful from kindergarten through graduate school, for slow learners as well as fast learners. Teachers should not assume that the handicapped learner should be kept on memory-type questions and the brilliant student on only higher level process questions; all learners need to use varied types of questions to the full extent of their ability.

The discussion thus far has included only the cognitive aspect of learning, and classrooms that emphasize only this can be barren indeed—if the affective and psychomotor aspects are minimized. In reality, these domains cannot be separated, each being dependent upon the other when significant learning takes place.

Acquiring Attitudes and Values

Knowledge alone is insufficient as a goal of any form of education. Unless constructive attitudes and values accompany it, knowledge is at least neutralized, and is even dangerous on occasion. Research supports the fact that the cognitive (intellectual), psychomotor (muscular), and affective (feelings, values, and attitudes) features of a child's learning are closely related and in many ways inseparable.

An attitude may be defined as a predisposition to respond in a certain way to objects, ideas, persons, or subjects. It may be conscious and willful, or subconscious; it may be rational or irrational.[9] Attitudes and values result from an individual's total experience. They are flexible, and change as the learner's experiences in living are expanded. They are, therefore, extremely personal.

Attitudes are involved with feelings and emotions which are included in the affective domain. There is general belief that they cannot be taught in a direct manner. For example, the importance or beauty of a musical selection is not taught by the teacher informing the children how important or beautiful it is, or by the children merely verbalizing on its importance and beauty. The children must *internalize* such importance and beauty to the extent that their conduct toward music, and their response to and understanding of other music, are affected.

Since attitudes and feelings are related, the affective atmosphere of the classroom must be one that furthers positive emotional growth. When the environment frustrates children by failing to meet social and emotional needs, there is little to contribute to the development of wholesome attitudes and values. A learning environment that permits destructive, negative opinions of any child's music or of people tends to further negative

---

[9] John Jarolimek, *Social Studies in the Elementary School,* 3rd ed. (New York: The Macmillan Company, 1967), p. 59.

attitudes and values. Attitudes, emotions, and values, whether good or bad, will be developed in the classroom; it is the teacher's responsibility that they be healthy and constructive. Therefore, teachers must plan for teaching children how to value. Raths, Harmin, and Simon [10] suggest that this can be done by using the following steps in teaching valuing processes:

> Encourage children to make choices and to make them freely.
> Help them discover and examine available alternatives when faced with choices.
> Help children weigh alternatives thoughtfully, reflecting on the consequences of each.
> Encourage children to consider what it is they prize and cherish.
> Give them opportunities to make public affirmation of choices.
> Encourage them to act, behave, live in accordance with their choices.
> Help them to examine repeated behaviors or patterns in their own lives.

Children's attitudes and values regarding music may reflect the attitudes of both the peer group and those of high status adults. Thus it is possible that a child's attitudes and values can be weakened by contradictory musical influences emanating from adults and peers (radio, television, and recordings). Since children's musical backgrounds and experiences differ, teachers should not strive nor expect to have all children acquire the same set of musical values.

The positive attitudes and values of teachers are highly important in the instructional process. The chance remark of a teacher might have a lasting influence on a child. The teacher's attitude toward music, with its great variety of values and uses in human life, will usually affect children's attitudes.

Different types of music affect people differently. Therefore, the teacher should work toward a classroom environment in which the varied opinions of children toward works of music are listened to with interest, valued, defended with musical knowledge when necessary. (Why did you like or dislike this music?) Such environment permits disagreements that can be expressed in ways that permit personal differences while arguing intellectual points in support of positions taken. Musical values and attitudes toward music cannot be separated entirely from respect, concern for the feelings of others, and the acknowledgment that people can hold differing values—especially in a classroom situation in which there is neither hostility nor aggression. An intellectually sound position for a music teacher to take is one that attempts to judge "good" music in accordance with how well it performs its function, and to operate in a climate of openness that admits the exploration of every type of music to attempt to find out what it is used for, how it is constructed, and how good it is in its

---

[10] Louis E. Raths, Merrill Harmin, and Sidney B. Simon, *Values and Teaching: Working With Values in the Classroom* (Columbus, Ohio: Charles E. Merrill Books, Inc.), pp. 38–39.

category. In this atmosphere every facet of music from Renaissance to jazz and electronic has a place, and their values are to be discovered by children in their personal learning of music.

The psychomotor domain will be treated in musical performance activities in chapters to follow.

Music in Other Areas

When children learn in their world, apart from adult direction, they learn in the way nature evidently intended them to learn—with an innocent disregard of subject boundaries, and their instincts are basically correct. Music *does* relate to other areas and vice versa in the real world. In the past, music suffered because of what sometimes became an exclusive *use* of music to enhance other subject areas and a corresponding neglect of music as a subject in its own right.

The move to explain all subjects in terms of their conceptual structures has helped teachers to know more specifically what they should help children learn, and has made clear when music assists learning in social studies, when social studies assists learning in music, and when learning in both subjects takes place simultaneously. The informal classroom has assisted children in learning relationhips of facts and ideas by permitting them to cross subject boundaries when necessary in seeking solutions to their problems.

A useful point of view in some informal classrooms is that the humanities can form a way of tying all parts of the curriculum together without hindering learning in any subject. Education pertains to humanity, and all subjects may come into logical focus when that is kept in mind. The IMPACT project mentioned in Chapter Two was an interesting experiment in placing the arts in a central position in a curricular organization in which no subject area was to be neglected.

Music has great value in communicating to children the dignity and worth of other cultures. The increasing emphasis on music of Asia and Africa has import beyond the knowledge of this music—it fosters respect and recognition of people whose cultures are equally significant to those of the West when judged from their own points of reference. The greater sophistication of rhythm and melody in those cultures balances very well with the emphasis on harmony and polyphony in music of the West. Children can become fascinated with Oriental scales and meters, and Afro-American music is now recognized as the greatest distinctly American contribution to world music. Part Five will deal with this in more detail.

By means of music, children can come to understand one of the ways man has kept historical records; what the Westward movement was; the meaning of the concept of the United States as a "melting pot"; the origins of patriotism; the Great Depression, and many more social concepts concerning events, people, region, nation, and world.

General Principles

Some general principles to use as guides for teaching and learning music follow. All teachers need to be aware of them and to use them as guides in developing music programs and lessons.

1. Music activities are selected that are on the child's physical, intellectual, and social maturity levels.
2. The teacher has obvious confidence in the child's ability to learn music.
3. The teacher employs a variety of activities and materials for individual, small-group, and whole-class activities.
4. The teacher arranges for musical problems to be solved by the children.
5. The children have musical experiences that are satisfying to them.
6. The children have good models with which to identify (other children, parents, teachers, other adults).
7. There is a planned, sequential, but flexible program of music instruction from level to level.
8. There is meaningful, varied, and frequent practice that is essential for learning music skills.
9. Teachers and parents work together to help children learn music; the musical and cultural environment influences to a significant degree children's musical perceptions and values.
10. Individual differences and levels of musical proficiency and aptitude are recognized, studied, and accommodated.
11. The children see meaning and relevance in what they are doing as they make immediate functional applications of these skills and procedures, as they become involved in establishing purposes, in the selection of appropriate activities and materials, and in assessing the degree to which the objectives have been realized.
12. Teachers are able to select and state what they are going to teach and the subsequent pupil-learning behaviors (objectives), how they are going to accomplish this (methods and materials), and then determine how well they have taught it (evaluation).
13. Children are taught the skill of asking different types and levels of questions and are encouraged and given opportunity to employ this skill.
14. The teacher is an active guide to learning, a co-learner, and a resource person who shares in class activities.
15. The children's musical activities are successful to them. The teacher plans activities in which children can be successful, in which they are interested, and through which they can progress in learning music.
16. The children develop favorable self-concepts through successful individual, small group, and class music experiences.
17. The learning of music is enhanced when the learner is motivated and personally involved in what is to be learned.
18. Children learn more readily when they study music content that is interesting and meaningful to them.
19. Learners are free to explore, discover, question, and to profit from making mistakes.

References

AUSUBEL, DAVID P., *Educational Psychology: A Cognitive View*. New York: Holt, Rinehart and Winston, Inc., 1968.

BEARD, RUTH MARY, *An Outline of Piaget's Developmental Psychology for Students and Teachers*. New York: Basic Books, 1969.

GAGNÉ, ROBERT, *The Conditions of Learning* (2nd ed.). New York: Holt, Rinehart and Winston, Inc., 1970.

HUNKINS, FRANCIS P., *Questioning Strategies and Techniques*. Boston: Allyn and Bacon, Inc., 1972.

O'BRIEN, JAMES P., "How Conceptual Learning Takes Place," *Music Educators Journal,* September 1971, p. 34.

PULASKI, MARY ANN SPENCER, *Understanding Piaget—An Introduction to Children's Cognitive Development*. New York: Harper & Row, Publishers, 1971.

REESE, SAM, "Discovering the Nonintellectual Self," *Music Educators Journal,* May 1974. Maslow's philosophy and music.

RYAN, FRANK, and ARTHUR K. ELLIS, *Instructional Implications of Inquiry*. Englewood Cliffs, N.J.: Prentice-Hall, Inc., 1975.

SANDERS, NORRIS M., *Classroom Questions: What Kinds?* New York: Harper & Row, Publishers, 1966.

ZIMMERMAN, MARILYN P., "Percept and Concept: Implications of Piaget," *Music Educators Journal,* February 1970, p. 49.

Individualized
Instruction
in Music

"Music teachers must adapt their programs to meet new curricular designs that do not always accommodate performance-centered activities for large groups. They must provide experiences for students working individually or in small groups and often without direct teacher supervision. The development of materials and other resources for individualizing instruction is the responsibility of the teacher."[1] Individualizing instruction is an attempt to actualize the educational principle of accepting all children "where they are" in musical responsiveness and permitting them to progress as far as they are capable. In such a program there are both teacher-directed and student-selected individual and group activities.

The following curricular trends can be used as evidences of the move toward a more informal classroom:

> From the teacher as informer and lecturer to the teacher as a guide and facilitator of learning.
>
> From few student records to extensive records on the problems and progress of each student.

[1] David J. Boyle and Robert L. Lathrop, "The Impact Experience," *Music Educators Journal,* January 1973, p. 47.

From emphasis on content to emphasis on process.

From rigidity in discipline to interdiscipline.

From predetermined, set objectives, to continually changing objectives.

From textbook centered to multisources.

From teacher source to multimedia source.

From teacher interest content to student interest content.

From emphasis on accumulating knowledge to emphasis on how to find and create knowledge.

From highly structured classes to less formal classes.[2]

The Informal Classroom

The informal classroom represents a distinct change in beliefs and techniques. While it consists of teacher-directed activities, the teacher addresses the entire class infrequently. The classroom is arranged into learning stations (centers, laboratories, and studios) and each contains an activity of challenge and interest. During most of the school day individuals and small groups move from station to station. Directions for each activity are in written or printed form. The activities are created by imaginative and resourceful teachers and students to match the maturity, needs and interests of each learner. Children are free to learn from each other, and in all areas of the curriculum, because learning is not compartmentalized into discrete areas. An elementary classroom may have as few as one or two music stations while a music room could have thirty.

Equipment In addition to the usual equipment for music study, the music stations require teacher preparation of various types of meaningful materials in the form of direction sheet, booklet, learning packet, chart, manipulative instrument or object. Some of these are housed in boxes. Questions used as criteria in preparing a station include: What musical concept will this activity assist the learner to develop? What musical behavior will the learner display to reveal formation of the concept? What musical experience will produce the learner's response? What is the level of achievement considered to be a successful response? The responses expected of learners should, if possible, be varied and permit choices that allow the students to operate at their own levels.

The sound-producing equipment should generate balanced sounds, with no sound source conspicuous by being distinctly louder than others. Some can be pointed away from the rest; some sounds can be absorbed in part by drapes and accoustically-treated walls; and others can be muffled by sound-absorbent partitions. The floor of the area should be carpeted if possible, to absorb more sound. The entire area demands accoustical study to

[2] The last eight points are from Deborah Wolfe, "Trends in Science Education," *Science Education,* March 1970.

balance and soften the many sounds that characterize individual and small group instruction. Fortunately, most of the classroom instruments are modest volume-producers. The use of closets, hallways, and vacant rooms helps to reduce the problem of undesirable sounds interfering with learning.

The stations are ordinarily arranged to serve one student, pairs of students, or groups of three or four.

Teachers' Responsibilities in Individualized Instruction

Individualized instruction places heavy responsibility on the teacher to diagnose each child's musical background, capabilities, needs and interests; to prescribe for and with each child performance objectives and selected and sequenced learning activities, to realize these objectives, and to provide appropriate instructional resources. The teacher must further assume the responsibility for establishing reasonable time limits for each task. Upon completion of the task, the teacher and pupil assess the degree of progress made, and then move forward through the same cycle described above, hopefully at a higher and more challenging level. The teacher who uses these procedures must not only plan and equip learning centers but must also keep varied, specific, and detailed records on each child. The child's learning is assessed by repeated observations over an extended period of time, and the old adage, "By his works ye shall know him" applies when evaluating the learner's progress. Teacher's aides and team teaching are often helpful in the task of keeping individualized instruction in successful operation. To individualize instruction means that the teacher plans learning experiences for each student whether or not the individual is in a group; it does not demand a one-to-one teacher-pupil relationship, although this may operate at times.

In individualized programs the teachers have control, authority, and responsibility quite the opposite of a *laissez-faire* approach. They are learning facilitators with the role of active participants who realize that they are only complementary to the learning processes of the student. They build structure as they provide learning materials, as they enter and depart from children's activities, as they arrange the classroom so that they can identify learning areas being used or neglected, and as they assist learners in finding music meaningful in terms of their own living. "The properly managed informal classroom is well-structured, albeit in its own way. . . . The atmosphere . . . can best be described as controlled but not regulated. Extensive planning and meticulous records are part and parcel of (effective) informal education." [3] Teachers "bear a heavy responsibility throughout. They plan and supply the learning environment and see that

[3] *The Open Classroom: Informal Education in America* (Dayton, Ohio: Institute for Development of Educational Activities, Inc.), 1972, p. 15.

it is continually renewed and kept challenging. They move about the room to supply help as required; supply feedback to pupils as needed so that they may evaluate the accuracy or appropriateness of their performances; keep records which show activities completed for each pupil; determine which children need help in developing knowledges, interests, and attitudes; and teach them in small groups that are relatively homogeneous with respect to achievement." [4]

Grouping and Scheduling

Grouping and scheduling need to be examined because the emphasis on the individual learner is sometimes confusing to those seeking to understand informal types of class organization. "The motivation for learning often comes from interaction with others. A music classroom where all activities are conducted in small groups or individually will eventually lose the satisfaction that comes from combining efforts toward a common musical goal or from receiving evidence of successful achievements through peer response. The teacher must plan a regular time when students can share the skills and understandings they have gained while working independently. . . . The connection between individualized tasks and classroom musical activities must be clearly understood by the individual student. Without this motivation for learning, the individualized atmosphere can become as sterile and as nonproductive as some feel the traditional music classroom has been." [5]

Perhaps because individualization of music instruction is still in its embryonic stages, many varying types of schedules are found. Some are the same as in traditional programs while others consist of a listing of events in an open, flexible school situation: choral singing; guitar class; recorder class; stereo listening; piano lab; composing with percussion; and so on. After initial guidance of students into the program, and after teacher observation of their responses, learners' needs and interests dictate their individual, small group, and large group involvements with music and a schedule is planned from this practical base. A typical schedule for a day in one program is described as follows:

1. With chairs arranged in a circle, children enter, sit down, and participate in a group activity for from 5 to 7 minutes.
2. Each child reviews the schedule to find his station-letter for the day. (The schedule is a large class list with a clip or a space for a strip of paper after each name.)

[4] Ralph C. Preston and Wayne L. Herman, Jr., *Teaching Social Studies in the Elementary School,* 4th ed. (New York: Holt, Rinehart and Winston, 1974), p. 38.
[5] Eunice M. Meske and Carroll Rinehart, *Individualized Instruction in Music* (Reston, Va.: Music Educators National Conference, 1975), pp. 95–96.

3. Each child takes his packet from the wall container, goes to the assigned station, and begins working.

4. Fifteen minutes before the end of the period, lights are flicked to signal quiet practice for ten minutes.

5. Pack-up time begins five minutes before the end of the period. Teacher and students examine the room to make certain it is restored to the condition in which they found it.

The Learning Station

When the decision has been made to enter an individualized music program, the teacher will find several ways in which it can be initiated. Individualized instruction can begin on a small scale, with one, then two and more learning stations added to the customary class group instruction until, if desired, a complete transition has taken place. A second way is to change to a fully individualized program at once, and a third is that the entire school curriculum be organized around the informal or open classroom concept.

The stations are to be arranged to facilitate movement without disturbing other learners; traffic flow is important. Decisions must be made concerning the number of tables, easels, carrels, and types of equipment; the lighting must be sufficient, and the general effect should be attractive and inviting.

The teacher plans for realization of the same instructional objectives and terminal goals as before. However, specific objectives for each learner pertinent to the attainment of the general goals are established by the children, the teacher, or cooperatively by children and teacher. Behaviorally stated objectives are excellent for use with the individual learner because the stated outcome of the activity can be observed and evaluated by both child and teacher. Many of the activities included in the stations can be self-correcting, thus providing for immediate and positive evaluation and feedback.

Cornell suggests activities such as adding an Autoharp [6] accompaniment to a new song learned via tape recording and notation; creating an original melody on the xylophone and playing it for a friend; comparing the rhythmic features of three different pieces of music; creating a melody on the piano black keys with the right hand with an accompaniment on the black keys played by the left hand; transposing a tune one can play on the piano or bells to another key; and experimenting with a synthesizer. She further states that there are infinite possibilities of this nature that teachers can create for students, but that some materials should be available without

[6] A source of learning station activities based on the Autoharp is *Teaching Music With the Autoharp* (Union, N.J.: Music Education Group).

specific instructions so that students can freely pursue their own interests.[7]

Matching Learners and Stations   Before students are assigned to or select a station or project, the teacher must know whether or not each learner is able to complete the task successfully. What musical knowledges, skills, and experiences are necessary as prerequisites? (What is the student able to do musically?) What other knowledges and skills are necessary? (Do the students have the vocabulary needed in order to follow directions? Can they operate a tape recorder?) How can the teacher answer the above questions? (See student records; give a pretest; reassign the student to another station; give the student information needed; place directions on a tape recording if reading ability is doubtful.) A logical task sequence must be organized so that the activity progresses step by step to a successful conclusion.

Each learning station should be continually evaluated. Teachers need to know if it is attractive to children; if the goals are clear and if the directions to achieve them are easily understood; if the station can accommodate different levels of maturity; and if the children's comments are favorable to its continuance and/or expansion. Children should have the opportunity to request other learning stations, and they need a balance between working alone and in groups that provides experiences in cooperation and accommodation in order to achieve the objectives.

Labeling Stations   There are many types of stations from which teachers can select to serve learning situations. They usually bear descriptive titles although some teachers give numbers or letters to theirs. Many are named from the musical elements to be studied: Rhythm, Melody, Harmony, Form, Tone Qualities, Dynamics, Tempo, and sometimes Music Fundamentals or Theory. Others may be Guitar, Ukulele, Keyboard Lab, Electronic Lab, Filmstrip, or Programed Materials. Many teachers invent titles that amuse children, such as Make and Play, Drums Away, Fun and Games, Keyboard Kapers, Read All About It, Play That Tune, Listen!, Composer's Corner, and Make a Tone Row.

An *exploratory-optional* station is one the learner is free to choose and for which the teacher does not point out the educational purpose before the child visits it. Such stations may assist teachers in observing the learner's musical attitudes and interests because the educational task is self-selected and reflects interest and preference.

When a music teacher establishes 30 one-level activity stations in a music room and moves at once into an individualized situation, this is *only a first step* toward organizing an individualized program of instruction. Such a program may require several years of evolution before learning is on a truly individualized basis. This first step operation represents an admirable effort, but it can be quickly perceived that while students are working at individual tasks, they are doing these in turn; their instruction

[7] Helen L. Cornell, "Drums and Dumpsters, Puppets and Pods," *Music Educators Journal,* April 1974, pp. 61–63.

has yet to be individualized in terms of the needs and learning styles of each student and it has done little to take into account their different rates of learning and ability levels. Even so, positive results have been reported though these may have been influenced favorably in part because the experience was new and excitingly different. One music teacher instituted the above first step program in a spring term. The evaluation of that teacher claimed that the experience resulted in:

1. more opportunity to interact with children.
2. more opportunity to learn to know each child.
3. more evidence of improved teacher-pupil and pupil-pupil relationships.
4. more opportunity to observe each student.
5. more independence on the part of the learners.
6. more enjoyment of music fundamentals by learners.
7. more interest in music, particularly at the sixth grade level.
8. more interest in singing because it became only part of a more balanced program.

The evaluations of the children included the following:

I like music because nobody tells you what to do.

I really like station D because I can listen to different kinds of music.

I really like music because it is organized; the stations are fun.

I like station H (composing) because it is a free station. I also like the quickie you do after you have done the work at your station.

I like every single station in the room; I think it is a good way to learn about music.

I like music stations because they are different from any other music activities.

I like it because you do other things than sing.

I like to be manager.

I like station G because I learn my notes faster.

I like station J because you try to find all four beats in it and draw lines to add up to four.

I like stations because I learn a lot and they are fun!

A plan for initiating fully individualized instruction is described in a publication by Floy S. Moore.[8] Combining group work with job cards for individuals, the author describes in detail how a teacher can initiate individualized instruction using everyday materials at little or no cost. The author states in the Preface: "The plan is quite structured so as to give definite limits to the students. . . . However, it contains opportunities for creative effort and for enrichment and can be (later) modified into a situation of more 'music lab' dimensions." Excerpts from the book are reproduced here with permission.

---

[8] Floy S. Moore, *Individual Studio-Stations in the General Music Class* (Portland, Ore.: Sumar Publications, 1974), 1152 N.E. 189 Place, 97230.

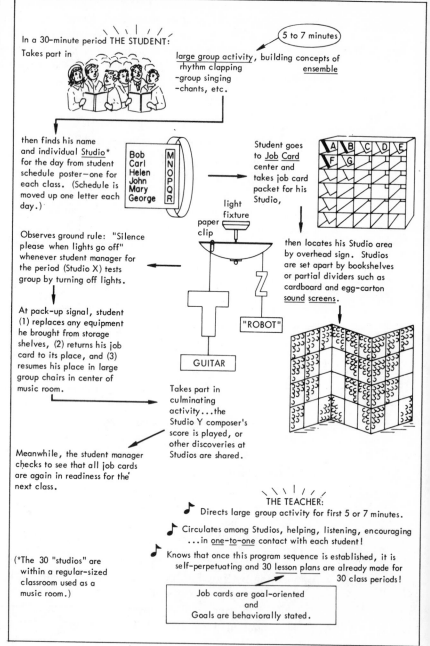

In a 30-minute period THE STUDENT:

Takes part in

large group activity, building concepts of
rhythm clapping
–group singing
–chants, etc.

ensemble

5 to 7 minutes

then finds his name
and individual Studio*
for the day from student
schedule poster—one for
each class. (Schedule is
moved up one letter each
day.)

Bob
Carl
Helen
John
Mary
George

M
N
O
P
Q
R

Student goes
to Job Card
center and
takes job card
packet for his
Studio,

A B C D E
F G

Observes ground rule: "Silence
please when lights go off"
whenever student manager for
the period (Studio X) tests
group by turning off lights.

light
fixture

paper
clip

then locates his Studio area
by overhead sign. Studios
are set apart by bookshelves
or partial dividers such as
cardboard and egg-carton
sound screens.

At pack-up signal, student
(1) replaces any equipment
he brought from storage
shelves, (2) returns his job
card to its place, and (3)
resumes his place in large
group chairs in center of
music room.

"ROBOT"

GUITAR

Takes part in
culminating
activity...the
Studio Y composer's
score is played, or
other discoveries at
Studios are shared.

Meanwhile, the student manager
checks to see that all job cards
are again in readiness for the
next class.

THE TEACHER:

♩ Directs large group activity for first 5 or 7 minutes.

♩ Circulates among Studios, helping, listening, encouraging
...in one-to-one contact with each student!

♩ Knows that once this program sequence is established, it is
self-perpetuating and 30 lesson plans are already made for
30 class periods!

(*The 30 "studios" are
within a regular-sized
classroom used as a
music room.)

Job cards are goal-oriented
and
Goals are behaviorally stated.

List of Studios

The following is a list of learning sources used in the individual studios of the pilot project. Obviously, not all schools will have the same set of equipment. Therefore teachers who use an individual studio plan will need to determine what sources are available at their schools and what alphabetical order is most workable for their situations. Section IV contains a detailed description of each studio learning source.

A	Musicology (library materials)
B	Banjo-uke (small banjo with 4 strings tuned as a ukulele)
C	"Play the Beats" game
D	"Play the Beats" game
E	Chord organ
F	Chord organ
G	Melody bells (a set of 8 diatonic tone bells C to C')
H	Autoharp
I	Chord organ
J	NOTES—a teacher-made bingo-like game
K	NOTES
L	Hand bells—a set of toy Swiss-type bells
M	Melodica
N	Computer—a Playskool computer toy with teacher-made cards of musical symbols
O	Scale Game
P	Puzzles
Q	Small Percussion
R	Resonator bells
S	Musicology
T	Guitar
U	Chord organ
V	Melody bells
W	Electronic sound generator (made from kit)
X	Manager
Y	Composer
Z	Robot
𝄞	Guitar
𝄢	String bass
♭	Melody bells
#	Acoustical engineer

Student Record

The teacher records in a grade book the studio at which students have worked, and, in brief notation on a segment of the page, some indication of their progress.

The following is one example:

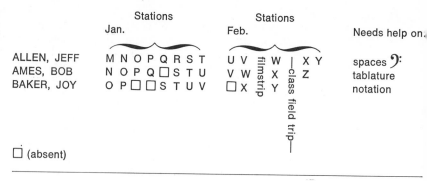

	Stations Jan.	Stations Feb.	Needs help on
ALLEN, JEFF	M N O P Q R S T	U V W X Y	spaces 𝄢
AMES, BOB	N O P Q ☐ S T U	V W X Z	tablature
BAKER, JOY	O P ☐ ☐ S T U V	☐ X Y	notation

☐ (absent)

The job cards contain very explicit explanations of activities. Many of them tell where to find materials; how to use them; how to use the time provided; where to obtain assistance; and how and what to do during the last five minutes of the class period.

By the second year of such a program the teacher will have evolved means to support better accommodation of individual differences. One teacher had, at this point, expanded the opportunities at each station to include three or more choices or levels of difficulty, thus moving nearer to individualization.

Learning packages have become available commercially and many teachers are making their own. While most are designed for school use, some can be taken home by children. Tapes are in wide use as a kind of learning package. Emphasis should be on musical experiences rather than stressing isolated and uninteresting facts such as, "A quarter note in moderate tempo receives one beat." With tapes, melodies are identified; the listener tells in what ways melodies are varied; whether the music is now faster or slower in tempo or higher or lower in pitch; whether the rhythm is even or uneven and if the music moves in two's or three's; instruments are identified. Other packages may be concerned with types of scales, building scales with the knowledge of their structure; writing descants; and identifying phrases. There are packages for individuals, pairs, and small groups.

Examples of the use of learning packages are:

Upper primary level children have a learning activity packet from which they learn to recognize the sounds and names of instruments. They listen to a tape, then place pictures of the instruments in correct order as they hear their tone qualities.

Intermediate level children work in pairs with a record player and a sound filmstrip for instruction in music reading. The activity is self-correcting and the children keep records of their accomplishment. Another package consists of taped lessons for electronic organ. Another concerns playing the bells.

As part of the study of variation form, a *learning contract* is distributed to a class of ten- and eleven-year-olds, and each child determines which option or options contract to fulfill. The children will work individually or in pairs. The following is part of a sample learning contract concerning variation form.

Theme and Variation #1

Name _____ *Completion Date*_____
I WILL:
_____ 1. Make two variations of "Canoe Round" by changing the rhythm.

_____ 2. Make three variations of my own choice in the melody of "Johnny Has Gone For a Soldier."

_____ 3. Play this theme on an instrument of my choice as a march, a waltz, and a funeral dirge.

_____ 4. Play a variation of "Hot Cross Buns" by changing it from major to minor.

To return to the topic of music stations, they should be present in both the regular classroom and the music room as a matter of availability to the learners. The one or two in the classroom may be described best by the term *music center* because of the probability of the inclusion of a number of different activities, while those in the music room may be stations or studios because of the probability that they would be limited in scope by comparison with the more general center in the classroom. However, this is a decision of the teachers involved. With this type of informal arrangement, the student has the benefits of guidance in music from both the classroom teacher and the specialist and can learn music in a more meaningful context.

Individualized instruction is sometimes used by music specialists as a welcome change from traditional class instruction by employing it one or two days of the week or everyday during the spring term only. Accommodations are commonly made to incorporate choral and other large group activities.

References

ASPY, DAVID N., "Toward a Technology Which Helps Teachers Humanize Their Classrooms," *Educational Leadership,* March 1971, pp. 626–28.
BARTH, ROLAND S., *Open Education and the American School.* New York: Agathon Press, 1972.

BOYLE, DAVID J., and ROBERT L. LATHROP, "The Impact Experience," *Music Educators Journal,* January 1973.

DUNN, RITA, and KENNETH DUNN, *Practical Approaches to Individualizing Instruction: Contracts and Other Effective Teaching Strategies.* West Nyack, N.Y.: Parker Publishing Company, 1972.

Individualization in Music Education issue, *Music Educators Journal,* November 1972.

Individualized Music Program. New York: Holt, Rinehart and Winston, 1975. Cassette tape, teacher's guide, duplicating masters, posters.

MESKE, EUNICE B., and CARROLL RINEHART, *Individualized Instruction in Music.* Reston, Va.: Music Educators National Conference, 1975.

MONSOUR, SALLY, *Music in Open Education.* New York: Center for Applied Research in Education, 1974. 521 Fifth Ave., 10017.

MOORE, FLOY S., *Individual Studio-Stations in the General Music Class.* Portland, Ore.: Sumar Publications, 1974. 1152 N.E. 189 Place, 97230.

Music in Open Education issue, *Music Educators Journal,* April 1974.

Open Classroom: Informal Education in America. Dayton, Ohio: Institute for Development of Educational Activities, Inc., 1972.

SHIPMAN, DAVID, CARMAN M. CULVER, and ANN LIEBERMAN, eds., *Teachers on Individualization: The Way We Do It.* New York: McGraw-Hill Book Company, 1974.

SILBERMAN, CHARLES E., *The Open Classroom Reader.* New York: Random House, 1973.

TALMAGE, HARRIET, ed., *Systems of Individualized Education.* Berkeley, Calif.: McCutchan Publishing Corporation, 1975.

In our teaching of men we hardly do more than the housemaid's humble chore of raising the blinds to let the sunlight stream into the house. The teacher's work is to remove impediments to a man's own seeing, to remove the things that would block the light. He cannot reach into another man's mind to insert knowledge; neither can he furnish the light to that mind by which it will see the truth. He merely sets nature free to work, as a doctor's medicine helps nature to throw off a disease; his is the humble work of helping nature, imitating its procedures, but never supplanting it. . . . He cannot offer the comfort of a superior intellect, as an angel can, for in fact his intellect is not superior; it is of exactly the same kind as that of the student.

St. Thomas Aquinas
1225–1274

Planning and Organizing to Teach Music

5

The intent of this chapter is to provide suggestions for planning, organizing, and implementing music programs for children. Ways of formulating objectives to guide children's cognitive, affective, and psychomotor learning are also presented.

Basic Phases of Program Building

A program building process for music has several interrelated parts.

Statement of Philosophy   A philosophy serves as a foundation and framework for building the program. For example, if a teacher declares the following to be a philosophical belief about music, then one must ask how this philosophy is reflected and implemented in his or her program for children. Two examples of philosophical statements follow:

> Music education is part of aesthetic education; aesthetic education is part of the general education of the child. Through experiences with music, the learner will be increasingly capable of feeling, creating, discovering, performing, learning, and thinking.

Through music, people can live more full and complete lives because of their sensitivity to the world of sound. Such persons will know music's language, its symbols, and be able to form concepts concerning the elements that comprise music—concepts that will serve as tools to find meaning and to add to their knowledge of music and the human experiences of which it is a part.

What type of program must be organized and activated to reflect each of the above stated philosophies? A well-constructed philosophical statement should give direction and enable teachers of music to make clear to their coworkers and the general public the importance of music; it should be the product of either the music staff or the classroom teacher or teachers responsible for and involved in developing the music program. The philosophical statement should serve as a guide for three phases of program development: specifying terminal goals, implementing and developing the program, and evaluating the program.

Specifying Terminal Goals

Terminal goals have the purpose of describing the music capabilities the learner can be expected to attain during a year or in grades K–6. These goals should be carefully stated with a number of considerations in mind. They should be based upon generalized goals held by the school and the community, and be in accord with public opinion concerning music's value and position in education. Other bases used in the specification of terminal goals are the needs of the learners for aesthetic expression and the structure of music as a field of study. Relevant research in music education should be used in the formulation of terminal goals; analysis of the community must also influence them. Cultural groups, home backgrounds, business activities, social activities, and music activities and resources should be reflected in the goals of the program. To keep goals relevant and current, teachers must incorporate applicable knowledge they acquire from professional study and research as well as information obtained from professional meetings, workshops, conferences, and conventions. Those who write and agree upon the terminal goals should do so with the intent that such goals reflect the accepted philosophical beliefs concerning both the school program and the music program. These goals should be stated specifically to serve as direction in designing present music programs. Nevertheless they should not remain in a rigid state, but be flexible enough to allow for suitable innovative changes.

Implementing and Developing the Program

The major purpose of this phase of developing a music curriculum is to identify the total learning environment that will make it possible for the learner to achieve the terminal goals. The major activities essential to this process for individuals, a class, or for grades K–6 are:

Specifying instructional and behavioral objectives
Selecting program content
Sequencing the proposed instruction
Suggesting types of learning experiences

Objectives as a Basis for Planning and Teaching

Introduction The Pictorial Model of Music Learning indicates the four major categories of music content: the elements of music as a discipline; musical skills; attitudes, values, and behaviors; and musical thinking. These form the framework from which the teacher selects justifiable objectives, then plans learning experiences which serve to promote them.

A Pictorial Model of Music Learning

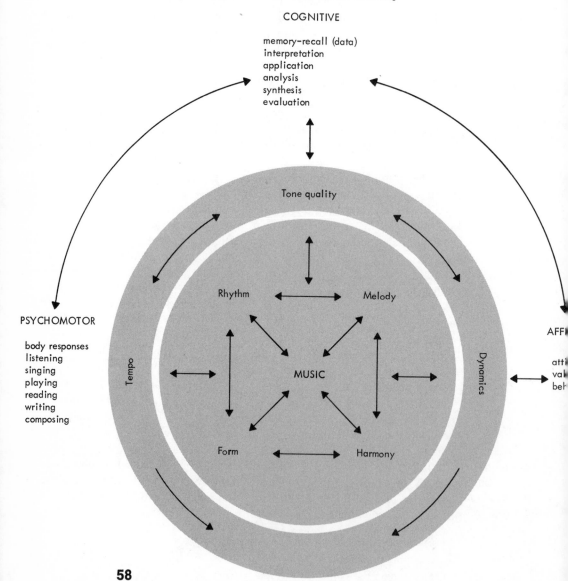

Objectives   Primarily, music teachers become involved with four distinct levels of objectives.

1. general school objectives (terminal goals)
2. music content objectives
3. instructional objectives (specific objectives for the teacher)
4. behavioral objectives (stated in specific and measurable terms as objectives for the children)

General objectives have already been discussed. *Music content objectives* are concerned with the principal aims to be realized in the area of music. For example, in the content area of music the objectives could focus on musical knowledge, the history of music, development of skills in listening, creating, and performing, appreciation of music, and problem-solving processes in music.

Since *instructional objectives* are closely associated with formulating and implementing plans for teaching, they are more clearly focused. Minimal precise instructional objectives of which the teacher is aware when planning and developing learning activities for listening are:

To help the students to

understand the necessity for listening as part of the process of communication.

differentiate between hearing and listening as a means of learning music.

respect listening as a means of learning music.

improve in the ability to listen to music with discrimination.

listen with specific purposes in mind (to appreciate, to interpret, to analyze, to discriminate, to solve problems, to evaluate).

listen to follow directions, make explanations, and to understand the music.

use knowledge of musical elements in analytical listening.

Specific instructional objectives state the purposes which guide the selection and development of behavioral objectives, and for selecting and sequencing content and learning experiences. They should relate to the terminal goals of the school and of the music program as a whole. Instructional objectives can be formulated and sequenced for use in designing a school music program, a program for a class, for a block of two to three grade levels, for a small group or for a daily lesson plan. They can serve as guides to the selection of objectives in the areas of knowledge, skills, and appreciations that are relevant and appropriate for each student. For example, such objectives could begin with the following ideas:

To acquire knowledge (understanding) of _____

To develop the skill of _____

59   To encourage appreciation (attitudes, values, behaviors) of _____

An example of the relationship of the four levels of objectives is found below:

General Goal of the School.[1]	To develop a sense of aesthetic taste in all aspects of life.
Music Content Objective.	To increase the students' capacity to control the availability of aesthetic qualities through music.
Instructional Objectives for a	
Class:	To demonstrate understanding of rhythm, melody, harmony, dynamics, tempo, tone quality, and form.
Lesson:	To identify brass, woodwind, and string instruments by their tone qualities.
Behavioral Objective.	Upon hearing a recording of the Third Movement of the Tchaikovsky Symphony No. 4, the student will identify the sections performed by the woodwind choir, brass choir, strings, and full orchestra by writing W, B, S, and O in correct order on a sheet of paper provided by the instructor.

Specific behavioral objectives are stated in terms of precise behavior to be manifested by the students, the learning to be attained, and the conditions under which learning occurs. In other words, a well-written behavioral objective states *what the students are expected to do, under what conditions they are expected to do it,* and *to what extent (how well) they are expected to do it.* A behavioral objective is precise and limited, such as, "After listening to these (specific) recordings, the students will identify the dominant woodwind instruments by writing their names in the spaces provided on the worksheet." The objective states something the students can do after an educational experience that they could not do prior to it.

Writing Behavioral Objectives The three parts of a behavioral objective were stated above as (1) what the learners will do, (2) under what conditions they will do it, and (3) how well they are expected to perform. What the learners will do should be identified by an "observable verb." Part two of an objective, the conditions section, should not have a time limit unless time is an essential part of the objective, and this is seldom the case. Part three, how well the learners are expected to perform, is best expressed by using the phrase "at least" when numerical criteria are desired. It is permissible to use two, three, or more sentences if these are needed to state an objective fully. It is also permissible to use pictorial means when these contribute to communicating the objective clearly. The word "correctly" is often redundant in stated objectives. For example, "The learner will name the wind instruments of the orchestra" is a better

---

[1] Adapted from Malcolm Besson, et al., *Teaching Music in Today's Secondary Schools* (New York: Holt, Rinehart and Winston, Inc., 1974), p. 59.

statement than "The learner will correctly name the wind instruments of the orchestra." Objectives should apply to the individual student rather than be stated "at least eighty-five percent of the students" will accomplish what the objective asks. Although there may be some pupil failures, it is not necessary to predict this on a class basis. When percents are applied to quantities, such quantities are only those that are expressed in numbers. For example, if there are ten items in a test, ninety percent can be used when referring to nine of the ten questions.

There may be subobjectives related to the major objective. For example, a subobjective related to the behavioral objective immediately above might be, "After listening to this (specific) recording, the student will identify the clarinet as the solo woodwind instrument by writing its name in the space provided in the worksheet." A subobjective is written in the same manner as the major objective, but is subordinate in relation to the major objective within this educational goal.

Cognitive objectives are those concerned with facts and knowledge, mental activities having to do with action verbs such as identifying, analyzing, listing, labeling, classifying, categorizing, describing, and evaluating. Teachers can plan activities in which students, by their overt (observable) responses will reveal whether or not, or to what extent, the activities were successful in helping them attain the objectives. Because concepts are personal, resulting from combinations and patterns of an individual's experiences, their cognitive behaviors are not necessarily synonymous with what is stated in the objectives.

Cognitive Behavioral Objectives

CATEGORY OF LEARNING	PERFORMANCE OBJECTIVE
Knowledge.	The students will identify eight instruments of the orchestra as they listen to each of them from a specially prepared tape.
Comprehension.	The students will differentiate 2/4, 3/4, and 4/4 meters by demonstrating the conducting pattern of each meter as they listen to musical examples of each of them from a prepared tape.
Application.	Given an eight measure chord sequence, the students will provide a melody consonant with the chords in a meter of their choice. Three or fewer errors in notation will be considered satisfactory.
Analysis.	Given the score of an unfamiliar song from a music series book, the student will identify sequence, ostinato, repeat sign, rhythm pattern, melody pattern, the key, and the scale tone that initiates the melody. Two or three omissions will be considered satisfactory.

Synthesis. Given the melody with its accompanying chords, the students will create a classroom orchestra score involving voices, piano, bells, Autoharp, and percussion of their choice.

Evaluation. Students will listen to the singing of the class while they observe the score of the song. They will then judge the performance in terms of intonation, pronunciation, appropriate tone quality, and rhythmic accuracy.

Psychomotor Objectives The term psychomotor unites mind and movement; it describes mental processes that have movement as the end result, thus including musical performance. There are a number of categories of psychomotor skills. At the lowest level is perception that eventually calls for a physical action, then follows the "set," which implies a readiness to act, the guided responses (an observable reaction), a learned response of habitual nature, a more complex overt response such as the automatic fingering on an instrument, then the advanced control of motions that results in adaptations or improvements, and finally, the ability to originate or develop new skills.

Musical performance requires cognitive processes, and this combination of mental processes with the resulting physical responses is called psychomotor learning. Such consequences can be evaluated in terms of observable performance. Ways of doing this include the use of behaviorally stated objectives that refer to individual and group musical performance or other body movement and certain creative activities. Checklists and rating scales can be used to evaluate the performance of individuals. Checklists for evaluation can be constructed, using such titles as Musical Skills, Instrumental Performance, Vocal Performance, Improvisation Skills, and Conducting Skills.

Affective objectives are those concerned with feelings, attitudes, appreciations, and values. When working in this area, teachers must remember not to indoctrinate learners, but to help them acquire information upon which to act and make judgments with increasing independence. Also, since such acts and judgments are often highly personal, the learner's privacy should not be threatened by the school. When students are reacting positively to music—that is, with personal enjoyment, it can be assumed that they are finding satisfaction in the experience in which they are involved, that they desire to hear more of this kind of music, that they identify with it, and that they desire to evaluate it. Since such personal responses are often covert (not observable), the behavioral objective may appear to be not applicable, or at least more difficult to construct, because of a lack of definite criteria to measure performance. In contrast to the observable verbs typical of cognitive objectives, nonobservable verbs such as the following are appropriate for affective objectives: appreciate, love, desire, choose, like, dislike.

Affective Behavioral Objectives Four learning categories to use as guides when constructing affective behavioral objectives for elementary schools have been identified, according to the Krathwohl-Bloom *Taxonomy:*

1. Receiving	Being receptive is made known by observable awareness, willingness, or attentiveness.
2. Responding	Active desire for an experience, voluntary action, lack of resistance.
3. Valuing	Forming personal preferences, developing firm convictions, recognizing traditional values, acting in accordance with convictions.
4. Organization	Comparing, relating, and synthesizing values; developing a personal hierarchy of values.

In the affective domain, teachers should commit themselves to the task of creatively devising ways for children to express covert (internal) learnings in overt ways. There are many ways in which pupils reveal their individual appreciations, attitudes, habits, values, and interests. See the examples which follow:

Affective Behavioral Objectives [2]

CATEGORY OF LEARNING (covert activity)	PERFORMANCE OBJECTIVE (overt manifestation)
Receiving (being receptive).	After several successful experiences in accompanying with the Autoharp, the student, at the teacher's suggestion, takes the instrument to a practice booth on his/her own time to work with a learning package concerning the Autoharp.
Responding.	When given the opportunity to choose to participate or to not participate in several types of group activities, the student chooses to join a recorder group.
Valuing.	After attending a school concert of the local symphony orchestra, the student voluntarily writes to the conductor, urging him to bring the orchestra to school for another concert.
Organization (of a personal hierarchy of values).	When provided the time and access to phonograph recordings, the student arranges them in order of his/her preference.

[2] David R. Krathwohl, Benjamin Bloom, and B. B. Masia, *Taxonomy of Educational Objectives: Handbook II: The Affective Domain* (New York: David McKay Company, Inc., 1964). Adapted.

While behavioral objectives are acknowledged to give precise direction to teaching and learning, they become controversial when used rigidly, stifling individuality. As stated above, they are somewhat difficult in the affective domain because many affective responses are not observable, thereby ruling out the clear evaluation typical of cognitive responses. Perhaps the matter can be summarized by saying that any good idea can be weakened by those who use it poorly, and that the teacher's judgment must prevail over rigidity of any kind in the human experience we call education.

Teachers should ponder the warning of Charles Leonhard not to over-emphasize the intellectual aspects of music: "We should exercise caution in abandoning the goals we have worked toward under the often vague term appreciation. One danger that I see in the current emphasis on concepts and structured learning is that we may become so involved in the specifics and minutiae of music that we forget that the musical experience is basically an affective experience. Whatever else it may achieve, music loses its value when it fails to touch the heart and stir the feeling of people." [3] Those words urge teachers to consider children's appreciative responses to music and to realize that these are often nonverbal in character. This is part of affective learning—the feelings and emotions aspect. Music is always a reflection of humanity; the technical aspects of music are only a means of communication. *Music is an aesthetic experience and a social language before it is an intellectual experience,* and competent teachers never forget this when they plan the music lesson.

Exploratory Objectives   There are objectives that are open-ended, therefore not as exact in nature, being focused upon experiences rather than on precise outcomes. These are *exploratory objectives* which free students to adventure into what are to them uncharted avenues of music learning. When students are engaged in music experiences of this type, there are certain characteristics of their efforts to learn. They are:

Seeking individual fulfillment through a musical experience.

Freely experimenting, exploring, and testing their own ideas.

Disclosing their imagination in creative ways.

Operating on hypotheses and intuition to create new musical sounds, forms, and interpretations.

Employing analytical thought processes to seek musical meanings and results.

Musical exploration and creativity can take many forms: improvisation, movement, composition, conducting, interpretation, and experiments with sounds and instrumentation. Exploratory objectives should encourage students to find new ways that involve inductive and intuitive thought processes. The Manhattanville Music Curriculum Program in Chapter Eleven provides examples of this.

[3] Excerpt from address by Charles Leonhard at the Conference to Improve the Effectiveness of Music Education in Oregon Elementary Schools, Gearhart, Oregon, April 27–28, 1967. State Department of Education, Salem, Oregon.

Selecting Program Content   The program content should be selected on the basis of what capabilities the learner must acquire to satisfy the instructional objectives. Such content will be selected from the structure of musical knowledge, which is included in this chapter, and will be appropriate for the experiences and activities through which the musical elements are experienced—movement, composition, musical performance, and analysis of music. Knowledge of the capabilities of each child is essential in order to select content that is appropriate.

Selecting Music Content   One of the major tasks of any teacher is the selection of appropriate content. Concepts of music provide the focus for the elementary music program. The conceptual structure of music involves the elements of music: tempo, dynamics, rhythm, pitch, harmony, and tone quality, with their formal communicative and artistic organizations and forms. Personal comprehension of specific concepts relative to the structure of each of the elements is fundamental to an individual's understanding of both simple and complex compositions.

Sequencing the Proposed Instruction   When instruction is thoughtfully sequenced there is a logical learning continuum which aids in comprehension and retention of learning. Learners are able to "accommodate" new musical learnings to earlier assimilated experiences and reach a state of equilibration, according to Piaget. Steps in a learning progression can be listed or drawn in diagram form. The many facets of music instruction make it difficult for any one example to be representative of the sequencing necessary to achieve the instructional objective. The following model shows one way to sequence instruction concerning major and minor triads.

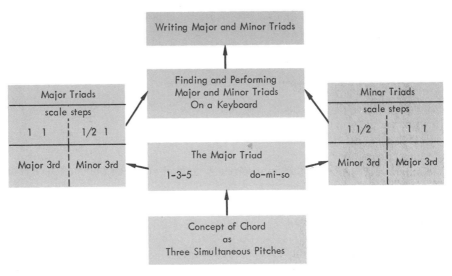

Model for Sequencing Instruction

The goals, instructional objectives, and program content dictate starting points from which the teacher or staff can select and sequence varied and appropriate learning experiences. The term *task analysis* has been applied to this process. The many experiences are encounters with music that result in active responses: moving, singing, playing instruments, listening, improvising, composing, conducting, and analyzing. These will be dealt with later.

**Day-to-Day
Performance
Objectives
and their
Relation to
Lesson Plans**
This is the point in planning where specific procedures (strategies) are selected by the teacher. There are many different possibilities for such planning, and the teacher normally chooses experiences and strategies suited both to the children under instruction and to his or her personality. No teacher will operate exactly like any other teacher; each is a unique personality. Thus the planning of the lesson will be a reflection of the particular teacher who prepares it, showing how that teacher's strengths are employed and how possible weaknesses are accommodated. Such plans may be for a daily lesson, a week's work, or a more lengthy unit. A sample lesson plan that may be used as a guide for devising a teacher's own plan follows:

AN INSTRUCTIONAL PLAN

THE EXPERIENCE: (The nature of the experience and the plan for conducting it.)

Designed for: Large Group_____ Small Group_____ Individual_____ Other_____

Time span needed for completion:

MATERIALS NEEDED:

OBJECTIVE(S): (State in performance terms the observable behavior of the learner, the conditions under which this takes place, and the extent of learning expected.)

Cognitive _____

Affective _____

_____

Psychomotor _____

_____

PRIOR KNOWLEDGE REQUIRED: (Competencies needed by the learner for the task.)

EVALUATION:

_____

In the above Instructional Plan *the experience* is to be stated in descriptive terms. The teacher lists special *materials necessary* in the conduct of the experience, and composes an *objective* or objectives in behavioral terms that spell out what observable activity or activities the learner will do as a result of the experience. The *prior knowledge required* section causes the teacher to reconsider the learning sequence to be certain that the learners have the necessary prerequisites that enable them to profit from the experience. When many such plans are assembled and sequenced, they could be the equivalent of a course of study.

The Structure of Music and the Sequence of Learning

The music teacher who understands the structure of music has little difficulty explaining to an administrator, board of education, and the public the content of music as an aesthetically and intellectually valid subject. By "structure of music" is meant the generalizations and supporting concepts and data that form the structure of the subject matter of music. These arise from the components of music: tempo, dynamics, tone quality, rhythm (duration), melody (pitch), harmony, texture, and form. Unless detail is placed in a structured pattern, it is rapidly forgotten. The cognitive structure of music is intended to refer to a flexible program of instruction. A sequential, logical, cyclical type of curriculum in which the learner proceeds from the simple to the complex is employed.

The Sequential Spiraling of Conceptual Learning In a spiral curriculum, a concept or generalization moves from the general to the more complex and specific as one advances to higher levels of learning. For example, learners will encounter duration of sound at each level, but with increasing complexity at each succeeding higher level. Students learn at different rates, therefore they may begin at a somewhat different level of comprehension. Once teachers recognize these variants, their plans should accommodate them with appropriate methods, activities, and materials. As stated earlier, the music program is based upon learning about the elements of music. This provides the teacher with a solid basis for curriculum planning that should be flexible, provide a wide variety of musical experiences, and employ a broad selection of musical literature.

**Specifics
of Music
Structure**

The major tasks confronting teachers are the selection, organization, and sequencing of content and learning experiences of a music program for children. Teachers need to justify to themselves the importance of what they teach. In the selection of music content and skills they may ask themselves:

> Does this help children to live better in today's world?
> Is this at the children's level of comprehension?
> Does this assist the children to acquire important musical concepts?
> Will this help to realize the objectives of the proposed program?

Children discover concepts and generalizations as they confront music through many planned experiences and through contact with facts in relation to those experiences. These are developed at various conceptual levels. The role of structure in learning lies in giving students an understanding of the fundamental structure of whatever subjects we choose to teach.[4] As important as this is, the teacher should remember that it must be combined with an understanding of the different learning styles of children and other individual differences.

Teachers choose portions of knowledge from the vast amount in existence. They should endeavor to select the most important and relevant information that will bring about maximum music learning. Music subject matter consists of data, concepts, and generalizations that make up the content of music, which Bruner calls the *structure* of the discipline. These three categories are explained below.

Data refer to particulars rather than to universals. They are propositions or statements that include things or situations of the present or of the past. Data can be tested and proved to be true or false.

Examples of musical data (facts) are:

> Bach died in 1750.
> A sharp placed before a note raises its pitch one-half step.
> In the same meter, a quarter note has the same duration as two eighth notes.

Some teachers place major emphasis on the learning of facts as ends

---

[4] Jerome S. Bruner, *The Process of Education* (Cambridge, Mass.: Harvard University Press, 1960), pp. 11–12.

within themselves. They fail to see the importance of using them as a foundation for organizing information into concepts. As a result, they may emphasize information of only minor import. Whether or not a fact is important to learn is usually determined by the context in which it is used. Therefore students should participate in learning experiences that help them tie together the facts they acquire to form more meaningful relationships.

The concept is first a nonverbal response to a stimulus. As this is repeated and varied, the concept grows and expands in the mind of the learner. In order to communicate and use the concept in human society, the learner will eventually find a name for it. The name of the concept, such as "harpsichord," is only a label for something that exists in a human mind. Thus, concepts represent characteristics common to a group of experiences; they are definitional when given word labels; they do not exist in reality, being only mental impressions; they are the mind's effort to give order to reality by attaching word-labels. They are thus mental constructs, and they include musical phenomena heard, seen, and felt by sensory perception. The effect of naming concepts is that communication is made easier and the complexity of the musical environment is reduced to manageable proportions. All concepts are not indicated verbally. Verbal or aural dimensions may lead one to experience a particular feeling that, although unnamed, is a concept. Later on the learner, perhaps a music listener, can analyze the concept and name it, thus making it more accessible and usable.

Young children understand concepts which relate to tangible things more easily than those which are abstract in nature. Teachers establish environments of musical stimuli that contain certain problems to be solved. In the ensuing experiences, the students encounter and solve problems, and in this process musical concepts and generalizations may be acquired. By observing the students, the teacher will know that the concept is understood even though unverbalized, because of their behavior (performance). Therefore, the concepts in the Conceptual Structure of Music listing soon to follow in this chapter are suggested for the teacher's use as a framework for planning and organizing experiences that will assist children in forming their own musical concepts. Listed below are theoretical steps in the development of the concept "melody."

The learners first experience a melody by hearing it, possibly many times.

They respond to it with body movement.

They experience other melodies and begin to form notions of what a melody is.

They experiment with performing melodies by singing, playing instruments, and body movement; they create their own melodies.

They compare their performances with melodies performed by others.

By further effort they are able to comprehend that rhythm unites with pitch to form melody.

They see a familiar melody in an understandable form of notation.

They revise and expand their concept of melody; they then use their newly revised concept in exploring other aspects of melody.

Generalizations are statements that contain two or more concepts and that show relationships among concepts. Like facts, generalizations can be substantiated or disproved by referring to concrete or obvious evidence. Both concepts and generalizations aid children in organizing and seeing relationships and meaning in music.

Main ideas or generalizations suggest relationships and offer insights into the way music is produced and into the ways it affects the life of man. Generalizations not only describe facts (data) but they give structure to them. Thus, careful consideration must be given by the teacher in the selection of valid and significant content objectives which include the discovery, processing, and mastery of relevant and worthy data, concepts, and generalizations.

The following conceptual structure of music outline is highly condensed and can easily be expanded. The generalizations stated in formal, adult language may be used by teachers in planning programs, courses of study, and lessons. They are rarely recited or presented to children. Examples of concepts and generalizations appear in the outline. The same concept or generalization may be sought and explored at very simple levels, progressing in spiral fashion to ever higher levels as children grow in musical responsiveness. *Most generalizations are tentative;* they will be tested, refined, and explored further. Bruner writes, "A curriculum, as it develops, should revisit these basic ideas repeatedly, building upon them." [5] Young children learn that "sound and silence have duration," but this generalization will be expanded, refined, and made more specific as children increase and refine their experiences in music. Teachers do not "teach" concepts; instead they plan experiences and guide children so that they may develop their own.

The outline to follow describes in conceptual terms a world of music from which teachers can prepare objectives in relation to content and suitability for an individual, a class, a level of accomplishment, a course of study, or for a complete music program. The Conceptual Structure of Music outline portrays music as a broad content area from which only a small part would be selected by the teacher for implementation within the boundaries of a music lesson or a year's course of study.

A CONCEPTUAL STRUCTURE OF MUSIC

Tempo

GENERALIZATION: Tempo (degrees of fast and slow) is found in all organized music.

[5] Bruner, *op. cit.,* p. 53.

Concepts:

lento	(slow)
largo	(broad and slow)
andante	(moderately slow)
allegretto	(moderately fast)
allegro	(lively)
vivace	(spirited)
presto	(very fast)
a tempo	(in original tempo)
accelerando	(gradually faster)
rallentando	(gradually slower)
ritardando	(gradually slower)

Dynamics

GENERALIZATION: Dynamics (degrees of loud and soft) is a characteristic of most music.

Concepts:

accent	> – ∧	(more than usual stress)
pianissimo	pp	(very soft)
piano	p	(soft)
mezzo piano	mp	(medium soft)
mezzo forte	mf	(medium loud)
forte	f	(loud)
fortissimo	ff	(very loud)
sforzato or sforzando	sf	(heavy accent)
crescendo	cresc.	(gradually increasing loudness)
decrescendo	decresc.	(gradually decreasing loudness)
diminuendo	dim.	(gradually decreasing loudness)
sign for crescendo:	◁	
sign for decrescendo:	▷	

SUBGENERALIZATION: There are relationships between changes of dynamics and tempo, and melody, harmony, and texture.

Rhythm

GENERALIZATION: Rhythm in music is a grouping of sounds and silences of varying duration, usually controlled by a regular beat.

Concepts:

beat
equal divisions of the beat
unequal divisions of the beat
one-to-two relation of note values
one-to-three relation of note values

one-to-four relation of note values
notated rhythm
dotted notes
rests
speech-rhythm
notated speech-rhythm
articulation such as staccato and legato
fermata ⌒

SUBGENERALIZATION: Musical sound has duration and pitch.

Concepts:

word-rhythms related to duration
word-rhythms related to duration and pitch
notation of word-rhythms
notation of melody

SUBGENERALIZATION: Accent or lack of accent governs types of rhythm.

Concepts:

metrical rhythm
meter, bar line, measure, upbeat (anacrusis), downbeat,
meter signature, duple meter, triple meter, primary accent,
secondary accent, rhythm pattern
asymmetrical rhythm ($\frac{5}{4}$, $\frac{7}{8}$, etc).
"measured" rhythm (no regular recurring beat, such as in
Gregorian chant)
free rhythm
rallentando (rall.)
accelerando (accel.)
rubato
no common metrical beat (such as some Oriental, Indian,
and Hungarian music which cannot be expressed in traditional notation)
syncopation as a disturbance of the normal pulse of meter,
accent, and rhythm

SUBGENERALIZATION: Devices related to rhythm are used by composers to
add interest to their compositions.

Concepts:

rhythm patterns
rhythmic ostinati
augmentation
diminution
canonic imitation
polyrhythm
free rhythm (rit., rall., accel., rubato, syncopation)
syncopation

SUBGENERALIZATION: There are rhythms which are characteristic of
peoples and nations.

Concepts:

distinctive rhythms in national songs

distinctive rhythms in national dances
(minuet, waltz, polka, schottische, square dance, etc.)
distinctive rhythms associated with ethnic groups

GENERALIZATION: Rhythm is universal and has meanings beyond music.

Concepts:

Rhythm in—
the seasons
waves of the ocean
the grain of wood
architecture
painting
the heartbeat
day and night
life cycles of plants and animals
the speech and movement of man

Melody

GENERALIZATION: A melody is a linear succession of tones which are rhythmically controlled and are perceived by the human ear as a meaningful grouping of tones. (Children might say, "A melody is a line of tones in rhythm that sounds right.")

SUBGENERALIZATION: Direction: The tones of melodies may go up, down, or remain the same in pitch.

Concepts:

pitch and vibration
high and low
contour
relation to tension, climax, and release
notation of pitch
staff, note, clef, numerals, and syllables to identify pitches

SUBGENERALIZATION: Duration: Melodies are formed by a union of pitch and rhythm.

Concepts:

relation of song melodies to word rhythms
note values (see Rhythm)
rhythm patterns in, or related to, melodies

SUBGENERALIZATION: The tones of melodies may have adjacent (scale-line) pitches or skips (chord-line pitches).

Concepts:

scale (major, minor, diatonic, modal, pentatonic, chromatic, the tone row derived from the chromatic, wholetone, ethnic, invented)
passive and active scale tones (tension and release)
tonal centers
home tone

key
key signature
accidental
intervals
relation to chords (see Harmony)

SUBGENERALIZATION: Form: Melodies are usually formed of distinct parts or sections.

Concepts:

phrase
phrase arrangement (repetition and contrast; unary, binary, and ternary song forms)
sequence
tonal patterns and their alterations

SUBGENERALIZATION: Devices: Melodies can be manipulated. (Children might say, "Melodies can be changed in different ways.")

Concepts:

transposition
diminution
augmentation
inversion
retrograde
melodic variation
rhythmic variation
harmonic variation
octave displacement

SUBGENERALIZATION: Melodies may reflect national or cultural styles.

SUBGENERALIZATION: Some melodies are functional in that they tend to communicate ideas and moods.

Harmony, Polyphony, and Texture

GENERALIZATION: Harmony pertains to the vertical aspect of music, the successions of chords and the relationships among them. (Children might say, "Harmony means chords and their changes.")

GENERALIZATION: Texture, a term derived from weaving, pertains to vertical and horizontal elements ("threads") in music which produce such effects as light, heavy, thick and thin, and which include styles of composition such as homophonic and polyphonic.

SUBGENERALIZATION: Homophonic music consists of one melody with an accompaniment.

Concepts:

accompanied song
accompanied instrumental solo
music of the nineteenth century
harmony suggested by chord tones in melodies

SUBGENERALIZATION: Polyphonic music has two or more melodic lines sounding at the same time; these melodic lines are connected in tonal music by harmonic relationships.

Concepts:

> round, canon
> counterpoint
> contrary motion
> fugue
> fugal entry
> music of Palestrina and J. S. Bach
> harmony suggested by chord tones in melodies
> descriptive terms: contrapuntal, imitative, canonic, fugal, atonal polyphony

SUBGENERALIZATION: A chord is any simultaneous combination of three or more pitches; some may be more agreeable to the ear than others. (Children might say, "A chord is three or more notes sounded together.")

Concepts:

> Chord construction—3rds, 4ths, 5ths, clusters, contrived chords
> inversions
> relation to key centers
>> triad
>> scale
>> major
>> minor
>> question and answer (V_7—I)
>> cadence: full, half, plagal
> relation to melody
>> harmonizing a tune
>> chord tones
>> passing tones
>> consonance
>> dissonance
>> primary and secondary chords
>> chording
> chords relating to no tonal center
>> atonality
>> chords as conjunctions of melodic lines
> parallel chords

SUBGENERALIZATION: Identical harmonies can be sounded at different pitch levels.

Concepts:

> transposition
> key signatures

SUBGENERALIZATION: Harmonies can be combined.

Concepts:

> bitonality
> polytonality

GENERALIZATIONS: Some kind of sound can be produced by almost every object in the environment.

Tone quality (timbre, tone color) is the difference between tones of the same pitch produced by different voices and instruments; it distinguishes the sound of one voice or instrument from another.

SUBGENERALIZATION: Sounds, voices, and instruments can be classified according to tone quality, range, characteristics, and the means employed to produce them.

Concepts:

Classification of unconventional sound sources
    paper
    rubber
    glass
    wood
    metal
    plastic
    food
    materials found in nature
    body sounds
    other

Classification of conventional sounds sources
    voices
        soprano
        alto
        tenor
        bass

    instruments
        strings
            plucked
            stroked
            bowed
            keyboard
        woodwinds
            flue
            reed
        percussion
        brass
        organ
        electronic

SUBGENERALIZATION: Instruments can be played in ways that produce different sounds.

Concepts:

legato
staccato
spiccato, as concerns bowing
mute, as concerns strings, trumpet, French horn, trombone
vibrato

use of extreme ranges of high or low
stop, as concerns the organ
glissando, as concerns the harp and other instruments
experimental ways

SUBGENERALIZATION: Voices and instruments may be combined to produce an infinite variety of tone qualities.

SUBGENERALIZATION: Composers and arrangers select different voices, instruments, and tone qualities for specific reasons.

SUBGENERALIZATION: The difference in tone qualities can be explained scientifically.

Concepts:

     resonance
     harmonics
     overtone series
     partials
     vibrato
     oscilloscope

Form

GENERALIZATION: Musical forms are similar to plans of construction made by architects.

Form in Music

SUBGENERALIZATION: Melodies may be divided into parts.

Concepts:

     motive
     phrase
     period

SUBGENERALIZATION: Melodies can be extended and altered.

Concepts:

     introduction
     coda
     interlude
     sequence
     repetition
     section
     diminution
     inversion
     retrograde
     thematic development
     augmentation

Forms of Music

SUBGENERALIZATION: Most musical form is based on the principle of repetition-contrast (same-different, unity-variety).

Concepts:

> a a
> a b
> a b a
> A B A sections
> rondo (A B A C A; A B A C A B A)
> variation

SUBGENERALIZATION: Some forms can be classified as contrapuntal.

Concepts:

> round
> canon
> fugue

SUBGENERALIZATION: A compound form comes into being when several movements are combined to form a complete musical composition.

Concepts:

> movement (of a larger work)
> instrumental compound forms
>   sonata-allegro
>   concerto
>   suite
>   classical dance
>   ballet
>   other
>   symphony
>   overture

An example of using this Structure of Music in the intermediate grades follows. The teacher has abstracted his or her generalization from the outline, "The family of reed instruments includes the oboe, bassoon, clarinet and saxophone." In developing this generalization, concepts of each of these instruments must be formed. When considering the bassoon, data such as these will be learned by the children:

Data	a long tube which doubles back on itself
	a double reed made of cane
	a conical bore
	a tone of cavernous quality
	a bass instrument
	a very wide range of pitches
Concept	the standard bassoon
Generalization	(assuming concepts of the four instruments have developed)
	The family of reed instruments includes the oboe, bassoon, clarinet, and saxophone.[6]

[6] Notice where the generalization is found in the Structure of Music. What might be termed a subconcept in the Tone Quality section was restated as a generalization. Find the source.

This generalization may later be refined and expanded if the teacher chooses to work with it further. For example, the discovery of the *metal* reed could be planned as a *discrepant event* which would bring the attention of the children to the function of reeds in the accordion, harmonica, and reed organ. Then the concept of the "family of reed instruments" will expand and the concept of "reed" will grow. Children can discover that each metal reed is constructed to produce a definite pitch, while each cane reed must in some way accommodate difference in pitch. Thus discovery grows out of discovery as the teacher guides the process in a helpful but unobtrusive way. The children are guided to discuss their findings and problems as they work with the tone qualities, range, appearance, and mechanical features of reed instruments. Such study as this is ordinarily *only a part* of a lesson plan which includes a variety of musical activities such as singing, playing instruments, body responses, and listening, all selected to assist progress toward specific objectives.

In developing concepts, children may listen to music, perform music, compose it, write it, analyze it, and discuss it. The aim is to clarify the mental image of the aspect of music under study.

**Organizing for
Conceptual
Learning**

Competent teachers of music have a logical plan to follow when they begin to organize their teaching efforts. They will:

1. Know, understand, and be able to describe each broad generalization upon which the structure of music is based.   generalizations

2. Know and understand each concept upon which the comprehension of each generalization rests.   concepts

3. State in their plans the behavioral changes that will result from experiences planned to achieve this.   objectives
                                                                (behavioral)

4. Choose the music experiences and music literature that will help the learner to develop each concept.   experiences

5. Select or develop evaluative techniques to measure the effectiveness of the musical experiences used to assist the learner in building concepts that in turn lead to the formation of generalizations.   evaluation

**Children's
Learning and
Teacher
Planning**

Thus far, the ways children learn have been emphasized; attention will now be given to the bases from which teachers plan. When children learn, they begin with facts (data), but when teachers plan, they begin with generalizations.

Despite the reverse appearance of the two columns, it should be obvious by now that the teacher's planning will reflect the learning process of children. The first step in learning is *perceptual*. The children learn facts by means of the senses, and the effective teacher plans to encourage children's use of every appropriate sense.

Children's Learning	Teacher Planning
1. **FACTS** (data) from which to acquire	**GENERALIZATIONS** reflecting structure of the discipline, to
2. **CONCEPTS** from which to form	**CONCEPTS** supporting the generalizations, to
3. **GENERALIZATIONS** reflecting the structure of the discipline	**FACTS** (data) necessary to build concepts

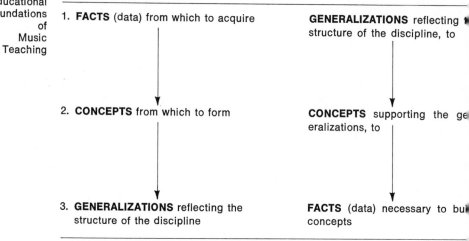

The second step requires *associative thinking* in that the images are retrieved from mental storage, reexamined, explored, and organized so that concepts may be formed from them. The third step has to do with *forming generalizations* based on experience with concepts, and applying these generalizations in new situations to test them and to change and refine them.

A major task of the teacher is to engage in a type of questioning that guides discussion, assists children in their comprehension of pertinent aspects of the matter at hand, helps them relate the parts to the whole, encourages them to explore, theorize, experiment, and so on. It is important that children verbalize their experiences. They work with musical facts, concepts, and generalizations in two ways: (1) listening to music, and (2) producing music by performing it and composing it. Habits, attitudes, and values are influenced by this process, the type of classroom environment (both physical and social), and the example set either consciously or unconsciously by the teacher's attitude toward music.

The selection of materials of instruction that most clearly reveal the essentials of the lesson is vital and poses another important task for the teacher. All of this is necessary to relate the learning process to the teaching process.

A balance of questions involving the various types of thinking are used by teacher and pupils as they assemble data and seek solutions to problems. In the exploration of problems they usually begin at the data level, move to the concept level, and then to the generalization level. Examples of different types of questions are indicated in the following illustration:

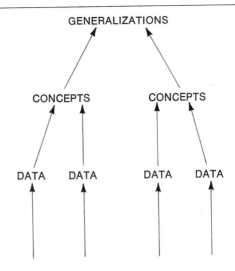

TEACHER'S QUESTIONS:
a balance of

Cognitive-memory Questions

"What is meant by this
term or symbol?"

Convergent Questions

"Under what conditions are
musical terms and symbols
used?"

Divergent Questions

"What would happen if there were
no terms or symbols?"

Evaluative Questions

"Are these the most appropriate
terms and symbols needed for
the best communication of
this song's message?"

Jerome Bruner writes, "Grasping the structure of a subject is under-standing it in a way that permits many other things to be related to it meaningfully. To learn structure, in short, is to learn how things are related." [7] ". . . the curriculum of a subject should be determined by the most fundamental understanding that can be achieved of the underlying principles that give structure to a subject." [8] Understanding the structure of music means being able to comprehend the relationship of the elements which comprise music and to use this understanding in dealing with music.

[7] Jerome Bruner, *The Process of Education* (Cambridge, Mass.: Harvard University Press, 1960), p. 7.
[8] *Ibid.*, p. 31.

Planning for Teaching

The teacher's knowledge of the competencies of children at the beginning of the year serves as a base for developing annual music programs, units or lessons. A model to use as a guide to planning for the optimum learning of each child follows:

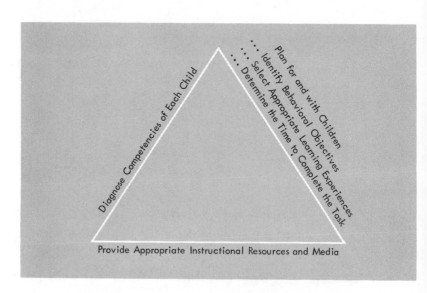

Model for Diagnosing and Planning for Learning

To know the children and their musical abilities at the beginning of the year, the teacher can utilize information from the following sources:

1. Health records	that may reveal any deviation from the norm affecting music learning, including eyesight, hearing, and muscular coordination.
2. Cumulative records	that begins when a child first enters school; they may indicate the scope and sequence of the child's musical learning.
3. Checklists	that indicate types of musical experience and levels of competency.
4. Tape recordings	of musical performances of the previous year.
5. Interviews with former teachers	that may reveal musical problems and experiences which relate to the present.

6. Interviews with private music teachers — that reveal abilities, interests, and attitudes.

7. Anecdotal records — that are dated records of significant observed behavior of the child by previous teachers.

Teachers may obtain information from:

1. Pupil-teacher conferences — to learn about children's interests, musical experiences, and family musical background.

2. Observations — of attitudes, facial expression revealing degrees of enjoyment, emotional involvement, ease of voice production, ability to stay on pitch, facility with instruments, ability in part singing, muscular coordination, rhythmic skill, and creative responses.

3. Class discussions — that reveal likes, dislikes, prejudices, problems, interests, appreciations, knowledge, and understanding.

4. Parent-teacher conferences — that reveal family musical interests and cultural and economic conditions affecting present musical responsiveness.

Lesson Plans

There are aspects common to all lesson plans. *First* is the instructional *objective* or objectives, the reason for the plan in the first place. The writing of instructional and behavioral objectives has already been stressed in this chapter. When they are properly written, they state the behavior by which the child evidences comprehension of the concept, under what conditions, and to what degree. *Second* is the selection of *activities* through which the child can engage in mental, physical, and affective processes that best assist forming a concept or concepts. An important principle is to plan for a variety of activities that keep the learners involved, interested, and happy. This requires that they are within the present abilities of the students so that the learner can experience success after due effort. *Third* is the selection of *materials* to use for the activities. In music education this term means all the musical, mechanical, and literary items needed, including songs (song material). Songs and recordings of musical worth should be chosen. All materials should be assembled and prepared in advance of the lesson to avoid confusion and loss of time. The *procedure* of the lesson is the *fourth* item. Sometimes this is stated in the activities section above. This is the learning sequence. An example based on an approach for a class would be:

1. A review of a favorite song, rhythmic response, or both that recall earlie
   learnings. Always try to add something new to review experiences.
2. A new problem activity usually related to or an outgrowth of the review.
3. Application of the problem in a new situation, such as in a different song, c
   on a different recording. This is done to evaluate the success of the childre
   in achieving the objective of the plan. From this the teacher will have clue
   indicating how to plan for the next lesson.
4. Close the lesson by singing a well-liked, familiar song.

Fifth is *evaluation*. This part of the plan may be incorporated into th
procedure, as above. The test regarding where it should be placed i
"Where can it be treated adequately?" It could conceivably appear in a
parts of a plan. Did the learners achieve the objectives? Were the learner
happy and satisfied with the experience? Which aspects of the plan wer
successful and which were not? What are the implications for the ne
music lesson?

Lesson plans can be organized in several ways, but all of the abov
parts should be present.

The first lessons of the year might center around pleasurable singin
and getting acquainted experiences. From the standpoint of music activitie
they might include something like the following:

First Day   Sing familiar songs.
                What did you learn to sing at camp last summer?
                What are your favorite songs from past years?
                Common repertoire songs.

Second Day   Review familiar songs; try to add something new to them.
                Discover or invent a rhythm pattern to be used with percus
                sion instruments with a song.
                Learn a new song.
                Begin to use songs or parts of songs for individual and grou
                tone matching.

Third Day   Sing familiar songs.
                Make up a tune for a short poem.
                Introduce a new recording for listening purposes; creat
                some appropriate physical responses.

The following suggested plan can accommodate all of the informatio
previously discussed in this chapter relating to associating objectives wit
the structure of music, learning data, the forming of concepts and (eventual
generalizations by children, behavioral objectives, and teaching pro
cedures that include questioning strategies.

Example I

DAILY LESSON PLAN

Name _____

Date _____ Grade _____ Time _____

Purpose (Instructional objective):

There can be more than one purpose and performance objective, and there can be sub-objectives.

Performance Objective (behavioral):

Materials Neeeded:

Teaching Strategies or Procedures:

    A. Beginning and motivating activities (setting the stage for learning).
       1. Planning activities with pupils.
       2. List of possible types of questions and their sequence.

    B. Developmental activities. Plan at least three different types for each lesson to accommodate individual learning styles and to realize instructional and behaviorally stated objectives written above.

    C. Summarization and evaluation activities.
       1. By students and teacher.
       2. By teacher to adjust his/her teaching of the next lesson.

Please use back of sheet for comments by student teacher and/or supervising teacher for evaluation, follow-up questions, etc.

Instructional Objective This states the purpose of the lesson from the standpoint of the teacher. Example: To expand knowledge of tonic dominant chord changes.

Behavioral Objective This identifies what will happen from the standpoint of the children. Example: After singing and accompanying with the Autoharp several (specific) familiar songs, some of which can be harmonized by (1) one chord, and (2) two chords, the learners will identify the tonic and dominant chords in these songs when the teacher plays them on the piano, the Autoharp, and from recordings. They will identify the tonic chord by raising one finger, and the dominant chord by raising five fingers, and will do this with their eyes closed.

Remember that behavioral objectives call for children to behave or perform in a variety of ways, such as: [9]

Identifying a musical instrument, term, symbol, or aspect of notation by picking it up, pointing to it, touching it, or communicating it verbally.

Naming an instrument, form, term, symbol, or relationship.

Arranging three or more phrases, terms, symbols, measures, or events in order based on a stated plan.

Describing properties sufficient to identify a type of song, phrase, term, symbol, or relationship.

Selecting an object, term, symbol, or phrase from two or more which might be confused.

Composing or *constructing* music, accompaniments, musical instruments, drawing, and written or verbal statements which indicate ability to infer, hypothesize, and evaluate.

Demonstrating the sequence of operations necessary to carry out a musical procedure.

Deriving an answer to a musical problem by employing the behaviors stated above, and organizing these into various types of data derived from such behaviors into a musical concept or generalization to be applied in the solution of other musical problems.

Materials List all media and/or materials needed for the lesson—projectors, films, slides, transparencies, tapes, recordings, charts, maps, books, poems, songs, paper, instruments, objects, etc. Teachers should be specific when listing sources; state the title of a book, with publisher and page numbers; state the manufacturer of a recording and the record number.

Teaching Strategies and Learning Experiences This is the "how to do it" part of the plan. What the teacher does and what the students are doing

[9] Robert E. Nye, Vernice T. Nye, Neva Aubin, and George Kyme, *Singing With Children,* 2nd ed. (Belmont, Calif.: Wadsworth Publishing Company, Inc., 1970).

in each activity is included here, as are the teacher's questions. The teacher tries to use as many different types of questions as are logically appropriate in exploring an idea or concept—knowledge, translation, interpretation, application, analysis, synthesis, and evaluative types of questions. This section can be divided into two distinct parts: (1) Introduction, which may include a review of a previous lesson, building readiness for the lesson of the day, and establishing purposes, (2) Developmental strategies, the work-study-game activities the children will engage in.

Evaluation It consists of concluding and evaluative strategies, specific techniques to be used to determine if the behavioral objectives of the lesson have been realized. Teacher and children generalize and summarize what has been accomplished or learned, what they planned to do but did not complete, how well they did what they did, where they could improve, as well as what they need to continue to work on in the next lesson.

The above plan is useful for beginning teachers because it assists in learning how to organize a lesson. Less detailed plans are used by experienced teachers because they know many of the details and procedures and do not need to write them.

Inexperienced teachers may feel that a great many things must be packed into a lesson in order that the year's objectives can be realized; thus they may err by striving to "cover" too much in a teaching plan. The fear of omitting something of importance can cause the acquisition of knowledge to become an objective rather than a process that nurtures the capacity to pursue profitable learnings. Such an approach negates the idea of conceptual learning because in order for concepts to grow and for generalizations to be formed, there must be studies in depth in which the main idea(s) is approached from every angle and by all appropriate senses. This is different from a random acquisition-of-information approach.

There are various types of lesson plan organizations. Most effective plans should be designed to free the teacher to establish a learning situation in which children can become involved in the exploration of music and in autonomous learning. Teachers sometimes become slaves of rigid lesson plans which emphasize musical content and musical skills as ends within themselves. It is important that the *process* of learning be emphasized. Overly rigid plans can be a major source of pupils' lack of interest in music and consequently their limited learning of musical concepts.

Example II: Descriptive Lesson Plan for Second or Third Grade
This plan includes some of the possible teacher-pupil interaction which obviously would not be written in a teacher's daily plan. It will be successful only if the children have previously mastered the concepts listed.

LESSON PLAN FOR SECOND OR THIRD GRADE

(30 minutes)

Generalization: The tones of melodies may have adjacent (scale-line) pitches skips (chord-line pitches).

Subgeneralization: (focus of the lesson) Some melodies move in skips or steps

Concepts	Data
high	line
low	space
skip	measure
step	etc.
scale	
melodic line	
chord	

Behavioral Objective: The children will differentiate between parts of selected melodies which move chord-wise and parts which move scale-wise by demonstrating with their hands and/or bodies and by recognizing such parts in notation

Pacing Teaching Strategies (expanded here for illustrative purposes):

five minutes:
A.   Introduction
     Teacher: What do we remember about the last song we sang yesterday
     (Teacher writes major points on chalkboard as children state them.
     Child: We sang "Taps" last.
     Teacher: Why did we sing it last?
     Child: Because it is a song to end with; it begins, "Day is done."
     Teacher: Today we are going to do more with this song. Let's sing it again
     Each of you think of a way to show the high and low pitches. Try to
     remember how the tune goes. Can you hear it in your head without
     singing it?
     Children demonstrate with hands, bodies, etc.
     Teacher: Where did you begin?
     Children: Low
     Teacher establishes the pitch and the class sings the song.

twenty minutes:
B.   Development
     Teacher directs students to sing "Planting Cabbages," and says, Sing it as
     you did last week, with part of the class singing measures one and two, five
     and six, the rest singing measures three and four, seven and eight. (The
     teacher has assigned the more difficult chord-line measures to good singers
     and the less difficult scale-line measures to the less certain singers.)

PLANTING CABBAGES

2. *You can plant it with your feet. . . .*

3. *You can plant it with your hands. . . .*

TAPS *(transpose to F major)*

Slowly   U. S. Army Bugle Call

Day   is   done,   gone   the   sun   from the   lake   from the hills,

from the   sky.   Safe - ly   rest   all   is   well   God   is   nigh.

Class sings the song as directed.
Teacher: Now comes the puzzle: In what way are these songs alike? (pause)
  Child: Could we sing the songs again?
Class sings the songs again.
  Sally: The tunes are different.
  Fred: The rhythm is not the same.
  Marie: The way we sing "Can you plant the cabbages so" is a little like "Day is done, gone the sun."
Teacher: Why do you think they are alike, Marie?
  Marie: The tune in both places skips instead of going in steps.
Teacher produces charts of the notation of each song and asks Marie to explain what she means by pointing to the measures.
Teacher: Does anyone have another theory? Let's sing these songs again, watch the notes, and think how it sounds when the melody skips lines and spaces.
Class sings the songs again.
Teacher: Was there any part of these two songs that didn't skip lines and spaces?
  Bob: The part I sing in "Planting Cabbages" doesn't skip.
Teacher: I see that you have examined this song carefully, Bob. Look at the chart and show us the part that you think doesn't skip.
Bob points to measures three and four.
Teacher: Play those measures on the bells, Pete. (He does)
        What did you discover?
  Pete: The notes were all next to each other; there were no skips.
Teacher: Play measures seven and eight. (He does)
        What do you find there?
  Pete: There is a skip in measure seven.
Teacher: Can you change the song so there isn't a skip there, Pete?
Pete experiments and adds an E between notes D and F to eliminate the skip. Teacher writes the E into the chart by making D and E eighth notes which are slurred on the word "same." Pete plays measures seven and eight as revised.
Teacher: Let's all sing measures seven and eight to see if we like them this way.
The class sings the measures and likes the change. Pete volunteers that it is easier to play on the bells this way.
Teacher: Can we analyze the melody of "Taps?" He holds up the chart of "Taps."
  Child: It's all skips; it has some repeated notes.
  Child: There are dotted notes.
Teacher: Let's examine "Planting Cabbages." Can you use the chart to explain what you find?

Children: It's half skips and half steps; measures 1–2, 5–6 are skips, and measures 3–4 and 7–8 are steps; it's in 6/8 meter.

Teacher: Everyone sing the measures that skip along chord lines and let Pete play the measures that step along scale lines.

The class does as directed.

The teacher next tests the class on its comprehension of chord lines and scale lines by the following process:

1. A familiar song is sung as the children move to show skips and steps as they hear them in the melody.
2. The class decides if skips or steps are present and states where they are found in the song.
3. The teacher shows a transparency of the notation on the screen to enable the class to verify its decision.

The children will find:

"A Hunting We Will Go"	to be	all steps
"Merrily We Roll Along"	to be	all steps except one skip at the end of the first phrase
"Little Tom Tinker"	to be	all skips and repeated notes until steps in the last measure
"Bow Belinda"	to be	a skip pattern one step lower, then one step higher, with steps in the last measure.

five minutes:

C. Concluding the lesson

Teacher: Let's see if we can state in one sentence all the important things we learned about melodies today.

Class: Some melodies move in steps, some move in skips, and some move in steps and skips. (Notice how the children summarized the day's lesson by stating their findings in the form of a generalization.)

The concluding activity is the singing of "Bow, Belinda" and clapping the beat while volunteer pairs of children improvise dances in turn.

Materials

Chalkboard

Songs the children know. Source: *Basic Music,* 4th ed., Nye and Bergethon, Prentice-Hall, Inc., 1974.

Charts of the notation of "Taps," p. 63, and "Planting Cabbages," p. 63.

Bell set

Transparencies of "Merrily We Roll Along," p. 78, "A Hunting We Will Go," p. 85, "Little Tom Tinker," p. 98, and "Bow, Belinda," p. 69.

Comments: Notice that the teacher plans to work toward *many more goals* than stated in the focus of the lesson. Besides working toward the generalization and behavioral objective stated, this teacher will give attention to:

Tonal memory (can you hear it in your head without singing it?)
High and low pitch
Body movement in relation to high and low in pitch
Grouping children in accordance with their degree of ability to sing accurately on pitch
Using notation to solve musical problems
Playing an instrument (why do you think the teacher chose Pete to play the bells?)
Manipulating a melody by changing it
Comparing measures seven and eight with the changed version to judge if the new version is acceptable
Emphasizing listening skills

A concluding activity which involves body movement in dance improvisation (creative), clapping the beat (rhythm), and which may involve "pure enjoyment" as well as possible application of melodic skips and steps and repeated notes to dance movements.

At this time the teacher does not plan to relate chord lines to chords; this is reserved for a later lesson. There may be question as to whether the teacher should have used the terms "chord line" and "scale line." Either the class has sufficient background so that no student would question the use of the terms or the teacher is using them in the hope that some student might ask about them; then a study of these would be proposed as a suggestion that came from the class. The teacher did not plan to develop the reference by the children to repeated notes or repeated note groups; the class was guided in activities that emphasized skips and steps—the stated purpose of the plan.

The concluding activity can be questioned if it leaves the children in an emotional state that would make their learning in a following subject difficult. It would be assumed that it will not, or if it did, this teacher would follow it with another concluding activity to quiet the children, or that the class is followed by dismissal for the day or for recess or physical education.

Example III: A Lesson on Cognitive Process Skills The following plan illustrates the use of various cognitive process skills. Teachers should not attempt to pattern all of their lesson plans after every step listed here, for some objectives do not lend themselves to all of the processes. They should, however, include all that are applicable to the realization of the stated objectives. The following plan is probably for eight- or nine-year-olds, depending upon their musical maturity.

LESSON PLAN III

Materials: drum, chalk and chalkboard, (specific) music book, recordings.

Teacher's Objective: To teach for the generalization that "regular accent determines meter."

    Concepts to support the generalization: beat, accent, meter signature (or time signature).

        Situation: Asking the class to listen and observe, the teacher plays a drum or claps hands with steady beat, sounding no accent.

        Observing: "How would you describe what you heard?"
"Could you tell what the meter (time signature) might be?"
"Why not?"

        Comparing: The teacher now repeats the performance except that he or she accents every other beat.

"How would you compare what you just heard with what you first heard?"

"What is the musical term for the stress I placed on some of the beats?"

Answer: Accent. "How often did I accent the beats" (every other beat.)

The teacher repeats the performance, but accents every third beat. "Compare what I did this time with what you heard the other times." (We have now heard no accent, an accent on every other beat, and an accent on every third beat.)

The teacher writes what he or she did the first time on the chalkboard:

| | | | | | | | | | | | |

A child is asked to draw a short line either above or below the note stem as the teacher plays the example again, stressing every other beat:

| | | | | | | | | | | |

The teacher again writes the series of note stems on the chalkboard and asks another child to come forward to notate accents. He or she plays an accent on every third note.

| | | | | | | | | | |

Classifying: How many classifications of accents do we now have? (three: no accent, an accent every other beat, and an accent every third beat.) The teacher now asks a child to draw a barline before each accented note.

What meter signatures can we place in front of these examples (none for the first, $\frac{2}{4}$ [or $\frac{2}{2}$ or $\frac{2}{8}$] for second and $\frac{3}{4}$ [or $\frac{3}{2}$ or $\frac{3}{8}$] for the third.)

What names can we say that conform to these two-beat and three-beat meters?

Ma-ry, John-ny, Jack-son, Ok-la-hom-a

Mel-o-dy, Ros-a-lie, Jon-a-than

The class repeats each name a number of times while clapping or stamping the accent. (Children suggest and experiment with others.)

Collecting and Organizing Data: The children open their music books and search for meters with two and three beats to the measure. These are listed on the chalkboard under each category.

Summarizing Statement: When a meter contains two beats, the numeral two appears high in the meter signature; when a meter contains three beats, the numeral three appears high in the meter signature. (An exception is fast $\frac{6}{8}$ which will be dealt with later.)

Recognizing Assumptions: The teacher says, "Some people say that all music 'swings' in two's or three's." How can this be when some of the meter signatures you saw in your books were $\frac{4}{4}$ and $\frac{6}{8}$ and perhaps others?" At this point, the books are opened again, and the children are helped to find that $\frac{4}{4}$ can be considered to be 2 + 2, and $\frac{6}{8}$ to be 3 + 3. The latter meter should be closely examined in the music for $\frac{6}{8}$ meter is practically always written in such a manner that the measure can be divided to illustrate that 3 + 3 characteristic (rather than a mathematically possible 2 + 2 + 2). Meters such as ⅝ and ⅞ should probably be reserved for study at a future date when this information becomes necessary.

Creative Thinking: The teacher suggests that the class invent meters up to six beats in a measure.

The class invents and labels a number of meters by placing regular accents at different intervals by clapping, stamping, or using percussion instruments.

Inferring from the Data: Students state in their own words: accent determines meter; regular accents result in meter; there are many meters.

Analyzing: The teacher plays recordings of short selections that clearly denote ⅔ and ¾ meters. The children are asked to "feel" the beats and accents, and determine the meter of the selections.

Application: The children find songs they like in their books and sing them with a "feel" for the meter; they might also conduct the meters. This will lead them to discover that some songs are more heavily accented than others, and that the strength of the accent is sometimes a matter of musical taste rather than a matter of musical mechanics.

**Music Skills
Objectives**   If students are to engage successfully in music learning activities they will need to learn a variety of music skills that will assist them in their growing understanding of music. Appropriate objectives should be formulated in the following areas of music skills:

Listening   Listening is the basic music skill because learning the skills of singing, playing, and moving to music are dependent on the learner's ability to listen to, analyze, and appreciate music.

Moving to Music   Children learn music by moving their bodies to its salient characteristics as they listen to it. They need to experiment with free interpretation, characterization, dramatization, fundamental movements, singing games, and dances.

Singing   Singing is one of the most satisfying of human activities. Children need to be able to sing on pitch with a tone quality suitable to the meaning of the words they sing. By the time they leave the elementary school they should possess the ability to sing independent parts of songs such as parts of a round, chants, and descants, and those necessary for harmonic part singing.

Playing Instruments   The desire to manipulate musical instruments seems to be in all children; they ordinarily find great pleasure in playing instruments. Through performing on percussion instruments, bells, xylophone, and recorder, they can contribute to their understanding of rhythm, pitch, form, dynamics, tempo, and melody. By chording on the Autoharp and piano they can learn much about harmony and chord construction.

Reading Music This skill relates to all the other skills in that music notation symbolizes what is heard and what is performed. There are music symbols for pitch, duration, meter, tempo, dynamics, and harmonization.

Composing Music Children can create their own music in the same spirit that they create their own stories, poems, paintings, and dances. They can create a melody; they can make a song from a poem, add percussion parts as accompaniments and create percussion compositions; improvise vocally and instrumentally; and assist in group projects such as creating an operetta.

Following is a suggested outline of a plan for teaching skills.

Example IV

LESSON PLAN FOR TEACHING SKILLS

The specific skill to be developed: _____

Performance objective(s) to be realized: _____

1. *Description and Demonstration*
   The skill is demonstrated or otherwise made known to the learners.
   a. The specific skill action is described.
   b. The skill may be demonstrated by a performer (such as the teacher or a skilled student) or by audiovisual means.
2. *Trial to Assess Degree of Skill and Need for Improvement*
   The learners are led to try out their present degree of skill in order that the teacher or the learners identify common errors or the general need for improvement.
3. *Practice for Mastery*
   The practice of the skill, how this is arranged for, and a listing of the drill activities. Remember that these are sometimes in the form of games.
4. *Application or Assignment*
   The use of the new skill in other settings, for variety, practical application, meaning, and for measurement of the degree of mastery of the skill by the learners.

Other Plans Lesson plans vary in complexity from the extremely simple to the highly intricate. However, the entire subject of lesson plans is complex because plans that are simple in design can be intricate in their development. A plan in which one song, one recording, or one rhythmic response appears may be too brief or too monotonous (because of the many repetitions of the single musical experience that take place). It is also possible that individual differences cannot be well accommodated in such a plan. Experienced teachers have learned that it is essential to a functional plan that more than one music activity be normally employed in order for children to respond to and analyze music in different ways. Many college teachers refuse to accept a one-idea plan, although some do when it is the initial attempt of the student. However, it is understood that as later plans are designed, they will reveal the student's ability to organize more complex plans in which several of the music skills appear.

An excellent source of materials of instruction for lesson plans is the "Music Examples" section of a book edited by Charles Gary.[10] Specific songs with their sources, specific recordings and other examples are stated in relation to concepts being developed. The simple one-song or one-recording plan is exemplified by some of the suggestions offered by Bergethon and Boardman,[11] but these are intended to be incorporated into more complex plans. Wheeler and Raebeck [12] present suggestions for plans of different levels of complexity. Students can profit from examining such plans and applying the following criteria when revising them for their own purposes.

Criteria for Use in Designing Lesson Plans   While there are always exceptions, most lesson plans can be evaluated by applying the following criteria:

1. The teacher's objectives are clearly stated. They are drawn from one or more of the four areas of music instruction: music subject matter, cognitive process skills, music skills, and attitudes-appreciations-values.
2. The teacher's objectives are, as far as possible, stated in specific terms which incorporate evaluation directly into the plan.
3. The teacher plans challenging and interesting ways to motivate interest in the lesson.
4. The teacher presents a variety of activities in logical sequence that employ all appropriate senses—the ear, eye, and muscular response.
5. The teacher balances activities in terms of intake types (such as viewing and reading), and expressive types (such as performing and creating).
6. The teacher accommodates individual differences.
7. The teacher states key questions.
8. The students are kept active mentally and/or physically during the entire lesson.
9. The teacher selects each activity to assist in the realization of a specific objective.
10. The teacher designs plans that contain general procedures such as what all participants are to do when children or teacher enter and leave the classroom. Distributing books, finding pages in books, getting instruments ready to play, and sounding the first pitch are some of the aspects to be planned.

[10] Charles L. Gary, ed., *The Study of Music in the Elementary School: A Conceptual Approach* (Reston, Va.: Music Educators National Conference, 1967).

[11] Bjornar Bergethon, and Eunice Boardman, *Musical Growth in the Elementary School,* 3rd ed. (New York: Holt, Rinehart and Winston, Inc., 1975).

[12] Lois Raebeck, and Lawrence Wheeler, *New Approaches to Music in the Elementary School,* 3rd ed. (Dubuque, Iowa: Wm. C. Brown Company Publishers, 1974).

For example, if song titles and page numbers are on the chalkboard, both time and the teacher's voice can be saved.

11. The teacher lists all necessary materials of instruction needed for implementation of the plan.

After teaching a lesson, a teacher might ask:

1. Did I encourage student inquiry and discovery of concepts rather than tell them in lecture style?
2. Did I encourage student creativity?
3. Did I keep the learners active?
4. Did I select appropriate activities for the realization of the objectives?
5. Did I and the students evaluate the lesson in terms of stated objectives?

The range of musical interests, aptitudes, skills, and knowledge is so extensive at any given grade level or age that nongraded plans of school organization present few difficulties to teachers who have been aware of students' individual differences and who have been providing for them in their previous grade level planning. Also, an accurate concept of team teaching is one in which the classroom teacher and the music teacher plan and work together for the good of the children.

**Checklist To Evaluate
the Effectiveness of an Instructional Plan**

		Weak	Below Average	Average	Strong	Superior
Clarity of Aims	The purposes of the lesson are clear.					
Appropriateness of Aims	The aims are neither too easy nor too difficult for the pupils.					
Organization of the Lesson	The individual parts of the lesson are clearly related to each other in an appropriate way. The total organization facilitates what is to be learned.					
Selection of Content	The content is appropriate for the aims of the lesson, the level of the class, and the teaching methods.					
Selection of Materials	The specific instructional materials and human resources used are clearly related to the content of the lesson and complement the selected method of instruction.					

Checklist To Evaluate
the Effectiveness of an Instructional Plan

	Weak	Below Average	Average	Strong	Superior
Beginning the lesson — The pupils come quickly to attention.					
Clarity of Presentation — The content of the lesson is presented so that it is understandable to the pupils. Different points of view and specific illustrations are used when appropriate.					
Pacing of the lesson — The teacher "stays with the class" and adjusts the tempo accordingly.					
Pupil Participation and Attention — The class is attentive. When appropriate the pupils actively participate in the lesson.					
Ending the Lesson — The lesson is ended when the pupils have achieved the aims of instruction. There is a deliberate attempt to tie together the planned and chance events of the lesson and relate them to the immediate and long range aims of instruction.					
Teacher-Pupil Rapport — The personal relationships between pupils and the teacher are harmonious.					

**Applying What
You Have
Learned About
Designing an
Instructional
Plan**

The songs to follow are presented to assist the student in designing a lesson plan. Whether the plan should be written at this time, or following study of Parts Two and Four is a matter for the instructor of the class to decide. However, some preliminary thought about lesson plans could be of value. Professional teachers will select for use the song or songs that best lead to a realization of stated objectives. Songs, or any other materials of instruction, are analyzed by teachers to find whether or not they are suitable for their purposes.

In this chapter, a number of principles for planning lessons were stated, most of which will not be repeated here. Using all appropriate senses (eye, ear, body) was one. Thinking in terms of cognitive, affective, and psychomotor learnings was another. Planning in terms of helping learners form concepts about or relating to the elements of music was an important principle. The Conceptual Structure of Music can stimulate the formation of objectives. How to write instructional and behavioral objectives, and various types of lesson plans have been discussed.

To help use the songs in lesson plans, the authors will make a few suggestions, realizing that the creative teacher will think of many more.

SONG	RELATED CONCEPTS AND ACTIVITIES
Little Ducklings.	melodic contour; scale tones; perform tune on bells
Jennie Jenkins.	tempo (fast) contour (disjunct melody line); chord roots; two-part form; improvise a chant on scale tones 5–6 (*so-la*); questions and answers in text suggest two groups of singers or solo and chorus
The Sow Took the Measles.	form; ₵ and 2/2 meters; chord tones in the melody (disjunct); experiment with *ritard* to better communicate the meaning of the text; chord roots to play and/or sing; tonic-dominant harmony
This Train.	provision for high and low voice ranges; the beat (marching); selection of appropriate percussion instruments to improvise an accompaniment; possible dramatization; syncopation; related recording for analysis
Kum Ba Yah.	part singing; improvising harmony; singing in thirds; I V₇ IV harmony

THE DUCKLINGS

JENNIE JENKINS

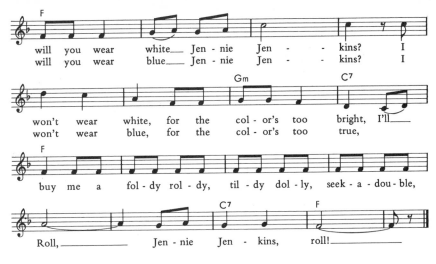

will you wear white___ Jen - nie Jen - - kins? I
will you wear blue___ Jen - nie Jen - - kins? I

won't wear white, for the col - or's too bright, I'll___
won't wear blue, for the col - or's too true,

buy me a fol - dy rol - dy, til - dy dol - ly, seek - a - dou - ble,

Roll, _____ Jen - nie Jen - kins, roll!_____

3. *Will you wear red—I won't wear red, it's the color of my head.*

4. *Will you wear green?—I won't wear green, it's a shame to be seen.*

5. *Will you wear purple?—I won't wear purple, it's the color of a turtle.*

More verses can be created describing different colors.

THE SOW TOOK THE MEASLES

American Frontier Song

How do you think I be - gan in the world? I got me a sow and

sev - 'ral oth - er things. The sow took the mea - sles and she died in the spring.

1. What do you think I made of her hide? The
2. What do you think I made of her nose? The
3. What do you think I made of her tail? The
4. What do you think I made of her feet? The

ve - ry best sad - dle that you ev - er did ride. Sad - dle or bri - dle or
ve - ry best thim - ble that___ ev - er sewed clothes. Thim - ble or thread___ or
ve - ry best whup___ that___ ev - er sought sail. Whup or whup socket or
ve - ry best pick - les that you ev - er did eat. Pick - les or glue___ or

a - ny such thing,
a - ny such thing,
a - ny such thing,   The sow took the mea - sles and she died in the spring.
a - ny such thing,

THIS TRAIN

American

This train is built for speed now, etc.
Fastest train you ever did see,
This train is bound for glory, this train.

This train don't carry no liars, etc.
No hypocrites and no high flyers,
This train is bound for glory, this train.

KUM BA YAH

Afro-American Spiritual

2. *Someone's crying, Lord, Kum ba yah!*

3. *Someone's singing, Lord, Kum ba yah!*

4. *Someone's praying, Lord, Kum ba yah!*

Summary

When a teacher plans music instruction, there are certain logical steps in the process:

1. The teacher must possess a rationale or philosophy concerning teaching

music to children. Why teach music to children? How should music be taught to children? What can music do for children that nothing else in the curriculum can do as well?

2. The teacher understands what children are like physically, emotionally, aesthetically, socially, and intellectually. How do chidren learn? How does the teacher diagnose the musical capabilities, needs, and interests of each child?

3. The teacher is knowledgeable of what should be taught. What are the appropriate data, concepts, and generalizations? What are the skills, attitudes, and values? What are the thought processes to be furthered? What are the objectives that encompass these?

4. The teacher selects and uses appropriate learning experiences and materials of instruction to realize the stated objectives.

5. The teacher evaluates the success of the music program for the individual or group, and sometimes for the school and community.

EXPLORATORY ACTIVITIES

1. How might a predetermined scope and sequence in music be a disadvantage to a teacher? How might it be an advantage?

2. Explain by example the difference between a fact, a concept, and a generalization in music. How are they related?

3. What is meant by the structure of a subject?

4. Evaluate this statement: "We have a wonderful music teaching guide in our school; it tells the teacher exactly what to do each day."

5. How might a sequence of music study that is well-organized in terms of subject matter fail to be sequential for a learner?

6. What are the advantages and disadvantages of a national curriculum in music?

7. It was pointed out that when a lesson plan is followed, a teacher will teach toward many goals other than those stated in the generalizations and behavioral objectives. Re-read the Lesson Plan for Second or Third Grade to find the place where the teacher works to *extend* the singing skill of the "less certain" singers. What other unwritten goals might a teacher work toward in a lesson?

8. Analyze the types of questions the teacher asks in the Lesson Plan for Second or Third Grade.

9. Read *Preparing Instructional Objectives* by Robert F. Mager; then formulate behavioral objectives for developing a musical concept.

10. Select three or four concepts or a sub-concept from the Suggested Structure of Music Outline. Show how you would develop these in a teaching plan. Follow the procedure suggested in this chapter. Do the same with a selected generalization.

11. Plan what you believe to be an appropriate and desirable music program for ages 5–12. Consider all the elements of music. Discuss your formulated program with others.

12. Examine the music curriculum guides used in the school system nearest you and appraise the suggested music learnings for each age and performance level. Compare these suggested learnings with those in a guide from an-

other school system. How might these be improved to meet the musical needs and conditions in your area?

13. Examine a music course of study used in a nearby school system to answer the following questions:

What musical content, facts, concepts and generalizations are stated or suggested?

Do you find serious omissions?

What suggestions are made for the spiral development of key ideas and concepts?

Are objectives stated in behavioral terms?

What teaching strategies, types of questions and methods of inquiry are listed?

What musical skills and abilities are indicated?

What musical attitudes, appreciations, habits, and values are encouraged and taught?

14. Relate the approach presented in *The Study of Music in the Elementary School: A Conceptual Approach* (MENC, 1967), with the Structure of Music Outline of this chapter.

15. Analyze the Structure of Music Outline and revise it to suit your purposes. Add or delete generalizations, subgeneralizations, and concepts, or reword them. Determine how you will use this suggested structure in teaching the elements of music.

16. In the history of United States music education, whenever teachers have concentrated exclusively on facts about music rather than on the beauty and the satisfactions of music, children's appreciation of this subject has declined. How can teachers prevent this negative development and still utilize the conceptual approach?

17. After learning the types of lesson plans presented in this chapter, study those in *New Approaches to Music in the Elementary School,* by Lois Raebeck and Lawrence Wheeler, Wm. C. Brown Publishers, Dubuque, Iowa, *Musical Growth in the Elementary School,* by Bjornar Bergethon and Eunice Boardman, Holt, Rinehart and Winston, Inc., and the implications for lesson plans in *The Study of Music in the Elementary School: A Conceptual Approach,* Music Educators National Conference. Explore the following features of these plans:

Objectives

Relation to the structure of music

Learning music skills

Relations to attitudes, feelings, and values (humanizing music)

Keeping the learner active

Intrinsic motivation

Extrinsic motivation

Facts, concepts, and generalizations

Teacher's questions

Provision for individual differences

Grouping

Evaluation

18. If possible, prepare a three-minute lesson in which one music concept is introduced and taught. Videotape it and present it to the class for an impersonal analysis.

References

Accountability Umbrella Section, Music Educators Journal, September 1972, pp. 42–73. Includes discussion of behavioral objectives.

BAKER, EVA, and W. JAMES POPHAM, *Expanding Dimensions of Instructional Objectives.* Englewood Cliffs, N.J.: Prentice-Hall, Inc., 1973.

BOYLE, DAVID, compiler, *Instructional Objectives in Music: Resources for Planning Instruction and Evaluating Achievement.* Reston, Va.: Music Educators National Conference, 1974. Chapter 6.

COMBS, ARTHUR, *Educational Accountability Beyond Behavioral Objectives.* Washington, D.C.: Association for Supervision and Curriculum Development, 1972.

FRAENKEL, JACK R., *Helping Students Think and Value.* Englewood Cliffs, N.J.: Prentice-Hall, Inc., 1973.

HOLT, DENNIS M., "Competency Based Music Teacher Education: Is Systematic Accountability Worth the Effort?" *Council for Research in Music Education,* Bulletin No. 40 (Winter, 1974), pp. 1–6.

"How Students Learn Music," *Music Educators Journal,* February 1970, pp. 47–63.

KIBER, ROBERT, *Behavioral Objectives and Instruction.* Boston: Allyn and Bacon, Inc., 1970.

LEONHARD, CHARLES, and ROBERT W. HOUSE, *Foundations and Principles of Music Education* (2nd ed.). New York: McGraw-Hill Book Co., 1972.

RADOCY, RUDOLPH E., "Behavioral Objectives in Music: Shall We Continue?" *Music Educators Journal,* March, 1974, pp. 38–40.

RATHS, LOUIS E., et al., *Values and Teaching: Working with Values in the Classroom.* Columbus, Ohio: Charles E. Merrill Books, Inc., 1966.

SIDNELL, ROBERT, *Building Instructional Programs in Music Education.* Englewood Cliffs, N.J.: Prentice-Hall, Inc., 1973.

SIMON, SIDNEY, LELAND W. HOWE, and HOWARD KIRSCHENBAUM, *Values Clarification: A Handbook of Practical Strategies for Teachers and Students.* New York: Hoit Publishing Co., 1972.

WOODRUFF, ASAHEL D., "How Music Concepts are Developed," *Music Educators Journal,* February, 1970, p. 49.

"You Can Build a Comprehensive Music Curriculum," *Music Educators Journal,* November, 1974, pp. 42–45.

Evaluation

6

The final step in developing a music curriculum is to establish means of evaluation. Evaluation is a process of assessing to what degree objectives have been attained. It is made in terms of specific and immediate objectives as well as in terms of terminal and program goals. Evaluation in music consists of assembling, interpreting, and using data to measure three aspects of the curriculum: student achievement, teaching success, and program adequacy. Assessment of student achievement is determined by the use of various tests and evaluative techniques. These devices are employed to determine the amount, relevancy, and quality of the learner's behavior as measured by the terminal goals and the precisely stated performance objectives. If objectives are clearly stated, they yield specific levels of performance from which criteria for student achievement can be established.

Evaluation is not an end within itself, it is a continuous process that is a useful tool in adjusting learning goals, objectives, and experiences. The major purpose of evaluation is to ascertain at various points the degree of progress achieved, and, when appropriate, to assist in the adjustment of plans and in the improvement of instructional activities and procedures. It is not presented here as an activity to be employed exclusively at the

conclusion of a program or any aspect of a program, but as an integral part of each of these. Therefore the subject will be developed in some detail.

There are music educators who deny that there is adequate means of measurement of musical growth because music is rooted in the affective domain, thus not easily measurable. Music teachers take three different positions concerning measurement by observable behavior: some deny that meaningful appraisal is possible; others believe that ways can be found to evaluate all music experience; while some believe that while the result of most musical experiences can be measured, the result of some which are covert will remain difficult to assess until creative teachers are ingeneous in preparing performance objectives that will indicate externally what students have internalized. Some experiences may continue to be impossible to appraise.

Evaluation can disclose the need for instructional provision for individual differences in both musical aptitude and learning styles. It can also disclose what aspects of the program need revision and refinement. A realistic evaluation of student achievement can lay the foundation for evaluating teacher success.

Results of evaluation can seldom be accepted at face value; they must be studied and interpreted. Perfection has never been achieved by man, but music teachers must strive to provide the most effective program possible under existing conditions, and evaluation should help to attain this goal. "Existing conditions" can refer to space, scheduling, equipment and supplies, which are also in need of appraisal, revision, and improvement as they relate to the learning process.

Leonhard and House [1] suggest the assessment of seven areas: philosophy; terminal goals; course division and program objectives; content, sequence, and instructional objectives; nature of learning experiences; scheduling and facilities; and plans for evaluation.

Suggested Guidelines

Any effective program of evaluation should be guided by several specific and significant criteria:

Evaluation Should be Made in Terms of Behavioral Objectives Examples of this type of objective are: the children indicate their understanding of the relationship between vertical and horizontal chord tones by successfully arranging the horizontal chord tones found in selected melodies vertically, finding and playing chord tones on keyboard instruments, and singing chord tones to accompany songs; the children demonstrate their understanding of the structure of the major scale by performing major scales without notation on the bells from several different pitches; the

[1] Charles Leonhard, and Robert House, *Foundations and Principles of Music Education,* rev. ed. (New York: McGraw-Hill Book Co., 1970).

children reveal positive attitudes toward worthy music by listening with interest at home to the televised Young People's Concerts, as demonstrated in their class discussion. The great value in stating objectives behaviorally is that they are described in simple, direct, and realizable *performance* terms that point directly toward evaluation.

Everyone Concerned with Learning in the Music Program Should be Involved in Evaluation   Learning is facilitated when a receptive environment for performance, composition, and analysis of music exists. Bringing about such an environment necessitates the formulation of a basic point of view, establishment of objectives and ways to realize them, and use of diverse techniques to appraise the degree the objectives have been attained. Administrators, parents, other adults in the community, teachers, and pupils should work together in this process. Teachers have the leading role, serving as guides and facilitators in this cooperative endeavor. Questions the teacher might ask include: Do the learners understand the objectives? Are they of personal importance to individual learners? How can I help the individuals to identify and analyze the various aspects of objectives and the difficulties entailed? What strategies can I use to help pupils become conscious of the next steps needed? How can I assist them to discover other meanings and possibilities related to the problem?

Children learn best when they are given opportunities to identify what they need to learn, have some choice in what they are to learn, plan how they are going to learn it, and appraise how well they have done so. Questions the learners might ask themselves include: What do I already know about this problem? What does the problem entail? What do I need to know? Where do I begin? What resources do I need? What is my next step? As a result of each bit of evaluative data collected, the pupil should become more secure and certain of what next steps should be taken.

Evaluation Should be Recognizing as Necessary Feedback and Put to Use   Children require feedback in order that they may adjust to their world, find reason to reorder or change the world about them, and to build their self-concepts. The school should provide a realistic, unbiased, and valid feedback to learners so that they perceive their condition accurately and become better able to set objectives and plan procedures to achieve them. Learners must be able to know, analyze, and assess the results of their attempts to learn; if they do not have this feedback, they do not know how to modify and improve their learning.

Records That Are Necessary for Furthering the Quality of Pupil Learning Should Evolve from the Various Means of Evaluation Used   "The traditional system of marking and grading and credit granting is so inadequate and distorting, such a nuisance to good teaching and learning, that we simply must have to throw it out and get ourselves something better." [2] Grading is increasingly seen as a report of doubtful accuracy created more

[2] Fred T. Wilhelm, ed., *Evaluation as Feedback and Guide,* 1967 *Yearbook* (Washington, D.C.: Association for Supervision and Curriculum Development, 1967), p. 234.

for the benefit of parents and academic bookkeeping than for the teaching-learning process. The reason a grade symbol has little meaning is that it is rarely supported by an explanation of how it was determined. In order for it to have meaning, one must state objectives, the type of evidence which indicates attainment of the objectives, and the analysis of the evidence. Most of what teachers are continually evaluating in their work in the classroom either cannot be summarized into a grade, or can be summarized only with extreme difficulty. Also, subjective influences such as personality, effort, and apparent interest may interfere with teachers' efforts to assess certain types of accomplishment accurately. In music there are many factors to consider. There can be goals and objectives of progress in understanding and using the elements of music, the skills of the program, types of thinking, and musical attitudes and behaviors. Even though a teacher analyzes each of these in relation to a specific child, the grade symbol may be as much a rating of the effectiveness of the teacher's strategies as it is of the child's progress.

An important principle is that when grades must be given, the child should know the basis for and meaning of the grade. If children understand that this is only one way of looking at themselves, and that certain other ways are more meaningful in terms of personal growth and worth, little harm may result. What children want to know in music is their progress in one or more of the many facets of the study; a C, B, or A is general in coverage and does not communicate specific meaning.

When children transfer from one school to another, their new teachers should receive a record of their progress in music. Also, there is a need to communicate children's progress through some form of record to their parents. Records do not need to be exhaustive; they should include only necessary and pertinent data. Records and data can be valuable in helping children to become more self-directed and exacting in their learning, if they are organized into meaningful feedback that serves as a guide for children in making decisions and seeking information on their own.

Tests comprise only one type of evaluation; they are no longer the major source of data. They have a place when they are used in conjunction with other evaluative devices to help children assess their progress and when they are used by teachers as one way of evaluating.

Many Different Types of Evaluation are Used   If learning in the three domains—cognitive, affective, and psychomotor—is to be assessed, there is cause to use varied evaluative techniques. Some possible means of evaluation follow:

Observation	Inventories	Case studies
Discussion	Samples of creative work	Tape recordings
Checklists	Teacher-made tests	Evaluative criteria
Diaries	Standardized tests	Cumulative records
Questionnaires	Group-made tests	Activity records
Charts	Anecdotal records	Attitude scales
Logs	Sociometric tests	Evaluative questions
	Musical performance	

Teachers decide what combinations of devices they need to use in accordance with the types of evidence desired. Tests used to measure and assess accurately should have the following characteristics:

Validity. They measure what they profess to measure.

Reliability. They measure accurately and consistently.

Appropriateness. They are designed in accordance with the level of the individual or group to which they will be applied.

Practicality. They are easy to use and are not unduly costly in terms of time or money.

Objectivity. They can be used by different persons with the same results.

Usefulness. They will reveal data that can be utilized.

Behaviorally-descriptive. They reveal data related to behavioral objectives and actions of the pupils.

Children practice self-evaluation by means of: group discussions; folders containing samples of work such as composition; tapes made of performances; verbal feedback from teachers and peers; criteria decided upon by the group; checklists; and diaries.

**Evaluative
Devices
Described**

One of the many devices used in evaluation is the essentially simple checklist or checksheet. For example, the 1974 MENC Standards [3] include lists of general standards, such as "Each elementary school provides two current basal series for each classroom." Such standards can be quickly useful in determining whether or not a school music program adheres to them by checking either a *no* column or a *yes* column opposite the standard. A checklist that appraises programs in more detail can be constructed with points under major headings such as Activities and Strategies in the Classroom, Measurement of the Child's Musical Growth, and The Teacher. These headings and points are at the left of the sheet, with columns to their right. Lines are drawn to provide spaces in which to check either *yes, partially, no,* and *plans for improvement?*

The same principle can be adapted for use with individuals. A check sheet can be constructed to reveal pupil responses to certain musical concepts, such as loud-soft, fast-slow, high-low, crescendo-decrescendo, woodwind, brass, and percussion. These can be listed under the heading *Behaviors,* with vertical columns to the right indicating the type of musical activities in which pupil recognition or use of these concepts took place, such as singing, composing, moving, playing, listening. Another device can be constructed to record the current level of competency attained in the mastery of a particular skill, such as playing a ukulele. The assessment should reveal what abilities the student possesses or lacks, such as naming the strings, tuning the instrument, and performing specific chords and accompaniments.

[3] *The School Music Program: Description and Standards* (Reston, Va.: Music Educators National Conference, 1974).

When written tests are constructed, the teacher should provide the learners with a very easy way to respond to the questions. Because most tests should be in the context of a musical experience, such as listening to music, the pupils should concentrate on the music, unhindered by possible struggles with writing at the same time. If writing is to be done, it should occur after the musical experience is concluded. Normally, the questions are likely to be of multiple choice or other type in which the students simply circle or check the answer.

Examples of portions of tests follow:

Examples

Program Evaluation

	yes	partially	no	plans for improvement?
The elementary music program has a sequentially organized program / has a well-qualified staff / has adequate materials of instruction				

Student Progress Evaluation

BEHAVIORS by means of:	SINGING	PLAYING	LISTENING	MOVING	COMPOSING
Recognition of: loud-soft					
fast-slow					
high-low					
cresc.-decresc.					
woodwinds					
brasses					
percussion					

Instructions: Listen carefully, then circle the best answer.

1. The contour of the melody is like:

2. The tempo is:
   fast   moderate   slow
3. The form of the piece is:
   A A   A B A   A B A C A
4. The added part is a:
   descant   ostinato   harmony part in thirds

Multiple Choice Test

A simple type of written test can be used before young children understand the staff. For example, if teachers' purposes have included expanding concepts of how pitches move in scale-line patterns, they can use the first three notes of "Three Blind Mice" and similar repeated patterns in songs the children have come to know well. Written correctly, this particular pattern could be drawn:

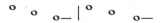

On the test paper, however, it might appear with one misplaced note, and the children would be asked to find and circle the error:

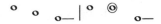

EXPLORATORY ACTIVITIES

1. Examine courses of study in music published by city, county and state education departments to learn what provisions are suggested for evaluation and to what extent evaluations are made in terms of purposes.
2. Indicate practical ways in which each of the criteria in this chapter may be used in music teaching. Which ones do you believe should receive more attention? Which do you think are the most difficult to employ?
3. How can you aid children in using self-evaluation in the lessons and units of work you plan?
4. Arrange to observe a class in music and discuss with the teacher the evaluative techniques used.
5. Examine a cumulative record form used in a local school system. What music data is recorded? What additional entries, if any, are needed?
6. Prepare a sample checklist, a guide for an observation, a questionnaire, and a chart that can be used in a music unit you plan to teach.
7. How can you use discussion as an evaluative technique in a unit or lesson you are teaching? Anecdotal records? Tape recordings? Open-ended questions?

Musical performance? Logs and diaries? Tests? Discuss these techniques critically with other students and with your teacher.

8. Formulate a lesson plan on the basis of pertinent objectives. Then devise ways to evaluate the success of the plan in terms of achieving these objectives.

References

BENTLEY, ARNOLD, *Musical Ability in Children and its Measurement*. New York: October House, Inc., 1966. Explains the origin of Bentley's *Measures of Musical Abilities* tests.

BLOOM, BENJAMIN S., ed., *Taxonomy of Educational Objectives: Cognitive Domain*. New York: David McKay Company, Inc., 1956.

CAMPBELL, DONALD T., and JULIAN C. STANLEY, *Experimental and Quasi-Experimental Designs for Research*. Chicago: Rand McNally & Company, 1963. For graduate students who are designing research projects.

COLWELL, RICHARD, *Elementary Music Achievement Tests*. Chicago: Follett Publishing Company, 1967. For grades 4–12.

———, "Musical Achievement: Difficulties and Directions in Evaluation." *Music Educators Journal*, April 1971, pp. 41–43, 79–83.

GORDON, EDWIN, *The Musical Aptitude Profile*. Boston: Houghton Mifflin Company, 1965. Designed to assess musical aptitude in grades 4–12.

KRATHWOHL, DAVID R., BENJAMIN S. BLOOM, and BERTRAM B. MESIA, *Taxonomy of Educational Objectives: Affective Domain*. New York: David McKay Company, Inc., 1964.

LEHMAN, PAUL R., *Tests and Measurements in Music*. Englewood Cliffs, N.J.: Prentice-Hall, Inc., 1968.

MICHAELIS, JOHN, *Social Studies for Children in a Democracy* (4th ed.). Englewood Cliffs, N.J.: Prentice-Hall, Inc., 1968. Chapter 17, "Evaluation."

The School Music Program: Description and Standards. Reston, Va.: MUSIC EDUCATORS NATIONAL CONFERENCE, 1974.

WILHELMS, FRED T., ed., *Evaluation as Feedback and Guide*. Association for Supervision and Curriculum Development, 1201 Sixteenth Street, N.W., Washington, D.C. 20036, 1967.

LEARNING MUSIC BY MOVEMENT AND RHYTHM

Movement, Rhythm, and Dance

To help children learn music concepts, the teacher has choices among a number of different approaches from which a teaching strategy will be developed. Based upon the level of attainment of the student, they are: *movement,* in which the muscles and nerves of the body are the medium, *improvisation and composition,* in which the learner performs various musicianly roles, *singing and playing instruments,* and *analysis* of music, a skill learned both concurrently with the other approaches and as a result of them. Listening is recognized as an essential part of all musical activities.

At the beginning of music instruction for young children, teachers have certain basic concepts in mind. Children can develop these by means of movement. They are:

Duration

Beat
Divisions of the beat
Meter
Rhythm pattern

Rest
Word-rhythm
Articulation
    staccato (detached)
    legato (connected)

Pitch	Tempo
High, low, same	Fast, slow
Up, down	Accelerando
Contour	Ritard

Dynamics	Form
Loud, soft	Same (repetition)
Accent	Different (contrast)
Crescendo	Phrase
Decrescendo	
	Harmonic changes

The importance of movement to learning was brought to the attention of music teachers in large part by Emil Jacques-Dalcroze (1865–1950), a Swiss musician, who found that unless the learner experiences aspects of music by body movement, the music that the individual later performs will be mechanical, without feeling, and the expressive responsiveness essential to genuine musicianship may never develop. Today, every teacher of early childhood education knows that children learn first by using their muscles.

Expressing rhythm through movement is an activity that music shares with physical education and creative dramatics. Music assists physical education by helping movement be more rhythmic; it assists creative dramatics by heightening the dramatic expression. When physical education gives children more control over their bodies, and when creative dramatics helps to free them to interpret what they hear in music, these areas can in turn contribute to understanding music. By moving to music children can learn to hear music with perception, to respond to it with imagination, and to explore the expressive ideas it contains.

Of primary concern is listening to the rhythm in music and responding to it with physical movement. When children aged five, six, and seven begin their school year, many of them will not be able to sing in tune. Therefore there is logic in first listening to music, then responding by physical movement to what is heard, and in the process becoming oriented to rhythm, pitch, and mood. This builds a background of experience for better singing a little latter.

There are important values in rhythmic responses other than the building of a background for successful singing. Among these are the development of body control, imagination, willingness to experiment, rhythmic responsiveness, and concepts of fast and slow, heavy and light, loud and soft, and long and short, in terms of body movement. Furthermore, rhythmic activity is a necessity in carrying out a balanced daily program of education for children. It is *unnatural* for boys and girls to sit quietly for long periods of time. There is evidence to show that teachers who guide their pupils in appropriate rhythmic responses, and who know the proper times to do this, can reduce pupil tension and fatigue to a marked degree, which makes learning much more likely.

"Fundamental movement" is a term used in physical education. It describes simple, basic movements such as walking, running, skipping, and galloping. Music books for kindergarten and first grade contain helpful song and piano material as well as suggestions for teaching such movements. Also, teachers can quickly learn to use percussion instruments or a few notes on the piano keyboard to improvise rhythms for the simple fundamental movements to which children learn to respond. In these grades the teacher should not expect every child to respond in the same way; some children need time to experiment before being able to do what the others do. Children need time in which to explore *their own* tempo. Thus, at first the teacher observes and uses the child's natural tempo before asking conformance to one predetermined by the teacher.

Music is not always required to initiate rhythmic response. For example, words for walking can be chanted, then clapped, then walked, before appropriate music is added in the tempo and rhythm of the children's walking. Other fundamental movements can be introduced by the teacher's drum beat or by word rhythms and learned by clapping before the children move to them with their whole bodies. The music can then be brought in after the rhythm is learned. The words of songs can be learned first in rhythmic speech, and the melody added later.

Further understanding of fundamental movements can be gained by using songs that suggest impersonation (imitative play). Children who are five and six years of age tend strongly to *be* what they impersonate, such as the horses that gallop and the rabbits that hop. The teaching of fundamental rhythms can continue also from the point of view of free rhythmic play. The teacher may tap a drum, play the piano, or use a recording, and ask the children what it "makes them feel like doing." From their prior experience should come such movements as clapping, walking, running, skipping, galloping, sliding, hopping, and jumping. Through freedom to respond to the rhythms of music they can discover other body movements which may include swinging, pushing, bouncing, pulling, bending, stretching, and striking. During all of this the teacher controls and guides the learning situation by helping the children relate familiar physical responses to the music they are hearing. The teacher should do this in such a manner that each child feels she or he has made a personal contribution.

In kindergarten and first grade the terms "walking note" and "running note" make sense to children because they represent body movements they know. Since children in these grades have limited knowledge about fractions, terms like "quarter" and "eighth" are without much meaning. However, learning the adult terminology should follow learning the "movement" terms *as soon as this seems practical.*

It takes time to develop skill in these activities; beginning teachers are likely to try too many things at first. They should "make haste slowly," striving for a simple and thorough approach. By the end of the first grade most children will have learned to walk, skip, run, and hop in time to music. During the second grade most children will have learned to slide, jump rope, and bounce a ball in rhythm. In third grade the ability to leap and step-hop is generally acquired.

Teachers may take a rhythm from something a child is doing, or from nature or machines outside the classroom, and repeat this on a percussion instrument or on a piano. The children are then asked to identify the rhythm and move to the playing of the teacher. Percussion instruments may be selected to accompany or to represent the rhythm. There are some simple guidelines to follow as children move, such as not to touch other children or get in anyone's way, and for all to move in the same direction. In a small classroom perhaps only four or five children will do the moving, after which the teacher can select others to take their places. The children not moving may create unobtrusive motions at their seats to interpret what the small group does.

The piano The piano can assist in promoting fundamental movements and other rhythmic responses. The recording, useful as it is, will never be a complete substitute for a teacher's flexible use of the piano. Even though a classroom teacher may have little or no piano training, the instrument can be used in improvisatory ways.

The black keys provide a ready-made pentatonic scale that has the wonderful quality of always sounding acceptable, no matter what one does with the various notes either singly or in chords or clusters. (With the entire forearm, for example, try pressing down on a large cluster of black keys.) With the right hand, find a combination of black keys that sounds satisfactory and play steady quarter notes for marching or walking; play the long-short 6/8 pattern ♩ ♪♩ ♪ :‖ quickly for skipping and galloping or slowly for swinging and swaying. Sound sixteenth notes for running. With the left hand, try adding single tones or open fifths in the bass below the patterns you have learned to play with the right hand. You will soon be experimenting with other sounds.

Another approach is to play a major scale for walking. Selected chords in the bass can portray characters or animals for rhythmic dramatizations, such as an elephant walking and a leopard stalking. When chords are played in time with jumping, an accompaniment to that movement results. Playing small parts of the scale up and down in rapid succession can do the same for running. Chords alternating between treble and bass (using both hands) can inspire swinging or the idea of a seesaw. Music textbooks for early childhood often contain helpful suggestions that assist non-pianists as well as formally trained ones. No recording can adapt tempo to a child's movements.

Children should not be asked to respond to rhythm until they have had the opportunity to listen carefully. Teachers often ask them to close their eyes while they listen. After this comes the question, "What did the music tell you to do?" There may follow a discussion, then the music will be repeated and the children will begin to contribute ideas to the group. The teacher will often help free rhythmic responses to develop by asking such questions as, "Does the music make you feel like walking or running or skipping?" "Is it happy, sad, fast, slow?" "How many different motions are good to use with this music?"

Free rhythmic responses are so numerous that it is doubtful that any listing of them can ever be complete, particularly since each of them can be varied almost endlessly. Some, in addition to those already mentioned, are:

trotting	tapping	stroking	swaying
dipping	reaching	patting	rolling
tripping	grasping	creeping	hammering
stamping	banging	rocking	whirling
tossing	circling	crawling	tumbling
skating	beating	turning	sliding

Others are rising and falling in terms of crescendo (gradually louder) and decrescendo (gradually softer) and in terms of rising and falling pitch. For example, one way in which crescendo and decrescendo can be acted out is by a circle of children coming together at the height of the crescendo, and being at the farthest point apart at the lowest level of the decrescendo.

Space is needed for freedom of movement, and it must be admitted that it is at a premium in some classrooms. However, good work can be done despite admitted handicaps, by keeping the following suggestions in mind. First, rhythmic activities need never be boisterous or unruly. Second, activities requiring space may be arranged in some larger room. The room should seldom be the size of a gymnasium because this can destroy the intimate feeling desirable for this type of music work. Third, many substitute responses can be made. Children can "walk" with their hands in the air above their heads, and they can "march" with their heels while their toes remain on the floor. When clapping is required, it can be done in quiet ways such as striking the tips of the fingers of both hands together rather than using the palms, or striking the fingertips of one hand on the palm of the other hand. Fourth, part of a class can do the rhythmic activity while others sing, chant, clap, evaluate, or perform a quiet substitute.

To sustain interest, variety is essential. Since no child enjoys skipping to the same music over a long period of time, a variety of accompaniments is also recommended. The teacher may use recordings, the piano, various percussion instruments, and the chanting of the voice. Still more variety may be attained. by changing the tempo of the music. Jumping ropes,

119

bouncing balls, scarves, flags, and balloons may be used to make appro
priate activities more colorful and impressive. These often aid the sel
conscious child by focusing attention on the object, and assist th
development of big, free movements. Scarves for this purpose are made o
silk or lightweight nylon, longer than the child. Such length permits man
uses, including dramatization.

It is important that teachers know the physical limitations of the ag
groups they guide in activities that require physical exertion. For exampl
if teachers are unaware that to "waddle like a duck" during a song about
duck is a strenuous exercise for children in the first grade (or any grade
they might easily continue this activity for too long and see children fa
down from exhaustion. Any teacher who intends to ask children to d
such activities should personally try them in advance.

Action Songs, Singing Games, and Dances

Action songs and singing games are emphasized in the primary grades, an
dances are emphasized in the intermediate grades because children age
nine to eleven have gained the physical control and coordination tha
enables them to perform and enjoy this more patterned social activity
However, each of these responses appears to some extent in all the grade
Their major musical purpose is to help children feel rhythm and to respon
to it with physical movements.

Although many action songs can be done without first acquiring a back
ground of fundamental movements, this is not true of most singing game
and dances. *Action songs* are those to which children can add appropriat
motions. *Singing games* are those that involve elements of game, chanc
and sometimes dance. *Dances* are more formalized. Teachers and childre
who have imagination will find that they can transform some "ordinary
songs into action songs, singing games, and dances of their own inventio

Most folk dances are easily taught in the intermediate grades. Some o
them are taught to primary grade children in simplified versions. Th
easiest "dance" would be the American Indian type in which six-year-old
do a thumping walk or hop. Occasionally a simplified waltz is introduce
in those grades also. However, most basic dance steps are taught in grade
four and five, and they are embellished in grade six. Children in thes
grades can easily learn the polka, schottische, minuet, polonaise, an
mazurka.

When children sing and at the same time do extensive body movemen
the result is usually detrimental to either good singing or good rhythmi
action or both. Consequently it is best to divide the children into tw
groups that alternate in singing and in doing the game or dance. The grou
that does the singing frequently adds hand clapping and percussion instru
ments to its accompaniment.

Many singing games and dances contribute to organized play on the playground. The song provides the accompaniment. When these activities take place indoors, the piano and recordings contribute variety.

One of the values of singing games and folk dances is the contribution they can make to social studies, for through them children can form a better understanding of the peoples of the world and their customs.

When dances are used in music class, they serve musical objectives; when they are used in physical education classes teachers use them to realize the objectives of physical education. Sometimes these objectives are related; sometimes they are not. Dances can be useful in the study of beat, meter, pattern, notation, instruments, syncopation, and in relation to dance rhythms utilized by composers. For example, the waltz and Johann Strauss, the mazurka and Chopin, the bolero and Ravel, the polka and Dvorak, Weinberger, and Shostakovitch.

Most of the formal dances are taught in the intermediate grades, although the simple waltz and minuet are sometimes introduced in the third grade. The waltz is first presented as a type of walk in which a large step then two smaller steps are made as dancers move in a circle. The teacher can learn how to teach dances from readily-available sources—the music text books, physical education books, record jackets, and from courses of study. In situations where children are reluctant to have only one partner throughout a dance, mixer-types are useful. Examples of these found in many of the books are "The Old Brass Wagon," "Red River Valley," (both in *Singing With Children,* Wadsworth Publishing Company) and "The Caller's Song" in *Music for Young Americans,* Book 6.

Examples of familiar dance songs are "Holla Hi, Holla Ho," "Stodola Pumpa," "Du Du Liegst Mir im Herzen," and the American songs "Buffalo Gals," "Four in a Boat," "Goin' to Boston," "Sourwood Mountain," and "Turkey in the Straw." Recordings include the RCA Victor Series *The World of Folk Dances,* Bowmar Records' *Singing Games, Singing Games and Folk Dances, Folk Dances, Singing Square Dances,* and *Play Party Games,* and many more from other sources. See *Sources of Materials* at the end of this part of the book.

There are folk dances from all over the world. The four American types are (1) play-party games, (2) round dances, (3) long-ways and circular formation dances, and (4) square dances. The origin of the *play-party game* is interesting; at a time in American history when dancing was sometimes frowned upon, people sang dance accompaniments instead of playing them, and called the dance a game, thus getting around the restrictions of those days. *Round dances* are performed with partners. They are "round" because to move easily about a crowded hall, the partners dance in the same circular direction. Examples of this type include the waltz, polka, schottische, rye waltz, and the varsovienne ("Put Your Little Foot . . ."). *Long-ways* and *circular* formation dances include the

Virginia Reel. The *square dance* is one in which eight dancers (fou
couples) salute, curtsy, and change partners in a square formation whi
performing many interesting figures. Possible steps in teaching a fo
dance follow:

1. In preparation, study the directions of the selected dance. It should be one
   which the children already know the basic movements required, but if the
   do not, be sure to teach these as separate rhythms as a preparatory step
   their learning the dance.

2. As you study the dance, practice the steps without the music. Then listen
   the music or learn the music, and do the steps in rhythm to it.

3. If necessary, write any difficult part of the directions on a small pad or ca
   that can be carried inconspicuously in the hand.

4. Teach the song (if it is a dance song) so that the children know the melod
   and words well before attempting to learn the dance.

5. Direct the children into the proper dance formation.

6. Have the children practice the first set of steps with no music. Then hav
   them do these steps while speaking the rhythm of the words of the song, an
   guide them to associate the word-rhythm with the steps. Repeat until th
   steps are learned.

7. Do this much of the dance with the music.

8. Repeat Steps 6 and 7 with the next set of steps. Continue this process unt
   the entire dance is learned.

9. Do the entire dance with the music.

Characteristic Dance Patterns

There are rhythms and dances characteristic of peoples of the worl
often related to their historical origins. The current interest in the rhythm
of Africa and Asia will inevitably produce new materials of instruction.
Latin-American Patterns

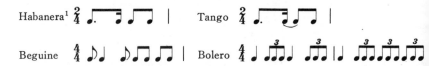

Basic Rhythms (combine the three)
1. Timbales (paired single-head drums)

[1] Recorded examples include "Habañera" from *Carmen* (Bizet) and *Jamaica
Rumba* (Benjamin), both in Bowmar 56, and *Grand Walkaround* (Gottschalk)
Adventures in Music, V. 5–1.

2. Maracas

3. Claves

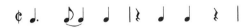

Traditional Dances [2]

Recorded Examples

Free rhythmic response.　My Playful Scarf, Franson Corporation CRG 1019
(ages 2–4)

Ravel: "Laideronette, Empress of the Pagodas" from
Mother Goose Suite, BOL 57 (Bowmar Orchestral
Library Album 57)

Moussorgsky: "Bydlo" from *Pictures at an Exhibition*, AM 2 v 1 (Adventures in Music, Grade 2)

Donaldson: *Under the Big Top*, BOL 51

Moussorgsky: "Ballet of the Unhatched Chicks" from
Pictures at an Exhibition, AM 1 v 1

Animals and Circus, BOL 51

Pierné: *Entrance of the Little Fauns*, BOL 54; AM
2 v 2

Pierné: *March of the Little Lead Soldiers*, BOL 54

Prokofiev: "March" from *The Love for Three
Oranges*, BOL 54

Pictures and Patterns, BOL 53

---

[2] These dance patterns are strummed and related to songs in *Teaching Music
with the Autoharp* (Union, N.J.: Music Education Group), pp. 23–30.

Walking.

Children may develop different types of walking b
pretending they are different characters or animal
Marching is an outgrowth of walking. Walking i
normally relaxed and swinging.

Thomson: "Walking Song" from *Acadian Songs an
Dances,* AM 1 v 1

Kabalevsky: "Pantomime" from *The Comedians* (bi
steps) AM 1 v 1

Moussorgsky: "Bydlo" from *Pictures at an Exhibitio*
(lumbering steps), AM 1

Prokofiev: "Departure" from *Winter Holiday* (fas
steps), AM 2

Herbert: "Dagger Dance" from *Natoma,* AM 3 v

Grieg: "In the Hall of the Mountain King" from
Peer Gynt Suite, AM 3 v 2

Marching.

While the interest of young children in marches fo
cuses on body responses, the older children may b
interested in comparing and analyzing different marc
styles. Military band marches can be compared wit
the favorite marches of the young children—those
having to do with toys, dwarfs, and such. Older chil
dren could add to these the march movements o
Beethoven's Third Symphony and Tchaikovsky's Sixt
Symphony as well as the "March and Cortege" from
Gounod's opera, *The Queen of Sheba.*

Rossini-Britten: "March" from *Soirees Musicales*
AM 1 v 1

Herbert: "March of the Toys" from *Babes in Toy
land,* AM 2 v 1

Vaughan-Williams: "March Past of the Kitchen
Utensils" from *The Wasps,* AM 3 v 1

Lully: "March" from *Ballet Suite,* AM 3 v 2

Sousa: *Semper Fidelis,* AM 3 v 2

Grieg: "Norwegian Rustic March" from *Lyric* Suite
AM 4 v 1

Gould: *American Salute,* AM 5 v 1

Coates: "Knightsbridge March" from *London* Suite
AM 5 v 2

Running.

Running on tiptoe is commonly stressed; the movement should be kept light.

Gluck: "Air Gai" from *Iphigenie in Aulis,* AM 1 v 1

Bizet: "The Ball" from *Children's Games,* AM 1 v 1

Hopping.

Hopping is done on one foot.

Moussorgsky: "Ballet of the Unhatched Chicks" from
Pictures at an Exhibition, AM 1 v 1

Bach: "Gigue" from Suite No. 3, AM 1 v 1

Gretry: "Tambourin" from *Cephale et Procris,* AM 2 v 1

Jumping.

Jumping is done with both feet together. Overly heavy movements are to be avoided.
Massenet: "Aragonaise" from *Le Cid,* AM 1 v 1
Bizet: "Leap Frog" from *Children's Games,* AM 1 v 1
Meyerbeer: "Waltz" from *Les Pateneuers,* AM 2 v 1

Skipping or Galloping.

Skipping is a step, hop, first on one foot and then on the other. Children enjoy a large fast skip that gives them the feeling of moving high in the air. When galloping, one foot is kept ahead of the other throughout, and the back foot is brought up to meet it. Heels never touch the floor.
Bach: "Gigue" from Suite No. 3, AM 1
Gretry: "Gigue" from *Cephale et Procris,* AM 1

Whirling.

Massenet: "Argonaise" from *Le Cid,* AM 1
Rossini-Respighi: "Tarantella" from *The Fantastic Toy Shop,* AM 3 v 2

Swaying, rocking.

These movements can relax children after the stimulation of the more active movements. Swaying trees, branches or flowers are often imitated, as are swings, the pendulum of a clock, rocking a baby to sleep, and rowing a boat.
Bizet: "Cradle Song" from *Children's Games,* AM 1 v 1
Fauré: "Berceuse" from *Dolly,* AM 2 v 1
Shostakovitch: "Petite Ballerina" from *Ballet Suite No. 1,* AM 2 v 1
Offenbach: "Barcarolle" from *Tales of Hoffman,* AM 3 v 1
Chabrier: *España* (for a spirited swinging), AM 4 v 1

Sliding, gliding.
Waltzing.

Prokofiev: "Waltz on Ice" from *Children's Suite,* AM 3 v 2
Tchaikovsky: "Waltz" from *The Sleeping Beauty,* AM 4 v 2
Khachaturian: "Waltz" from *Masquerade* Suite, AM 4 v 2
For specific suggestions, study the Teachers Guides for the *Adventures in Music* albums. Older Children can study the waltz with the purpose of expanding that concept. The *Adventures in Music* albums provide many different types to study. Contrast the Viennese and American concepts of waltz.

Review of fundamental movements.

When working with recordings that illustrate sever
different movements, small groups of children can t
asked to respond appropriately whenever their a
signed movement is heard.
A Visit to My Little Friend, Franson CRG 101
(ages 2–4)
Animals and Circus, BOL 51
Marches, BOL 54
Nature and Make Believe, BOL 52

Rhythmic Dramatization

Rhythmic dramatization implies that children are able to respon
physically to rhythm, melody, mood, tempo, dynamics, and instrumenta
tion. First they listen to the music to ascertain how an action or a story i
suggested. Then they associate the action or story with related aspects c
the musical elements. In the instance of a story, some call these "cues.
Finally, they create a dramatization. The Teacher's Guide for *Adventure
in Music* recordings is helpful.

Dramatization.

Bartók: "Bear Dance" from *Hungarian Sketche:*
AM 3 v 2
Ibert: *The Little White Donkey,* AM 2 v 1
Kabalevsky: "March and Comedian's Gallop" fron
The Comedians, AM 3 v 1
Debussy: "Golliwog's Cakewalk" from *Children'
Corner* Suite, BOL 63
Grieg: "Ase's Death" from *Peer Gynt* Suite No. 1
BOL 59

Imitating animals seems to be a natural interest of young children
thus recordings such as those that follow have possibilities for listening
moving-dramatizing activities. Older children should be asked, *"How doe:
the music describe the animal?"* Their answers should be in terms of th
elements of music—rhythm, melody, tempo, dynamics, harmony, and
instrumentation. The question encourages analysis of the music.

Animals.

Rimsky-Korsakoff: *Flight of the Bumble-Bee,* BOI
52
Respighi: *The Birds,* Mercury 90153; "Prelude"
from, BOL 85
Liadov: *Dance of the Mosquito,* BOL 52
Griffes: *The White Peacock,* AM 5 v 1
Saint-Saëns: "The Swan" from *Carnival of the Ani
mals,* AM 3 v 2

Machines.

Villa-Lobos: "Little Train of the Caipira" from
Bachianas Brasileiras No. 2, AM 6 v 2
Honneger: *Pacific 231* (a railroad locomotive of
World War I)

Nature.

Mossolov: *Iron Foundry,* on *Sounds of New Music,* Folkways FX 6160

Debussy: "Reflections in the Water" (piano music and an example of impressionist style)
Debussy: "Nuage" (Clouds), BOL 70
Thomson: *The River,* Vanguard 2095
Debussy: *La Mer* (The Sea), section from, BOL 70; AM 6 v 2
Ives: *Three Outdoor Scenes,* Composers Recordings CRI 163
Grofé: *Death Valley* Suite, Capital T–272
Grofé: *Grand Canyon* Suite, BOL 61
Vivaldi: *The Four Seasons*

Percussion
Instruments

8

Percussion instruments can be considered as extensions of the body. The body can produce sounds of rhythmic value. Hand clapping of various kinds (flat-palmed for loud, cup-palmed for lower pitches, and fingers only for soft) provide some possibilities. The sound made in pulling the tongue away from the roof of the mouth can be done in ways to produce high- and low-pitched "clicks" which imitate the ticking of a clock. Stamping feet, tapping toes, slapping thighs, and snapping fingers contribute their sounds too, and all of these can be done with a beat and with accents to form beat groups. Although making such sounds and using rhythmic speech help to build a feeling for rhythm, they are limited in tone quality, and children are happy to explore and use the sounds of the many percussion instruments, usually with great interest. The teacher can assist this exploration by asking: "How many ways can you play it?" and "How many different sounds can you make with it?"

128

**The Early
Years**
Children in nursery school, kindergarten, and first grade should be encouraged to experiment with the sounds made by miscellaneous objects of wood, paper, metal, glass, and stone when they are tapped, shaken, and struck. The teacher who is encouraging concept formation of high and low pitch will group the sound producers accordingly at either end of a table. Later the children will play the ear training game of sorting these according to different classifications such as high and low pitch. Others could be types of tone quality such as ringing, scratching, rattling, jingling, and booming. After handling, sounding, and naming all these sound producers and instruments, the children can face away from the table and piano while the teacher plays a game with them to test their ability to identify and describe the different sounds. They may also identify instruments that have short and long duration of sound.

A first-grade teacher made these comments concerning activities in her room that culminated in the successful use of this equipment:

> The children are given many opportunities to initiate their own rhythmic activities. Duration, volume, accent, tempo, and moods are felt with hands, fingers, feet, and moving bodies. Percussion instruments are but extensions of tapping feet and clapping hands. Thus the children *gradually* use drums, bells, woodblocks and sticks to accompany or to create rhythm patterns. By careful listening children find one drum lower or higher in pitch than another. They discover differences in quality as well as in pitch by tapping different places on their instruments. They suggest that part of a song reminds them of a bell or a gong. Tambourines and other instruments can be used for spontaneous self-expression and interpretation during story time.

In this first grade the children had done "drum talk"—beating out the rhythm of words in drum language; they had walked, run, or tapped instruments as they spoke their names in rhythm; they had used scarves, streamers, and balloons to help them to feel and see other rhythms. Instruments were introduced slowly over several weeks, one at a time. Clapping generally preceded playing at first. Early playing was informal; each child played each instrument at one time or another. Songs such as "Little Miss Muffet" were used in which the light-sounding instruments played first, then the heavier-sounding wooden instruments took their turn as the climax of the song approached, and the two were combined in the concluding climax. Among the many other steps in learning to play the instruments was having those holding wooden instruments play on the primary accents and those holding metal instruments play on the other beats. After this, further discriminations between instruments were made, sometimes selecting those that seemed best to play with a piano piece, a song, or a recording. When the music changed, a need for a change in instrumentation developed. Some children made suggestions concerning the use of specific instruments.

Not until the second grade do most children perform either the metric beat *or* the melody-rhythm of a piece when asked. Prior to this, these phenomena are worked with separately, although many children can walk the beat while singing the melody.

Children are encouraged to explore percussion instruments that can be substituted for body movements such as walking, marching, and skipping. They sound them to feel the beat. They find that chopsticks can make a sound suggestive of rain falling on a roof, that sand blocks can imitate a train, that rattles and drums seem necessary to make some American Indian songs sound complete, and that words of songs sometimes suggest certain accompanying instruments or percussion sound effects. They find that instruments can be played to produce accents which will eventually outline the meter, and that instruments can reproduce the rhythm of the melody—usually the rhythm of the words. As they grow older, by keeping their toes on the floor they can make the *heel-clap* sound for two-beat meters, the heels sounding the downbeat and the hands clapping the upbeat. Dances are sometimes accompanied in this way. Transfer can be made to low drum-high drum for the same rhythm; other less heavy-sounding instruments can substitute for the high drum. Notation is brought in to explain what has taken place only after children have first heard and felt the rhythm pattern they are to see. After their experience with it, a picture of it (the notation) helps them visualize the concept.

In the early years the instruments are introduced slowly in connection with small or large group work, one or two at a time. This initial group work with the instruments is of necessity teacher-directed. Music books for these levels contain songs with which to introduce instruments. Since the emphasis today is upon children's growth in creative ability and in musical discrimination, fully written published scores for percussion instruments are rarely used. It should be made clear that there is nothing wrong with a teacher using such scores to introduce children to the potentialities of group instrumental performance; it is wrong only when this is continued to the exclusion of opportunities for children to grow in listening, discriminating, and in analyzing music in order to create their own scores. One logical approach to such scores is where in place of standard notation, tiny drawings of the particular instrument tell the child when to play it.

The mass rhythm band activity for kindergarten and first grade which was once popular, was never appropriate for that age group. Children at this age level are individualistic rather than fully cooperating members of a large group; the score had to be dictated by the teacher, which meant children's creativity and discrimination were practically absent; and there were sometimes aspects of exploiting little children for the entertainment of adults.

**Later Years:
Ages 9–12**

By the third grade children can create their own percussion scores for small and large ensemble use, based upon their growing understanding of rhythm, playing instruments, the tone qualities of instruments, notation, form and general musical taste. To add instruments to recorded music, the children first listen carefully, discuss what they have heard, theorize on what tone qualities and dynamics may be appropriate, experiment by performing with the instruments, and finally decide upon the completed score. Certain criteria should be used, such as:

> Is the effect musical?
>
> Can the recorded music be clearly heard when the instruments play?
> Are there musical reasons for the selection of the instruments?
>
> Is the form of the music reflected in the choice and use of the instruments—when they play and when they are silent?
>
> Is the general effect of the music—heavy, light, thick, thin, high, low—reflected in the choice of the instruments?

There is opportunity in this activity to utilize rhythmic music of all types, from selected music by "name" composers to ethnic music of the world and to jazz.

Using percussion instruments to contribute to the interpretation of songs continues through the elementary school into junior high school. Sound effects heard on radio, television, and in the movies form a very real part of everyday living. Children at all levels enjoy the challenge of adding or creating descriptive sound effects to help communicate the message of certain songs. One or two drums can add immeasurably to an American Indian song; a tambourine or two can lend atmosphere to a Gypsy song; a combination of tambourine, drums, claves, and maracas can vitalize a Latin American song. A rhythm pattern drawn from the music at hand can be both experimental and creative to the children who are guided to discover it. This experience can relate to note reading skill when the pattern is written on the chalkboard in notation to be analyzed—so that "we can see what we did" or so that "our work can be saved and remembered for tomorrow's lesson." This develops associations between playing instruments, feeling rhythm, and visualizing it. Percussion accompaniments may be constructed from part of the melody rhythm, from the meter, or from a combination of these. Two or three simple patterns may sound complex when combined. Contrasting rhythms can be played on two or more different instruments or groups of instruments and the combinations of two or more patterns with the rhythm of the meter can be challenging, interesting, and tests of rhythmic growth. *Polyrhythms* may be either two contrasting rhythms within the same meter, or two different meters used at the same time, sometimes called "polymetric."

**Percussion
Instruments
Described**   The successful use of percussion instruments demands knowledge of a variety of sounds. The teacher needs to know the tone qualities that can be produced by each instrument, and how to play each of them. In general, commercially made instruments are superior to those made by teachers and children, although some of the latter can be quite suitable for temporary use, and a few can be of permanent value.

132

Learning
Music
by
Movement
and Rhythm

Percussion Instrument Sound Chart

Wooden instruments that "click" and
have short duration

Sticks
Claves
Castanets
Coconut shells
Wood blocks
Tone block
Xylophone

Metal instruments that ring or jingle
and have longer duration

Finger cymbals
Triangle
Jingle bells
Jingle clogs
Tambourine
Gong
Cymbals

Instruments that swish or rattle

Sandblocks
strip rattles
Maracas and other rattles

Instruments that "scratch"

Sticks
Guiro (notched gourd)

Hawaiian instruments
Pu'ili (slit bamboo sticks)
'Illi-ili (stones)
'I pu (large gourd)

Instruments that "boom"

Drums

Wooden
Instruments

Rhythm sticks can be made from dowel rods of from 3/8″ to 5/8″ in diameter, purchased from lumber yards. They are usually cut in 12″ lengths. Hardwood produces the most resonant sounds and will not break as easily as softwood. Ends can be smoothed with sandpaper; they can be enameled any desired color. Children hold one in each hand and strike them together. They should explore differences in pitch and sound by tapping different places on the sticks, and by tapping the sticks on suitable objects such as the floor and desk.

Claves are paired resonant sticks about an inch in diameter. They can sometimes be satisfactorily made from six-inch lengths of a broom stick or from doweling that is an inch in diameter. The professional method of playing is to hold one clave loosely in the partly closed left hand, resting on the heel of the hand with the other end resting on the fingernails and on the thumb and index finger, and to strike this one with the other clave held stick-like in the right hand. This instrument is seldom used in primary grades. It has its major place in Cuban songs and Latin American dances of the intermediate grades. A favorite example of claves rhythm that can be learned through speaking the rhythm of words is:

Shave, hair—— cut, six bits!

A more intricate claves rhythm is played in 4/4 meter on the underlined numbers representing eighth notes: 1 2 3 4 5 6 7 8 1 2 3 4 5 6 7 8.

Castanets used by children and by adult orchestra players are mounted on a handle. The instrument is made of a pair of cupped pieces of resonant hardwood, usually chestnut, attached by a cord. Of Spanish origin, the adult Spanish dancer holds a pair of unmounted castanets, one in each hand. The skilled dancer-player produces a variety of exciting effects from a sharp click to a sustained muffled rattle. Those played by children will produce only the sharp click. One castanet is sufficient, because of its penetrating sound. A recording of Chabier's *España* rhapsody will illustrate its use in the adult orchestra.

Coconut shells are useful to imitate hoofbeats of horses. Ripe coconuts can be purchased at food stores and the outside fibers can be removed, if desired, by a coarse kitchen "scratcher." They are then cut in half with a saw and the meat is scraped out. The two halves are then struck together to make a "clip-clop" sound. Children should explore the variety of sounds possible by striking them together in different ways including inside out, and striking them with sticks. Two paper cups can imitate coconut shells with a softer sound.

Woodblocks are best obtained from commercial sources, although imitations can be made from sections of old baseball bats. Woodblocks are sometimes held suspended by a cord to increase vibration. They are

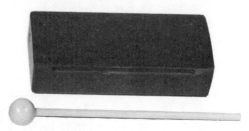

struck lightly with a hard rubber mallet at the hollow side near the edge over the slot. They can be played resting on a desk, preferably on a piece of felt, or held in the palm of the adult hand.

Children should experiment by striking them at other places, and with different beaters. They are useful to enhance songs about such subjects as ponies, cowboys, and clocks.

The *tone block* is produced commercially. The instrument is held in the left hand with the cut side toward the player. It is struck lightly on top with a stick, above the cut opening. Different sizes have different pitches, and this fact can be useful in song accompaniments.

The *xylophone,* a keyboard melody instrument, should be purchased for best results although it has been made experimentally by teachers and students in upper grades from redwood strips or one-inch doweling resting on ropes. In early primary grades it is often used for a special *glissando* effect to describe such incidents in songs as "The mouse ran up the clock," in "Hickory Dickory Dock." Later on it is used as a melody instrument. The *marimba* is a xylophone of Latin American origin that has metal tube resonators. (Illustrations of these instruments are shown in Chapter Fourteen.)

**Metal
Instruments**

Finger cymbals are tiny replicas of the larger cymbal, and are usually obtained commercially rather than made by teachers. One is usually held in each hand, and they are struck together lightly at the edge or flat together for different effects. They can also be played with one hand, with the two cymbals fastened to fingers that can strike the instruments together. This latter way enables a dancer to accompany his own dancing with delicate metallic punctuations. Finger cymbals are useful for subtle effects in Oriental songs and to portray elves or angels.

The *triangle* is struck lightly by a metal rod on the inside corner of the base of the instrument. A large nail or spike will sometimes make a satisfactory substitute. It is held suspended by a cord. The tone can be continued by moving the beater back and forth rapidly on the inside edges of the two sides. It can be silenced by touching it.

Jingle bells are purchased. They are played by shaking them vigorously. Some are mounted on sticks while others are worn around the wrist or ankle. A small tinkling sound can be produced by holding

them toward the floor and moving them back and forth with a gentle motion of the wrist.

Jingle clogs are more easily purchased than made. Their major use is in primary grades. They are held in one hand and tapped against the palm of the other hand in a manner that leaves the jingles free to sound. When teachers make them from metal discs used in roofing, fastened loosely on a stick, they will gain added resonance if the discs are bent slightly. Sometimes the discs are alternated with bottle caps.

The commercially produced *tambourine* is best. It is held at the place on the instrument where there are no metal jingles. To play it, the head is struck against the heel of the hand, or it is shaken. The instrument strikes the hand; the hand does not strike the instrument. Experimental effects can be produced by tapping it on the knee, tapping it with fingers, and using a rubbing motion with the thumb followed by striking, tapping, or shaking. The head is coated with shellac and powdered rosin when professional drummers use the thumb roll. Tambourines lend atmosphere to Gypsy, Hebrew, Spanish, and Italian songs.

The true *gong* is relatively expensive. A large one could be borrowed from the high school band, perhaps. A gong can be made from German silver about one foot square. Cut a circle from this. Drill holes for the cord that will suspend it. Then hammer the edges, testing the sound

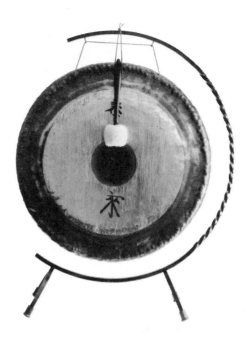

from time to time, until the edges curve inward about two inches. A substitute can be found in the metal lid of the heavy barrel-like cardboard containers often used as waste baskets in schools. Ask the school custodian to save one of the containers (to use as a drum) and the lid to use as a gong. Drill a hole by which to suspend it. A suspended length of iron pipe can be another substitute. This instrument is used with songs about cathedral bells, huge clocks, and the Orient.

Cymbals of the best tone are commercially made, although some teachers have found good tones in aluminum pan lids. They are held one in each hand and struck together in a glancing blow with hands moving up and down in contrary directions. Other effects can be found by striking the cymbal on its edge, and with different beaters or sticks.

Sandblocks, used largely in primary grades, can be made from any soft wood from 3/4″ to 1″ thick and about 3″ by 3″ square. Handles can be door or drawer pulls, spools, leather, or small pieces of wood. Fasten the handle with screws, and place No. 1–0 sandpaper or emery cloth (this lasts longer) on the rubbing side of the block with thumb tacks. Hold a block in each hand and rub the rough surfaces together. Some teachers believe that the motion of the arms required to play sandblocks is a superior means by which the five- and six-year-olds can achieve rhythmic control in a very short time.

Maracas can be purchased or made from a pair of gourds by placing in them a suitable amount of dry seeds, pebbles, or bird shot. They are necessary for many Latin American dance songs. Maracas are held either by handles or by the neck of an elongated gourd, and are usually shaken in a steady eighth-note rhythm. The arms move back and forth; the wrists

are stiff. For a soft effect they can be tapped by the fingers rather than shaken. Gourds from which to make maracas and guiros can be purchased from the Pearson Gourd Farm, 1409 North Merced Avenue, Box 310, El Monte, California. The catalog of this firm gives directions for the construction of these instruments. A single maraca on a long handle is **138** used as an American Indian rattle. It can be decorated with feathers and furs. The *cabaca* or *cabaza* is a large enameled gourd that has small wooden beads strung loosely around it. This form of rattle is a Latin American instrument. *Strip rattles* can be made from walnut shells and bottle caps suspended alternately on 3″ to 4″ cords suspended from a band. They are worn on the wrist or ankle in American Indian dances. *Other rattles* can be made from spice cans, typewriter ribbon cans, pill boxes, ice cream and cottage cheese cartons, salt boxes, etc. A maraca-like rattle can be made from a large electric light bulb. Cover it with papier mâché: when dry, break glass.

Instruments That Scratch

Rhythm sticks make a light scratching sound when they are stroked across notches. The notches appear in most commercially made sticks, and can be added to teacher-made ones by making a row of shallow saw cuts on one of each pair of sticks. These can be filed to the proper depth and smoothness, and the smooth stick is then stroked over the notched stick.

A *guiro* is a large gourd with ridges cut along its side. It is played with a small stick or a wire scratcher scraped back and forth across the ridges. It is a Latin American instrument. Besides the scratching sound it can be made to produce a tap-scrape-tap rhythm.

Hawaiian Instruments

Pu'ili are slit bamboo sticks. They can be made from two 18″ bamboo sticks that are 1″ to 2″ in diameter. The lowest large joint is the handle. It can be drilled out and sanded. Holes 1/4″ to 3/8″ in diameter are drilled above this joint to serve as guides for cutting out corresponding slices from the holes to the tip. The sticks are struck softly together and used in graceful motions as an extension of the arm. *'Illi-ili* are pairs of small rounded volcanic rocks to be held in the palm of the hand and clapped or rubbed together. Using many players gives an interesting effect. The *'I pu* is a drum made from a wide, jar-shaped gourd. The top of the stem end is cut off and the seeds and pulp are removed. It is played by slapping the side of the gourd with the palm of the hand. *Uli-uli* are feathered gourds.

Drums

There are many kinds and sizes of drums, manufactured and teacher-made. Some have one head, others two. They come singly and by two's and even three's. For different effects they can be struck off-center or in the center, with the fingertips, the heel of the hand, or with various types of padded beaters. There should be at least two drums in every classroom; one of low pitch and one of high pitch. The many types of commercial drums include the tom-tom, tunable drums, bongo, and conga drums. Homemade drums of varying quality may be devised from chopping bowls, wooden kegs, lard cans, and wastebaskets with goatskin (soaked 24 hours), real calfskin or heavy rubber thumbtacked, nailed, or laced on. Old drumheads can be used, salvaged from stores or from the high school bandroom. To paint skin drumheads, use water-color paint applied on the *wet* head. Color is an important element in constructing any of the instruments because it makes them more attractive to children. Smaller drums can be devised from oatmeal boxes or other cardboard containers, used as they are or with ends covered with a rubber sheet or very heavy paper. Flowerpot "drums" can be made by stretching and taping wet heavy paper across the opening; the paper tightens as it dries. Ready-made drums of fair quality are found in the very heavy cardboard barrel-like cartons used to ship chinaware, seed, ice cream mix, and sweeping compound. These are stood open-end-down on two books (to raise them off the floor in order to increase resonance) and pounded. They can be useful as drums, and have added utility in that the metal cover can be used as a gong. These potential drums are often found as wastebaskets in school corridors.

Drum beaters can be purchased. They can be made from sticks of doweling of sufficient diameter cut to proper length, and soft rubber balls. The doweling is glued into a hole made in the ball. Instead of the rubber ball, a ball of cotton, covered with muslin and tied, can be used, or a ball can be made of aluminum foil covered with muslin and painted with two or three coats of the nitrate liquid used by airplane manufacturers.

The *conga drum* is a large long Cuban drum played with the palms of the hands, usually with the left hand with flat fingers striking the edge of the head and the right hand also with flat fingers striking the center of the head.

The *bongo drum,* another Latin American instrument, is a double drum; one is larger than the other. Held between the knees with the

small drum on the right, it is played with the tips of the fingers and the thumbs. The bongo is used in Latin American music.

Some of the many possible songs for introducing and expanding the use of percussion instruments are the familar "Hickory, Dickory, Dock," "Jingle Bells," "Jingle at the Window," "Ten Little Indians," various songs about trains, "This Old Man," "Toodola," "When the Saints Go Marching In," "Mister Banjo," "Down the River," "Sandy Land," and "Tinga Layo."

Summary We have described some of the contributions that percussion instruments can make to children's explorations of tone qualities, dynamics, pitch, form, rhythm, and the interpretations of songs in which their use is appropriate. Concepts of the phrase, repetition, and contrast can be enhanced by creating percussion scores which reflect these aspects of form. Feelings for mood can be reflected in the choice of and the manner of playing the instruments. Notation can be learned and understood better when children find it useful to them in playing and composing percussion scores. Every concept of rhythm may be strengthened at times by the use of these instruments.

Learning
Music
Concepts

Tempo and Dynamics

Tempo and dynamics can be clearly associated with rhythm and melody. Fast-slow and loud-soft are among the first music-related concepts young children are asked to learn at the beginning of their school music instruction.

The teacher can help children discover their own natural tempo by playing a drum or the piano to their steps as they walk across the room, perhaps on some errand or as part of a game. After the relation between their steps and the sound the teacher makes has been learned, the children will be able to govern their steps in accordance with the tempo the teacher plays, and can walk slower or faster. This can be a challenging game at this stage of development. The character of slow and fast music can be examined by comparing two songs, one of them slow and the other fast. Children can be guided to discover that much fast music is "light" and much slow music is smooth, calm, or perhaps "heavy." These descriptions of slow and fast music should be discovered through and reinforced by

142

physical responses to music, and these responses may include aspects of impersonation and dramatization, often of animal movements. Body movement, percussion instruments, and hand clapping are used to develop the concepts *accelerando* (gradually faster) and *rallentando, ritardando,* and *ritard* (gradually slower). These can be felt and seen when two children throw and catch a large ball as the music changes tempo. They come closer together for a more rapid bouncing for fast tempos and farther apart for slower tempos.

Loud and soft are easily-understood concepts, and from them are gradually learned the gradations of relative degrees of loud and soft. Percussion instruments and hand clapping can assist in learning about

crescendo ◁══════ (gradually louder) and *decrescendo* or *diminuendo*

══════▷ (gradually softer). Some teachers have children imitate them as they clap hands or sound an instrument softly when held low, near the floor, then gradually increase the volume as the hands move higher. This becomes *crescendo* and its reverse becomes *decrescendo.* These aspects of musical expression should be related to, or discovered and identified in, songs and recordings at once, and reviewed and identified repeatedly. *Accent* is a quality of dynamics easily taught in relation to loud-soft and to meter. *Adventures in Music* recordings which can help teach this concept include "Petite Ballerina," Shostakovitch; "Can Can," Rossini; "Departure," Prokofieff (all from II), "Dagger Dance," Herbert; and "Tarantella," Rossini (from III).

From the third grade up, recordings such as "Pacific 321," Honegger, (concerning a railway locomotive of World War I vintage), and "Fêtes," Debussy (concerning a festival) can be useful in studying tempo and dynamics on a large scale. Attention should always be given to their function in the music being studied. Songs should be selected which exemplify their use. Indexes of music textbooks will be helpful. The teacher can draw the attention of the children to tempo and dynamics by well-planned questions: "Would this song be better if it were sung (slower, faster, softer, louder)? "Let's try it that way." "Was it better, or not as good?" "Why do you think so?" "Can you think of other ways we might try it (perhaps utilizing accent, crescendo, decrescendo)?" "Let's try to find the very best ways to sing the song expressively."

As for terminology, English terms are ordinarily learned in the primary grades and their Italian counterparts introduced in the intermediate grades. Some of the terms in more common use are listed in the Structure of Music Outline, Chapter Five. Such a vocabulary should be a *useful* one—not one to be learned because a book lists terms. They are terms that need to be employed by teacher and children to describe the tempo and dynamics of any given piece of music, to explain *how* fast or slow, loud or soft the children's own compositions should be performed, and to be able to discuss music intelligently. Memorization of this terminology is usually boring and self-defeating, but practical use of it makes good sense. In the intermediate grades a glossary of music terms should be made available to the children to help them solve the musical problems and to enable them to answer their own question Some music series books have such glossaries. Other terms related to t character of performance are:

cantabile	in a singing style	*maestoso*	majestic
dolce	sweetly	*molto*	very much
grandioso	grand, pompous, majestic	*poco*	a little

Some teachers and children have made imaginative posters illustrati terminology. For example, *adagio* might be illustrated by the turtle, *alleg* by a swift-flying bird, *accelerando* by a rocket taking off, and *grandio* by a regal king.

As work on tempo and dynamics continues through the years, rel tionships between these and the other elements of music should be di covered, and appreciation of them should grow. There are relationshi between tempo and dynamics, and between them and melody, harmon form, and texture. These are waiting to be explored through experienc planned by teachers.

The Beat and Its Subdivisions

Adults are apt to overlook or underestimate the need children ha for a great deal of experience with the regular and continuous beat th is characteristic of most music. To the adult, this regular beat seems be too simple for much consideration and some teachers tend to give little attention. The result of this becomes obvious when children ha difficulty understanding division of the beat and meter, and when a lar number of adults cannot march, keep in step or walk in a natural, rhythm manner. All children need extensive rhythmic experience, and they ne teachers who realize how important it is to musical growth, as well as physical and personality development.

Beat and pulse are terms most people use interchangeably. The autho will use the term beat in this book, in the sense that in moderate temp the 4/4 meter has four beats.

The ear, the eye, and the body are employed in building the concept the beat. Children *listen* to the teacher's playing on a drum, the piano, clapping hands. They also listen to selected recordings which stress t beat. They *see* the teacher play on a drum or clap hands and try to imita those motions, and by so doing, learn little by little to be "in time" wi the motions. Children explore and analyze the beat for themselves throu their body responses and by experimenting with various percussion instr ments. They also see the beat pictured in simple notation:

(Notice that these simple 4/4 measures are written in a manner corresponding in miniature to the printed page of a reader.)

The body is employed in a number of ways. The children *feel* the beat with their whole body by walking, marching, swaying, hopping, or by clapping, slapping thighs, and making other hand-arm movements. They can also respond with words that reflect the beat and its subdivisions which are repeated over and over, such as:

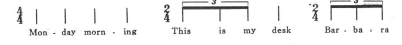

or

* Percussion instruments or hand clapping are often employed when a rest falls on the last beat of the measure.

An aim of the teacher is to have all children feel the beat together. It is a *good* feeling, enjoyed by people all over the world.

Word Patterns [1]

Chant	Play Instruments
Chant in a deliberate manner, emphasizing the last word in each line of the following:	*Six children, each with a different instrument, play in turn the underlying beat, while the class chants.*

Bonefish, bluebird, black sheep, CROW	Triangle	
Chickadee, doodlebug, robins in a ROW	Tambourine	

[1] From *This Is Music for Kindergarten and Nursery School,* by Adeline McCall. Copyright © 1965 by Allyn and Bacon, Inc. Used by permission.

146

Learning
Music
by
Movement
and Rhythm

Word Patterns

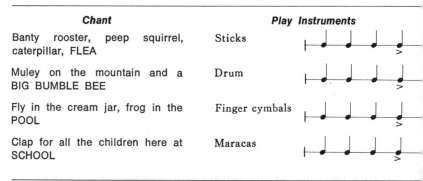

Chant		*Play Instruments*
Banty rooster, peep squirrel, caterpillar, FLEA	Sticks	
Muley on the mountain and a BIG BUMBLE BEE	Drum	
Fly in the cream jar, frog in the POOL	Finger cymbals	
Clap for all the children here at SCHOOL	Maracas	

From street calls and jingles most children have experienced th
beat and many of its divisions. For example:

> One potato, two potato, three potato, four;
> Five potato, six potato, seven potato, more.

Teachers should bring such playground rhymes into the classroom an
make use of them.

The quarter rest can be introduced by challenging the children t
invent motions to do when the beats are like this:

Mrs. Richards, in her *Threshold to Music* materials tells of Hungaria
children throwing their hands up and away and saying "Sw-sh." Childre
will think of many ways to express or act out the quarter rest. Afte
involving the children this way, and deciding on a motion, the symbo
for the rest   is written in. Another approach is with pictures. Mr
Richards' Chart 4 of the First Year Charts, with the empty dog house
as rests, has become a favorite.

Music series books for the kindergarten and first grade provide eas
piano pieces which encourage responses to the beat, and their publisher
provide recordings of marches, march-like songs and dance songs whic
do the same for all grade levels. Other commonly-used recordings includ
the RCA Basic Record Library for Elementary Schools, the Adventure
in Music albums (also RCA), and the Bowmar Orchestral Library
particularly Album 54, Marches. The teacher should seek out these collec

tions, study the suggestions provided for teachers, and select the music most appropriate to the needs of the class.

Echo-Clapping   Echo-clapping is one appropriate introduction to rhythmic instruction because normal children of school age have the physical coordination to do it with ease (although a few six-year-olds need to be taught how). If children can imitate the teacher's clapping perfectly, the teacher knows that they are comprehending the rhythms and that they possess the physical coordination to respond. Children of all ages are interested when the teacher suddenly says, "Listen to what I clap; then you clap it." First, establish the beat, then:

Soon children will be able to clap improvised patterns to be echoed by the class.

Another interesting type of echo-clapping is the question-and-answer, in which the teacher or a child claps a rhythmic question to be answered creatively, such as:

This activity leads to discovering and creating questions and answers in melody, and to increasing comprehension of the phrase.

Later on, echo-clapping in canon form can develop rhythmic memory. In this activity the class echoes perhaps one measure behind the leader

147   and in so doing must (1) remember what was clapped and repeat it later *while at the same time* (2) hearing and remembering what the leader doing at the moment. For example:

Children can take the part of the leader, and percussion instrumen can be used instead of the clapping.

Some Possible Responses Relating to Note Values

Note	Clapping	Speaking	Stepping
Whole	clap-squeeze-squeeze-squeeze	ta-a-a-a or who-o-ole-note	step-point-point-po
Dotted Half	clap-squeeze-squeeze	ta-a-a or half-note-dot	step-point-point
Half	clap-squeeze	ta-a or half-note	step-bend
Quarter	clap	ta or quart-er	walk
Eighth ♫	clap-clap	ti-ti or eighth-eighth	run-run
♩ ♪	clap-clap	ta-ti or skip-ty	skip-ping
♫♩	clap-clap-clap	tri-o-la	run-run-run
♫♫	clap-clap-clap-clap	ti-ri-ti-ri	run-run-run-run

After children have learned to respond to note values in the abo ways, they can analyze the notation of simple songs by clapping, speakin and stepping. Songs such as "Hot Cross Buns" can be studied in this w: by young children.

Body Movements, Rhythm Words, and Notation

Movement	Line Notation	Words	Music Notation	Meter
walking				
thigh slapping	— — — —	ta ta ta ta	♩ ♩ ♩ ♩	$\frac{2}{4}$ or $\frac{4}{4}$
hopping				
clapping				
running				
clapping	– – – –	ti-ti ti-ti ti-ti ti-ti	♫ ♫ ♫ ♫	$\frac{2}{4}$ or $\frac{4}{4}$
tapping	– – – –	ta-ti ta-ti ta-ti ta-ti ti-iri ti-iri ti-iri ti-iri		$\frac{6}{8}$
skipping, galloping	– – – –			$\frac{2}{4}$ or $\frac{4}{4}$
swaying				
sliding	————	ta-a-a	𝅝	$\frac{3}{4}$
skating				
rocking				
swinging				
step-bend	————	ta-a ta-a	𝅗𝅥	$\frac{2}{4}$ or $\frac{4}{4}$
jumping				

Some teachers make charts such as the following for children to stud

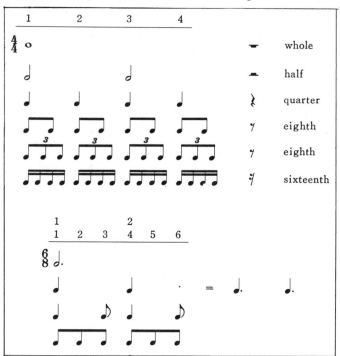

BINGO

American Folkso

There was a farm-er had a dog, And Bin-go was his name - O,

B - I - N - G - O, B - I - N - G - O,

B - I - N - G - O, and Bin-go was his name - O.

Teaching the Concept "Rest"

At the time this song is learned, the beat and the rhythm of the melod can be experienced by marching to the song and clapping. Point out th repeated pattern long long short-short long and sing it: tah tah tee-tee ta

(♩ ♩ ♫ ♩). Clapping softly with the fingers, not the palms, th

class sings the song as written, then on its repeat, omits singing "B" an

squeezes fists instead of clapping on that beat. On the next repeat, th letters "B" and "i" are not sung, the fists clenched on those beats. This is continued until silently clenched fists are squeezing the complete pattern. The name "rest" can be attached to the short and long silences the children have felt with their muscles. A dance can be created for the song.

**Divisions of
the Beat**

The necessity for divisions of the beat appears very soon after learning the concept of the steady beat. Although the beat may be fast or slow, the impressive aspect of divisions of the beat comes from relative length. Words such as "Rain, rain, go a-way" demand | ⋅| ⊓ | and provide learners with obvious instances where the short-short sound is equal to one long sound. Another way of picturing this is in short and long lines: __ __ _ _ __. The Hungarian methods "speak" the quarter note beat *ta* (tah) and the eighth note as *ti* (tee). Thus, the above rhythm pattern would be *ta ta ti-ti ta*. Young children can easily read and write this introductory form of notation. Later on, they can add a slanted line to form the note head ♩ . The triplet | ♩♩♩ | was once regarded as a complexity to be taught in intermediate grades but today young children can easily identify it as *tri-o-la, tri-pl-et,* or *tri-ple-ti* and begin to comprehend that in this division of the beat they find three notes to one beat.

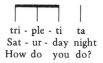

tri - ple - ti   ta
Sat - ur - day night
How do   you do?

From this beginning, the seven year old can eventually use and understand the concept of four-to-one or

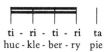

ti - ri - ti - ri ta
huc - kle - ber - ry pie

and its variants.

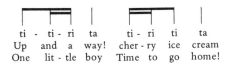

ti - ti - ri ta   ti - ri ti   ta
Up and a way! cher - ry ice cream
One lit - tle boy Time to go home!

Any division of the beat should be studied in relation to words, body movement, songs (melody-rhythms), and children's improvised percussion patterns. For example, let us say that the children are guided to sense and observe the rhythm of the melody of "Hey, Betty Martin," which begins with a fast *long short-short long* or, in this instance, a *ti ti-ri ti ti* pattern.

Later they can find that "Ten Little Indians" is constructed from th
same rhythm pattern used in a different way, with the first part of
repeated many times.

Dotted Notes   While the rhythm of the dotted quarter note may hav
been felt for some time and practiced by imitation, emphasis on this co
cept is usually in third and fourth grades. A familiar song like "America
is useful. By writing it in notation, the fact of the dot being worth ha
again the value of the note it follows is pictured. Also, the class should b
guided to discover where the second beat-point falls (on the dot). A
teacher-made chart can then be studied. It could be:

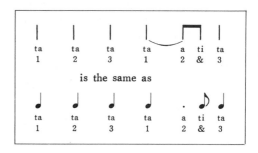

All uses for the dot should be explored in the notation of songs, and th
fact that the dot adds again the original value of the note it follows shoul
be reviewed as frequently as it is needed to understand the music bein
performed or composed by the children.

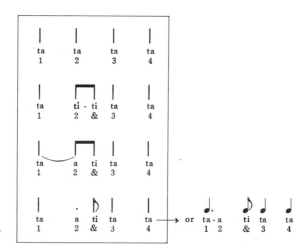

When this relationship of notes and beats has been established, it is no
difficult to apply it to the dotted-eighth-and-sixteenth note pattern. This i
identical to the dotted-quarter-and-eighth pattern except that it is ordinari
(but not always) twice as fast. "Battle Hymn of the Republic" is a son
often used in this study. The children should have numerous experience
with the rhythm of this melody, singing it, clapping it, listening to recorde

versions, and listening to performances of it by members of the class. They might conduct experiments with changing the rhythm, such as singing it in even eighth notes, then discussing if this would be preferred to the uneven rhythm of the written song. They should examine the notation carefully. After comparing the even eighth notes with the dotted-eighth-sixteenth notes, the following teacher-made chart should be studied:

By means of the chart the children should be able to analyze the divisions of the beat by dividing it into halves (eighth notes) and then into quarters (sixteenth notes) to understand mathematically and visually the dotted note rhythm they already "know" from previous listening, clapping, and singing.

By means of the types of activities mentioned above, children can be discovering and identifying beat units and divisions of the beat. They can find them in words, with clapping, by playing on percussion instruments, and in the melodies of songs. By looking at notation of music they have worked with and know, they will find that beat units can be written in different note values:

$$\quad \text{♩} , \quad \text{♩.} , \quad \text{♩} , \quad \text{♪} .$$

They will discover equal division of the beat:

$$\quad \text{♩♩} , \quad \text{♫} , \quad \text{♫} , \quad \text{♬} ,$$

and unequal divisions:

They will also find that three notes of equal value can occupy a beat unit normally divided in two's:

Competent teachers know that it is much more fun for learners to find these for themselves than to be lectured about them.

Staccato and *legato* can be included in the study of the duration of sounds. These are expressive aspects of music having relationships with note values. They are ways of *articulation,* staccato being detached or disconnected sounds and legato being smooth and connected, with no silence between the sounds. The German folk song "My Hat" can be sung in either staccato or legato style; the children can "think over" and evaluate the effect of each of these kinds of articulation in this and other songs and instrumental pieces.

MY HAT[2]

German Folksong

Among the many recordings which illustrate articulation are:

Legato (articulation).   Also music for resting
Stravinsky: "Berceuse" from *Firebird* Suite, AM
1 v 1

[2] This becomes an action song by touching the chest for "my," the head for "hat," holding three fingers high for "three," and drawing the three corners in the air for "corners." After this, the actions are continued, but one of the four action words, probably "hat," is omitted, leaving only silence in its place. The next time another word is omitted until all four words are indicated only by the action.

Fauré: "Berceuse" from *Dolly,* AM 2 v 1
Bizet: "Cradle Song" from *Children's Games,* AM 1 v 1
Offenbach: "Barcarolle" from *Tales of Hoffman,* AM 3 v 1

Staccato (articulation). Moussorgsky: "Ballet of the Unhatched Chicks" from *Pictures at an Exhibition,* AM 1 v 1
Anderson: *The Syncopated Clock,* Keyboard Junior Recordings
Stravinsky: "Dance Infernale" from *Firebird* Suite, BOL 69; Keyboard Junior Recordings
Vaughan-Williams: "March Past of the Kitchen Utensils" from *The Wasps,* AM 3 v 1
von Suppé: *Light Cavalry* Overture

Another aspect of duration of sound is the *fermata,* or hold (⌢). This is found in some familiar songs such as "Erie Canal" and "We Three Kings of Orient Are." It can be identified in recorded compositions when the regular beat stops for a time and one tone or chord is sustained before the beat and the melody continue.

Rhythm and Pitch

Rhythm is an integral part of melody. As soon as pitch is added to a rhythm pattern some kind of melodic fragment or tune results. Because of the ease in singing the descending minor third interval, this descending pitch pattern has become an important beginning point in relating rhythm and pitch.

These two notes represent *high* and *low* pitch concepts, thus the beat, divisions of the beat, and high-low pitch concepts can be taught or involved simultaneously.

When the descending minor third is introduced, it can be related in game form to clapping and thigh-slapping (patchen), *so* (scale tone 5) to clapping, and *mi* (3) for slapping. After establishing the pitches and relating them to the motions, the teacher can make the motions while the class, group, or individual listens and watches, after which the learner responds with both making the motions and singing the pitches. Also, the teacher can sing those pitches using a neutral syllable (la, loo) and the students can respond by singing the syllables or numerals, imitating the rhythm sung by the teacher. Eventually students can take the part of the

teacher. This activity leads directly into steps in learning the Curwen
hand signs, as will be discussed in Chapter Twelve. Many simple words
can be sung in quarter-and-eighth note patterns:

Young children need musical (singing) conversations like this, and enjoy
having teachers sing instructions to them rather than always speaking them.
They also enjoy the creative possibilities in singing answers to the teacher's
statements; they need not always reply with the same pitches the teacher
sings. The experience with 5–5–3 is quickly expanded to include other
pitches; the next one is usually scale tone 6 or *la*. In the classroom, working on problems of rhythm and pitch are often integrally related. For
example, speak the following words to decide upon their natural rhythm:

> *Star-light, star bright,*
> *First star I see to-night;*
> *Wish I may, wish I might,*
> *Have the wish I wish to-night.*

Then ask a few classmates to sing the words in this rhythm, using only
scale tones 5 and 3. When the class agrees that a version so improvised is
logical and pleasing, notate it. Next, have some other students improvise
tunes using scale tones 5, 3 and 6. Notate a pleasing version of this.
Finally, ask others to improvise tunes with scale tones 5, 3, 6, 2, and 1
and notate the best tune. Remember that what the college class can do
in a few minutes may take weeks at elementary school levels.

Accent, Meter, and Rhythm Patterns

Rhythmic
Exercises
    Beginning with very easy movements, teachers help children to feel
basic rhythm by having them perform thigh-slapping, finger-snapping,
desk-tapping, and heel-stamping sounds, first as exercises, then in connection with verse, songs, and recordings. A major purpose is to build concepts of metrical rhythm. The long-term objective has three stages,
beginning with the concept of symmetrical meters—those divisible by two
or three—because they are easiest and therefore the logical starting point.
These include the familiar 2/4, 3/4, 4/4, and 6/8. Next the children meet
the interesting stage of discovering, exploring, and devising alternation
and combinations of these meters. The third stage is learning asymmetrical
meters such as 5/4, 7/8 and others not divisible by two or three, which
have irregular accents. Ten and eleven-year olds will discern that these are
formed from the familiar two and three beat groups they know from their
study of the more conventional meters, but now arranged in a different

less regular order. Movement, spoken words, or phrases can be found or invented to help the children learn to feel these meters just as appropriate movement and words helped them with the common ones. Such meters are commonly used in the musics of Africa and Asia and they comprise an important element in Western music being written today. Thus, school music has been freed from the metrical straight-jacket of earlier years and is ready to undergo an exciting expansion in rhythm. Some examples of rhythmic exercises follow.

March rhythms such as "This Old Man," "The Caisson Song," and "Pop! Goes the Weasel!" can be felt by:

Clap
Heels

Clap
Thighs

Waltz rhythms such as "Ach du lieber Augustin" ("The More We Get Together") can be moved to by:

Clap

Tap Desk

Slap
Right Knee

Left Knee

Finger-snap

Clap

Slap-thighs

Snap fingers

Clap

Slap thighs

Tap desk

The above pattern could be written as two measures in 5/4 meter. Other rhythmic exercises:

Clap
Tap Desk

Finger Snap
Clap Hands

Clap
Stamp

Percussion instruments can be used instead of body movements to produce the sound in such exercises. Even tone bars or bell sets can be employed. While the class does one pattern softly in unison, one child can improvise rhythmically by clapping or by playing a percussion instrument. If the basic beat is felt and understood, children should be able to place many of their patterns in notation. They should be guided to discover that the natural accent produces the measure by dictating where the bar lines are placed.

**Rhythmic
Development
of "Hickory
Dickory
Dock"**

The approach of Carl Orff to music for children includes body percussive sounds such as stamping feet, slapping thighs (patschen), clapping hands and snapping fingers. (Notice that the sounds have four levels of pitches from low to high: stamp, patsch, clap, and snap.) These motions not only help children feel the beat and rhythm patterns, but the physical action adds to their pleasure.

Speak clearly and convincingly:

thighs   clap   thighs snap-snap   thighs   clap   thighs snap-snap
Hickory dickory dock (tick-tock); the mouse ran up the clock (tick-tock)

    thighs   clap   thighs   clap   thighs   clap   thighs snap-snap
The clock struck one, the mouse ran down; hickory dickory dock (tick-tock)

After this has been mastered, some of the class can add the percussion instruments suggested with the song.

A new melody for the song can be improvised on a small keyboard instrument on the pitches of the C pentatonic scale: C D E G A. In this learning sequence one progresses creatively from speech sounds and word rhythms to adding body percussion, then percussion instruments, and finally a melody. Find other rhythmic speech patterns and experiment similarly with those of your choice.

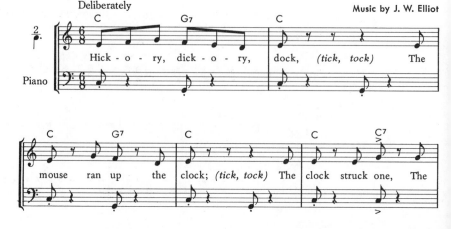

HICKORY, DICKORY, DOCK

Words from Mother Goose

Music by J. W. Elliot

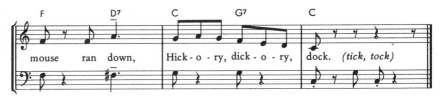

mouse ran down, | Hick-o-ry, dick-o-ry, | dock. *(tick, tock)*

Suggestions

For generations this Mother Goose song has been accompanied by children playing rhythm sticks slowly, two beats to the measure, in imitation of the clock which is a big old grandfather's clock that really ticks and tocks. In addition, one child is privileged to be the mouse and will play *glissandos* on the bells—going up in pitch when the mouse runs up, and down in pitch when the mouse runs down. The tick tock indicated during the rests can be performed by a child playing on two tone blocks, one higher than the other in pitch. Which tone block will play the "tick" and which one the "tock"? (Tick is a higher vocal sound and tock is a lower one, so the tone blocks should imitate these different pitches.) Try to have the children discover this. Also have them decide what to do on the accent; perhaps a different instrument should play at that point.

Conducting

Conductors' beat patterns are another rhythmic response to the meter, usually in intermediate grades, and after they have been learned they can be used by the children to identify meters they hear from recordings. The entire class can perform these with songs or recordings. The primary (heavy) accent of each measure is indicated by a downbeat, as illustrated. A drum played on this beat (marked *1*) will help the children to hear and feel the accent. A secondary accent occurs in 4/4 and slow 6/8 meters on beats 3 and 4, respectively.

Left-handed children will conduct all left and right motions as right and left—the reverse of the drawings. Such an exercise by children while

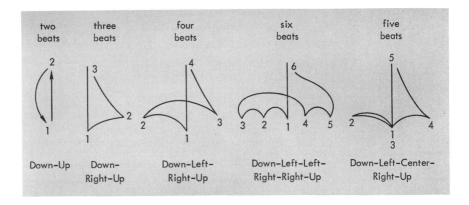

singing a song will assist them in giving each measure the correct number of beats. One of the Dalcroze exercises consists of children's conducting different meters while marching.

Word-Rhythms The use of word-rhythms is a natural way to introduce rhythmic response. There is rhythm to be discovered in the spoken word, and children use and enjoy this rhythm in their play. The *sound* of words attracts children in the early primary grades, and people of all ages react to them, as testified by the rhythmic cheers at athletic events. Also, the rhythms of both simple and complex note values can be assimilated with ease when teachers relate these to familiar words.

Examples:

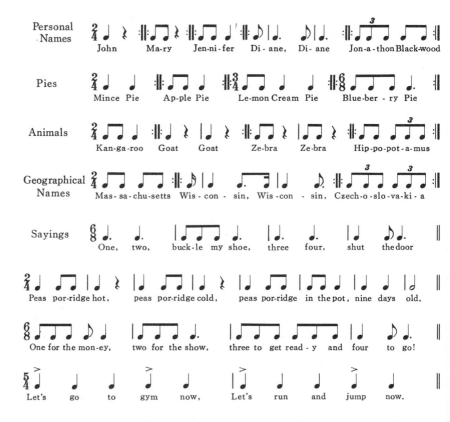

Percussion instruments, clapping, and the use of feet can be added to enhance the rhythm and add to the interest—for names can be "said" with feet and instruments. The teacher should be alert to the fact that most of these word-rhythms can be altered according to different ways of accenting words. For example, "Lemon cream pie" might be:

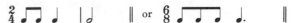

160

Several different rhythms may be correct for one word. Rhythms of some radio and television commercials are interesting to work with; they have the advantage of being well-known by the children.

*Exploring
Common
Meters*

When short word rhythms are repeated and when longer groups of rhythmic words are spoken, there is a natural tendency to group the beats by accenting some of them. In their most common usage these accents are spaced regularly, at intervals of two or three beats. If children lower their hands on the accents and raise them on beats between the accents they can find whether the beats are grouped in two's or three's. This can be done with songs or recordings but the teacher may find it appropriate to introduce the search for meter with a drum. From these groupings, formed by accents, they can theorize on what the meter may be.

Songs and recorded music useful for exploring common meters are very easily found because most of the music for elementary school exemplifies such meters.

Number of Beats	*Duple Meter*	*Triple Meter*
1		3/8 3/4 (tempo di valse)
2	2/4 2/2	6/8 6/4
3		3/8 3/4 9/8
4	4/8 4/4 4/2	12/8

What do meter signatures mean? They tell us only how many of a certain kind of note or its equivalent can be found in one measure. If the signature is 3/4, there are three quarter notes or their equivalent value in the measure. Whether each receives one beat or not is usually not revealed by the meter sign alone. Most of the time they will receive one beat, but when the tempo is very rapid the entire measure would receive only one beat. If the meter is 6/8, we know that there are six eighth notes or their equivalent in each measure, but we do not know from the meter signature whether there are two or six beats in those measures—whether each eighth note receives one beat or one third of a beat. Thus, the upper figure does *not* always tell us the number of beats in a measure, and the lower figure does *not* always tell us the kind of note that receives one beat. Meter signatures tell us only the number of a certain kind of note or its equivalent that can be written into one measure.

There is a possibility that in stressing meter accent teachers limit the capacity of children to think beyond its regularity. One way to begin to overcome this is to have them listen for accent in a rendition of "America" from a recording or played on the piano by the teacher. The correct performance will reveal little or no meter accent. To add a definite accent to the first beat of each measure would destroy the solemnity and dignity of this melody. Hearing recordings of Gregorian chant will reveal no regular recurring beat or accent. Aspects of music which tend to make rhythm more free—less bound to the rigidity of regular beats and accents—include *rallentando* and *ritardando* (gradually slower) and *accelerando* (gradually faster). *Rubato* is a term which implies that the performer treats the tempo and note values very flexibly, employing many slight accelerandos and ritardandos. This may be done in two ways, either by applying this freedom to the melody while the beat remains stable, or by applying it to the music as a whole. Many jazz players illustrate the former; Liszt and Chopin, among many other nineteenth century composers, employed the latter. There is some Oriental, Indian, and Hungarian music which has no metrical beat. Syncopation upsets the normal meter and accent by deviating from the regular recurring accent; it shifts accents to normally weak beats. The familiar "Hokey-Pokey," "Dry Bones," and "Rock Island Line" are among the many songs from which older children can learn about syncopation. Again, the teacher should examine the indexes of music books for the heading "syncopation." Recorded selections such as Gershwin's "I Got Rhythm" and "Anything Goes," and many selected popular and jazz tunes of the day can be useful, as are standard selections such as Gottschalk's "Grand Walkaround" (Adventures in Music 5 vol. 1). When possible, the rhythmic notation should be written on the chalkboard to help children analyze syncopation. The *beat points*—the place or note in the measure where the metric beat falls—should be indicated, and the accents clearly marked.

Latin-American music is a useful source in studying syncopation, and some Negro spirituals are excellent for this function. An important matter concerning the performance of syncopated music is that performers should relax and permit themselves to be natural mediums for transmitting the rhythm. The more they tense themselves and "try very hard," the less success they are apt to have.

Music of our day reflects a desire for some contrasts to the more commonplace meters and rhythms. Thus there is new emphasis on exploring less familiar meters once the common ones have been mastered. Some examples of songs and recordings are:

Meter	Title	Source
5/4 (3+2)	"Rune"	*Music Near and Far,* Silver Burdett
5/4 (3+2)	2nd Movement	Sixth Symphony, Tchaikovsky
7/8 (3+2+2)	"Donkey Cart"	*Music Around the World* Silver Burdett
7/8 (3+2+2)	"The Shepherd Boy"	*The Spectrum of Music, Junior High School Book,* Macmillan
5/4, 7/8	4th Movement	*Trio,* Ravel
2/8, 3/8 (2+3+2+2)	"Little Bird Go Through My Window"	*Together We Sing, Lower Grades Book,* Follett
5/4, 6/4	"Promenade"	*Pictures at an Exhibition,* Moussorgsky
5/4, 3/4	"One May Morning"	Book Six, *Birchard Series*
5/4	*Take Five*	Desmond. The Dave Brubeck Quartet Columbia CS 8192
5/8, 6/8	"Summer Has Come"	*Voices of the World,* Follett

Experiments in Music Creativity, Contemporary Music Project, MENC, 1966, lists rhythmic recordings recommended for classroom study on page 23. Some record jackets of Asiatic Indian music explains the metrical organization of that music, and the indexes of the music textbooks guide the reader to songs and recordings having composite meters. For further study of polyrhythms and polymetric concepts see *The Study of Music in the Elementary School: A Conceptual Approach,* MENC, 1967, pp. 47–50.

Older children enjoy experimenting with less common meters, composing percussion pieces and songs having such beat groupings. Composite meters are normally combinations of 2 and 3 beat groups. 5/4 is either 3+2 or 2+3; 7/8 either 2+2+3, 2+3+2, or 3+2+2. An interesting challenge for a class is to devise a logical conductor's beat for 7-beat and other less standard beat groups. An assignment for individuals and small groups could be structured as shown in the blank score to be filled in. The first experience with this should be very simple, using only two or three instruments for four measures. By means of an opaque projector the entire class can study, read, perform, and evaluate such scores.

Percussion Score in 5/4 Meter

	1 2 3 4 5	1 2 3 4 5	1 2 3 4 5	etc.
Triangle				
Tambourine				
Wood block				
Bongo drums (or small drum)				
Conga drum (or large drum)				

Alla breve meter (¢) is really 2/2 meter. It could also be considered as 2/4 written in 4/4 so as to be more easily read, the notation being "less black" in that it has fewer eighths and sixteenth notes to decipher. 3/2 is not uncommon; songs such as "Kum Ba Ya" are written in that meter, and 9/8 is the meter for "Down in the Valley." Familiar songs can and do change meter, as testified by "Goodbye, My Lover, Goodbye," and "We Three Kings of Orient Are."

Chart of Meters

	Simple				Compound				Composite		
	♩	♪	♫		♩	♪	♫		♩	♪	♫
2	2/2	2/4	2/8	6	6/4	6/8	6/16	5	5/4	5/8	5/16
3	3/2	3/4	3/8	9	9/4	9/8	9/16	7	7/4	7/8	7/16
4	4/2	4/4	4/8	12	12/4	12/8	12/16	11	11/4	11/8	11/16

The most commonly-found meters are 2/4, 3/4, 4/4, and 6/8. Technically, the 9- and 12-note compound meters can be changed to become composite by alternating normal accents. In composite meters one finds two or more meters in some form of alternation.

GERAKINA

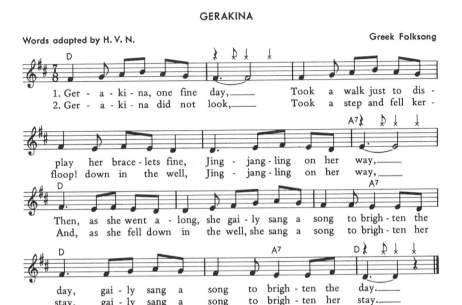

Words adapted by H. V. N.

Greek Folksong

1. Ger - a - ki - na, one fine day,_____ Took a walk just to dis -
2. Ger - a - ki - na did not look,_____ Took a step and fell ker -

play her brace - lets fine, Jing - jang - ling on her way,_____
floop! down in the well, Jing - jang - ling on her way,_____

Then, as she went a - long, she gai - ly sang a song to brigh - ten the
And, as she fell down in the well, she sang a song to brigh - ten her

day, gai - ly sang a song to brigh - ten the day._____
stay, gai - ly sang a song to brigh - ten her stay._____

3. *Gerakina gave a shout, Soon a young lad pulled her out for all to greet,*
   Jing-jangling on her way.
   Then, as she thanked the lad, she gaily sang a song to brighten his day,
   gaily sang a song to brighten his day.

4. *Gerakina took a look, Looked and felt her heart go floop! then very soon,*
   Jing-jangling, they were wed,
   So, all through life, they say, they gaily sang a song to brighten
   each day, gaily sang a song to brighten each day.

The original Greek song ends less happily. Gerakina (pronounced "Yehr-ah-kee-nah") went to the well to bring fresh water, with her bracelets resounding. When she fell, shouting, into the open well, young and old ran to the rescue, and the singer, who felt miserable because he was in love with her and she had ignored him, ran with them to help her but never succeeded in attracting her attention.

What instruments would you choose to depict Gerakina's jingling bracelets?

The tempo is rather fast; it will be found that counts 1, 4, and 6 mark the beat points.

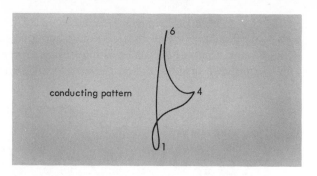

conducting pattern

From *Toward World Understanding With Song.* Reproduced by permission.
Copyright 1967 by Vernice T. Nye, Robert E. Nye, and H. Virginia Nye.

Rhythm Patterns

One of the ways children become conscious of definite rhythm patterns is by means of such activities as echo-clapping, described earlier. Teachers help children to recognize the patterns found in selected songs. For example, they can discover the patterns in "Jingle at the Window" from which the entire rhythmic structure of the song is derived.

three times

ten times

three times

JINGLE AT THE WINDOWS

Moderato   Singing Game

Pass one win - dow, ti - de - o, Pass two win - dows, ti - de - o,

Pass three win - dows, ti - de - o, Jin - gle at the win - dows, ti - de - o,

Ti - de - o, ti - de - o, Jin - gle at the win - dows, ti - de - o,

Ti - di - o,   ti - de - o,   Jin-gle at the win-dows,   ti - de - o.

"Au Clair de la Lune" consists of a four-measure phrase rhythm pattern which is used four times; it is the rhythmic unifying element for the entire song.

All of "Ten Little Indians" except the concluding two measures consists of the pattern:

With the exception of the final three measures, "I Love the Mountains" is constructed upon two rhythm patterns:

Younger children can identify patterns and teachers can write them on the chalkboard if the children are unable to notate the rhythm of what they hear. Older children can look for these repeated patterns in notation, as well as identifying them when listening to songs and recordings.

All songs do not contain such distinct patterns. Teachers must seek songs and recorded music which are best suited to build specific musical concepts. Words of songs can assist in performing rhythm patterns. A simple example is the song "Sally Go Round," in which seven-year-olds decide they want to use the rhythm of the first four notes as an ostinato (repeated pattern) played by sticks throughout the song.

English Singing Game

Sal - ly go round the sun._____ Sal - ly go round the moon,_____

Sal - ly go round the chim - ney pot on a Sun - day af - ter - noon._____

The children can remember the rhythm of the pattern by repeating silently the words "Sally go round" (   ). They might decide to have a wood block play the rhythm of the last two measures over and over along with the one the sticks play. It could be remembered by the rhythm of the words "Sunday afternoon" (𝄆 ♩ ♪♩ ♪|♩ 𝄿 𝄽 𝄿 𝄇). A rhythm pattern has been defined as a specific grouping of sounds related to an underlying beat.

Some of the many songs usable for the identification and study of rhythm patterns are "When Johnny Comes Marching Home," "Jingle Bells," "Over the River and Through the Woods," "Hanukkah," "The Old Brass Wagon," and "Skip to My Lou." Examples of the many recordings which serve the same purpose are "Country Gardens," arranged by Grainger, RCA Rhythm Album 6, "The Little White Donkey," Ibert, Adventures in Music 2, "Habañera," from *Carmen,* Bizet, Bowmar Orchestral Album #56, and "Golliwog's Cakewalk," Debussy, Bowmar #63.

An Expanding Concept of Rhythm

Besides expanding their concept of rhythm in music, children should be helped to find rhythm in other areas of living. There is rhythm all about us —in the waves of the ocean, day and night, life cycles of plants and animals, the heart beat, moving oars, the grain of wood, in machinery, poetry, speech, dance, and when we walk. How does Debussy compose music that reflects the rhythm of the ocean? Hear his *La Mer.* How do composers of art songs manage the rhythm of the poems they set to music? Might there be a relation between the beat, its divisions, and certain architecture? Are there evidences of unity, balance, and variety in man's many experiences with rhythm? There is a world of rhythm to be explored.

Preparing to Teach
Rhythmic Activities

Individual Differences

Since children are different in makeup, teachers can expect that what is an easy rhythmic response for one child may be a difficult one for another. To assist children who find rhythm difficult, teachers seek to guide them to success either in the same rhythm at a slower tempo, or with a different and more simple action to which they can respond at their own natural tempos. When they succeed, they should then be helped to synchronize their movements with gradually slower and faster tempos. It helps some children to produce the sound of the rhythm by clapping, singing, speaking, chanting, or making up sounds; their sounds and actions are then more easily synchronized and a habit of doing an action with a sound begins to develop.

Sometimes six-year-olds do not understand that there is supposed to be a definite relation betwen the sound they hear and what their muscles are to do. Therefore, they cannot march in time with music until they are **169** guided to discover this relation, possibly by the example of other children.

Teachers should remember that when children are asked to move in time with music, they are expected to (1) control a specific movement, (2) listen to the music, and (3) synchronize the two. It is natural that some children find the teacher's request confusing, and the teacher must help children by permitting them to learn the movement well before asking them to add the other two aspects. Sometimes the use of a paper streamer or a scarf will help children to comprehend a motion that they cannot understand by use of the arm alone.

When some children cannot clap their hands in time with music, they can sometimes succeed by striking both hands on the thighs. Some teachers slow the speed of recordings for action-responses of subnormal children. When this is done with songs, it also lowers the pitch. Thus, the pitch cannot be lowered out of the natural vocal range if the recording is to be used for singing with the action. For children who are above average in physical control, the teacher encourages responses of a creative nature of which they are physically capable. Body movements and playing percussion instruments can provide means for successful participation other than singing for children who need to experience success.

Normal Expectations

Early Childhood

Rhythmic activities are free and informal; they emphasize use of the big muscles in large, free motions. The children do imaginative and creative play in imitation of men, animals, and things. They become able to respond to simple patterns played on the drum, piano, tone block, or record player with actions such as walking, marching, running, jumping, hopping, skipping, galloping, and tiptoeing. Concepts of high-low, heavy-light, long-short, and soft-loud can be acquired. Simple directed action songs and singing games are played, such as "The Elephants," "Eensy Weensy Spider," and "Hey Diddle Diddle." Such songs are found in quantity in nursery and kindergarten series books. Dramatizations, finger plays, and hand movements are done. Children learn to use some percussion instruments to tap in time with music and for sound effects that add interest and variety to musical experiences.

Levels One and Two

Ability to respond to fundamental movements with large free motions: walking, running, jumping, hopping, skipping, and combinations of these.

Performance and enjoyment of action songs (such as "If You're Happy") and singing game songs (such as "Wee Little Man," "My Pretty Little Miss," "Looby Lou," "Clapping Land," and "Pony Land").

Ability to respond to rhythm with movements such as swinging, bending, twisting, swaying, stretching, pushing, pulling.

Creative response to rhythm (rhythmic dramatization).

Ability to do simple dance steps, skills, and formations including galloping, sliding, skipping, bowing, circling, singing games, circle with partner on the right.

Understanding of the relation of rhythmic movement to quarter, eighth, and half notes (walking, running, and step-bending or bowing), and ability to use these rhythms by playing them on percussion instruments.

Growth in ability to suggest suitable percussion accompaniments for piano pieces and for recorded music.

Comprehension of whether the music "swings" in two's or three's (duple or triple meter).

Ability to combine movement and some percussion instruments with greater skill and for more specific purposes in level two.

Awareness of repeated rhythm patterns and repeated and contrasting phrases or sections of music in level two.

**Levels Three
and Four**

Mastery of rhythmic concepts and skills taught in kindergarten through levels one and two.

Knowledge of many action songs, singing games, and simple playparty games and dances.

Ability to create and notate simple percussion scores.

The transfer of rhythmic understanding gained from body responses to note and rest values, including the dotted note.

Continued development in understanding beat, patterns, accent, meter, and form through body responses.

Development of increased awareness of the differences between descriptive music and pure ("pattern") music through creative rhythmic dramatization.

Knowledge of conductor's patterns for 2, 3, and 4 beat meters.

Ability to perform combined movements of walk-step, step-hop, skip-hop, step-slide, slide-hop, and to use these movements in dances and dramatizations.

Ability to march to duple and quadruple measures, accenting the first beat of each measure.

Recognition and identification of 2, 3, and 4 beat meters in recordings or in the singing and playing of the teacher.

Ability to step the melody rhythm of selected familiar songs.

Ability to clap, step, and write in notation simple rhythm patterns played by the teacher.

Recognition of the musical phrase through body movement.

Ability to create and notate percussion scores to songs and recordings.

Ability to interpret songs and recordings with rhythmic movement.

Ability to use percussion instruments to play both metric and melody rhythms.

Ability to use percussion instruments with discrimination.

**Levels Five
and Six**

Mastery of rhythmic concepts and skills of the earlier levels.

Ability to dramatize work songs and ballads.

Ability to notate more complex rhythm patterns.

Knowledge of meter, notation, and melody rhythm in relation to the beat.

Creative interpretation of music's emotion and structure through movement.

Ability to use conductor's beat patterns in all common meters.

Ability to create more complex and tasteful percussion scores and to use percussion instruments with discrimination for sound effects with music.

Understanding the concept of syncopation through movement and the use of percussion instruments.

Increased skill in moving to and in reading the notation of more complex patterns.

Growth in comprehension and use of asymmetrical meters.

A repertoire of many American play party games and dances and folk dances of the world; an understanding of the place of these in the world of music.

Ability to play and enjoy Latin-American percussion instruments.

Selected Songs for Experimentation

DOWN AT THE STATION

English Song
for Kindergarten through Second Grade

Down at the sta - tion, ear - ly in the morn - ing,
See the lit - tle puf-fer bil - lies all in a row See the en - gine driv - er
turn a lit - tle han - dle, Chug, chug, puff, puff, Off they go!

SOME SUGGESTED RHYTHMIC ACTIVITIES
Children

Clap the meter, four beats to the measure, as in measure 7; say "Chug, chug, puff, puff."

Clap the word-rhythm as you say the words.

Combine 1 and 2 by selecting appropriate percussion instruments for these rhythms.

Teacher

Select a rhythm pattern such as the note values in the first measure and have this played on a percussion instrument throughout the song. Children can learn it by repeating the words "Down by the station" in the rhythm of the first measure.

Nine-year-olds can step the note values, first of selected measures, then in two-measure parts until the entire song can be stepped.

Older children can identify each rhythm pattern, step it, and notate it.

SOME SUGGESTED RHYTHMIC ACTIVITIES

Children

Sway in time with the music.

Clap hands or use percussion instruments on the first beat of each measure and in the rhythm of the meter in three beats to the measure.

Teacher

Encourage the children to invent with hand clapping or percussion instruments an appropriate way to mark the end of each of the four phrases, thus teaching phrase awareness.

Have the class conduct 3/4 meter.

Teach a simple waltz run or step. Example:

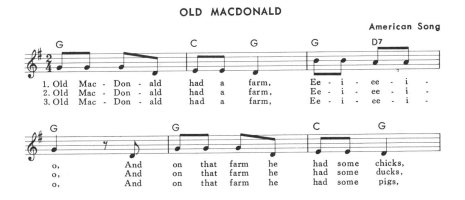

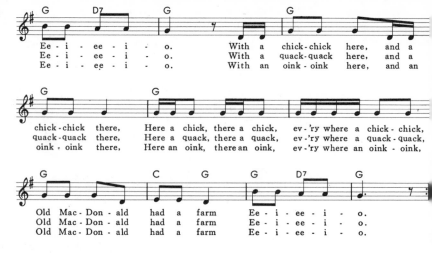

Ee - i - ee - i - o.	With a chick-chick here, and a	
Ee - i - ee - i - o.	With a quack-quack here, and a	
Ee - i - ee - i - o.	With an oink-oink here, and an	

chick-chick there, Here a chick, there a chick, ev-'ry where a chick-chick,
quack-quack there, Here a quack, there a quack, ev-'ry where a quack-quack,
oink-oink there, Here an oink, there an oink, ev-'ry where an oink-oink,

Old Mac-Don-ald had a farm Ee - i - ee - i - o.
Old Mac-Don-ald had a farm Ee - i - ee - i - o.
Old Mac-Don-ald had a farm Ee - i - ee - i - o.

SOME SUGGESTED RHYTHMIC ACTIVITIES

Children

Sing the song, discuss aspects of it that may influence a percussion accompaniment, then create a percussion score and notate it.

Invent actions each time "Ee-i-ee-i-o" is sung. Dramatize the song.

Teacher

Review the basic beat by having the class conduct the meter.

THE PAW-PAW PATCH

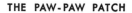

Kentucky Singing Game for Grades Three through Five

Where, O where is pret-ty lit-tle El-lie? Where, O where is pret-ty lit-tle El-lie?

Where O where is pret-ty lit-tle El-lie? Way down yon-der in the paw-paw patch.

2. Come on, boys, let's find El-lie, etc.

3. Pickin' up paw-paws, put'n'em in a bas-ket, etc.

4. Here she comes, we'll all go with her, etc.

SOME SUGGESTED RHYTHMIC ACTIVITIES

Children

Create a dance-dramatization of the song.

Teacher

Use the song to teach the relation of word-rhythms to note values; use the different word-rhythms of the verses in a percussion score for the song.

RIG-A-JIG-JIG

SOME SUGGESTED RHYTHMIC ACTIVITIES

Children

Create a dance; learn and compare 2/4 and fast 6/8 meters in the process.
With percussion instruments, enhance the leisurely walking effect of the verse and the excited skipping effect of the refrain.

R.E.N.

TO PUERTO RICO

Song for Grades Five and S[...]

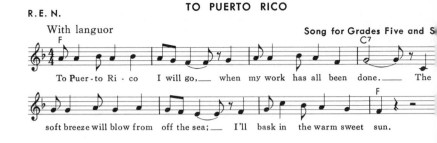

To Puer-to Ri - co I will go,___ when my work has all been done.___ The
soft breeze will blow from off the sea; ___ I'll bask in the warm sweet sun.

SOME SUGGESTED RHYTHMIC ACTIVITIES

Children

Devise a Latin American percussion score and notate it. Possibilities
include:

maracas   conga drum

castanet   or claves

Teacher

Teach for the concept of syncopation.
(For part-singing, improvise a new part a third higher than the melody.)

THE COUNT

Brazilian Song for Grades Five and S[...]

1. He wrote me a let-ter, ca-ram - ba! It asked for my
2. This he told my fa-ther, ca-ram - ba! Fa - ther shook with

hand.   I wrote him my an-swer, ca - ram - ba!
wrath.   He broke ev - 'ry pot in the kich - en;

Said, "No wed - ding band."   I ran down the path!

SOME SUGGESTED RHYTHMIC ACTIVITIES

Children

Devise a Latin American percussion score.

Teach the ♪ ♩ ♫ ♩ rhythm pattern through use of the word "caramba," while children enjoy emphasizing in the song.

Teach ♫ ♩ ♫ ♩ by comparing it with ♪♩ ♪♩ ♩ in "To Puerto Rico"; it is the same rhythm twice as fast. The generalization is that the same pattern can occur in lesser or greater note values (in diminution or augmentation).

Additional Activities and Suggestions for Lesson Plans

A primary problem with music lesson plans is how to guide children toward the learning of musical facts and skills and the developing of concepts and generalizations in ways that truly attract children to music. All competent teachers intend that children *enjoy* their experiences with music. Perhaps we can learn from the Manhattanville Music Curriculum Program ideas which help music lessons become interesting, profitable, and fascinating to the learners. This program deals more with ways of learning than with specific strategies. Its concept of a music class is that of a laboratory for discovery, dealing with sounds and skills. It is a place where children can explore music on their own terms and on their level of understanding by performing, composing, and evaluating music. Teachers are assumed to be guides who create problems for children to solve. They stimulate rather than dominate; they encourage rather than dictate; they question more than they answer; and they are as sensitive to the learner as they are to the subject matter. Every student is involved at times as a composer, a performer, a conductor, and a critic. Each student makes musical judgments at some time which are often hypotheses to be tested through creative exploration and evaluation. Some part of most lesson plans should reflect aspects of the Manhattanville exploratory approach. (See Part III)

Learners may imitate, explore, discover, recognize, identify, inquire, contrast, differentiate, classify, verbalize, recall, and evaluate. They may utilize one or more of the following activities to do these things: singing, playing instruments, moving, creating, reading, dramatizing, impersonating, improvising, composing, and discussing. Utilize all the appropriate senses in a lesson plan: hearing, seeing, feeling with body muscles. Plan so that children listen before they attempt to respond with movement or with voices. Avoid presenting too much in one lesson.

Help children sense the beat by sounding some type of clearly stated rhythmic introduction to performance-type activities. This can be done with hand clapping, stroking the Autoharp, with percussion instruments, with counting, and with the teacher's singing or playing.

In the following pages readers will find activities listed which are related to the Structure of Music Outline in Chapter Five. They should not

feel responsible for knowing how to work with each of these; the activitie
are presented as a list from which to choose. Some of them will requi
teaching experience to do well. Therefore, those activities and suggestio
can be dealt with in part in the college class, in part during student teac
ing, and in part during later years of professional teaching. They combi
both American and European teaching strategies and are listed in ord
of increasing difficulty.

TEMPO

A Developmental Plan

The children discover their natural tempo	The teacher adapts drum or piano a companiment to the natural tempo the individual learner.
The children recognize relative fast and slow in songs, drum beats, and in recorded music.	The teacher provides the opportuni for the children to compare two son one fast and one slow; and two cordings, one fast and one slow.
The children discover the concept of tempos appropriate for imitating animals or describing activities. The eye aids the ear.	The teacher uses songs and recordin that suggest appropriate rhythms f the movements of animals and ma The teacher draws chart-pictures tempo vocabulary: a marching soldi —Di Marcia; a turtle—Adagio; sleeping baby—Largo; a jet liner Presto; a spinning top slowing do —Rallentando; a rocket taking off Accelerando, and so on.
The children see and identify tempo designations in the musical score and understand them.	The teacher selects music which e courages such identification.
The children are able to provide appropriate tempo names for music sung and heard.	"What would happen if the tempo this song is slowed down?" "Let's it." "Is the result better, or worse "Why do you think so?" "Can y think of ways to vary the tempo t might improve this song?" "W terminology can you use to descri the changes in tempo?"

Behavioral Objective: The children reveal their understanding of concepts degrees of fast and slow by . . . . . (what specific p formance, under what conditions, and to what exten

A Developmental Plan

The children begin to understand the difference between soft and loud and degrees of softer and louder by hearing and by acting this out in body movements. The comprehension of variations in dynamics increase; the children are able to express these in creative ways such as in body movement and in drawings.

piano (p)—soft
forte (f)—loud
The teacher plans experiences in which the children find these terms useful. Songs and recorded music offer experiences to build increasing comprehension of the variations in dynamics.

Vocabulary additions become useful to the learners in their own compositions.

Accent, crescendo (cresc.), decrescendo (decresc.), mezzo piano (mp), pianissimo (pp), mezzo forte (mf), fortissimo (ff).

Increasing ability to enter into a deeper analysis of music with respect to dynamics.

The children will suggest dynamics for their musical interpretations, and they will experiment with dynamic levels for the purpose of communicating ideas by means of music. They will listen analytically to several selected recordings and compare the use of dynamics heard in them.

Behavioral Objective: The children reveal their understanding of concepts of loud and soft by . . . . . (what specific performance, under what conditions, and to what extent.)

Crescendo,
decrescendo.

Listen to recorded music that clearly portrays these dynamics, such as "Bydlo" from *Pictures at an Exhibition,* Moussorgsky, Adventures in Music 2, vol. 1. Have the students decide how to act them out with body movements of their choice.

BEAT, DIVISIONS OF THE BEAT, RHYTHM PATTERNS

Beat (pulse).

The teacher adapts clapping, a drum beat, or piano improvisation to the natural rhythm of the learner's walk.

Beat.

After children have learned to respond physically to a steady beat, they are asked to dramatize an activity that is done to a steady beat, such as chopping wood, shoveling snow, hammering, sawing, and rowing. They will do different dramatizations in appropriately

Fast, slow.

different tempos, adding to their concepts of fast and slow.

Heart beat.

Find, feel, and imitate the heart beat. Have childre find out when the heart beats slow or fast.

Beat.

Dramatize the beat by walking, "How many differe ways can you walk?" (tired, slow, lightly, fas heavily, like a toy soldier, like a rag doll.)

Notating the beat.

After young children have learned to walk in tim with the beat, ask them to draw their original pictur or notations of the beat.

Beat.

Utilize rhythmic speech with rhymes such as "Hic ory Dickory, Dock," and "Sing a Song of Sixpence speaking the words and clapping and/or walking t beat on the word syllable accents.

Eighth notes.

Dramatize running. "How many ways can you run (as if in a race—fast, as if you are tired—slow, jo ging, quietly so no one will hear you, etc.)

2-to-1 relationship.

Select children's names that have one and two sy lables. Have children speak the names while drur ming or clapping on the first syllable:

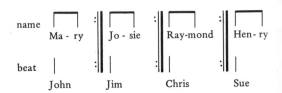

*Beat, word-rhythms,
rest.*

Chant, step, and/or contrive motions for rhythm verse such as "Ding Dong Bell," (invent a motion the end of appropriate phrases for the rest); "T Bear Went Over the Mountain"; "Pease Porric Hot" (rest concept also); and "Wee Willy Winkl (| ☐ and ♪).

Drum talk.

Children play their names on a drum as they spe them. Other children answer, speaking and playi their names. The experience is heightened by usi two drums, one of high pitch and the other of l pitch available to each child as he speaks and pla Example:

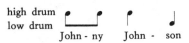

After this experience has been absorbed, the child can begin to use drum talk to say things such as:

I live in Chi - ca - go, Chi - ca - go, Ill - in - ois.

Two such statements can be combined as an experiment in sound.

Fundamental movements.

The teacher improvises with drum or piano; the children respond with the appropriate motion: walking, running, skipping, galloping, hopping, swaying, rowing, as they are able. When the piano is used, the black keys provide an easy way for the nonpiano player to improvise acceptably. Galloping is done with one foot kept ahead of the other, the back foot being brought up to meet it. Children pretend they are ponies or horses.

Divisions of the beat.

The teacher writes a simple quarter note or quarter-and-eighth note pattern. Children first act it out in their own original ways. Then they write it on paper either with the *ti-ti ta* notation or with invented symbols such as large and small circles:

Notation.

ta   ta   ti - ti   ta

Beat and divisions of the beat.

A beat is established by everyone clapping, and the tempo is held steady. The teacher says, in time with the beat, "My náme is Dán-iel Éck-hart," and the students will echo, "His náme is Dán-iel Éck-hart." Each student does this in turn, stating his or her name in accord with the beat, and the class restating it in echo fashion. Later on, names can be written in abbreviated notation, and still later, in traditional notation without the staff.

Relate the rhythm of names to movement and eventually to notation.

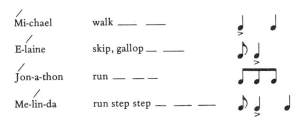

Divisions of the beat.
(eighth notes)

Teacher and children can make up patterns for th
class to read with the *ti-ti ta's* and with percussic
instruments. Example:

| | | | |⊓ | ⊓ | || | | | |

⊓⊓| ⊓⊓| || | ⊓ | 𝄾 ||

Triplet (tri-ple-it,
tri-o-la, or *tri-ple-ti)*

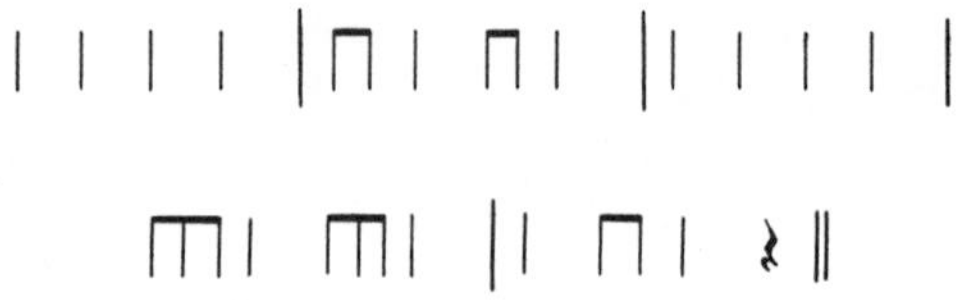

Find many interesting words to write in this simp
notation. Examples:

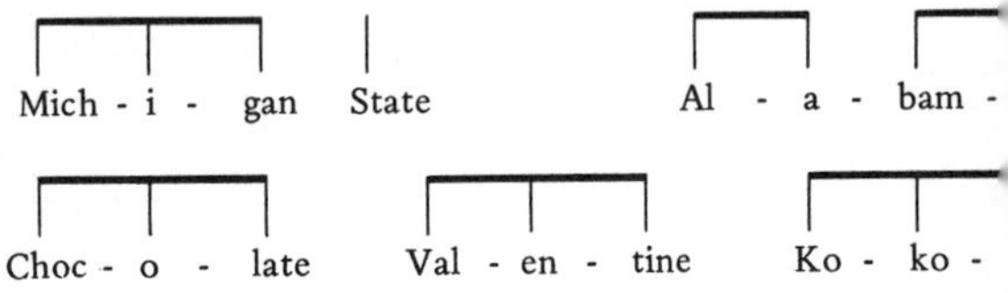

Mich - i - gan   State   Al - a - bam -

Choc - o - late   Val - en - tine   Ko - ko -

Rest.

Young children can be helped to understand *rest* b
the use of sheets of colored paper.

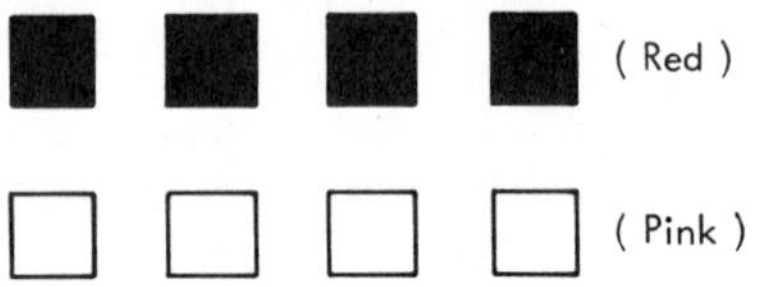

(Red)

(Pink)

Learn about rests by removing a sheet or sheets
paper.

Accent.

Learn about accent by the use of two shades of a
one color.

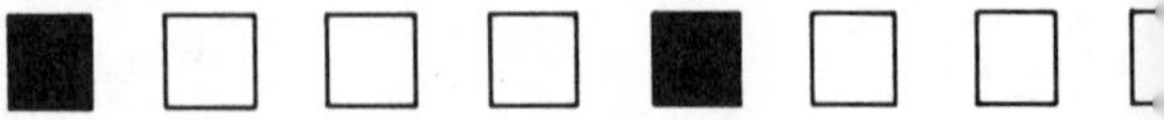

Then go into any meter the teacher wishes.

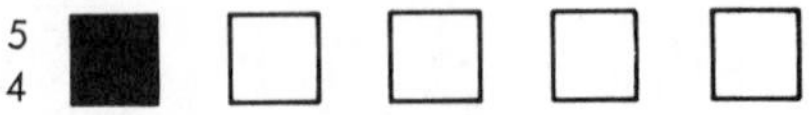

5
4

183 *Divisions of the beat.*
eparing to Teach
ythmic Activities

Divisions of the beat.   Use paper cutouts for note values.

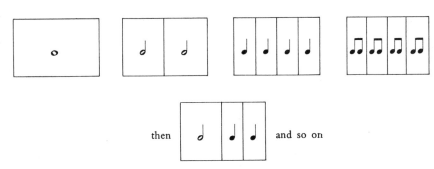

then [♩ ♩ ♩] and so on

Children play games by arranging these note values and performing them. However, the note groupings cannot be larger than the whole sheet as illustrated by the whole note.

Beat.

The class beats a slow steady beat with clapping, pounding lightly on desks, or with percussion instruments while each child says his name twice in time with the beat. Next, the class translates the rhythm of some of the names into the *ti-ti-ta's* and the *tri-o-la's*. The teacher selects some of these to be written in quarter and eighth note abbreviated notation (without note heads). This last step requires that names be screened by the teacher because some demand a complexity beyond the present ability of the children to notate them. In such cases a nickname might be substituted, or only a first or a last name would be used. The class could chant the complex names but not notate them at this time.

Rhythm pattern.
Percussion score.

Young children can invent percussion scores through use of word rhythms such as:

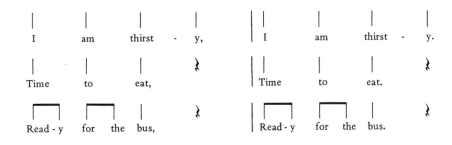

Rhythm pattern.

Such patterns can be transferred to percussion instruments, hand clapping, thigh slapping, etc.

One child creates a rhythm pattern within limits
by the teacher, such as using only *ta* and *ti-ti*. A se
ond child creates a different one that "fits with" t
first one. The two patterns may be written on t
chalkboard; the students and/or the class plays
claps them in sequence, then in combination. Pe
cussion instruments of contrasting tone qualities m
be selected to play them.

Improvising patterns.

Game: Establish a steady beat in a specific met
Give each child in turn an opportunity to clap a p
tern to "fit with" the beat. Each pattern must
different from what anyone else has clapped.
meter would probably be an easy one to start wi
Each child continues clapping his or her patte
until the result equals the amount of complex
the class can absorb, then the game begins aga
The teacher may wish some of the improvis
patterns notated. They can be transferred to perc
sion instruments for further exploration of patte
combinations of patterns, and their instrumentatic

pattern

beat

Rhythm pattern.

Utilize words whenever they can assist childre
comprehension of the pattern. Examples:

violet, daffodil, peppermint, bumblebee

marigold

water-lily

"Sit in a circle and clap your hands"

wisteria

*Rhythm pattern,
improvisation.*

Several students will take percussion instrumen
One will establish a basic pattern to be perform
throughout an original percussion composition wh
others will enter and depart at different times to a
interest and variety to the piece.

Divisions of the beat.

Let children manipulate colored sticks or color
sheets of paper cut in sizes to represent the relati
values of whole, half, quarter, and eighth notes. St

dents are to arrange sticks or paper into various combinations with the stipulation that no combination can be of larger size than the largest stick or sheet. Students can place these on the floor and walk or step them as they count the beats of the measure. More advanced students can chart short songs in this manner.

Divisions of the beat.

Use *Threshold to Music* Experience Charts, First Year, charts I–XI. These assist the understanding of the beat, and quarter note, eighth note, and quarter rest values. The teacher plays a series of measures by beating a drum. The children respond by translating these into the *ti-ti ta's.*
"Which one did I clap?" The teacher asks children to identify the measure he claps:

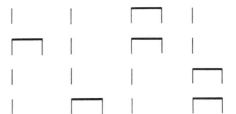

Note values and note reading.

"Which one did I play?" The children select the correct rhythmic grouping or pattern from six different small cards or small charts at their desks or from six large charts on the wall. This can be done in traditional notation.

Rhythm pattern and note memory.

Use flashcards with simple rhythm patterns. The teacher shows a card, then conceals it. The class then claps it, thus promoting note memory.

Divisions of the beat.

Experiment with clapping one note value while stepping another note value with the feet.

Rhythm patterns.

Experiment with clapping a simple rhythm pattern while doing another one with the feet.

ACCENT AND METER

Accent.

Use selected words to discover accent. Examples:
mu-sic a-rith-me-tic ge-og-raphy

Regular accents result in meters.

Try accenting beats grouped in two's and three's:

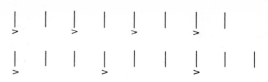

(This can be related at once to familiar songs.)

Words can help too:

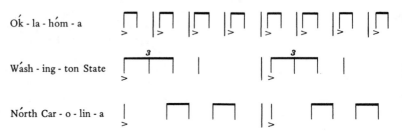

Ok - la - hóm - a

Wásh - ing - ton State

Nórth Car - o - lin - a

Such examples can introduce children to the conc
that in normally accented music, the bar line is pla
before the heavily-accented beat, and that variety
rhythm can be accomplished in any meter by cha
ing the accents to accommodate a different meter
a time. For older children:

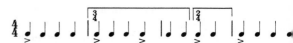

There are many meters. Invent a number of meters by placing regular acce
at different intervals by clapping, stamping, or us
percussion instruments.

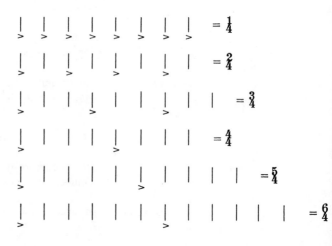

Inventing responses to meter.

Ask children to invent ways to respond to the beats and accents in various meters. Possibilities:

²⁄₄ touch knees, then head

¾ touch knees, hip, forehead

¼ clap above head for the first beat, clap normally (opposite chest) for the second beat, slap thighs for the third beat, and touch knees for the fourth beat.

For all meters: push both hands high into the air for the first beat and pull back for the other beats.

Changing meters.

Assign children the task of composing a percussion score with an unusual meter pattern such as one measure each of ¾ and ¼ in succession throughout. Try other "different" meter combinations.

Syncopation.

Syncopation can be introduced and explained by using a song the children know, such as "Li'l 'Liza Jane."

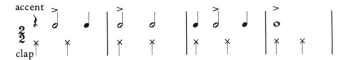

The children should be able to deduce with the aid of the teacher's questioning that while the clapping is regular because it is on the beat, the accents are not. They may be able to discover that syncopation takes place when the accent falls on a part of the measure not usually accented. Some people call this a *displaced* accent. After this, the children may wish to employ syncopation in their percussion compositions. They can experiment with syncopation in several ways:

Writing accent marks on beats not normally accented. Beginning a measure with an eighth note followed by a quarter note.

Using a tie to connect a weak beat with a strong one:

Placing a rest at the beginning of the measure as in "Li'l 'Liza Jane."

Ordinarily, the longer the note value, the more stress it receives (the louder it is in relation to the other shorter note values).

Polymetrics.

Polymetrics result from unlike rhythms sounding a
the same time. They can be introduced by wor
rhythms.

Children can write simple polymetric scores to pla
tape record, and evaluate in class.

*Accent, meter,
patterns, form.*

Utilize dance. Children can create dances based upo
specific accents, meters, rhythm patterns, and form

Some dance improvisations based on these element
can be done by couples with hands on each other
shoulders. Traditional dances can be learned, an
their notated rhythm patterns can be observed an
related to body movement.

Rhythm, analysis of.

Listen to two contrasting recordings and compar
the rhythmic aspects heard.

FORM

Phrase.

The students listen to a phrase of music, and selec
a place in the room to move. The manner of move
ment to the music is decided upon. As the phrase i
sounded again, the students move to their selecte
place so that they arrive there at the time the phras
ends.

Phrase and cadence.

The students decide upon a movement or body posi
tion to reflect whether the phrase ending (cadence
rests on the tonic (I or home) chord, thus giving
feeling of repose (a *perfect* cadence), or whether i
rests on some other chord, usually the dominant (V
V_7—an *authentic* cadence) or the subdominant (I\
—a *plagal* cadence), giving feelings of being incom
plete or not being final. The phrases can be "acte
out" and the different cadences described by move
ment and/or body position.

Rhythm pattern.

The class or group agrees upon a rhythmic patter
to be used as a basis for a rondo. This pattern i
"A." After A is performed, a previously selecte
child creates in body percussion sounds a new par

Rondo.

called "B." Then A is performed again, after which part "C" is created in body percussion by another child. Thus the composition develops into A B A C A D A E and so on until each child selected has had opportunity to create and perform his or her part. Next, the body percussion patterns can be transferred to percussion instruments appropriate to the pattern. Variations: One or two rhythm patterns can be combined with A. Crescendo could be incorporated into A. Parts B, C, D, and E could include melody instrument improvisations. The resulting piece could be tape-recorded, listened to, and discussed. A dance could be created to reflect the patterns and their sounds. Recordings of rondos could be studied as sources of more ideas to incorporate into future rondos.

Additional Recordings for Teaching Specific Concepts

Tempo, fast.

Corelli: "Badinerie" from *Suite for Strings,* BOL 63
Kabalevsky: "Intermezzo" from *The Comedians,* BOL 53
Rossini-Respighi: "Tarantella" from *The Fantastic Toy Shop,* AM 3 v 2

Tempo, slow.

Ravel: "Pavanne of the Sleeping Beauty" from *Mother Goose* Suite, BOL 57
Corelli: "Sarabande" from *Suite for Strings,* BOL 63

Fast and slow.

Slow Joe, Franson YPR 9003 (ages 6–10)

Accelerando.

Grieg: "In the Hall of the Mountain King" from *Peer Gynt* Suite, AM 3 v 2; BOL 59

Accent.

Prokofiev: "Departure" from *Winter Holiday,* AM 2
Rossini-Respighi: "Can Can" from *The Fantastic Toyshop,* AM 2 v 1
Herbert: "Dagger Dance" from *Natoma,* AM 3

Percussion reviewed.

Strike Up the Band, Franson CRG 5027 (ages 5–8) Children can play a game to identify percussion instruments. The order on the recording is drum, cymbal, wood block, jingle bells, sticks, triangle, tambourine

Beat (pulse).

Gounod: "Waltz" from *Faust Ballet* Suite, AM 3 v 1
Herbert: "Dagger Dance" from *Natoma,* AM 3 v 1
Dvořák: Slavonic Dance No. 7, AM 4 v 2
and various marches

*Fermata, ritard,
accelerando.*

These interrupt the regular beat.
Brahms: Hungarian Dance No. 5, BOL 55
Shostakovitch: "Petite Ballerina" from *Ballet Sui*
No. 1, AM 2 v 1

Meter.

Game: Select recordings that are clear examples of
specific meters. Play these, asking the children to
identify the meter they hear. One way to help them
solve the problem is to tell them to make the hand
and arm go *down* on the strong accent of the first
beat of the measure, then raise the arm slightly for
each of the intervening beats until the next strong
downbeat comes. They should count the downbeat
as "one," and continue to count the intervening beats.
The last number before the next downbeat tells the
listeners the number of beats in the measure. From
this they may be able to determine the meter (time
signature).
Sousa: *Stars and Stripes Forever,* AM 4 v 2 (²⁄₄
meter)
Bach: "Gigue" from Suite No. 3, AM 1 v 1 (two
beats, ⁶⁄₈ meter)
Delibes: "Waltz of the Doll" from *Copelia,* AM 1 v
1 (³⁄₄ meter)
Ippolitov-Ivanov: "Cortege of the Sardar" from
Caucasian Sketches, BOL 54 (four beats, ⁴⁄₄ meter)
Offenbach: "Barcarolle" from *Tales of Hoffman,*
AM 3 v 2 (⁶⁄₈ meter)

Changes in meter.

Cailliet: *Pop Goes the Weasel* (variations) AM 4 v
(⁶⁄₈, ³⁄₄, ⁴⁄₈, ³⁄₄, ²⁄₄)
Copland: "Street in a Frontier Town" from *Billy the*
Kid, AM 6 v 1
Piston: "Tango of the Merchant's Daughter" from
The Incredible Flutist (⁵⁄₈), Mercury 90423

Less common meters.

Ginastera: "Wheat Dance" from *Estancia,* AM 4 v
Copland: "Hoe-Down" from *Rodeo,* AM 5 v 2
Guarnieri: *Brazilian Dance,* AM 6 v 2
Brubeck: *Time Out,* Columbia CL 1397
Brubeck: *Time Farther Out,* Columbia CL 1690 (⁷⁄₈

Polyrhythms.

Copland: "Street in a Frontier Town" from *Billy the*
Kid, AM 6 v 1
see *The Study of Music in the Elementary School:*
A Conceptual Approach, Charles L. Gary, ed.
(Music Educators National Conference, Washington, D.C., 1967), pp. 47–50
see *Source Book of African and Afro-American Ma-*
terials for Music Educators (Music Educators Na-

tional Conference, Washington, D.C., 1972) for
two beats against three, p. 34.

Rhythm patterns.

Bartók: "Bear Dance" from *Hungarian Sketches,*
AM 3 v 2
Cui: *Orientale*
Tchaikovsky: "Fourth Movement" from Symphony
No. 4
Beethoven: "Second Movement" from Symphony
No. 8
Ibert: "The Little White Donkey" from *Histories No.
2,* AM 2
Bizet: "Habañera" from *Carmen,* BOL 56
Milhaud: "Copacabana" from *Saudades do Brazil,*
AM 4 v 2 (Ask children to find and identify the
four major patterns used by the composer.)

Bolero pattern.

Ravel: *Bolero*

Beguine pattern.

Porter: *Begin the Beguine*

Habañera pattern.

Bizet: "Habañera" from *Carmen*
Gottschalk: "Grand Walkaround" from *Cakewalk,*
AM 5 v 1
Benjamin: *Jamaican Rhumba,* BOL 56

Syncopation.

Gottschalk: "Grand Walkaround" from *Cakewalk,*
AM 5 v 1
Debussy: "Golliwog's Cakewalk" from *Children's
Corner* Suite, BOL 63
Copland: "Hoe-Down" from *Rodeo,* AM 5 v 2; BOL
55
Charbrier: *España,* AM 5 v 1 (also for study of the
beat)

Sources of Materials

BOMAR RECORDS, INC.
622 Rodier Drive
Glendale, California 91201
> See catalog for recordings for rhythmic responses, singing games, folk and
> ethnic dances. Also march and dance music in the *Bowmar Orchestral
> Library.*

CHILDREN'S MUSIC CENTER
5373 W. Pico Blvd.
Los Angeles, California 90019
> Several helpful catalogs of tested materials.

CHILDREN'S RECORD GUILD AND YOUNG PEOPLE'S RECORDS
Franson Corporation
225 Park Avenue South
New York, New York 10003
Recordings for children ages 2–10.

EDUCATIONAL ACTIVITIES, INC.
Freeport, L.I., New York 11520
This helpful catalog contains recordings of Hap Palmer and many others.

FOLKWAYS RECORDS
701 Seventh Avenue
New York, New York 10036
Rhythmic recordings including those of Ella Jenkins; also a source of ethnic recordings. See catalog.

METHODIST CHURCH PUBLISHING HOUSE
407 Church Street
Nashville, Tennessee
Source of *World of Fun Folk Dances* and *New World of Fun Series*.

LYONS
530 Riverview Ave., Industrial Park
Elkhart, Indiana 46514
Offers a comprehensive catalog. Distributor of *Listen, Move, Dance* Vols. 1, 2, for movement and electronic sounds.

RCA VICTOR *Dance-A-Story* RECORDS (storybook-record combination)
Ginn and Company, Boston, Mass. 02117
Ginn and Company, 35 Mobile Drive, Toronto 375, Ontario, Canada

RCA VICTOR EDUCATIONAL SALES
155 E. 24th Street
New York, New York 10010
The World of Folk Dance series.

Sources of Percussion Instruments

CONTINENTAL MUSIC
150 Aldredge Blvd.
Atlanta, Ga. 30336

KITCHING EDUCATIONAL
1100 East 31st Street
LaGrange Park, Ill. 60525

MUSIC EDUCATION GROUP
Garden State Road, Union, N.J. 07083

PERIPOLE, INC.
P.O. Box 146, Lewiston Road
Browns Mills, N.J. 08015

RHYTHM BAND, INC.
P.O. Box 126
Forth Worth, Texas 76101

823 South Wabash Ave.
Chicago, Ill. 60605

EXPLORATORY ACTIVITIES

1. Miss Smith is teaching rhythm to her class today. First she tells the children that she is going to play walking music and they are to walk to it. Next she tells them to listen to the running music she will play, and instructs them that they are to do tip-toe running. After this the children are informed that they will skip to the teacher's playing. The last activity is a more complex one in which the children are told that the music tells them to walk for eight steps, skip for eight counts, then walk for eight steps. After practicing several times, the class does quite well. Rewrite this lesson so that it becomes a creative-exploratory one for the children.

2. Observe a lesson in rhythm in an elementary school. Identify the concepts being learned, determine which are being stressed and ascertain what strategies are used to develop them. How would you develop these concepts if you were the teacher?

3. Develop a resource unit on rhythm for a specific achievement level. Include the following: generalizations, concepts, typical data, behavioral objectives, types of questions, teaching strategies and activities, and materials.

4. List ways to encourage children to create rhythm.

5. In every song there are ordinarily three distinct aspects of rhythm: the first beat of the measure (primary accent), the rhythm of the meter, and the rhythm of the melody or words. Try writing a percussion score for a familiar song on this basis. Select instruments to play on the first beat and select others to play on the two rhythms. Experiment by dividing instruments into groups of similar pitches and into groups of similar type. Find which of the instruments are most appropriate for each rhythm.

6. Compile a file of recordings for use in teaching concepts of rhythm.

7. Appoint class committees to investigate the origin of folk and traditional dances in which they are interested. Each committee will report its findings, demonstrate the dance, play related music, and present ways to use these to expand children's concepts of rhythm.

8. If you were in a classrom that contained no percussion instruments, what potentialities for sound could you find in the materials around you? Examples: the sound of paper held in the air and tapped with a pencil, buckles or heavy jewelry struck with another object, the waste basket and sounds made with the body. Use these to create an interesting percussion score.

9. "Orchestrate" the following words with speech and percussion instruments:

> 6/8 *Life pays in kind,*
> *Life pays in kind; A*
> *song for a song, a blow for a blow,*
> *Life pays in kind.*

10. Create a story and use percussion instruments for sound effects. Example: The alarm clock (triangle) wakens us in the morning. The clock (gong or finger cymbals) strikes eight. Mother calls, "Are You Sleeping?" (sing the song to the accompaniment of the clock ticking—woodblock,

rhythm sticks). On the way to school we hear a train (sandblocks) and horses (coconut shells). Such a story is another way to help children learn the appropriateness of specific percussion instruments.

References

ABRAHAMSON, ROBERT M., *Rhythm Games for Perception and Cognition, Book 1*. New York: Music and Movement Press, 1973, 210 Fifth Ave., 10010. 36 pp. The first of a series of small books designed to encompass all of the elements suggested by Dalcroze.

BURNETT, MILLIE, *Melody, Movement and Language*. San Francisco: R. and E. Research Associates, 1973, 4843 Mission St. For early childhood and primary.

CHASE, RICHARD, *Singing Games and Play Party Games*. New York: Dover Publishers, 1967. 57 pp.

DALCROZE SCHOOL OF MUSIC, Hilda M. Schuster, Director, 161 E. 73 Street, New York City 10021.

DOLL, EDNA, and MARY J. NELSON, *Rhythms Today*. Morristown, N.J.: Silver Burdett Co., 1965.

FINDLAY, ELSA, *Rhythm and Movement: Applications of Dalcroze Eurhythmics*. Evanston, Ill.: Summy-Birchard Company, 1971.

FOWKE, EDITH, *Sally Go Round the Sun*. Garden City, N.Y.: Doubleday & Company, Inc., 1969. Singing games, skipping rhymes, ball bouncing ditties, clapping games, foot and finger plays, counting rhymes, etc.

GARY, CHARLES L., ed., *The Study of Music in the Elementary School: A Conceptual Approach*. Vienna, Va.: Music Educators National Conference, 1967, pp. 11–50.

HUMPHREYS, LOUISE, and JERROLD ROSS, *Interpreting Music Through Movement*. Englewood Cliffs, N.J.: Prentice-Hall, Inc., 1964.

JACQUES-DALCROZE, EMILE, *Rhythm, Music, and Education*. New York: G. P. Putnam's Sons, 1921.

JONES, BESSIE, and BESS LOMAX HAWES, *Step-it-Down*. New York: Harper & Row, 1972. Games, plays, songs and stories from the Afro-American heritage.

KENNEY, MAUREEN, *Circle Around the Zero*. Play chants and singing games of city children. Order from 63 East Clinton St., New Bedford, Mass. 02740, 1974.

LANDIS, BETH, and POLLY CARDER, *The Eclectic Curriculum in American Music Education: Contributions of Dalcroze, Kodály, and Orff*. Vienna, Va.: Music Educators National Conference, 1972, pp. 5–38. Contains bibliography pp. 208–9.

RAEBECK, LOIS, and LAWRENCE WHEELER, *New Approaches to Music in the Elementary School* (3rd ed.) Dubuque, Iowa: Wm. C. Brown Company Publishers, 1974, Chapter 4.

RICHARDS, MARY HELEN, *Threshold to Music:* Experience Charts for the First Year, Teachers Text/Manual *The First Three Years,* Fearon Publishers, Belmont, Calif.: 94002, 1964.

SHEEHY, EMMA DICKSON, *Children Discover Music and Dance*. New York: Holt, Rinehart & Winston, Inc., 1959. Chapters 7, 8.

SWANSON, BESSIE, *Music in the Education of Children* (3rd ed.) Belmont, Calif.: 94002. Wadsworth Publishing Company, Inc., 1969, Chapters 3, 4.

WILLOUR, JUDITH, "Beginning with Delight, Leading to Wisdom: Dalcroze," *Music Educators Journal*, September, 1969.

Films *Building Children's Personalities with Creative Dancing*, University of California Extension Division Film 5844. For teachers. May be obtained from UCLA Educational Film Sales Department, Los Angeles, California, and from Dance Films, Inc., 130 West 57th Street, New York, N.Y., 10019.

Dance Your Own Way, UCLA Educational Film Sales Department; also from Dance Films, Inc.

Discovering Rhythm, United World Films, Universal Education and Visual Arts, 221 Park Ave. South, New York, N.Y., 10003. Concepts in rhythm for children from preschool to seven years.

Hello, I'm Music: EMC Corporation, 180 E. 6th St., St. Paul, Minn. 55101. Six color filmstrips, six records or three cassettes, 240 worksheets and a teacher's guide. Melody, rhythm, harmony, form, and tone color are presented to children.

Let's Begin With the Beat, EMC Corporation, St. Paul, Minn. 55106. A sound-filmstrip.

Pantomimes, Brandon Films, New York, N.Y. 10019. How the body communicates ideas.

Reading Music: No. 2 Finding the Rhythm, Coronet Films, 65 E. S. Water Street, Chicago, Ill. 60601.

What is Rhythm? and *Discovering Dynamics in Music*, BFA Educational Media, 2211 Michigan Avenue, Santa Monica, Calif. 90404.

Refer to *Film Guide for Music Educators*, Music Educators National Conference. Reston, Va., 22091.

195

LEARNING MUSIC BY IMPROVISING AND COMPOSING

III

A New Pathway to Music

A New Point of View

Improvising and composing as a major pathway to music learning was a part of the revolt against an older type of music teaching that consisted primarily of singing songs from books and some listening experience. It had been found that as children grew, they resented this rather simple approach and that finally, many teachers as well as children seemed to suffer boredom and frustration. Critics of the former method claimed that a better way to music learning should include children's engaging in basic musicianly activities. They should:

discover musical sounds and how they are produced.

improvise and compose music.

use their voices, bodies, and abilities to play instruments to perform music they create.

interpret and evaluate what they create.

be able to notate what they create.

199

More precisely, they should learn music by acting out the roles of the musician—singing, playing, improvising, composing, listening, conducting, interpreting, and evaluating music. Those who promoted these theories believed that learners must *produce* music as well as *receive* music from others. The learners were to come to realize that music is a continuously evolving art; thus they would be actively involved with contemporary music as well as with the art, ethnic, and folk music of the past. These learners were to be adventurers, explorers, and innovators in music who would be free to take risks in their creative endeavors.

Early promulgators of these ideas were the American composers Henry Brandt and Lionel Nowak. Following their pioneering efforts, the Contemporary Music Project (CMP), an outgrowth of a young composers in residence program that began in 1958, was in operation from 1963 to 1969, financed by the Ford Foundation. This project included seminars and workshops for music educators and pilot programs in elementary and secondary schools to study methods of presenting contemporary music and to explore music learning by means of creative experiences. The results of three pilot programs appeared in *Experiments in Musical Creativity,* a 1966 publication of the Project and MENC. A conclusion made by the San Diego pilot program was, "Activities related to contemporary music, such as composition for percussion instruments, synthetic scales, and new sound sources provide a unique medium for creativity. The student with little or no background . . . can 'create' with enthusiasm and success, thus gain a first-hand contact with music that he might otherwise miss" (p. 61). CMP did much to make these ideas known, but the most powerful thrust toward new methods of instruction was made in 1965–1970 by a government-financed project, the Manhattanville Music Curriculum Program (MMCP), USOE V-008 and USOE 6-1999.

The reader may question how prevalent are teachers who base their entire music programs on improvisation and composition? The answer is that while a few do, the large majority do not. The quotation from Lowell Mason at the beginning of this book states what generally takes place: "The best teacher will not be confined to any particular predetermined plan, but will from the different methods make one of his own . . . one that he may modify and adapt to the varying wants and circumstances of his different classes." Perhaps the reader will encounter classes to which improvisation and composition comprise the *only* acceptable pathway for them; in most classes these activities may be an important *part* of a music program. A music textbook series that exemplifies this is *Comprehensive Musicianship Through Classroom Music,* published in 1972 by Addison-Wesley. This series resulted from the Hawaii Music Program, a state-financed project. Each elementary level teacher's book contains a Table of Contents Scope and Sequence Chart that includes the concepts to be learned, the songs and recordings that may assist this learning, and the musicianly roles to be assumed by the students. In the "musicianly roles" column the reader can quickly discern how improvisation and composition are integrated with the other activities that comprise a balanced program of music instruction.

What is the sequence of activities that lead learners toward composing music? There is logic in the young child's attempting to imitate what is heard, taking steps to explore the sound-producing possibilities of the environment, evaluating these sounds, then using them to improvise, and finally to compose. Understanding the term improvisation requires some thought, because when an improvisation has been notated, it becomes a composition. By definition, improvisation is the production of music without the aid of notation or memory. While this is true of percussion music of indefinite pitch, it does not explain that in more complex melodic music, memory of the underlying harmony is often a part of improvisation, notably jazz improvisation, in which performers invent their own melodic variations based upon a given or remembered succession of chords. Bach, Beethoven, and Handel were as renowned in their day for their improvisations as for their compositions. But children in our classrooms are not famous composers, they are only young people who can be fascinated by working with sounds. MMCP has made composing possible for them by a definition that defines music as *some kind of organization of sounds and silences intended to be music.* This places composition in reach of everyone.

The Manhattanville Music Curriculum Program

The Manhattanville Music Curriculum Program is an approach easy to initiate and can be adapted to any age group. Like all methods, it requires some years to develop its full potential. Aspects of it should be experimented with in the methods class in order that the college student may understand how musical learning takes place when the learners are actively involved in making their own music. For a complete explanation of this approach to music teaching of young children aged 3 through 8 read *MMCP Interaction: Early Childhood Music Curriculum,* Media Materials, Inc., P.O. Box 533, Bardonia, New York 10954. The first experiences to follow are preparatory to the program.

CONCEPTUAL IDEA	LEARNING EXPERIENCES FOR YOUNG CHILDREN 3–8
Sounds are everywhere.	While in the classroom or on a short field trip have children listen to and describe sounds of the environment. "Are they high, low, soft, loud, dull, short, steady, rumbling?, etc." Vocabulary is needed in order to express sound and tone qualities.
Pitch.	Search the classroom for objects that can produce sounds. Classify these into those producing definite and indefinite pitch.

Our bodies can be used to make sounds.

Have children explore the many sounds that can be made with the body. These will include clapping hands, slapping thighs, snapping fingers, rubbing palms, stamping feet, clicking tongue, hissing, "shh," and others. Ask that several of these be organized into a short composition. When it has been practiced it can be tape-recorded and played for the children's evaluation.

Imitating sounds.

Children can imitate sounds better than many adults. Have them imitate sounds from their environment such as fire sirens, police cars, birds, garbage trucks, and jet planes. Develop a repertory of sounds to draw upon later. Try to avoid the stereotyped sounds adults have built into the child's world such as "oink, oink" and "cock-a-doodle-doo" because these are not authentic imitations of animal sounds. Let the children create their own.

Objects can produce different kinds of sounds or tone qualities.

In order to increase sensitivity to tone qualities, ask young children to identify sources of sounds in listening games. The teacher might use a cardboard screen to hide the sound source. Suggestions of such sources might include those such as an egg beater, air escaping from a balloon, pouring water, crinkling paper, as well as more conventional sounds.

Vibration.

After children know the game, they can be assigned in pairs to develop sounds they can challenge the class to identify. Later on the teacher can make the game more complex by producing somewhat different sounds from the same object. Children might discover that some percussion instruments should normally be held in a way in which they are free to vibrate.

Analyzing instrument sounds.

With young children select, for example, a tambourine and make sounds with it. Ask questions such as "Can it sing a song?" (no) "Can it play softly?" (yes) "Can it play loudly?" (yes) "Does it make jingling sounds?" "Can it make a short sound?" "Can it make a long sound?" After this, find uses for the tambourine in a song or as a sound effect in a story. Do the same with other instruments.

Percussion instruments can be classified in many ways.

Young children can classify percussion instruments in accordance with the type of sound. Which instruments click? ring? jingle? swish? rattle? boom? Which instruments have sounds that are light? heavy? medium? This activity can relate to the functions of instrument tone qualities in accompanying songs and recordings. Older children might use adult classifications and decide to group percussion instruments under headings such as membrane, hollow, solid, and keyboard. Let children suggest other possible classifications; there are many more.

Sounds can be the same or different.

The teacher prepares a number of sound producers *in pairs* to assist young children to recognize similarities and differences in sounds. There may be identical-sized jars or cans or plastic containers with the same and different numbers of peas or beans in them. Some could contain pebbles or marbles or beads. The task is to shake them, listen to them, and classify the pairs that sound alike.

Tone qualities relate to sound effects.

Young children can decide upon the suitability of specific instruments or other sound sources for sound effects. They can select them to correspond with characters in stories such as The Three Bears, Three Billy Goats Gruff, and Three Little Pigs. (Older children can create stories in sound such as "My Day," "A Storm in the Mountains," "A Day at the Seashore," "A Haunted House," "Halloween Night," "Space Journey," and "Little Red Riding Hood.")

Every voice sounds different.

Plan for young children to listen to different speaking voices in the class. With eyes closed, can these voices be identified? Plan such listening games, emphasizing the uniqueness in the vocal sounds of each person. Encourage children to classify the speaking voices in terms of low, medium, and high. Children can relate these to choric reading that emphasizes differences in the tone qualities of the speaking voice.

MMCP Interaction.

The material to follow explains in brief the strategies involved in the Manhattanville Music Curriculum Program for children aged 3 through 8.

Music consists of sounds and silences presented in some organized manner.

The *free exploration* of sound sources (paper, metal, body, rubber, plastic, glass, and materials from nature) is recommended. This comprises the first of a series of steps that lead to experiences with every component of music. The second step is *guided exploration,* in which the teacher encourages the children to find additional sounds, to find more ways to produce sounds (this involves skills), to label new sounds (this involves vocabulary), to classify new sounds in various ways, to listen and react to sounds produced by other children and by the teacher, and

*There are many kinds
of sounds. Sounds can
be classified.*

to learn to respect the efforts of others. The purpose
of evaluation is not to point out failure, but to clarify
and extend children's ideas and judgments. The
teacher assists the children's learning by such actions
as presenting clues and examples, presenting words,
asking questions, showing pictures and other types
of illustrative material, and presenting musical examples. Contrasting words (walking-running, crawl-
ing-skipping) suggest different movements in time;
those such as whispering and shouting suggest different dynamic levels and different ways of producing
sounds.

*Sounds can be
organized and related.*

*Two or three people
may produce more
varied music than only
one person.*

*We can compose music
as individuals or in
small groups.*

Step three is *exploratory improvisation.* The child is
encouraged to repeat sounds he enjoys and to relate
them to other sounds. This relationship might be
contrasting sounds, through which the child may
learn that contrast can heighten the expressive implications of sounds, or it might be that by combining
two or more sounds a new and different effect can be
achieved.

Step four is *planned improvisation.* In this phase children are to be gaining performance and memory
skills necessary to produce compositions that are
aesthetically satisfying. They are guided by the
teacher to organize groups of sounds into meaningful
music ideas, to identify the ways these sounds are
arranged, to criticize constructively the arrangement
of the sounds, and to use this experience to suggest
other ways of improvising their own music.

The teacher accepts and works with whatever the
child produces, regardless of its quality, remembering
that these exploratory experiences are important and
real to the child, and that the type of learning is
basically intrinsic, not dictated by the teacher. After
a trial run of a student composition, teachers might
ask questions such as: "How do you know when to
start and stop?" (This helps them to discover the
need for a conductor if they do not have one.) "Do
you have a leader?" "Did you hear a change of
tempo?" "What kinds of sounds did you hear?" "Did
it sound the way you wanted it to sound?" "Would
you want to change this piece if you had a chance to
do it over?" "Are you satisfied with it?" The composing and performing of a composition can bring
into focus problems in duration, pitch, tone quality,
dynamics, and tempo, and teach compositional tech-

niques such as the *ostinato* in a practical setting that is honest and logical to the child.

The fifth step is *reapplication*. As children continue to compose their own music, they will discover and find need for all the component elements of music as well as skills in musical notation. First they will find a need to save their compositions, and will invent notation for this purpose. Eventually standard notation will be necessary for them to do what they want to do with their musical ideas. When children are trying to invent their own notation, teachers ask questions such as: "What if you wanted to show a thin texture in your music?" (Use a thin symbol.) "What if you wanted to show a thick texture?" (Use a thick symbol.) "What if you wanted to show low?" (Use the bottom of the page.) "High?" (Use the top of the page.) "Short?" (Use a short symbol.) "Long?" (Use a long symbol.) "Rising pitch?" (Use a rising symbol.) "Silence?" (Use a blank space, a circle, or?) "Falling pitch?" (Use a descending symbol.)

This same type of beginning in musical learning can be used by the older children also. Even the junior high school student can enjoy the thrill of experimenting freely with music.

There are immediate problems with this approach, one of which is the noise factor. MMCP calls this "creative fallout." As the group work expands, there must be space for the children to work, and in many schools this is not easily found. However, many teachers have discovered that children are able to concentrate in group composition while all groups are in the same classroom, one group in each of the four corners while others occupy the center area. The size of the group will vary in accordance with the assigned task. It can be from two to six, with four and five commonplace.

MMCP Interaction suggests that the teacher can organize the activity so that at a given time the class will explore sounds coming from paper, metal, or the voice. Other possibilities include those made by rubber, glass, plastic, outdoor materials, and other sound sources. It states possible questions the teacher might ask to stimulate interest and creativity.

The following example is reproduced from *MMCP Interaction.*

Unconventional Sound Sources

Paper	Rubber	Wood	Metal	Outdoor Materials
construction paper	bands	ruler	sheet metal	dirt
wax paper	balloons	spatula	saws	pebbles
tissue paper	hose horn	yard stick	tools	stones
newspaper	balls	bowls	can tops	leaves
light-weight cardboard	innertubes	bamboo sticks	pie plates	grass
brown, bag paper	tires	tongue depressors	oven shelves	snow
white stationery paper	toys	pencils	wire	rain
sandpaper		blocks	cans	twigs
cardboard strips		whistles	pails	branches
napkins	**Glass**	toys	baking pans	pine cones
magazines		tables	cookie sheets	eucalyptus pods
cardboard dividers	soda bottles	chairs	pipes	water
foils	jugs	clothespins	strips	
cardboard boxes	toys	poles	whistles	
paper balls		popsicle sticks	toys	**Other**
old books	**Plastic**	broom handles	tables	
egg crates		kitchen utensils	chairs	string
cardboard cylinders	funnel (horns)	containers	washtub	rope
toilet tissue cylinder	ruler	strips	nails	twine
paper towel cylinders	straws		broom handles	flower pots
carpet cylinders	food containers		screws	calfskin
material cylinders	bottles	**Food**	washers	chamois
corrugated cardboard	sprayers		bottle caps	
fruit crates	toys	condiments	paper clips	
straws	brushes	seeds	funnels	
milk containers	buttons	kernels	scissors	
papier mâché	combs	rice	bolts	
toys	old records	coffee	foils	
paint buckets	plastic strips	sugar	kitchen utensils	
ice cream containers	boxes	corn flakes	waste basket	
cigar boxes	tools	bread crumbs	springs	
cups	cups	grains	machines	
		macaroni		
		coconut shells		

Source: MMCP *Interaction*

ALTERNATE SERIES: METAL ENCOUNTERS

Phase I—Free Exploration

Instructional Objective: To explore a wide variety of sounds using metal sound sources.

Procedure: 1. Place a variety of metal objects, such as old kitchen utensils, large nails, horseshoes, pipes of varying sizes and lengths, metal bars, keys on a key ring, pans, pan lids, tea trays, empty coffee cans, etc., in a place designated as the sound materials center.

2. Encourage pupils to select and explore the objects for sounds. This may be done on an individual basis during the course of the school day, or pupils may select metal objects and share sounds in groups.

3. After adequate time for initial sound explorations, the following questions may serve to stimulate discussions of the sounds:

Were any sounds alike? If so, how were they alike?

Why were some sounds different? Could the differences be described?

Pupils will identify the differences and similarities in sounds in many different ways, including the physical techniques involved in performing them, relating sounds to personal experiences, and their acoustical characteristics, i.e., timbre, pitch, duration, volume.

4. Suggest that pupils find other metal objects, metal toys, pie plates, paint cans, etc., to add to the sound materials center.

5. All new objects should be explored for the variety of sounds they can produce.

Phase II—Guided Exploration

Instructional Objective: To explore a wide variety of metallic sounds and sound-producing techniques.

Procedure: 1. Invite pupils, as a class or in small groups, to find two very different or contrasting sounds with the metal objects they have selected from the sound materials center.

2. Allow an appropriate amount of time for exploration.

3. After individual pupils perform their sounds, other group members or the entire class should attempt to imitate the two contrasting sounds on other metal objects.

4. Discussion during and after perform
ance and imitations may deal with th
following:

How was the sound made? Did the beat
make a difference?

Can the sound be made in any other way
Are any imitations exactly the same?

Note: A few minutes of exploration may t
desirable before volunteers are ready
imitate a performed sound.

5. Pupils should be given two or thre
minutes of exploration time to investiga
each of the following questions posed t
the teacher:

What kind of sounds can you find that r
mind you of a clock ticking; wat
dripping; a baby walking; a father's heav
footsteps; a ball bouncing; teeth clatterin
a horse galloping; a snake crawling?

6. After each question and a period (tw
or three minutes) of pupil exploratio
volunteers can be invited to perform the
sounds.

7. After all sounds have been performe
and taped, listen to the tape and try t
identify the sounds, i.e., clock tickin
snake crawling, etc.

Phase III—Exploratory Improvisation

Instructional Objective: To explore a variety of ways of producin
and combining repeated patterns.

Procedure: 1. Pupils should select three sounds whic
they can play over and over again in th
same manner with metal objects.

2. Allow an appropriate amount of tim
for selection of sound sources and sound
and for rehearsals of the desired patterns.

3. As a class, or in small groups, listen t
the repeated patterns performed by ind
vidual pupils.

4. Discussion can be centered on th
following: Were any of the sound pattern
difficult to repeat? Why?

If some were difficult to repeat, can you suggest an easier way of playing them?

Which two patterns do you think would sound well together (one after the other)?

5. Experiment with combinations of sound patterns as suggested by the pupils.

6. Tape combined performances of repeated patterns for immediate playback and discussions.

7. Play for the students some recording containing a repeated pattern of metallic sounds, such as the *Symphony of Machines —Steel Foundry* by Alexander Mosslov.

8. Discussion of the listening example can be focused with the following questions:

What did you hear? Did you hear any repeated patterns?

How could we build a sound machine?

Phase IV—Planned Improvisation

Instructional Objective: To arrange repeated patterns in ways which are expressive and meaningful.

Procedure: 1. Build a sound machine. A sound machine is a game in which a number of sound patterns, organized in various sequential combinations, aurally represent the moving parts of an imaginary machine. The patterns developed in the previous encounters may be used, or new patterns may be investigated.

2. Pupils may work in groups of three, four or five, or the teacher or volunteer pupils may construct a sound machine by conducting members of the class in a sequential performance of their patterns. Students may wish to physically display the motions of the machine as well as their sounds.

3. Tape all the performances for listening and comparison of the differences and similarities.

Were the sound machines different? If so, how were they different? If not, what

could we do to make the sound machine
sound different from one another?

Were the sound machines the same in any
way? If so, how were they the same?

4. When appropriate extend the discussion
with the following:

Were the conductors satisfied with their
results? Did performers do what was expected of them?

If not, discuss how better results might be
achieved. Pupils should lead these discussions as much as possible.

Note: In order to successfully control entrance
and exits of groups of performers, pupil
conductors may have to develop simple
gestures for starting and stopping performers.

5. The following questions posed individually during follow-up encounters may
stimulate further thought and experimentation:

What would happen if:

some patterns or sounds were played at the
same time?

all metal objects were silent some of the
time?

the sound machine slowly broke down
rather than suddenly stopped?

we had two sound machines—a big one
and a little one?

MMCP Synthesis

For students aged 9 and older, the Manhattanville
Music Curriculum Program has developed another
publication, *MMCP Synthesis*. This consists of a
spiral-type curriculum that considers the elements of
music on gradually advanced levels called "cycles."
As in *MMCP Interaction* composing of music on the
child's level is the major activity. The students compose, conduct, perform, and evaluate music. Sample
strategies are suggested for teaching music at 16
levels (cycles). These begin with the same type of
sound exploration described earlier, but move quickly
into compositions that are taped in order that the

composers and the class can hear them and evaluate them.

In cycle 1 the student begins with activities such as finding sounds made from objects in the classroom, performing different sounds from the same object, and experimenting with dynamics (degrees of loud and soft) and with combinations of sounds, adding a steady beat to ordered combinations of sounds. In each of the suggested activities, the book suggests questions to ask the students and recordings of music of all types and times that are intended to stimulate interest and furnish information needed by the student composers.

It is of importance that the college class experiment with some of the sample lessons provided in *MMCP Synthesis* in order that the prospective teacher understands this type of approach to learning music. It stresses children's understandings of the following aspects of music: timbre (tone quality), dynamics (degrees of loud-soft), duration (degrees of long-short and rhythmic elements), pitch (including melody, harmony, and polyphony), and form. Teachers are assigned the task of being guides, creators of problems to be solved by the children, and resource persons. They are to stimulate rather than dominate, and to encourage rather than to control. They are to question more than answer, and to be sensitive both to children and to the art of music. The classroom is to be a laboratory in which children act as musicians who have a world of sound to explore.

Examples from *MMCP Synthesis* follow.

SAMPLE STRATEGY

Cycle 1.   The quality or color of sound, the timbre, is a major factor in the expressiveness of music.

Each student selects an item or object in the room with which he can produce a sound. Preferably, the item or object will be something other than a musical instrument.

After sufficient time has been allowed for students to experiment with sounds or selected objects, each student may perform his sound at the location of the item in the room.

Focus on "listening" to the distinctive qualities of sounds performed. Encourage students to explore other sound possibilities with the item of their choice.

Discuss any points of interest raised by the students. Extend the discussion by including the following questions: How many different kinds of sounds were discovered?
Could the sounds be put into categories of description, i.e. shrill, dull, bright, intense, etc.?
After categories of sound have been established, experiment with combinations of sounds.

Is there any difference between sounds performed singly and sounds performed in combination?

In listening to the recorded examples focus on the use of timbre.

How many different kinds of sounds were used?
Could we put any of the sounds in this composition into the categories we established earlier, i.e. bright, dull, shrill, etc.?
Were there any new categories of sounds?
Could we duplicate these?

ASSIGNMENT: Each student should bring one small object from home on which he can produce three distinctly different sounds. The object may be a brush, a bottle, a trinket or anything made of wood, metal, plastic, etc.

Suggested Listening Examples:
Steel Drums—Wond Steel Band; Folk 8367.
Prelude and Fugue for Percussion—Wuorinen, Charles; GC 4004.
Ballet Mécanique—Antheil, George; Urania (5) 134.

SAMPLE STRATEGY

Cycle 1.   The pulse is the underlying beat that may help to create a feeling of motion in music.

Allow 30 seconds for each class member to think of an unusual vocal sound. The sound can be made with the throat, voice, lips, breath or tongue.

Each student may perform his sound for the class. Focus "listening" on the distinctive qualities of the vocal sounds performed.

Discuss any points of interest raised by the students. Extend the discussion by including some of the following questions:
Did anyone perform his sound long enough to communicate a feeling of motion?
How would you describe the motion?

Divide the class into groups consisting of 4 or 5 students. One person in each of the groups should be a conductor. Each group will concentrate on producing their individual sounds to the motion of an item of their choice or one which has been suggested to them, i.e. the steady motion of a carpenter hammering a nail, the steady motion of a worm crawling, the steady motion of a person jogging, the steady motion of a horse galloping, etc.

Allow approximately 10 minutes for groups to plan and practice their improvisations. At the end of the designated time each group will perform.

Tape each improvisation for immediate playback and analysis. Discuss any comments made by the students. Extend the discussion by including the following questions:
How would you describe the motion, slow, medium, fast?
Did it have a steady beat or pulse?

Summarize the discussion by introducing tempo as the characteristic which refers to the speed of music and pulse which is the underlying beat (sometimes not heard but only sensed).

In listening to the recorded examples focus attention on the use of tempo.
How would you describe the tempo—slow, medium, or fast?
Did the pulse or underlying beat change before the end of the composition? What was the effect?

Suggested Listening Examples:
Flight of the Bumblebee—Rimsky-Korsakov, Nicolai; Epic LC 3759.
String Quartets Op. 76, No. 5, No. 79—Haydn, Joseph; Turnabout TV 34012S.

Careful planning is the rule when teachers utilize improvisation and composition to achieve the forming of music concepts. This interesting way to learn has the potential of leading the learner to explore every aspect of musicianship in active ways. Part Two contained many basic learnings, some of which may be regarded as necessary before students embark upon improvisation and composition. However, basic musical concepts can be developed by these creative activities from the outset of a pupil's musical experience if they are designed with thoughtful care.

Whether the activities to follow are to be accomplished by individual, small group, large group, or by the entire class is largely left to the teacher's judgment. The noise factor in the classroom can be upsetting at times; yet it has been found that children can concentrate despite surrounding noise when they are interested and if the volume is not too great. Some rooms have partitions that can be moved to make booths in which to work; others have several practice rooms attached; and still others have convenient side rooms or even hallways that can be pressed into service. In many situations all activities must take place within one room, with individuals and groups occupying corners and middle of that room.

The tasks are given time limits. Some of those to follow can be accomplished in two or three minutes, others in five or ten or fifteen minutes, while there are those that will require two or three class periods. Some assignments can be completed by individuals working at home or at school after regular hours or after other work has been done. There must be a predetermined signal, such as switching lights on or off, at which time the class reassembles to hear the results of the individual and group work and to analyze them.

Listening to recordings becomes listening *to find out* how other com posers solved similar problems, thus there is an active, purposeful type of listening that should encompass all musical styles. It is obviously for a different purpose than simply trying to understand a composer or hearing certain music only because someone thinks you should. Improvisation and composition are personal matters, thus they can be of primary importance to students and can thereby become a major pathway to learning.

Improvising and Composing

Accompaniment. — Provide an appropriate percussion accompaniment for selected poems and stories.

Beat and divisions of the beat. — Have small groups create a piece by using rhythm patterns derived from names.

Repetition and contrast. — Employing either vocal or instrumental sounds, plan a composition that begins and ends with the same sounds, but has different sounds in the middle. Invent a way to notate it. Tape the result; listen to it and analyze the different ways in which contrast is achieved.

Beat, pitch, chant. — Establish a steady drum beat over which individuals create a chant based upon *so mi,* using G and E on the bells to play the chant.

Word rhythms. — Create new words to known songs. Example: "If You're Happy." Use words denoting action or motion with this song, and perform them.

Imitating. — Listen to "Leap Frog," from *Children's Games* by Bizet, Adventures in Music 1 v 1. After acting out the music, compose a piece with similar sounds by experimenting with bells, piano, or Autoharp.

Muscular response. — Improvise a dance to a recorded composition or song that suggests dancing.

Dynamics, pitch. — Improvise music with percussion instruments to demonstrate concepts such as crescendo, decrescendo soft, loud, low pitch, high pitch. Following this, compose music, using *f, p,* $\diagup\!\!\!\diagdown$ and $\diagdown\!\!\!\diagup$ to interpret the score.

Some of the activities in this section are inspired by those in the *Comprehensive Musicianship* music series published by the Addison-Wesley Publishing Co. The reader is referred to the teachers' books of this series for a detailed, sequential treatment of the subject. See page 201.

*Pentatonic melody,
dynamics, duration.*

Improvise music on the black keys of the piano or bells in which dynamics and duration (long, short) are illustrated.

*Repetition, contrast,
duration, dynamics,
notation.*

Improvise in small groups vocal pieces, using different mouth, tongue, and throat sounds, demonstrate long and short sounds in this music. Devise symbols and notate the sounds. Rehearse the compositions and tape them. Listen to the taped performances and have students evaluate them. After this, perform them again with the emphasizing of *p, f,* ———— and ════════ to add interest to the scores.

*Music can be
improvised by a
conductor.*

The teacher distributes from 4 to 6 percussion instruments having contrasting types of tone qualities. A student conductor will establish a steady beat, then will point to those children who are to play, cueing the players in and out, having them play alone or in combination. From this experiment should come interesting sound sequences and an attempt to organize a composition. This can be done with an entire class by assigning specific instruments to groups.

*New or unusual sounds
can be produced when
tone qualities are
combined.*

The teacher selects four sound producers, either invented ones, simple instruments, or a combination of these. Each sound producer will have a distinctively different tone quality. Assign groups of children to combine them in a musical score, experimenting with the sounds singly and in combination. It may be necessary to devise notation. Tape the results and evaluate them in class discussion.

*Repetition, contrast,
duration, notation.*

Compose in groups a composition using nonpitched percussion instruments, inventing a symbol for each instrument and ways to indicate the duration of the sounds.

*Tone qualities, beat,
rhythm patterns.*

Groups will improvise accompaniments to familiar songs with percussion instruments. Roles played by students include singer, instrument player, and conductor. Actors could be added for songs easily dramatized. Work songs are good for this.

*Beat, tone quality,
dynamics, articulation.*

Improvise an appropriate percussion accompaniment to a selected recording, demonstrating soft, loud, legato, staccato, and the beat.

Using line notation that suggests pitch levels ar
duration, each student will draw a score, explain h
notation, and will interpret it vocally or conduct t
class in a performance of it. The scores can b
placed on transparencies for the class to view, an
lyze, and perform.
Example:

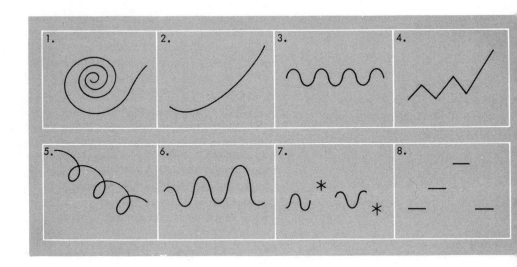

*Dynamics, pitch,
duration, mood.*

Improvise vocal sounds for moods such as angry, sad,
and happy. Analyze these in terms of dynamics,
pitch, and duration.

*Notation, pitch, tone
quality, dynamics,
duration.*

Pairs of students will compose sound frames such as:

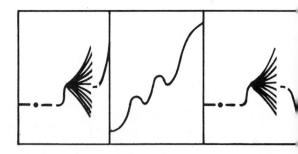

Perform these vocally, tape them, and discuss the
relationship between eye and ear—how the visual
describes the aural, and how the aural reflects the
visual.

Melody, playing.

Compose short, three-note (G A B—*do re mi*) melodies on the Song Flute or other small winds. Notate
them on a staff with quarter, half, and whole notes.

Sounds.

Improvise a vocal sound piece that describes Halloween.

*Melody, phrase,
playing, stave.*

Compose a two-phrase piece for a small wind instrument, using G A B C D, and write it on a two-stave staff. (This can be extended to a three- or four-stave staff if appropriate.)

Meter, coda.

Compose a piece for small winds in either ⅔, ¾, or ¼ meter. Employ G A B C D. Add a coda.

*Accompaniment,
ostinato, harmony.*

Improvise an accompaniment for "Row Your Boat" using G and E on bells. Is it an ostinato? Or is it harmony?

*Contrast, dynamic
levels, crescendo,
decrescendo, rhythm
pattern.*

Groups will improvise a percussion accompaniment for a parade march, such as "Parade" from *Divertissement*, AM 1 v 1, stressing the drum and unconventional percussion, rhythm patterns, dynamic levels, and crescendo and decrescendo.

Pentatonic mode.

Improvise tunes on piano, bells, or xylophone using notes G A B D E. Relate selected Chinese songs that use this scale.

Rhythmic ostinato.

Create ostinato rhythmic patterns (repeated patterns) in simple and compound meters. Notate them. Rhythmic words can be used as a basis for an ostinato if this aids the learner. Perform them with body sounds and/or percussion.
Examples:

Ev-'ry bo-dy likes   can-dy   Pe - ter the. jel -ly fish went for a swim.

*Recordings to stimulate
children to compose
percussion music.*

Toccata for Percussion, Carlos Chavez, Columbia CMS 6447; HBR 21003, 2 discs
Concerto for Percussion and Small Orchestra, Darius Milhaud, Capitol HBR 21003, 2 discs
Ionization, Edgard Varèse, Columbia MS 6146, also on Folkways' *Sounds of New Music,* FX 6160

Improvising melody.

Improvise what you believe could be an American Indian melody on a small wind instrument, using four notes, middle C, D, E, and G.

Rondo.

Compose an A B A C A B A rondo with percussion instruments. Divide the class into three groups, A, B, and C. Each group will compose its section of the rondo; ¾ meter will be used by all groups.

*Tone qualities,
new sounds.*

With the goal of composing unusual music, possibly for Halloween, listen to the following compositions on Folkways FX 6160, *Sounds of New Music,* then compose a piece on Autoharp or piano that explores new sounds: *Banshee,* by Cowell (piano); *Dance,* by Cage (prepared piano); and *Sonic Contours,* by Ussachevsky (piano sounds altered by recording).

*Unconventional
sounds, form.*

Groups will compose a piece having one of the following forms: ABA, ABC, AABB, ABAB, ABACA. No melody will be employed, only different unusual sounds. Try for new sounds on piano, bells, Autoharp, as well as from unconventional sound sources. Record the pieces; listen to find which form was used.

Dorian mode.

Individual students will compose a melody for small winds in the Dorian mode. Notate on a transparency for class viewing, performance, and discussion. (The Dorian mode has an organization corresponding to a scale on piano white keys that begins and ends on D.)

*Phrygian mode,
introduction.*

Compose a melody as above in the Phrygian mode and notate for viewing, performance, and discussion. (The Phrygian mode has an organization that corresponds to the piano white key scale that begins and ends on E.) Next, create a text for a song to be in either the Dorian or Phrygian mode. Write the song, then add a short introduction to it.

*Rhythm pattern,
accompaniment.*

Improvise rhythm patterns for familiar songs. Analyze them to find if they are indigenous to the song or if they contrast with the melodies' rhythms. Evaluate their effectiveness in accompanying the songs.

*Harmonic listening,
accompaniment.*

Improvise accompaniments to familiar songs of simple harmonization, using percussion instruments, Autoharp, piano, and ukulele. Tape these for evaluating the singing and playing in terms of balance and articulation. How can the accompaniments be improved?

*Jazz improvisation,
analysis.*

Listen to a selected recording that features jazz improvisation. Answer questions such as: What did the performers do with the melody? What instruments were used? Which instruments provided the rhythm? Was there repetition or contrast (or both) in the harmony? Improvise a suitable percussion accompaniment to the recording.

Accompaniment, notation.	Select a known rhythmic spiritual; improvise a foot stamp and clap accompaniment. Notate the finalized accompaniment.
Melodic and rhythmic improvisation, phrase, playing instruments.	Working in pairs, the players take turns improvising rhythmic and melodic patterns with recorders, using pitches G, A, and B. Later, extend the patterns into phrases, and imitate those.
Melody, chord line or disjunct.	Compose a melody of bugle-call type, based on the tonic chord (I-chord). Notate it and play it on the recorder, bells, xylophone, or piano.
Pentatonic mode, scale, phrase.	Using recorders, improvise answers to given phrases, using a pentatonic scale, either 12356 or 61235 of a major scale. Later, improvise both the question phrase and the answer phrase.
Ostinato.	After hearing the recording *Ostinato Pianissimo* by Henry Cowell, Time Records S/8000, *Concert Percussion,* have students improvise a similar ostinato.
Chords, harmony.	Improvise chording accompaniments on Autoharp or ukulele for familiar songs requiring I and V_7 or I IV V_7 harmonization.
Variation.	Using the melody instrument of one's choice, improvise variations to "Hot Cross Buns." Listening to recorded variations such as *Laideronnette, Empress of the Pagodas,* Ravel, AM 4 v 2, and *Pop! Goes the Weasel,* Caillet, AM 4 v 2, will assist the young composers in their search for techniques. The teacher asks questions about what is heard in terms of texture (monophonic, homophonic, and polyphonic), melody, ostinato, countermelody, major, minor, tempo, and meter.
Harmony in thirds.	Improvise a parallel third harmony part to songs easily harmonized in this way, such as "Sally Go Round" (one version), "San Sereni," "Marching to Pretoria," and "Polly Wolly Doodle."
Canon.	In pairs, improvise a two-part rhythmic canon in ⁴⁄₄ meter using body and vocal sounds.
Countermelody.	After singing a song with a countermelody, select a familiar song requiring only I and V_7 chords for harmonization, and improvise a countermelody. Try having the class sing or hum the melody while one

student attempts the improvisation. After several students have found successful ones, try combining two or three. Then discuss what seems necessary to produce a successful countermelody.

Composite meter.

Create a piece illustrating composite meter such as ⅞ or ⁵⁄₄. Use G A B on the recorder, bells, or xylophone.

Rondo.

Listen to *Sleeping Beauty Waltz,* by Tchaikovsky AM 4 v 2, as an example of an A B A C A B A rondo. Compose and notate a simple percussion rondo.

*Round, tonic,
subdominant.*

Using the round "Lovely Evening" as a model, compose your own round, using the song's chord pattern as a model. Make up words for your round if you wish.

*Tone row, polyphony,
canon.*

Listen to a recorded composition such as *Double Canon for String Quartet,* by Stravinsky, Columbia MS 6272. Analyze it to find that there is no tonic (home tone), that it is polyphonic, and that there is a canon. Then build a 12-tone row with resonator bells; the row must not suggest traditional tonal music; none of the pitches are repeated. Write the row on a staff, then write it in inversion. When the row is inverted, the pitch direction is reversed, but the intervals remain the same.
Example:

beginning of original row   beginning of inversion of row
etc.   etc

Improvise and play a short piece on the row and its inversions; utilize different rhythms, such as those of familiar songs. Write the composition on the staff. Then try playing it in canon form. Attempt to sing it and play it. Write and play it in retrograde (backwards). Write the row in retrograde inversion (backwards and upsidedown) by writing the inversion backwards.[1]

[1] *Making Music Your Own* (Morristown, N.J.: Silver Burdett) Book Six, p. 202 is an example of how a textbook introduces the tone row. For a report of a sixth grade's experience, see Mary Val Marsh, *Explore and Discover Music* (New York: Macmillan, Inc.), pp. 131–38.

Quartal chords, round.

Analyze the harmonic structure of a familiar round and generalize as to the structure of rounds. Then compose one based on quartal chords (chords made of fourths). Perform it and evaluate it.

Example:

Try constructing chords in fifths.

Cadence.

Write a piece to demonstrate complete phrase endings (end with a tonic chord), and incomplete phrase endings (end with V_7 or IV chord). The phrase ending is the cadence.

Ostinato.

Improvise rhythmic and tonal ostinatos to selected songs such as "Swing Low, Sweet Chariot," and "Leaving Old Texas."

Blues.

Compose a text and tune using a 12-bar blues chord progression in the key of C major. Be sure that you have a good rhythm pattern to accompany your three-phrase blues song. The chord sequence given below may be varied somewhat if this improves your song. Sing it with Autoharp accompaniment.

I	I	I	I_7
IV_7	IV_7	I	I
V_7	IV_7	I	I

*Serialization of the
tone row.*

Make a 12-tone row. Compose music based on the row to include serialization of duration by planning a specific note value for each note that is on a line, a space, a flat on a line, a flat on a space, a sharp on a line, and a sharp on a space.

Pitch, tempo.

Make a recording of the expressive reading of a short poem at 3¾ per second. Make two copies; play back at other speeds, 7½ and 1⅞. Discuss the result. Use three tape recorders to hear the three speeds sounded at once, and tape this on a fourth recorder. Discuss the possibilities of this for composing music.

Harmony.

Do vocal improvising over a rhythmic piano accompaniment of simple and easily comprehened harmonization.

Tone qualities. Learn to make sounds of various pitches on a synthe
sizer. Select several of those you like and tape them
Then alter the taped sounds to produce an electronic
composition.

Rhythm-Related Compositional Devices As children compose, they
have an interest in and a need for some of the devices used by the adul
composer. The terminology may seem complex at first, but it is rathe
simple when once explained. Consider the terms *augmentation* and
diminution. To augment something, one makes it larger; to diminish some
thing, one makes it smaller. This is what happens in rhythm. If young
composers are writing a score for percussion instruments based on the

pattern ♩ ♫♩ ♩ , they find that they can, if they choose, apply dimin-

ution by making the pattern one half its original value and repeating it
Writing this down, it looks like this:

The extension of the original pattern by repetition adds considerably to a
feeling of tension the children want to achieve. They might follow this
with an application of augmentation by making the original twice its duration, and thus construct a four-measure composition which builds up to a
climax followed by a feeling of release. Next they could utilize a canonic
treatment of the pattern, and assign this to the woodblock player. They
might decide that a continuous eighth-note pattern played by maracas
would add some stability and help to unify the piece. They could choose
to experiment with polymetrics by adding a hand drum playing quarter
note beats in 3/4 meter. Now the composition is complete. The childrer
have done what many adult composers may do—used diminution, augmentation, canon, and polymetrics. All they need is a group of classmates to
read, perform, and evaluate their composition. Learning music can be
exciting, creative, experimental, and intellectual—all at one time.

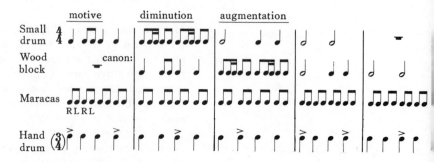

*The above 3/4 part is written in 4/4 meter by using the bar lines of the
other parts. The accent dictates the true meter.*

The Synthesizer and the Electronic Studio

The Synthesizer

There is increasing acceptance of the synthesizer as an important tool to help children learn music concepts. At the sixth grade level many students find the instrument to be of tremendous interest; accordingly, they are attracted to electronic laboratories where they can experiment with sound and compose music to their liking. The teacher should be sufficiently knowledgeable of the device so that it can be utilized with children from the age of six, and surely from the age of eight. Any strange or new sound is likely to attract children's interest, and since the synthesizer is rich in different types of sound, the instrument possesses a natural attraction when specific uses for it are planned. The oscilloscope should at times be a companion to the synthesizer because it gives a visual representation of the sound wave form of every sound producer. The device can be involved in experiments such as:

Tone quality The effect of attack, decay, harmonics, vibrato, and tremulo on tone quality.

Melody The relation of tempo, tonality, and tone quality to melody.

Harmony Major, minor, harmonics, intervals, and experiences in ear training.

Transposition Manipulation of transposition.

Synthesizers are available today in many degrees of complexity, from the sophisticated models suitable for a professional electronic laboratory to simplified models that are relatively inexpensive. The latter are easily portable, and are sometimes carried from school to school, permitting one to be shared by many children.

The Electronic Studio

An electronic music studio may be housed in part of a room, in an unused office or practice room, or in an otherwise vacant room. When this equipment is of marked value, special security is necessary to prevent theft or damage. There must be electric outlets and a table on which to place equipment. A bulletin board is necessary not only to schedule use of the equipment but to place assignments and directions for individuals and small groups. No chalk should be used in the area because chalk dust can accumulate on sensitive equipment, particularly recording equipment. To eliminate chalk dust, pins are used to attach notices to bulletin boards, or dust-free plastic boards that employ wax crayons are obtained. Tape recorders with multitracks are part of most laboratories because they widen the possibilities for use of the synthesizer to include composition and further experimentation. Since most synthesizers include no speaker system, they must be attached to a portable public address system, a guitar amplifier, a small electric organ or electronic piano, or to a phonograph that contains its own speakers. Stereo equipment should be standard. A good quality four-channel stereo recorder is considered basic, although some teachers have done well with more limited equipment.

223

Tape, a tape splicer, and a roll of leader tape will be with the tape recorder. The recorder's head must be able to monitor tracks already recorded while recording those tracks still open, that is, to synchronize the tracks so there will be no rhythmic disagreement among them. Teachers and students who use the laboratory need to know the techniques of editing tapes and the ways to manipulate them, such as playing and recording at various speeds to gain certain effects, creating tape loops, recording backwards, and time delay (possible on certain machines only).

Music teachers who have not yet had the opportunity to know the synthesizer may wish to consider attending summer courses in which they can learn to use and experiment with the instrument. It is an undeniable part of the present and there is no doubt of its expanded use in the future. Time Lab, Inc., Port Washington, N.Y. is one of the producers of introductory electronic devices.

Materials

Films *Discovering Electronic Music* (Discovering Music Series: RSC-774).
New Sounds in Music (Churchill Films).

Filmstrips *Creating Music Through Use of the Tape Recorder.* Keyboard Publications, 1346 Chapel St., New Haven, Conn. 06511. Two color sound filmstrips, one recording, eight study prints, one teacher guide.
Electronic Music. Keyboard Publications.
New Sounds of the Classics. Keyboard Publications.

Recordings *Electronic Music*
BADINGS: "Ragtime" from *Evolutions.* Epic BC 1118.
LeCAINE: *Dripsody.* A drop of water makes music on a tape recorder. On *Electronic Music,* Folkways FM 3436.
LUENING: *Gargoyles,* for violin and synthesizer. On *Columbia-Princeton Electronic Music Center,* Columbia MS 6566.
LUENING and USSACHEVSKY: *Poem in Cycles and Bells for Tape Recorder and Orchestra.* Composers Recordings Inv. CRI 112.
VARÈSE: Déserts, Angel S-36786

Unconventional Sound Sources
CAGE: Second Movement, *Amores.* Wood sounds. Time 58,000.
CAGE and HARRISON: *Double Music.* Eight rice bowls. Time 58,000.
HARRISON: *Canticle No. 1,* on *Concert Percussion.* Time 8,000.
OLIVERES: *Sound Patterns.* Mouth sounds. Oddyssey 3216–0156.
PARTCH: *The World of Harry Partch.* Hand-made instruments; an invented tonal organization of 43 tones within the octave. Columbia MS 7207.
Sounds of New Music (Cage, Luening, Ussachevsky, Varèse). Reverberation, tape loops, music concrete. Folkways FX 6160.

Prepared Piano
CAGE: *Amores No. 1.* Children can be inspired by this to try for new sounds on the Autoharp.

COWELL: *Banshee.* A banshee is a female ghost that warns of approaching death. Children can think in terms of Halloween and use the Autoharp to imitate the sounds made on the prepared piano. On *Sounds of New Music,* Folkways FX 6160.

Miscellaneous

Country Moog: Switched On Nashville. Gilbert Trythall. Athena 6003.

Electronic Music: Vox Productions, Inc.

Silver Apples of the Moon: Morton Subotnick. Nonesuch Records H-71174.

Electronic Sound: George Harrison. Zapple Records ST 3358.

Music for Voices, Instruments and Electronics: Kenneth Gaburo. Nonesuch Records H 7199.

Also see Record Album for Book 6, *Exploring Music,* Holt, Rinehart and Winston, Inc.

References

Electronic and Experimental Music

DENNIS, BRIAN, *Experimental Music in the Schools.* London: Oxford University Press, 1970. 76 pp. Introductory experiments; use of tape recorders.

Electronic Music issue. *Music Educators Journal,* November 1968.

FRIEND, DAVID, ALLAN R. PEARLMAN, and THOMAS D. PIGGOT, *Learning Music With Synthesizers.* New York: Hal Leonard Publishing Corp. Copyright 1974 by ARP Instruments, Inc., Newton, Mass. (ARP is a manufacturer of electronic instruments and equipment.)

PALMER, MARY, *Sound Exploration and Discovery.* New York: The Center for Applied Research in Education, Inc., 1974.

PAYNTER, JOHN, and PETER ASTON, *Sounds and Silences.* New York: Cambridge University Press, 1970. Thirty-six projects in creative music for intermediate grades through college.

SCHAFER, R. MURRAY, *Ear Cleaning.* Don Mills, Ontario, Canada: BMI Canada, Ltd., 1967. 46 pp. Explores sound; contains teaching suggestions.

———, *The New Soundscape.* Toronto: BMI Canada, Ltd., 1969.

———, *When Words Sing.* Scarborough, Ontario, Canada: Berandol Music, Ltd. Speech, poetry, and vocal sounds as means of communication.

SELF, GEORGE, *New Sounds in Class.* London: Universal Edition, 1967. 41 pp. New music notation, scores included.

WILLMAN, FRED, *Electronic Music for Young People.* New York: Center for Applied Research in Education, 1974. 521 Fifth Ave., 10017.

Catalog

Lyons Teachers Guide. Elkhart, Ind.: Lyons, 530 Riverview Ave. 46514. Contains a page of components for classroom electronic music: square wave generators, triangle wave generator, sawtooth wave generator, white sound generator, theremin, filter, electronic switch, ring modulator, envelope control, amplifier, speaker with reverb unit, sequencer. Also includes a page of audiovisual materials for exploring the new types of music.

LEARNING MUSIC BY PERFORMING

IV

Learning Music by Singing

In Part Two it was stated that there are relationships between body movement in response to music and learning concepts of pitch and melody. By means of such movement the learner can improve his ability to listen to music and to grasp tonal and other relationships. From this foundation the teacher assists children to hear pitch accurately and to reproduce vocally what they hear, to sing with understanding and to use their singing voices for self-expression in daily living.

Recent Research An opinion survey included as part of a research project [1] by A. Oren Gould of Western Illinois University agrees with earlier estimates of the approximate percentage of children that teachers classify as "nonsingers"; it was 50 percent for the first grade with a steady reduction to 5 percent in the sixth grade. The percentage of children that teachers classified as "problem singers" was 36.6 percent in the first grade with a gradual reduc-

---

[1] A publication produced from the completed project is *Finding and Learning to Use the Singing Voice: A Manual for Teachers* by A. Oren Gould (Washington, D.C.: Office of Education (Ditew), Bureau of Research, OEC 6–10–016, 1968).

tion to 11 percent in the sixth grade. This study claims to have established two basic principles of learning to sing: (1) the child must *learn to hear his/her own voice* in speaking and singing and to control high and low pitch levels with it, and (2) the child must experience unison with another voice or instrument and *learn the sound and feeling of his or her voice as it matches the pitches heard.* Both visual and tonal associations are needed to develop concepts of high and low in speaking and singing. Recommended activities include speech-to-song activities; repeated patterns in play or game songs such as found in echo songs, songs about animals, and roll call songs, use of humming and neutral syllables, body movements of many types which dramatize pitch and tonal direction, and mechanical devices such as bells and piano keyboard to hear and visualize pitch changes. The survey revealed "a certain amount of consensus" in the following:

1. All children can be helped to participate to some extent in singing activities with enjoyment and success.
2. Inability to sing a prescribed pitch does not prove that the child cannot hear pitch differences; it may mean only that he or she has not yet learned "what it feels like" to use his or her voice in unison with another.
3. The most common vocal problem is that of the low speaking voice coupled with the child's inability to sing comfortably at the higher pitch the teacher prescribes for the class.
4. Many of the children's psychological inhibitions toward singing can be traced to attitudes and remarks of parents and teachers.
5. Remedial measures in the group are more easily employed during kindergarten through grade three; in later grade levels more individual attention is necessary.

A study by Dr. Robert B. Smith at the University of Illinois, *The Effect of Group Nursery School Music Training on Later Achievement and Interest in Music: A Ten Year Progress Report,* found that in general the children sang lower pitches more easily than high pitches—"low" meaning the range from middle C up to A, and "high" meaning the range from G above middle C to D, a fifth higher. Furthermore, girls were more advanced than boys, as a group, at all grade levels. However, the experimental group boys appeared to close the gap at the fifth grade level. Tentative conclusions in the ninth year of the study included:

1. Lower tones should be used in those songs selected for younger children. (The control group boys found relatively good pitch accuracy only in the range of low B♭ to first space F.)
2. It is possible that songs emphasizing the upper range pitches should not be a major part of the song repertoire until the intermediate grades. (All boys were improving at the fifth-grade level.)
3. Teachers should be conscious of sex differences as they plan singing programs for young children. Boys are usually slow beginners and make less

progress than girls in the early years. It was indicated that boys can "catch up" to the girls in pitch accuracy at about the fifth grade level if vocal ranges appropriate for them are used.

The Child Voice

The child voice is often described as light in quality as well as in volume. It is also an extremely flexible mechanism, as illustrated by the strident cries of the playground. The teacher, then, is confronted by a voice that is capable of expressing many moods in song. Since there are many moods to express, this child voice can be sweetly soft and ethereal as it sings "Lullaby and goodnight" and can be momentarily harsh as it sings "David *killed* Goliath!" A logical way of deciding upon the voice quality desired in any song is for the teacher and children to discuss what manner of voice should be used to express the meaning of the words properly and to evaluate this continually when they sing. Although the child voice is light in quality, it should not sound weak or overly soft.

Many of the problems related to singing are soon solved when one adds to the above idea the following:

1. To make a generally pleasing sound (simple, natural, and clear).
2. To sing in a manner that avoids strain and tenseness.
3. To take breaths where one does when speaking the words (usually as the punctuation indicates); do not interrupt the phrase by breathing in unnatural places.
4. To enunciate clearly, but pronounce r's as some Southerners do [ah(r)], and sound final consonants distinctly and in unison.

Voice Range and Production

Classroom teachers insisted for years that songs in the older books demanded too high a range for a great many of the children's voices. As the years passed, these teachers observed a gradual lowering of the ranges in later books. However, individual voices vary greatly in range, particularly in the ability to sing high pitches. A minority of children can sing well above the top line of the staff, but in *group* singing this line is the upper limit for most classrooms. Three-year-olds generally sing in a range of three to five notes; four-year-olds sing in a range of five to six notes; five-year-olds can expand this to an octave. Because most preschool children sing within the following range, it follows that it will be useful *at the beginning* of the first grade for group singing.

The range within which most songs in series books are written is the following:

This range seems to be a basic one; it suits most adult voices well, and is also the playing range of many of the small wind instruments. The one that most children are able to sing by the sixth grade follows. However, some of the boys cannot sing as high if their voices are in the first stage of change.

Ranges children can sing successfully and which include those of many "problem singers" are:

There should be no hesitancy on the part of teachers to use these ranges for all of the children *some* of the time. It is obvious that there are different ranges for different age groups and for boys and girls at some levels. However, all children, even in kindergarten and first grade, should be encouraged to use all of their comfortable range, especially that of middle C to fourth line D.

Teachers often search for songs of limited range with which to initiate easy singing experiences. Examples follow:

3-note range:	Hot Cross Buns
	Merrily We Roll Along
	Good News (refrain)
	Trampin' (refrain)
	Fais do do (Go To Sleep) (first part)
4-note range:	Sally Go Round
	A-Hunting We Will Go (one version)
	Hokey Pokey
5-note range:	Go Tell Aunt Rhody
	Cradle Song (Rousseau)
	Lightly Row
	Sleep, Baby, Sleep
	Mary Had a Little Lamb
	Oats, Peas, Beans, and Barley
	Flowing River
	Green Gravel
	Whistle, Daughter, Whistle
	Grandma Grunts
	Old Woman (some versions)
	When the Saints Come Marching In
	Jingle Bells (refrain)
6-note range:	This Old Man
	Baa Baa Black Sheep

Old MacDonald
London Bridge
Lovely Evening
Hey Betty Martin
Skip To My Lou
Goodbye, My Lover, Goodbye
O Susanna
Old Brass Wagon
Pop! Goes the Weasel
Hickory Dickory Dock
Looby Lou
Caisson Song
Jolly Old St. Nicholas
Up On the Housetop
Au Clair de la Lune
Susy, Little Susy
Cindy
The Mocking Bird

When a textbook presents a song in a particular key, the writers have selected that key with the vocal range in mind. While it is indicative of a proper range for children's voices, there are considerations that lead teachers to change this range. Most of the songs in recent books are pitched in an easy, fairly low range. Therefore, after a song has been learned, the teacher should pitch it and other songs gradually higher, by half-steps, until teacher and children have extended their range into that considered normal for voices that have had help in developing the range to its natural span. Other songs will be printed in keys that demand a high range. Should a class be as yet unable to reach this range, the teacher will pitch these songs somewhat lower—usually not more than two whole steps at the most—then gradually pitch them higher as the singing range of the children improves. In today's music fundamentals classes for classroom teachers, simple transposition of the key by building the tonic chord (1-3-5) on the new keynote on bells or piano or singing it from a note sounded on a pitchpipe is commonly taught. Teachers need to be able to change the key of a song when the stage of development of the children's voice range makes this advisable.

The matter of correct pitching of songs becomes more complex in the sixth grade, where some of the boys may be in the first stage of voice change. The full range of these voices will normally fall approximately a fourth; thus a well-developed singing range of B♭ below middle C up to top line F will drop to a range of from F on the bass staff extending up to an octave above middle C.

Since the highest and lowest pitches of any range are somewhat mor
difficult to sing than the middle pitches, teachers select music that does nc
stress these extremes. The implications of this are two: first, that many c
the melodies in sixth-grade song books cannot be sung by boys in the rang
in which they are written, and second, that part-singing thus becomes
necessity. To sustain interest in singing, the teacher plans vocal parts boy
can sing easily in their range and takes special care to provide for thi
type of individual difference. Low harmony parts and chord root part
are helpful in this instance.

A successful music specialist declares that the natural range of th
voice—both the children's and the classroom teacher's—is fairly high whe
properly developed, and that normal voices should be able to sing the I
on the top line of the staff with ease. She states that vocal range is largel
a matter of correct breathing, breath support, and voice production. I
her intermediate grade classes, the children enjoy standing, then bendin
deeply with arms hanging limply, taking breaths—inhaling and exhaling—
while noting the fact that the diaphragm, not the chest, is primaril
involved in breathing. Then, remembering to breathe with the diaphragm
they stand erect, closed fists held near the shoulders with arm muscle
taut, inhale, then pretend to "chew" the air while slowly exhaling at th
teacher's signal. At other times, instead of "chewing" air, they place th
index finger of the right hand on the lips and slowly and steadily exhal
against the finger. These and other exercises, such as holding a piece c
thin paper against a wall with the breath for gradually longer periods c
time, are done to develop breath control. The teacher's approach appeal
to the boys, for she emphasizes that they should take part in sports an
in physical development to acquire the muscles they need in order to sing
There is truth in this, and the trained vocalist will not use the word "relax
that is employed in this chapter, but substitute "flexibility" instead, a wor
having somewhat different connotations.

To extend the range further, this teacher has the children vocalize u
and down the first five tones of the major scale with vowels such as "ah,"
"oh," and "oo," one-half step higher each time, as one hears adult vocalist
practice. When the higher range is reached, the children are instructed t
relax their faces to look as if they "had no sense at all," with the jav
held naturally and loose. The teacher takes special care not to injur
voices by vocalizing them too high or too low, and she can tell by the facia
expression when the children attempt pitches beyond their range at a give
stage in vocal development. In this way, this teacher extends the voca
range of her students to one believed suitable by the vocally trained.

A problem of some classroom teachers is that they have not learne
to use their singing voices properly, and therefore hesitate to sing pitche
they consider high. Many have used only a chest voice which they tr
to force upward in an attempt to sing higher pitches. They need to lear
how to sing in their high voice. Usually when these teachers try singin
high pitches softly in what can be termed a "half-voice" (i.e., it feels a

though one is using only half the voice he is accustomed to using; it is the head voice without the chest voice), they find that they can soon sing in a high voice that is very comparable to the child voice, and that eventually they will sing the high pitches with ease.

The teacher needs a clear, natural voice. Children are attracted by singing that sounds natural and normal. The male teacher's voice is no longer as rare as it once was in elementary school music. Most children are well-oriented to listening to and singing with this octave-lower voice on recordings, television, and radio as well as at home with their fathers. Once in a while a child will be confused by it and try to match its pitch. When this occurs, the male teacher should explain that his voice changed, and that he cannot sing as high as the children. He should play the song on an instrument that gives proper pitch, or have a child who knows the song sing it. In instances where teachers believe they cannot sing well enough to use their singing voices in teaching music, they can employ substitutions such as recordings, musical instruments, and children who sing well.

The following are physical requirements for good singing:

1. *Posture.* Place feet on the floor with the weight of the body somewhat forward, not on the back of the chair. Sit up straight, but not in a stiff or tense way. If standing, place the weight of the body toward the toes, not on the heels.
2. *Breathing.* Fill the abdominal region with air first (i.e., breathe "low," not high in the chest). This is the kind of breathing we do when lying flat on the floor or flat in bed. The goal in breathing is a controlled, continuous flow of breath. A husky or breathy sound indicates wasted breath.
3. *Open Throat.* Use the open, relaxed throat one has when about to yawn. Sing with the mouth open wide, but not so wide that it causes tension. Use "oo" and "ah" to relax the throat.
4. *Good Enunciation.* Open the mouth and use lips *generously* in pronouncing words. Be sure to pronounce final consonants distinctly.

Poor results often come from singing too loudly, singing too softly, not opening the mouth sufficiently, a slouching posture, a stiff and tense posture, a lack of interest, an unhealthy room temperature, and failure of the teacher to let the children comprehend the pitch and harmonic background of a song before asking them to sing it. The above physical requirements for good singing require that children are seated on chairs most of the time, rather than on a rug, because of the effect of posture on the proper use of lungs and diaphragm. Standing is also good.

Pitch Discrimination and Learning to Sing

The Out-of-Tune Singer

To adults who learned about high and low long ago, these concepts which are vital to listening and singing appear to be extremely simple. Yet, some seven-year-olds will confuse them. Young children often confuse *high* with *loud* and *fast* and *low* with *soft* and *slow*. When adult analyze this they find that high and low in pitch are abstractions; the asso ciation of high and low pitch with high and low physical levels is artificial however necessary for understanding. To make these experiences concrete for children it is essential that they be made "real" in terms of high and low physical position both with the body and with objects, in pictures and by relating to things in the child's world such as airplanes, trees, and stars (high), floor, rug, and grass (low). Step bells and ordinary bells held on end with the large bars down can relate high in pitch with the high bars and low in pitch with the low bars; this is effective because bells serve as audiovisual aids. Teachers employ songs in the kindergarten which children dramatize and later relate by discussion to high and low One of them is "Red Birds Flying."

RED BIRDS FLYING

Red birds fly - ing, red birds fly - ing, Now they stop on the ground.

Children are taught to play little action games in first grade such as:

I can reach high; I can reach low.

The above example relates high and low to widely spaced pitches illus trating these words and dramatizing them in terms of physical movement The following example is relatively more complex:

Clouds are up high; rain - drops fall down.

Many simple examples of song material useful in teaching these basic concepts are to be found in books on the kindergarten and first-grade levels. However, teachers can improvise their own songs for this purpose.

Acting out the melody line of songs in terms of pitch levels is a device that aids people of all ages to be more conscious of differences in pitch. The hand is used with a generous motion to move up, down, or to stay the same according to differences in pitch. When children are guided to respond in this manner their concepts of pitch relationships often im prove to a remarkable degree. In the above example the hand would move vertically as follows to reflect the melodic contour:

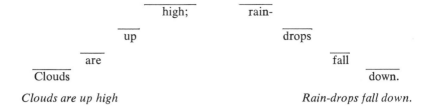

Clouds are up high   *Rain-drops fall down.*

The fact that at a certain stage of development a child does not sing in tune in no way proves lack of being musical. Instances can be cited to illustrate that it is possible for an out-of-tune singer to be an excellent musician. Among examples known to the authors are the concert master of a symphony orchestra and an eight-year-old pianist who played Bach with understanding, composed music of some quality, and who was an opera enthusiast. There is also the story of the secondary school music specialist who assumed that the superintendent could not hear how his music groups sounded because the man could not match tones. The specialist was wrong; the superintendent listened to them with critical judgment. Apparently these people never learned to relate their vocal mechanisms to what their ears heard; they did not know how this felt. Other reasons for people being unable to match tones with their singing voices are said to be general immaturity, a deprived musical environment, psychological blocks imposed by adults who tell them they cannot sing, lack of interest, failure to try as a result of fear, boredom, or of deprived background, and physical abnormalities which require attention of physicians. At another stage of musical development the child is something of a borderline case. If the teacher establishes a favorable environment, the child can sing in tune. However, if the teacher does not establish the pitch, if there is an accompaniment that confuses, or if the psychological situation is one in which muscles become tense, the child will probably fail to match tones.

In theory, inability to sing in tune should disappear during the elementary school years if children are given consistent help. There are skilled music specialists who insist that there should be no out-of-tune singers by the end of the second grade. However, in today's schools there are often a few children who cannot match tones well in each of the upper elementary grades. Teachers should be ready to assist these students toward pleasurable and accurate singing at whatever level they find them. A few children may not find their singing voices, or cannot control pitches accurately, until they are in high school. Teachers sustain the musical interest of such students through a program of varied activities—rhythmic responses, playing instruments, creating music, reading about music and musicians, and continuing to try to sing. There should be three major points of emphasis in helping them: they should participate in music

activities that are happy, interesting, challenging, and successful; they
should have many experiences in which they listen carefully to pitches and
to pitch differences; and because they learn by singing, they should be
encouraged to try.

During some stages of development, these children do not sense the
pitch of their own voices and often sing loudly (and happily) off key.
There arise the following problems: (1) how to help them to listen, (2)
how to keep these voices from hindering other children who are trying
to keep on pitch, (3) how to help them to make as real a contribution
to the group as the children who sing well, and (4) in the intermediate
grades, how to help them with their errors in such a way that they are
encouraged to try and remain confident of eventual success.

For young children who have not yet learned how to sing, the chanting
of old rhymes such as "Humpty Dumpty," "Mary, Mary Quite Contrary"
and "Rub-a-Dub-Dub, Three Men in a Tub" can be helpful. Children
like the *feel* of rhythmic or repetitious words; they enjoy saying them
together. If the teacher will establish the pitch of a low note such as middle
C and help them to *chant* the words on that pitch, a beginning can be
made in singing such one-pitch songs. In a few days the words can
be sung to the pitches of two tones, C and D, as follows:

Ma - ry, Ma - ry, quite con-tra - ry, How does your gar - den grow?

To accomplish this, the teacher may conduct in pitch levels, helping by
the ups and downs of the arm to indicate the low pitch and the higher
pitch. Next, this might be done on three pitches—and soon the children
will have learned not only to find their singing voices but to sing a song as
well.

Ma - ry, Ma - ry, quite con-tra - ry, How does your gar - den grow?

Many of the children who cannot match tones try to sing with the same
voice they use when they speak. Therefore, it is the task of the teacher
to help such children find their "high" or singing voices. This may be
done in a game situation. A favorite device is to have children pretend
to be the wind, a bird, or a siren. Children often sense pitch differences
more keenly through actions such as the teacher's lifting a child's hand up
high, or the children's starting from a squatting position (low) and moving
to a standing position (high). Another popular device is to have a child
pretend to call someone who is far away. When this is done, a sustained
speech results—and when speech is thus sustained (vowels held) singing
takes place.

When a child sings, but sings low and does not match the anticipated pitch, the teacher and class should *match the child's pitch* and sing the song in that key. This will often begin a procedure that brings success with the gradual raising of the pitch by singing the song in successively higher keys over a period of time.

The term "tone-matching" is not intended to convey emphasis upon an isolated drill technique. It is the authors' intention that it be thought of as "songs and games" for helping uncertain singers. Such a song or game may be sung by a class and a child may be selected to sing a part at the correct time. The part will sound at the right time because the teacher will sing with the child in case of faltering. Little or no attempt is made to correct faulty pitch while the song is being sung. It takes patience and faith on the part of a teacher to wait weeks and months for some children to sing correctly.

A commonly used device for listening and tone-matching is the calling of the roll in song and having each child answer on the same pitches. If someone is absent, the entire class responds by singing "absent," thus adding variety to this game. The teacher varies the pitch of these conversations-in-song, singing to each child in the range in which success will be most likely. Later, the purpose of the teacher will vary according to the progress of each child, and for some will be working to extend the range of already successful singers. Some successful singers may begin to improvise answers on pitches other than those the teacher sings; little question-and-answer tunes are created in this manner.

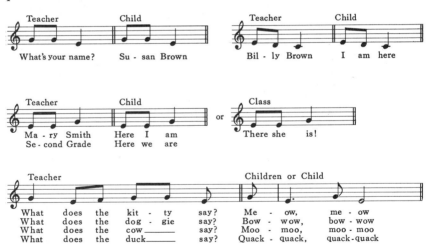

Another well-known tone-matching game is one in which the teacher places various objects in the hands of the children, who may be told to put their heads down on their desks and close their eyes. The game is played by the teacher singing, "Who has the _____?" and the child who possesses the object sitting up and singing, "I have the _____." An additional listening experience is to ask the class to identify an unseen child by the sound of the singing voice.

After learning to play this type of song-game, the teacher can sing questions such as, "What did you do last Sunday?" and "What did you have for breakfast?" and the child can create an answer with rhythmic and melodic variety. When a child has difficulty in matching tones with the teacher in any of these tone games, matching tones to another child's singing may do the trick. It is not wise to remain working with any one child too long in any of these procedures. To do so would make the other children restless because the progress of the game would be stopped, and it would unduly draw the child's attention to a relative lack of success. This refers to primary grades. A further aid to listening is the suggestion that the children "tune in" their voices just as they tune in radio stations. This is a concept children can understand because they know that the dial must be in exactly the right place for the station to "come in" properly. Another suggestion is to sing a familiar grouping of tones (or even a single pitch) for the children while they listen. Then ask them to listen with their "inner ears" while this is repeated for them. Next, ask the children to sing it. Finally, ask them if they sang exactly what they heard. Some of the children who cannot yet match tones will know that they have not sung what they heard. This process when repeated over weeks and months has notably improved the ability to listen and to match tones, especially when the teacher plans so that part of the class listens to and evaluates the singing of groups of children within the class, thus involving every child in the room with either singing or listening. Spontaneous tone games such as creating a "song" from children's words—i.e., "Johnny has a hair cut,"—and having children sing these words or additional words of their own in turn can sometimes help.

Picking out melodies or parts of melodies on the bells or piano can be a listening experience of value. These instruments can be used with songs that contain tones or tone patterns which are both played and sung. Listening for the proper time to play the instrument, and being sure the correct pitches have been sounded constitute a good listening experience in a situation of challenge and interest, and it helps build the background that leads to eventual singing on pitch.

There are certain tonal groups that are particularly easy for children to sing. It follows that if the teacher selects songs that contain these tonal groups, especially if they are repeated in the songs, and if these songs are pitched in easy singing range, there should result more than average success in group singing.

Among these are:

Number 1 is the easiest interval for children to sing; it is the descending minor third (5–3 or 1–6₁). Number 2 is an extension of number 1; it is sung by children all over the world in their natural, undirected play. Number 3, a descending series of three tones in whole-step arrangement, and Number 4, the ascending fourth, are easy to sing. Number 4 is often found in 5–8 position in major scales. Number 5, a pentatonic mode, is an important aspect of music children create spontaneously; songs based on it are easy to sing because no half-steps are involved. "This Old Man" and "The Caisson Song" emphasize the minor third. "Three Blind Mice" and "Mary Had a Little Lamb" stress the 3–2–1 note group, with the ascending fourth also stressed in "Three Blind Mice." The popularity of many songs can be traced to their utilization of these easily sung tonal groups. It follows that if easy-to-sing songs are pitched in easy-to-sing keys, they can speed the progress of children in becoming more skilled in tone-matching, which is hearing what is sounded, and reproducing this with the voice.

At times it is impossible to prevent the voices of out-of-tuners from hindering to some extent the progress of those children who are farther advanced in singing skills. A decision that is only of temporary value is to select out-of-tuners to make such contributions as the "zz" of a bee, the "tick tock" of a clock, the "ding dong" and other sound effects instead of singing. Since faulty singers learn to sing by singing, this device is no solution to their problem. Furthermore it would be unwise to make any obvious division of a class into singers and those who do something else. Careful listening is essential, but listening and never singing will not produce singers. Out-of-tuners should have many opportunities to listen to good examples of singing. These include the use of small groups or solo singers as examples to be listened to and constructively evaluated, and the inclusion of some good singers with the out-of-tuners when such temporary groupings are made. When out-of-tuners respond rhythmically to music, when they play the Autoharp, bells, and percussion instruments, and when they offer ideas for interpretation, dramatization and experimentation, they are making real contributions to group music even though they do not yet sing well. Teachers should give them full credit for what they contribute so that they feel they are first-class members of the group.

The traditional seating arrangement for music classes was dictated by concern for the out-of-tuners. They were seated in a group in front of the room, with the good singing voices of other children behind them and with the good singing voice of the teacher in front of them. It was supposed that this seating arrangement, which gave them correct pitches from both behind and in front, was of aid to them. Its disadvantage seems to have been that the obvious segregation of the out-of-tuners was a greater psychological block than the seating was an aid. It has been largely abandoned today. If children are seated in this manner, such seating is done in a way that presumably makes them unaware of its purpose. Actually the increasing informality of seating in today's classrooms tends to make any rigid seating plans for music unlikely. The arrangement should permit the teacher to move freely among the class so as to listen to each singer.

In the intermediate grades a problem may be how to continue to help the out-of-tuners without discouraging them. One teacher begins each year with "making a joyful noise." The entire emphasis is upon the joyous participation of every child with no regard as to singing on pitch, although the teacher is learning and studying the capabilities and problems of each child during this time. As soon as the first objective is achieved, work begins in assisting every child to sing on pitch. The teacher walks among the children as they sing, giving help to those who need it. While the singing is in progress, Jimmy is told that he is singing lower than the song is sounding, to listen with more concentration, and perhaps to sit with his friend Billy and tell Billy to help him. All of this is done in good spirit without setting anyone apart and always emphasizing to Jimmy that he is going to sing in tune soon—to keep on trying. Usually this teacher has eliminated out-of-tune singers by January.

Older children who cannot sing in tune know very well that they cannot, and they appreciate any help adults can give them as long as they are not embarrassed before their peers. Therefore, small group work apart from the class is desirable. A plan that has proved helpful is for the teacher to work with out-of-tuners in groups of two or four, with each child paired with another of like voice quality and range. With four, the teacher will place each child at a far corner of the room. The activity may begin with a story of children who have become separated in the woods or in the hills, and who are trying to find (call to) each other. One child is then asked to call in sustained speech (which is singing) to a partner across the room as though the partner were a city block distant. The call will ordinarily be sung in two pitches—the descending minor third pattern. The partner is to answer on the same pitches; this is the game. When this contact through tone matching has been established, they next begin singing other information back and forth, such as "Where are you?" "I'm over here," "Are you hungry?" and so on. The two children in the other corners of the room first listen to the pitches sung by the first two, then take their turn. Most of these children will find that they can hear the pitch given them in this way, and that they can answer it with surprising accuracy. After this introduction comes the repetition and extension of the singing back and forth, then eventually the singing of easy songs pitched in a range comfortable to the voices, and soon four more accurate singers have been added to classroom music.

Individual work with bells, including step bells, trying to match tones with the pitch of different metal bars in experimental fashion, can help. Time and relative privacy should be provided for such individual learning.

Time in which to practice hearing only one voice seems necessary for some as a prerequisite for group singing. That this has not already occurred may indicate a lack of singing in the home. The singing of a mother to her baby and to her young children is highly important in musical development. Music education begins at home, in the cradle.

When a problem singer can experiment over a period of time with singing into a tape recorder and playing back what was taped, the interest generated can result in ultimately singing on pitch. "The excitement from hearing one's voice on tape may lead the problem singer or reluctant singer to work diligently toward improvement of that sound, especially if the recording is made when alone or in a corner of the room, or even at home, with no one else to criticize or laugh. The child who never sings in person may proudly present the teacher with a recording revealing success." [2]

Some boys have psychological difficulty that stems from attempting to imitate their father's low voices and wanting to sound like men, not like their mothers, their female teachers, or girls. This can be overcome by explaining to the boys that their voices ordinarily change in grades seven through nine, and that shortly before the change begins, they will have better high voices than the girls, a soprano voice that signals the change to come. In fifth and sixth grades this is important to boys, and their understanding of this may determine whether they will use their still unchanged voices naturally or whether they will attempt to sing "down in their shoes." It is best to avoid using the adult terms "soprano" and "alto" and use instead "high" and "low." In three-part singing the parts are "high, middle, and low" rather than the terms descriptive of adult voices.

Establishing Pitch for Singing One of the most common failings of teachers is that of not giving the children sufficient time in which to hear the beginning pitch of songs a class is reviewing. This is because the teacher will "hear with the inner ear" the song in its proper harmonic setting, but will forget that the children, or many of them, are not hearing this. Too often these teachers sound a pitch and start the singing long before children have had time to orient themselves to this pitch, its relation to the scale in which the song is to be sung, and the harmonic setting of the first tones of the melody. This failure to help the children sense the

2 Eunice B. Meske and Carroll Rinehart, *Individualized Instruction in Music* (Reston, Va.: Music Educators National Conference, 1975).

pitch fully places some of them at such a disadvantage that they are out-of
tune singers when they need not be. When reviewing a song with a class
the following procedure is recommended:

1. Sound the 1-3-5 (tonic) chord built from the keynote [3] of the song by means
   of the piano, the bells, or by singing it. Sound 1 3 5 3 1. This is to establish
   a feeling for the key, that is, a feeling for the home tone in relation to the
   scale. The playing of the chord sequence I V₇ I on the piano or Autoharp
   does this excellently.

2. Sound at some length the keynote of the song. This should be sounded
   on an instrument such as the piano, bells, or pitch pipe.

3. Sing the keynote with the neutral syllable "loo."

4. Ask the children to sing this pitch, helping those who have difficulty. They
   can also sing 1 3 5 3 1 (and 1 5₁ 1 if the range permits).

5. Sing or otherwise sound the first note of the song if it is a note other than
   the keynote.

6. Ask the children to sing it and help them to match it.

7. Set the tempo by counting, directing, or clapping the rhythm of the meter
   and saying "Sing!" or, in rhythm, "Ready, sing!", after which the singing
   begins on the beat following the instruction "sing." Another way is for the
   teacher to sing the first two or four measures of the song as an introduction
   and direct or say "Sing!" as stated above. Doing this establishes the tempo
   and spirit of the song.

**Selecting
Songs for
Tone-Matching**

The teacher must analyze the melodies of songs to determine whether
or not they may be useful in "listen-then-sing" activities. There are songs
with easily sung repeated-note patterns and phrases, songs with parts that
can be echoed, songs with a limited range, songs with final measures that
can be repeated to create aesthetically satisfying codas, question-and-
answer songs, and dialogue songs. These permit the children to take
turns in singing and in constructive critical listening to the singing of
others.

Three song examples follow, the first two for primary level and the
third for intermediate level. The third example, "When the Saints Come
Marching In," has a tone pattern repeated twice in the original melody
and can be used in this form. However, it is printed here in a specially
arranged form to repeat the pattern four times, and to add another repeated
pattern near the end. It is an example of how teachers arrange songs
to adapt them to tone matching. The song has a small range, and rhythm
and spirit that children enjoy. The second group must listen carefully to
the first group, and is challenged to echo the tone pattern perfectly. Other
examples include "Old Texas," page 300, which is an echo-type song when
sung as a canon, and "The Keeper," page 298. These and others are in
many of the textbooks.

[3] See page 274 for how to find the keynote.

I HAVE A LITTLE BIRD

Peggy Burgess

Elementary Education Class
University of Oregon
Arr. R. E. N.

I have a lit-tle bird, who is well-known to you. He
lives with-in a clock, and each hour he sings cuck-oo.

CODA — Class or Group — Teacher — Group — Child

Each hour he sings cuck-oo. Cuck-oo cuck-oo cuck-oo.

THE ECHO

Kate Forman

Old Children's Air

Teacher — Class — Child

1. Ech-o I can hear you, hear you, hear you,
2. Now the rain is fall-ing, fall-ing, fall-ing,

Class — Child

Though I can't get near you, near you, near you,
So I'll stop my call-ing, call-ing, call-ing,

Teacher — Group — Child

You're so far a-way, a-way, a-way,
Won't you say good-day? good-day? good-day?

WHEN THE SAINTS COME MARCHING IN

New Orleans Song
Arr. R. E. N.

March tempo

Group One
Oh when the saints come march-ing

Group Two
Oh when the saints

in Everyone
come march-ing in, Oh when the saints come march-ing

in Lord, I want to be in that num-ber.

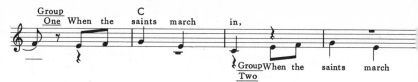

Examples of other echo-type songs are:

in *Singing With Children:*

"Are You Sleeping?"   "How Do You Do?"
"By'm Bye"   "If I Ask You"
"Barnyard Song"   "Getting Acquainted"
"Sipping Cider Through a Straw" "What Did You Do Last Summer?"
"Three Blind Mice"   "John the Rabbit"
"Today is Monday"   "The Sparrow's School" (Chichipapa
"Who Did?"   "Follow On"

Examples of other repetitious songs are:

in *Singing With Children:*

"Good-bye, Old Paint"   "Angel Band"
"Hot Cross Buns"   "Clickety-Clack"
"Rain, Rain, Go Away"   "Grandma Grunts"
"Old Woman's Courtship"   "Hole in the Bucket"
"Polly Wolly Doodle"   "Hush Little Baby"
"Tideo"   "Whistle, Daughter, Whistle"
"Tisket, a Tasket"
"Trampin' "

Tonal Memory is necessary for the singer. Teachers can assist the
development of tonal memory by such activities as:

1. Humming a familiar tune and asking the children to identify it; then asking
   children to hum it back to the teacher.

2. Arranging a signal whereby children stop singing during the performance
   of a familiar song, but continue to *think* the tune for a phrase or two. Then
   the teacher signals them to change from thinking the tune to singing it
   and so on.

3. Playing a game in which children hum a tune for the class to identify.

4. Having the class sing songs with neutral syllables (*la, loo*) rather than the
   words so that the singers can concentrate on the melody.

5. Challenging the class to sing songs with numbers and/or syllables.

6. Challenging individual children to explore the black keys of the piano—to work alone to find the melodies of pentatonic tunes they know such as "Old MacDonald," "All Night, All Day," "Get On Board," "Auld Lang Syne," "Land of the Silver Birch," "The Campbells Are Coming," and "Swing Low, Sweet Chariot." They can also create and try to remember tunes of their own.

7. Asking children to notate parts of well-known tunes from memory when they are sufficiently advanced for this activity.

Hand Signs

Pitch discrimination and the concepts of high and low are often explored by beginning with the descending minor third interval, 5–3 (*so-mi*). First, many names, nursery rhymes and other poems or words are sung on the two pitches. Next, hand signs may be performed by the children in response to them. The teacher sings *so* or *mi* and the children learn to identify both as high or low and with the hand signs. After children have learned the hand signs individual children can "think" the pitches and give signs to the class to be translated into pitch. Next, *la* (6) is added, and the three pitches are used in many ways in improvising short songs, setting poems to them, learning the hand signs, devising ear training games with them as described for *so* and *mi* above, and seeing the relation of the pitches in notation. Notice that the eye, ear, and body are all involved in learning pitch discrimination. Eventually *re* and *do* are added,

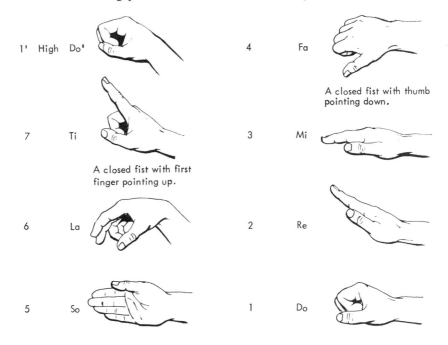

1'   High   Do'

7   Ti

A closed fist with first finger pointing up.

6   La

5   So

4   Fa

A closed fist with thumb pointing down.

3   Mi

2   Re

1   Do

and there are the hand signals, notation, improvisation of little melodie
playing of the pitches and the tunes on bells and xylophones, and usin
the five pitches of the common pentatonic scale. Rhythm patterns per
formed with body and percussion sounds can be utilized all the wa
through this process; the learning of notation and its description of th
duration of pitch (note values) can be applied throughout this develop
mental experience with pitch. Children can discover that rhythm an
melody are integrally related; that one cannot have a melody unless th
pitches are assigned duration, which is basic to rhythm.

The low *do* is formed at waist level. The signs move upwards step b
step in the illustrations below. *So* is made approximately even with th
mouth. High *do* is made even with the forehead.

To illustrate how rhythm syllables, Latin syllables, and hand sign
are used by many teachers, the following excerpts are reproduced fror
Twenty-Two Music Lessons, published by the Nova Scotia Department c
Education.

LESSON 15

Using Roll-Call to Reinforce So-Mi and Hand Signs

1. Teacher says: "I will clap the Rhythm Pattern of someone's name.
would like that person to (stand and) answer by saying and clapping it.
(There may be several people whose names have the same Rhyth
Pattern—let them all respond at once.) Then the whole class responds b
clapping and saying the rhythm syllables (ta & ti-ti)

Examples:

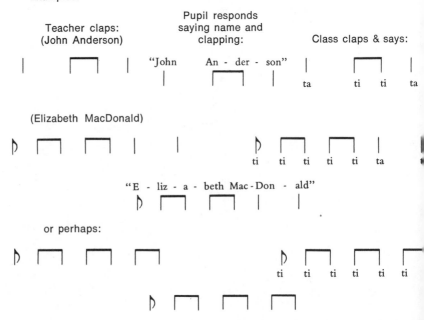

(Rosemary Stewart)

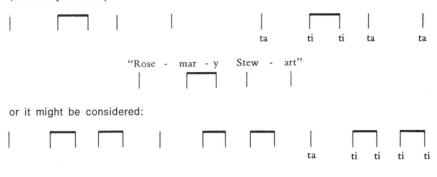

ta ti ti ta ta

"Rose - mar - y Stew - art"

or it might be considered:

ta ti ti ti ti

2. Using *so* and *mi,* the teacher calls each child by name (full name preferably), and each child echoes, as in the examples below:

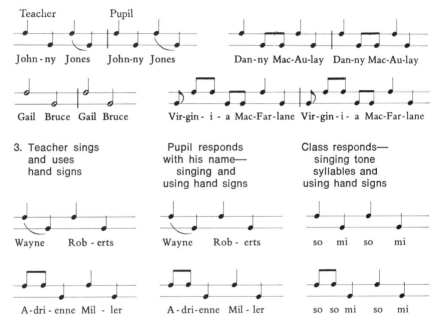

Teacher   Pupil

John - ny Jones   John-ny Jones

Dan- ny Mac-Au-lay   Dan-ny Mac-Au-lay

Gail Bruce Gail Bruce

Vir-gin - i - a Mac-Far-lane Vir-gin-i- a Mac-Far-lane

3. Teacher sings and uses hand signs	Pupil responds with his name— singing and using hand signs	Class responds— singing tone syllables and using hand signs

Wayne   Rob - erts

Wayne   Rob - erts

so   mi   so   mi

A - dri - enne Mil - ler

A - dri-enne Mil - ler

so so mi   so   mi

4. Teacher sings as before, but now instead of the echo, the child responds to the teacher's question, singing and using hand signs. The class responds, as in (3):

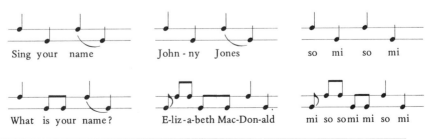

Sing your name

John - ny Jones

so mi so mi

What is your name?

E-liz-a-beth Mac-Don-ald

mi so somi mi so mi

PART OF LESSON 19

Added suggestions: using recorder, melody bells, piano, or "loo":

1. Give a four-beat rhythmic pattern using *so* and *la*.
*indicates *so:*

2. Now try the roll-call patterns, employing *mi, so,* and *la,* as outlined in Lesson 15. Here are some examples:

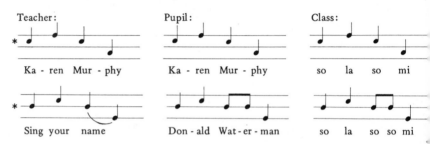

Teacher: You will find that the children will usually echo your tonal pattern. You will have to do the hand signals with them, at least at the beginning.

How Do Melody Tones Move?

Young children can discover that the tones of melodies move in three ways: they can repeat, they can move in steps (scalewise or conjunct), and they can move in skips or leaps (often chordwise or disjunct). When these concepts are being developed, the teacher selects songs and recorded music that most clearly reveal these tonal movements. Prior to this the children's first discovery may be that melodies move in single lines, horizontally. While the contour of a melody may move up and down or stay the same for a while, there is a steady linear progression. In songs such as "That's the Way Tunes Go" and "Space Ship" the concepts of both repeated tones and stepwise progression can be studied by the children in response to the teacher's question, "In what different ways do you think this melody moves?"

THAT'S THE WAY TUNES GO

Tunes may go up a step or two, or on one note they stay a while, They
skip some-times to high and low! That's the way tunes go.

SPACE SHIP

Wilma Wittemeyer
Arr. R. E. N.

1. We passed thru the son - ic bar - ri - er, my
2. Our speed was ten thous - and miles per hour strapped

as - tro - naut and I, In our
in our cap - sule tight, We are

aer - o - space ship, the X - fif - teen, We went
writ - ing our names in hist - or - y, In our

zoom - ing in - to the sky.
rock - et pow ered flight.

From *Exploring Music with Children* by Robert E. Nye and Vernice T. Nye. © 1966 by Wadsworth Publishing Company, Inc., Belmont, California. Reprinted by Permission of the publisher.

251

"Taffy" is another scaleline song with repeated notes; it is also usef
for experience with the octave leap.

TAFFY

From *Singing With Children* (2nd ed.) by Robert and Vernice Nye, Neva Aubin, an
George Kyme. © 1970 by Wadsworth Publishing Company, Inc., Belmont, California. R
printed by permission of the publisher.

Suggestions for use: "Taffy" can be used to introduce children to th
C scale. Children find the C scale easy to play on the piano because of th
consecutive white keys.

After the song is learned, one child can sing the first measure, anothe
the second measure, another the third and fourth measures, and so on
Children enjoy this method, which also serves to strengthen tonal memory

"The Hat" exemplifies a chordline song; it contains skips and leap
besides repeated notes. By experimenting, older children can find that F
A, and C are notes that can be played together on bells or piano to accom
pany the song, and thus begin to relate chordline melodies with accom
panying chords.

THE HAT

Have you seen Bu-geaud's cap up-on his head?
As tu vu la cas-quet' du père Bu geaud?

See how he wears it, Tra la la la la, See the cap up-on his head.
Si tu ne l'as pas vue, tu la ver-ras, La cas-quet-te, la cas-quet',

See how he wears it, Tra la la la la, See the cap up-on his head.
Si tu ne l'as pas vue, tu la ver-ras, La cas-quet du père Bu-geaud.

What Is a Scale, and How Many Different Kinds Can You Find?

The term *scale* means "ladder." It refers to an arrangement of rising pitches. Children soon become familiar with the major scale through experiences with scale songs and playing the C scale on bells and xylophone. They quickly find that one can sing or play down the scale as well as up. The bells and piano keyboard are effective audiovisual devices for children to use in determining a definition or description of the C major scale as consisting of both whole steps and half steps, and for the eventual discovery of their precise arrangement. Following this could be "trying out" the major scale pattern, beginning on notes other than C to find if it sounds the same. Although F and G are often the notes tried next, there are eleven black and white keys other than C with which to experiment. The fact that the major scale can be played from any black or white key is an important discovery. The children may find that the major scale consists of one repeated pattern: whole step, whole step, half step, (whole step) whole step, whole step, half step. There should be provision in the classroom for individualized study of this scale (diatonic) pattern. Some teachers use so-fa hand signs to explore the scale and its intervals. The advantage is said to be that signs have somewhat the same function as fingering on an instrument, and it is assumed that they make scale tones less abstract to the learner; a disadvantage is that pitch movements expressed in hand signs must be done rather slowly to be seen and understood.

The major scale should be compared with a pentatonic scale in which there are no half steps. Both the keyboard and charts are needed to explore and explain these scale patterns. A large chart of the keyboard, placed in a commanding position in the classroom, is considered an essential piece of equipment by a great many teachers. They refer to it frequently during music class to explain tonal relationships visually.

In any study of scales there should be an immediate association with

Major Scale	1	2	3	4	5	6	7	8
	d	r	m	f	s	l	t	d

Pentatonic Scale	1	2	3		5	6		8
	d	r	m		s	l		d

Visual Spacing
of the
Major Scale

8	d
7	t
6	l
5	s
4	f
3	m
2	r
1	d

Where are the half
steps?

song materials to explore how a scale is used in music. Because so many American children's songs are in major keys, this association is fairly obvious. The less commonly used tonalities need to be sensed in like fashion through songs that employ their scale structures. In working with a song built on a scale which is strange, the children might first determine on which note the tonal center (key note) seems to be, then try to construct the scale from that note, utilizing notes from the melody to complete it. Minor keys are not "strange" to the children; they have heard them many times from their environment. Eight-year-olds can begin to learn their precise structures through experiences with songs which are built on them. There are two ways to conceptualize the relationship of minor scales to major scales. (Since adults argue about them, it should be interesting for the teacher to watch how the children's thinking about them evolves.) One way is to consider every minor scale a relative of a major scale, that is, every minor scale can be thought of as beginning on the sixth step (*la*) of a major scale. Thus, it would be sung from *la* to *la* or from 6 to 6. This way of thinking has adherents because the syllables and numbers remain stable—attached to the major scale concept. Another way is to think only of the minor scale, call the home tone 1 or *do,* and sing it as though it began on the same scale step as a major scale does. This is of advantage when it comes to piano chording because the I-chord corresponds by number to scale tone one. Either way can be used. Most adults believe that the "best" way is the one they have been taught. Let the children explore both ways and decide which seems to be the most logical to them.

With selected song material (see the indexes of books), the three kinds of minor scales in common use can be worked with, and the children should use them to write their own compositions. Sometimes recordings will initiate an exciting exploration of a minor scale; Cui's *Orientale* is one example.[4] A problem for children to solve is "What feelings are communicated by use of minor tonalities in music?" They should find that

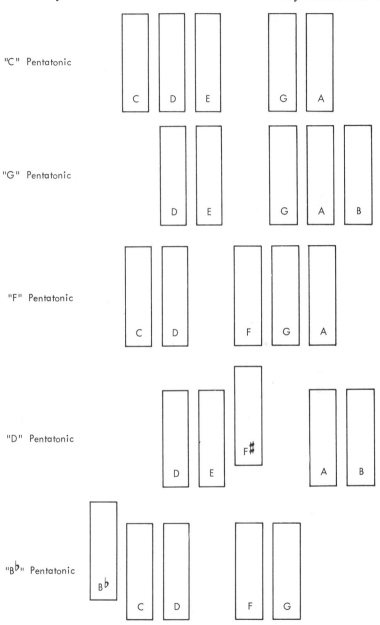

"C" Pentatonic

"G" Pentatonic

"F" Pentatonic

"D" Pentatonic

"Bb" Pentatonic

Pentatonic Scales on the Keyboard Instruments

[4] *Orientale* also has a rhythmic ostinato.

Major scale of	B♭	F		C	G
	B♭	F	do	C	G♮
	A	E	ti	B	F♯
	G	D	la	A	E
	F	C	so	G	D
	E♭	B♭	fa	F	C
	D	A	mi	E	B
	C	G	re	D	A
	B♭	F	do	C	G

How are syllables and letter names related?
Play these on the bells. Find the same scale
starting on a note not written here; play it.

there are at least as many communicated by minor keys as by major keys, and that minor is not necessarily associated with "sad."

By the teacher's creating an environment in which children are stimulated to discover and explore these scales for themselves, the same subject matter that under other conditions can be a rather puzzling, teacher-pressured memorization of three kinds of minor scales (natural or pure, harmonic and melodic) can be part of a thrilling adventure in expanding the concept of "scale." Learners can discover for themselves the truly fascinating ways in which man has structured many different kinds of scales for expressing and communicating feelings.

Passive and Active Scale Tones; Charts of Minor Scales

A typical scale involves a specific tonality. Children learn easily to identify the home tone as the most important pitch to which all the other scale members are related. Through expanding musical experiences, children will rate scale tone 5 as the next most influential, and scale tone 4 would be third in general importance. However, when persons sense the tonality of scales thoroughly, they come to feel that certain of the pitches tend to give them a sense of satisfaction and stability, while certain other pitches give them the feeling that they should move on to an adjacent pitch above or below. Using the major scale as an example, the *passive* tones are those of the tonic (I) chord, 1, 3, 5, and 8. The active tones are 2, which tends to move down to 1 or up to 3; 4, which tends to move down to 3 or up to 5; 6, which tends to move down to 5 or up to 7;

and 7, which pulls strongly to 8, and is called the *leading tone* because of this. These qualities of scale members can be discerned by children. Older children feel them more strongly than young children because their harmonic sense is more developed. To explore the passive and active qualities of scale members, ask the children to sing slowly up and down the scale, directing them to stop at different scale tones. Then ask them which way they feel the pitch should move—up, down, or stay the same. The movement of melodies with regard to active and passive scale tones relates to beauty, ease of singing, note reading, use of tones in their own compositions, and to expanding concepts of scale and tonality.

ONE MAY MORNING

English Folksong

Flowing (♩=152)

As I went out____ one May morn-ing, One May morn-ing____ be-time, I met a maid,____ from____ home had stray'd,____ Just as the sun____ did shine.

From *Birchard Music Series,* Book 6, copyright © 1962 by Summy-Birchard Company, Evanston, Illinois. All rights reserved. Used by permission.

What scale is this? Find it on the bells.
2 whole steps, 1 half step, 3 whole steps, 1 half step

1	2	3	4	5	6	7	8
1	2	3		4	5	6	7	8
1	2	3		4	5	6		7	8
1	2	3	4	5	6	7	8

Try to play these on the bells. What are the names of these scales?
How would you sing them with the syllables?

Scale Study

Compare this scale chart with the others. Which suits you best? Why?

MAJOR			do	re	mi	fa	so	la	ti	do
PENTATONIC			do	re	mi		so	la		do
MINOR la natural	ti	do	re		mi	fa	so	la		
MINOR la harmonic	ti	do	re		mi	fa	si	la		
MINOR la melodic	ti	do	re		mi	fi	si	la		

How are minor scales alike? How are they different?
How would you sing them with numbers?

Pentatonic Melodies   The term "pentatonic melody" is sometimes puzzling because they may be classified into four types. The first is the tune which is clearly pentatonic in both melody and any accompanying pitches and in which no harmonization (chord change) is desired. Second is the melody which has been harmonized; tunes in this classification can be treated successfully as either those in which no chord change takes place or as those in which harmonization can be applied. Third is a melody which contains a few nonpentatonic tones—such as major scale steps 4 and/or 7; these appear in unimportant places in the melody (not on the beat) so that no harmonization need take place. Fourth is the type which has a melody within the pentatonic scale but in which harmonization seems essential. Each type is useful in one or more ways in teaching. Pentatonic songs will be found listed in classified indexes of books. Examples not mentioned earlier include "Goodbye, Old Paint," "Grandma Grunts," "The Riddle Song," "Nobody Knows the Trouble I've Seen," and "Night Herding Song." As stated earlier, they can be played on the black keys of the piano, an activity which assists the development of tonal memory.

PENTATONIC SCALES

Tonal center ↑   ↑   ↑

Key Signatures   Children who have explored the scales and understand their organization will have no difficulty in determining why key signatures are necessary. When they fit the major scale pattern to different places on the keyboard they find black keys essential. From these, key signatures can be derived. Unless children find use for scales and key signatures, they will soon forget them. One logical use is in their own compositions. Another is in the performance of instrumental music; one must use the key signature in order to know what note to play and what fingering to use. Vocal music does not demand the same analysis of key signatures that instrumental music does; all the singer needs to know is the beginning pitch and *where that pitch is in the scale*. However, in order to know where the pitch of a new song is in the scale, one needs to know the key signature. If the teacher knows this, the children hardly need to, for the teacher can then give them the pitch and tell them where it is in the scale by having them sing first 1–3–5–3–1, then up or down the scale to the beginning note. Thus, in a purely vocal approach the teacher must invent situations in which the signature is of use to the learner. One is to select a student to be the teacher of a new song and ask the class to help the teacher plan what to do. Usually the need to know where the beginning note is in relation to the scale will appear early in the process. It is best to use two or more songs, each beginning on a different scale tone. For how to identify the key from the key signature, see p. 274, this chapter.

The Less Common Modes

Some scales were used more frequently in earlier centuries than recently. Today both contemporary composers and folk singers have brought them to a more prominent position in the music that surrounds us. They can be utilized to compose songs and instrumental pieces with a "different" flavor and to reflect older periods. For example, a troubadour song could be written with both words and melody that communicate feelings from that time in world history. Indexes in books guide teachers to modal songs. The Ionian mode is the major scale pattern; the Aeolian is the pure minor scale pattern. The less common modes are the following scales:

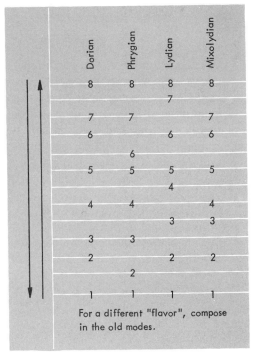

For a different "flavor", compose in the old modes.

Some examples of songs written in less common modes are the folk songs "I Wonder as I Wander," "Every Night When the Sun Goes In," "The Shanty Boys in the Pine," "The Days of '49," and "Ground Hog." Plain chants from church sources which exemplify the older use of the modes are in some of the books.

Accidentals, Chromatic, and Whole-Tone Scales

Accidentals (sharps, flats, or cancel signs not stipulated by the key signature) are to be found in two of the minor scales, in songs written both in these minor keys, and in major keys as well. A song such as "I Heard the Bells on Christmas Day," contains some half steps with accidentals. This can lead to exploring the *chromatic* scale which consists entirely of half steps. Another approach to this scale can be through a recording of "Flight of the Bumblebee" by Rimsky-Korsakov (BOL #52).

CHROMATIC SCALE

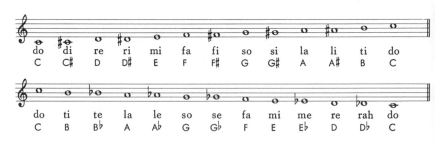

WHOLE - TONE SCALE

The chromatic and whole-tone scales can be used as "discrepant events" following the study of active and passive scale tones. These scales lack the feeling of tonality characteristic of major and minor scales. When children analyze why songs based on major and minor scales have home tones, they will find that the half steps have something to do with this feeling of tonality. When they analyze the chromatic scale they will find nothing but half steps; neither the whole-tone scale nor the pentatonic scale has half steps. Interesting generalizations may come from this. When would a composer not desire a feeling of tonality? What kinds of feelings would he be trying to communicate? *Mists*, by Howard Hanson, is a composition which utilizes the whole-tone scale.[5] The whole-tone scale can be compared to the common pentatonic, and children can determine which has the larger degree of key feeling. (The authors always assume that

---

[5] From *For the First Time*, Mercury Recording. A song constructed on whole-tone scales is "The Cage" by Charles Ives. It appears in several of the music textbook series of recent date.

when they write of scales or any other of the "music fundamentals," the teacher will be utilizing related songs and recordings which bring the study of the concept to musical life, and that the children will be using these in their own compositions for specific reasons. The good teacher knows that unless these aspects of music are truly interesting or useful to the learner, little will be gained from studying them.)

Ethnic Scales

The concept of *scale* is further expanded when ethnic scales are discovered or introduced. There are many of these scales; music education is only at the threshold of beginning to recognize them. They relate very well to some aspects of social studies. For example, in the study of Japan, children can listen to music and compose music based upon ethnic scales of that country. One is the already-known pentatonic scale. Another type of pentatonic scale is that used in the song "Sakura" (BOL #66). Beautiful "Japanese" songs can be composed by children who use this scale:

Much of the popular music of Japan is based on this pentatonic scale:

A gypsy scale:

A scale of Afro-American origin:

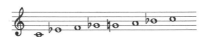

A source of some selected ethnic scales is Gertrude Wollner's *Improvisation in Music,* Doubleday & Company, Inc., Garden City, New York, 1963, Chapter Five, "Adventures in Unusual Scales." Pentatonic, whole-tone, four-tone, chromatic, Hungarian, Arabian, Hindu, Asiatic Indian, Egyptian, Irish, and modal scales are notated. The explanations on some of the record jackets of Asiatic Indian music explain the scale structures utilized in this music. To invent an *original* scale upon which to base songs and instrumental compositions, the learners plan to have either an irregular arrangement of whole steps, half steps, and other intervals as in the above examples, or a regular arrangement such as a consistent alternating of whole and half steps or a consistent use of an interval such as the minor or major third.

The Tone Row   This scale is an invented one, often based on the 12 steps of the chromatic scale. The elementary school learner can use resonator bells. Place the bars in an order that when sounded will not remind the listener of any tonality; this will require moving the bars about until the new scale sounds "atonal,"—that is, without any definite tonal center. The row will include all 12 tones, but not in the original consecutive order. Experiment with this arrangement of scale tones by playing familiar melody rhythms such as "Three Blind Mice" to discover new melodic sounds. Then attempt composition with your new scale, using the succession of pitches over and over again in different ways. (Your scale can also be constructed with fewer than 12 tones.) When one listens to this type of music from recordings, it will be found that certain compositional techniques of long standing are employed to manipulate melodies. Manipulation of traditional melodies will be discussed later; the same techniques apply to tone row music. Composers have used some of them for centuries. With the tone row, traditional harmony is absent; a new concept of harmonization is constructed, often being built from the vertical "happenings" of multiple melodic lines instead of the chords of old.

Tone Patterns and Intervals

Understanding and being able to use tone patterns and intervals relate to learning to read music effectively. When children can comprehend tonal and rhythmic groups as they comprehend words of English, they are learning to read music. Rhythm patterns were discussed in the previous chapter. Tonal patterns found in songs can be taught as parts of those songs. Tone patterns common to many songs include the following:

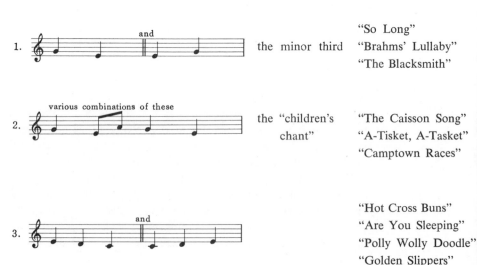

1. the minor third

"So Long"
"Brahms' Lullaby"
"The Blacksmith"

2. the "children's chant"

"The Caisson Song"
"A-Tisket, A-Tasket"
"Camptown Races"

3.

"Hot Cross Buns"
"Are You Sleeping"
"Polly Wolly Doodle"
"Golden Slippers"
"Shortnin' Bread"

262

"Star Spangled Banner"
"Blue Danube"
"Dixie"
"Goin' to Boston"
"Bow, Belinda"

"There Was a Little
  Woman"
"Dixie"
"The First Noël"

When the children have identified these and other tone patterns and can find them in songs and hear them from recordings, the next step is to identify variant uses of the patterns. For example, with reference to pattern number 5 above, the teacher may ask, "Find out how this scaleline pattern is used differently in 'Twinkle, Twinkle, Little Star,'" and "Look for it in 'Joshua Fought the Battle of Jericho'; how is it different in that minor song?"

Intervals   In order of using and learning melodic intervals, the young learner usually begins with the descending minor third. The second is part of any scale line pattern; the octave, the fourth, and the fifth are commonly used in children's songs. The sixth, then the seventh, would probably come next in order of usage. They are learned through associations with their use in familiar songs, followed by games of interval identification. To be certain they have identified the interval correctly, children can test their decision by beginning with 1 or *do* and "singing up to it."

The minor third is exemplified in "Brahms' Lullaby," "The Caisson Song," and "Lightly Row"; the major third in "Mary and Martha," "Little David," and "Swing Low, Sweet Chariot"; the fourth in "Taps," "I've Been Working on the Railroad," "Auld Lang Syne," and "Hark! the Herald Angels Sing"; the fifth in "Twinkle, Twinkle, Little Star," and "Baa, Baa, Black Sheep"; the sixth in "My Bonnie," "Bendemeer's Stream," and "It Came Upon the Midnight Clear"; and the octave with "Annie Laurie," and "Wait for the Wagon." The minor sixth is often identified by thinking the major sixth first, then comparing it with the half-step smaller interval. The minor and major sevenths are often identified by comparing them with the octave.

Ability to read music through knowledge of intervals becomes essential in the instance of contemporary melodies that do not move in the scalewise and chordwise manner of traditional melodies.[6] If syllables are used with this music, the teacher should consider using the *fixed do* system in which C is always *do*.

---

[6] That is, music with no tonal center.

The usefulness of tone patterns and intervals in reading music can be understood when songs are analyzed with these aspects in mind. For example, "Love Somebody" contains several tone patterns, the interval of a perfect fourth numerous times, and the interval of a perfect fifth once. Anyone knowing these and the rhythm patterns discussed in Part Two can sight-sing the song. How many times do each of the tone patterns occur? How many times is the interval of the fourth used?

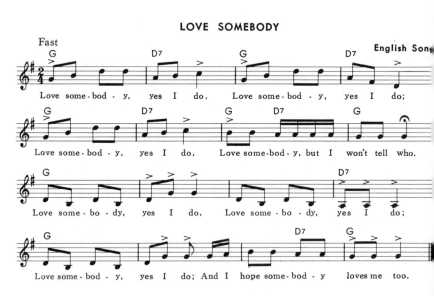

LOVE SOMEBODY

Chord-line melody patterns are another helpful factor in note reading; this will be referred to in the next chapter. "Love Somebody" contains G and D chord-lines and an inversion of the G chord appears in the last two phrases. Analyze "Alouette" in terms of tone patterns and intervals.

ALOUETTE (Skylark)

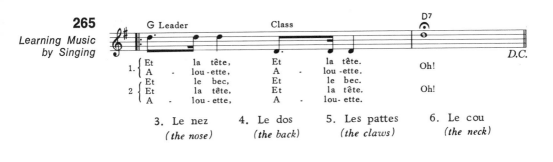

1. Et la tête, Et la tête. Oh!
  A - lou-ette, A - lou-ette.
  Et le bec, Et le bec.
2. Et la tête, Et la tête. Oh!
  A - lou-ette, A - lou-ette.

3. Le nez 4. Le dos 5. Les pattes 6. Le cou
(the nose) *(the back)* *(the claws)* *(the neck)*

Forms of Melodies

The answers to the questions, "Is the tune the same or is it different now?" and "How is it different?" guide children into learning concepts of the different ways melodies are put together. Very young children can answer these questions. The mind seeks a sense of order, and music is one of the better ways to foster the concept of form. Children can listen for form, hear it, analyze it, and apply it in their own compositions. The concepts of same, different, repetition, contrast, and variety can grow through finding the phrases of songs and comparing them. This is done first through the ear; later it can be seen in notation. In Part Two body movement was shown to be a means of discovering these similarities and differences, and percussion instruments were used to emphasize them.

It is important to remember that one-part (unary), two-part (binary), and three-part (ternary) song forms have many variants. Teacher and class should expect to find songs with phrase orders which are modifications of these model forms, and songs with different forms. For a simple example, "Whistle, Daughter, Whistle," has a unary form in which the same phrase is repeated note for note; it could be described as *a a*. "Hole in the Bucket" is also unary, but the phrase ends differently, hence it could be described as *a a'*.

HOLE IN THE BUCKET

American Folksong

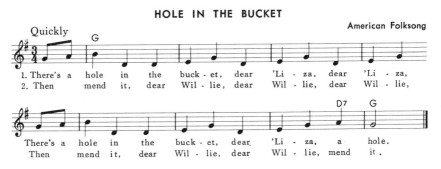

1. There's a hole in the buck - et, dear 'Li - za, dear 'Li - za,
2. Then mend it, dear Wil - lie, dear Wil - lie, dear Wil - lie,

There's a hole in the buck - et, dear 'Li - za, a hole.
Then mend it, dear Wil - lie, dear Wil - lie, mend it.

"Go Tell Aunt Rhody" is an example of binary form in which there are two unlike phrases, thus *a b*. "Li'l 'Liza Jane" is a variant of this, with four phrases, *a a' b b'*.

GO TELL AUNT RHODY

American Song

1. Go tell Aunt Rho - dy, Go tell Aunt Rho - dy,
2. The one she's been sav - ing, The one she's been sav - ing, The

Go tell Aunt Rho - dy, the old gray goose is dead,
one she's been sav - ing to make a feath - er bed.

There are many examples of ternary (three-part) form, of which "O Tannenbaum" is one, *a a b a*. The important aspect is a melodic statement, contrast, then a return to the beginning. Theorists ignore the first repetition of *a,* consider the form to be *a b a,* and compare it to an arch in architecture. "O Tannenbaum" includes another aspect of melody structure, the *sequence,* part of the melody repeated at a higher or lower pitch level. This is a device children can use in their compositions. "I Love the Mountains" is a song which is sequential in character.

O TANNENBAUM (O Christmas Tree)

Singing Game

Firmly

O, Christ-mas tree, O, Christ-mas tree, How faith-ful are thy branch - es!

Your boughs so green in sum-mer time, Stay green in win - ter's snow-y clime.

O, Christ - mas tree, O, Christ-mas tree How faith-ful are thy branch - es!

O, Tannenbaum, O, Tannenbaum,　　　　*Du Grünst nicht nur zur Sommerzeit*

Wie treu sind deine Blätter !　　　　　　*Nein auch im Winter, wenn es schneit*

O, Tannenbaum, O, Tannenbaum,　　　　*O, Tannenbaum, O, Tannenbaum,*

Wie treu sind deine Blätter !　　　　　　*Wie treu sind deine Blätter !*

Exploring the Manipulation of Melodies

In the preceding chapter certain aspects of music composition were explored with percussion instruments in a nonmelodic situation. These were augmentation, diminution, and canonic treatment. See p. 222, "Rhythm-Related Compositional Devices." These can be applied to melodies in the same way as described there, and older children can experiment with them in their compositions. Other composer's techniques which children can learn to employ include *transposition,* placing the melody in another key, *inversion,* writing it upside down, *retrograde,* writing it backwards, giving it a *variations* treatment by altering it rhythmically, melodically, or harmonically, and using *octave displacement,* which is distorting the melody with octave leaps. Octave displacement, inversion, and retrograde are illustrated below with "London Bridge." Stravinsky's "Greeting Prelude" exemplifies octave displacement with the familiar tune, "Happy Birthday to You," and it is useful at every elementary school level. One series, *Exploring Music,* 1966 edition, has it recorded for the first grade book, and page 73 of the Teacher's Book suggests treating "Hot Cross Buns" this way. "Greeting Prelude" is included on the Columbia Record *Instrumental*

LONDON BRIDGE

Singing Game

Miniatures, a group of short pieces by Stravinsky. Materials useful in exploring variation form include *Hot Cross Buns,* Young People's Record 5005, Lucian Calliet's *Variations on Pop Goes the Weasel,* Adventures in Music 4, vol. 1, excerpts from variations Mozart wrote on a French folk tune we know as "Twinkle, Twinkle, Little Star," [7] the *Second Movement* of Haydn's *C Major* (Emperor) *Quartet,* which uses a familiar hymn tune, and Charles Ives' *Variations on America.*

The most popular approach in introducing the manipulation of melodies is by means of very simple and well-known songs. Some additional examples include "Baa, Baa, Black Sheep," "Three Blind Mice," "Are You Sleeping?" and "Mary Had a Little Lamb."

What Do Melodies Communicate?

Songs are the union of poetry and melody; their words describe rather clearly the thought being communicated. Children should be encouraged to form judgments about how well the melody reflects the message of the words. "This song is said to be a lullaby." "How does the melody suggest that it is a lullaby?" "How well does it succeed in communicating this idea?" A song such as "Sleep, Baby, Sleep" could be used as an example. When such questions are stated, the teacher is relating man and music in recognition that most of the music of the world is functionally used rather than set apart as an art for the connoisseur. How does the melody of a work song, a street vendor's song, a dance song, suggest the message of the

SLEEP, BABY, SLEEP

2. *Sleep, baby, sleep ! The large stars are the sheep.*
   The little ones, the lambs, I guess,
   The gentle moon, the shepherdess,
   Sleep, baby, sleep ! Sleep, baby, sleep !

[7] "Ah! Vous dirai-je Maman." Odyssey Y-30289.

words? How well does it do it? The first question stimulates analysis and the second a value judgment. Analyze "Sleep, Baby, Sleep" to find how the relative instance or absence of fast, slow, note values, range, dynamics, form, repetition, contrast, climax, release, and other aspects affect the communication of the song's message.

Teaching Rote Songs

Selecting Songs for Rote Teaching

When one tries to describe the teaching of rote songs it will be found that there are almost as many approaches as there are songs. Many short songs can be taught as complete songs rather than in sections. However, one of the easiest types to begin with is the song which calls for an answer. "John the Rabbit" is one in which children reply, singing the words "Yes, ma'am." "Old MacDonald" is another. Children want to sing "Ee-i-ee-i-o" while the teacher sings the rest of it.

OLD MACDONALD

American Song

After the children have learned to sing the three-pitch "Ee-i-ee-i-o" part, the teacher may suggest that they learn the one-pitch "Here a chick, there a chick, ev'rywhere a chick chick" section. Soon part of the class can sing the first two measures, "Old MacDonald had a farm," and another part can sing "Ee-i-ee-i-o"—and everyone will sing "Here a chick, etc." As the learning progresses, the teacher will ask questions which assist the children in reviewing or learning the words. "What did Old MacDonald have?" (A farm) "Sing it: Old MacDonald had a farm." (They sing.) "What did he have on his farm?" (He had some chicks.) "Sing that part." (They sing.) "Where were those chicks?" (A chick chick here and a chick chick there.) "Sing it." Soon the entire song can be sung by the class. It is always fun—and it adds variety—to have different groups sing different parts. "Girls, you sing the parts about Old MacDonald and what he had on his farm. Boys, you sing 'Ee-i-ee-i-o.' All of you sing the 'chick chick' parts." Sometimes all the girls with red dresses can sing a part, or all children with brown eyes or white shoes; this adds to the pleasure of the occasion.

Young children will react in individual ways. Some may want to begin singing too soon, before they have listened to what they are to sing; there must be an understanding that they are to listen carefully "before their turn comes." Some may not sing; they need to listen longer, or their interest needs to be further stirred. Most of them will want to contribute actively as soon as possible; this is why songs with easy answering parts or parts suggesting simple physical responses are enjoyed and usually learned rather quickly. The logical procedure is to always work from the easiest parts first.

The echo-type song is one in which children sing parts which repeat pitch for pitch what the teacher has sung. "Are You Sleeping?" is one of this type. Every measure of this song is followed by an exact repetition. Thus the teacher presents it as a complete song first, then eventually asks the class to sing each part in imitation. Signals are developed that indicate the teacher's turn to sing and the children's turn. "Old Texas" can be sung in the same general way; six-year-olds who can sing on pitch will perform it well. "Follow On" is an echo song for older children. When they have learned the song, some of the children will sing with the teacher, and ultimately the class can be divided into two groups, one of which will sing the teacher's part.

FOLLOW ON!

Repetitious songs are easily taught by rote. "A-Tisket, A-Tasket" is a young children's song centered about the 5–3–6–5 tone pattern. Its sing-song repetitiveness makes it easy for children to learn. Other songs of this type include "Tideo," "Rig-A-Jig-Jig," "Pick a Bale of Cotton," "Hole in the Bucket," and "Standin' in the Need of Prayer." "Trampin'" is also an example.

After the teacher introduces "Trampin'" by singing it all the way through, the children may begin entering on the chorus part, "Tryin' to make heaven my home." In reviewing the words and meaning of the song the teacher may ask, "What is the singer doing?" (trampin') "What does that mean?" "What is he trying to do?" "Has he ever been to heaven?" "What has he been told about it?" Later on, a child or group of children will sing the teacher's solo part, with everyone singing the chorus. "Trampin'" is a call and response song; "Swing Low, Sweet Chariot" is another of this type for older children.

TRAMPIN'

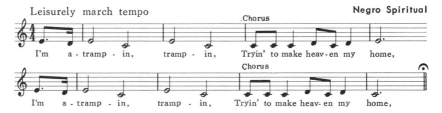

I've nev-er been to heav-en but I've___ been told,

Tryin' to make heav-en my home, That the streets up there are

paved___ with gold; Tryin' to make heav-en my home. D.

Songs such as "O Tannenbaum" and "Lightly Row" which have
phrase organization of *a a b a,* and other songs of longer length than these
are commonly taught by phrase-echoing. The teacher sings the song or
plays a recording of it, discusses its meaning with the children, and then
sings the first phrase; the children echo this. The teacher sings the second
phrase; the children imitate this also. Then the children are asked to sing
both phrases, and they do.

The teacher next sings the *b* phrase, which seems more difficult because
it is different; the children echo this. The process continues, phrase by
phrase until the song is learned. More complex songs may require a
combination of these different approaches. Teachers need to study each
song, analyze each thoroughly, then plan the best strategy for learning the
particular melody.

**Music
Concepts
and Rote
Teaching**

While rote singing is a necessary step in musical growth—and it is a
honored procedure from the standpoint of the history of man—if teacher
go no farther than this type of teaching, the result can be only a form of
music illiteracy. Phyllis E. Dorman writes, "There is a certain dignity and
logic in the simplest song. A song, any song, makes use of the same tools
present in the most complicated of the musical classics. Every element is
there: rhythm, melody, form, tonality, texture, dynamics, color, and
aesthetics. Songs should be used to teach musical concepts." [8] She recom-
mends that *music* be taught instead of only songs.

Although singing of rote songs may take place at any level and at any
age, more of this type of learning is necessarily used with very young
children who can do little or no reading of notation. However, every song
contains elements of music the teacher can use in some way to prepare for
or begin work with understanding music and learning about notation. The
following can be considered steps in teaching young children rote songs
keeping music concepts in mind while doing so.

Establishing the Pitch Because the range of any song is a crucial
matter, the teacher *must* establish the key and the beginning pitch acc

[8] Phyllis E. Dorman, "A Protest Against Musical Illiteracy," *Music Educato
Journal,* November 1967, p. 99.

rately. This means using pitchpipe, bells, Autoharp, piano, or some other reliable instrument. At any level of instruction the teacher should hum the tonic chord (1–3–5–3–1; *do mi so mi do*) or play it on the bells. In keys such as D, E♭, E, F, G, and A♭ the low 5 (5₁) can be sung or played to further reinforce the key feeling (1–3–5–3–1–5–5₁; *do mi so mi do so₁ do.*). In minor keys this process begins on *la,* the sixth step of the major scale according to the key signature. Older children should be able to do this after the teacher gives them the key note; it is an ear training experience and it is good to involve the class in establishing the pitch. In this process concepts of pitch, tone pattern, and key feeling are being nurtured.

Motivating Interest   There are many ways to motivate interest in songs. Sometimes the teacher announces the title and tells briefly with what it is concerned. Sometimes it is all a surprise—the children listen to the songs to find out what it is about. It is wise to take a little time for this. Pictures may help. After the teacher sings the song the children may be asked what its story or message is. A series of questions illustrated earlier may then follow.

Beat and Meter   The teacher might walk quietly in place to the beat while singing the song again as the children do likewise or imitate walking with creative adaptations, such as with the hands in the air, fingers on desks, or silently clapping hands. Accents may call attention to the meter, whether or not children understand what meter is at the earliest levels.

Phrase   As the teacher sings the song again, the phrase order can be stressed. For young children, the teacher may ask them to stand and imitate—move arms to depict a phrase ⌒ , step the beat while turning the body, reverse directions for a contrasting phrase, hold up a finger for phrase one, add a finger for each subsequent phrase, and so on. Some of this can be done with older children; however, those with good music backgrounds can sense the phrase order by listening, using their better-developed tonal memory. Logical questions to ask include, "How many phrases did you hear?" "Are there any that are the same?" "Similar?" "Different?" "Which ones?"

Melodic Direction: Contour   The teacher can ask the children to show by their hand positions what they think is the up and down direction of the melody. In a later lesson their analysis can give them answers to questions regarding steps and skips in the melody line and if certain phrases conclude up or down in pitch.

Independent Singing   After the children have heard a song several times with this kind of analytical guidance, they should sing it without the teacher's voice. The teacher can assist by high and low hand positions, but will join in singing only if absolutely necessary. A goal is to assure the children's independence of both the teacher's voice and the piano. Also, teachers cannot listen to children's singing if they too are singing.

Texture   The next time the children sing the song, the teacher may
use accompanying instruments to provide different textures. If the piano
sounds exactly the same as the melody the children sing, it is sounding only
the melody in unison with their voices. It is an example of *monophony*.
If the Autoharp or guitar sounds a chordal accompaniment which supports
the melody, there is *homophony,* a quite different texture. "Did it sound
the same or different this time?" "What made it sound different?" comprise a way to begin a discussion of texture even though the children may
not know the adult terminology. Different types of accompaniments can
be discussed, described, analyzed, and evaluated for their suitability for
the melody. Two or more melodic lines sounding at once constitute
polyphony.

Tone Quality   Tone qualities of voices and of accompanying instruments can be evaluated in terms of their suitability to express the meaning
of the song or in terms of beauty.

Dynamics   The children can be encouraged to sing the song at different dynamic levels—loud, soft, crescendo, decrescendo, with accents
and so on. They should determine the dynamics most suited to the song
thus learning about interpretation and aesthetic discrimination.

Thus the teaching of rote songs becomes "rote-note" teaching because
it can expand children's music concepts to the place when what they already have sensed and worked with is described in notation which, after
all, is only a kind of picture-description of the melody.

Finding the Keynote in Major Tonalities   This is necessary to enable
the teacher and children to establish the pitch and key feeling (tonality) of
a song.   The ways to find the keynote (home tone) from key signatures are:

1. The sharp farthest to the right is scale tone 7 or *ti*. Count up to 8 or *do*
   or down to 1 or *do*. The letter name of 8 or 1 is the name of the key.
2. The flat farthest to the right is scale tone 4 or *fa*. Count down to 1 or up
   to 8; the letter name of 8 or 1 is the name of the key. A quicker way for
   key signatures containing two or more flats is: the next-to-the-last flat on
   the right *is* the keynote.

Songs in major tonalities ordinarily end on 1, 3, or 5.

Finding the Key in Minor Tonalities

1. Find the major tonality indicated by the key signature.
2. Find the sixth degree of the major scale (6 or *la*). This note is the keynote
   of the relative minor tonality.

Songs in minor usually end on *la,* and rarely on *do* or *mi*.

Learn the song thoroughly before attempting to teach it.

Have the children participate actively in some way as soon as possible.

Don't plan too much to do with the same song on the same day; this can
become boring.

Possible activities for children to do while they listen to a teacher intro-duce a new rote song by singing it to them include:

Clapping hands (tips of fingers) soundlessly to the beat;

Clapping hands soundlessly to the rhythm of the words or melody;

Standing in place and trying to discern phrases by making heart-shaped movements with the hands and arms;

Conducting the meter or determining the meter by trying to conduct it;

Determining whether the music swings in two's or three's;

Acting out pitch levels and/or melodic contour with hands and arms;

Analyzing what is heard in terms of scalewise and skipwise patterns;

Listening for outstanding rhythm patterns;

Listening for outstanding tone patterns.

Take breaths generally at the end of phrases. People do not "break a phrase" by taking a breath during it when speaking; neither should this be done when singing. Periods, commas, and semicolons often point out the proper places to breathe.

Encourage children to suggest ways for better interpretation of the song.

Seeing What
We Hear

The above discussion has considered the teaching of songs by means of guided repetitions. The teacher's plans lead from purely rote singing to understanding music concepts that help children toward reading notation. Some activities that build notational concepts include having children:

1. Compare the notation of two familiar songs of the same tempo, one which uses many eighth and sixteenth notes and another which has whole notes, half notes, and quarter notes. Guide them to discover that the "whiteness" of notation relates to long note duration and the "blackness" of notation relates to short note duration.

2. Look for familiar rhythm patterns and note patterns in the notation of selected songs.

3. Look at the notation of phrases of known songs to find out that when phrases sound the same they look the same, and when they sound different, they look different.

4. Watch the notated melody line and follow it on the page with an index finger, all the while relating high and low in pitch with high and low on the staff.

5. Relate the keyboard to notation by providing easy songs to play on the bells by number, by the note names stamped on the bars, and eventually by notation.

Using
Recordings
of Songs

Recordings can be substituted for teachers' voices in teaching songs. Children learn some songs from recordings they play at home, and from radio and television programs. Singing commercials are frequently learned also. However, when recordings are used, many of the flexible techniques suggested above cannot be employed.

The children must sing softly in order to hear the recording. The volume of the record player can be gradually turned down as the children learn a song so that they will become increasingly independent of the recording. A test to determine how well the children have learned a song is to have them begin singing with the recording, then lift up the needle and have them continue without its help.

It is well to emphasize teaching the words when songs are learned by rote from recordings; they are frequently written on the chalkboard. Another technique, useful as a later step in the learning process, is to have small groups of children, no more than six, stand by the record player and sing with it while the remainder of the class listens to evaluate their effort constructively and awaits their turn at doing the same thing.

The recordings that accompany the series books as well as some other song books can be of genuine value in teaching songs. They usually provide worthy examples for children to hear and imitate: they often bring to the classroom fascinating instrumental accompaniments that could be provided in no other way. They aid the teacher who studies them even though not using them in the classroom, because with their assistance songs are learned correctly, both rhythmically and melodically. Beginning teachers should study the recordings that accompany the books they are to use in their classrooms. Before the fall term begins, if they hear these over a period of days they will have absorbed a repertoire of songs they need to know, and will have saved time by not having to pick out each song on a keyboard instrument and learn it without a model to follow. When a child tends the record player the teacher is free to move about the room to listen to individual voices and to direct class activities. The teacher can stop singing and listen to the children—something every teacher of music needs to do. No matter how well qualified a music specialist may be, there are times when a recording will provide an effective way to teach some songs. However, recordings cannot completely take the place of the teacher's voice; younger children sometimes find it difficult to understand the diction of voices strange to them. In all of the grades, a machine is no substitute for the personality of a teacher who sings.

The Piano and Other Voice Substitutes

The piano or bells may be substituted for the voice or recording by teachers who lack confidence in their singing voices and do not have recordings of songs they need to teach. Words for such songs may be learned by rote or written on the chalkboard. The teacher will then play the melody of the song. This may be repeated while the children do several of the activities of the rote singing process already described in this chapter, the instrument thus taking the place of the voice or recording. For a song of some length the phrase method may be desirable. After the playing of the entire song, the melody of the first phrase will be played; the children will mouth the words silently as it is played again. Then the children may sing this phrase with the piano; and next, sing without its support. This can be continued throughout the remaining phrase, combining some of them along the way. As the song is learned, the support of the instrument is gradually withdrawn to gain independence from it. A child in the class may be a teacher's assistant by singing to the class phrases or entire songs learned from the teacher's playing the piano, bells, or recorder.

Although it is highly desirable to have a piano available, the instrument is not essential to teach or to accompany songs. In a normal situation where the teacher sings, the piano has its greatest use at the end of the learning process. A song may be introduced by playing it on the piano in a simple manner. Since younger children find it difficult to hear a melody when an elaborate accompaniment is played, a simple accompaniment that permits the melody to predominate distinctly is the most effective style of playing. Most of the time the piano has little use, for two reasons: (1) when the teacher is playing the piano the children cannot be heard well enough to determine if each child is singing correctly, and (2) the teacher is in a stationary position and is unable to move through the class to hear and to help children with their problems. Another reason for not using the piano much of the time is that if it is used constantly the children cannot sing independently of it, and may become semihelpless in its absence. However, after a song has been learned, the addition of a piano accompaniment can be a thrilling and satisfying experience, adding greatly to the musical effect of the performance.

The piano is an important means of enrichment and a tool for developing many music concepts. Thus, it has its rightful place in the well-equipped classroom, but not as a dominating instrument.

Creating Songs

Teachers at all elementary levels are alert to children's spontaneous creating of songs and calls. They notate or tape-record those believed to be of value to the child or to the class so they can be saved for later use.

Jumping-rope verses and nursery rhymes can be set to music; original songs from the playground can be taken indoors.

One sunny morning a little girl in the first grade was holding her teacher's hand as she left the building to go to directed play. Deeply affected by the beauty of the day, she sang:

A BEAUTIFUL DAY

First Grade, Washington School
Eugene, Oregon

Oh what a won-der-ful day, Oh what a won-der-ful day! Oh what a beau-ti-ful day!

The teacher asked the child to repeat her song and they sang it together s
that they could remember it when they returned to the classroom and shar
it with the others. Another teacher of a first-grade group had just con
cluded a reading lesson in which children had learned new words. It wa
shortly before lunch, and the children suddenly related the new words t
their interest in food:

    1. One   two   three,   come eat   with   me.
    2. Blue   and   red,   will we   be   fed?

The above examples illustrate the point that creating simple songs is a
ability children possess and one that grows under the guidance of capabl
teachers. It is only a short step from spontaneous creative activity to th
point where a teacher says of a well-known poem, "Let's sing it toda
instead of speaking it," and the setting of poetry to music becomes
classroom activity.

The classroom teacher is in the most strategic position to establish a
environment in which children can create music. This teacher knows th
interests of the children and has most to do with encouraging creativ
responses as normal aspects of the entire school day. Children ar
normally creative, and when they find they have the ability and skill t
compose simple songs or instrumental pieces, they will frequently do thi
at home as a play activity, bringing their compositions to school.

Short verse that has a clearly defined rhythm should be selected. As
background for this activity children should have sung many short poem
and simple word rhythms. The words are spoken by the children in
regular beat pattern set by the teacher. The teacher establishes key feelin
by chording the familiar I V₇ I sequence in a key of his choice, and ma
sing the first word of the poem, thus suggesting to the children the be
ginning note of the song-to-be. While the teacher beats time (it is basi
to the method that the rhythm never be interrupted) individual childre
are asked to sing the poem. The other children may be urged to continu
to speak the words softly while they listen to the song being born. Th
rhythm is stressed, the assumption being that if the rhythm is maintaine
a melody will appear from each child which can be as spontaneous an
uninhibited as speech. It is further assumed that it is as natural for childre
to have many musical ideas as it is for them to have many ideas expresse
in language. This approach to song creation can be effective on any lev
and is believed by some to possess virtues that are superior, from the stan
point of creativeness, to the phrase approach, which will be described late
If children experience this type of creative expression, which keeps th
rhythmic flow proceeding without interruption, there might be fewer adu
musicians who lack a feeling for rhythmic consistency.

Instruments such as the bells and piano are sometimes of aid i
stimulating the creative process. A teacher used four tone bars from a se

of resonator bells with a first-grade class. The children were interested in new shoes, which several of them wore that day, and with the aid of the four tones they created a song on the subject called "New Shoes," which they also learned to play on the bells. Its repetitious words are typical of first-grade children. This song was sung throughout the term whenever one of the children came to school with new shoes.

NEW SHOES

Laboratory School
University of Wisconsin
Milwaukee

Melodies without words are created by children who have opportunities to experiment with tuned water bottles, xylophones, bells, piano, recorder-type instruments, and the instruments of the band and orchestra.

Teachers save worthy compositions by writing them down in music notation. If a teacher has had ear training, he or she can "take dictation" when the children create a song—that is, associate at once the tones with degrees of the scale. For instance, several song examples in this chapter are based on the same note pattern—the familiar 1–3–5 chord or the *tonic* chord. The recognition of this fact makes notating such songs a simple matter. Since few classroom teachers have had much of this kind of training, most of them rely on other means. For example, the teacher who heard Ann sing "A Beautiful Day" sang it with her so that when she returned to the classroom she could find the song on the bells or piano. To help remember the melody of a child's song, the inexperienced teacher can invent pictorial ways to record melodies by such means as drawing a continuous or a broken line showing the directions of the pitches and by drawing short and long dashes to represent comparative note values. Some teachers write melodies with numerals or syllables and determine the notation later. Some use tape recorders and "take it off" the tape later. Others have the children help them remember the song until a special music teacher or another classroom teacher has time to help notate it. Some children in the intermediate grades can be of help. There is always a way to notate these songs, and any teacher who tries will improve in skill with practice.

An activity that deserves respect is adding original verses to songs. When children do this, they must feel the fundamental rhythm and accommodate words and melody to this rhythm. It is good preparation for later activities in which poems are set to music. Words must be set music so that accents we use naturally in speech fall on musically-accente beats. For example, "the" and "a" are normally unimportant words; the will be sung on parts of the measure of little rhythmic importance—almo never on accented parts of the measure or notes of long duration, since th would give them emphasis to which they are not entitled.

As soon as children understand and can use notation, the son creating process in the classroom should include the notating of the so on the chalkboard or a transparency where everyone can participate some degree in seeing that it is written in a manner that correctly pictur what was created. Also, when good songs are notated in or transposed keys that children find easy to use when playing recorder-type instrument such songs may be duplicated and given to the children. When childr take such songs home to play for their parents on these instruments or the piano, they are learning about music notation as a by-product of the creative activity.

A SUNSHINY DAY

Second Gra
Eliot Scho
Portland, Oreg

When children can compose poetry and songs, the writing of simp operettas is not beyond the possibilities of the intermediate grades. A other opportunity is more teaching about musical form. Since the for of most of the songs children compose is simple in structure, often bei a question-and-answer type with repeated phrases, teachers can gui children to discover elements of form in music by having them exami their own compositions. To analyze song form is interesting to childr when it concerns a song they have written.

The procedure many teachers follow when they guide children in gro song writing in grades three and above is as follows:

1. Choose words that are simple, have steady rhythmic flow, and are unde stood by children.
2. Write the words on the chalkboard under the staff. Discuss the meaning the words, seeking ideas that will influence the song writing. Such ide will include mood and anything that may reflect descending or ascendi pitch.

3. Have the class read the words in unison so that a definite rhythm is established. Use clapping or stepping if necessary. The most heavily accented words or word syllables can be underlined. Measure bars can be drawn before (to the left of) these words or word syllables.

4. If this activity is comparatively new to the children, sound the tonic chord by singing 1 3 5 3 1 (do-mi-sol-mi-do), or by playing it on Autoharp or piano. If these instruments are used, it is better to play the chord sequence I V₇ I to establish a definite key feeling. If the children are experienced in song writing, this step is not necessary because they "hear with their inner ears" what they create, and the arbitrary setting of a key may interfere with the creative process.

5. Ask for suggestions to start the song. There are several approaches. In the earliest stages of learning to compose, a teacher may have all or part of the first phrase written and ask the class to finish that section of the song. This can be done by the class *thinking* what the rest of the song might be (after singing the first part several times) and finally singing it, the teacher accepting the majority opinion. Soon individuals will have melodic suggestions to offer, and the process becomes one of both group and individual contribution. The group is the controlling force, however, and exercises discrimination in choosing between versions of parts of the song that are volunteered by individuals. The composition generally proceeds phrase by phrase with the group singing frequently from the beginning of the song. The teacher notates the song as it grows in length. Those teachers who can take musical dictation will write stemless notes on the staff. Since it is necessary to proceed with rapidity to avoid lagging interest, these are usually little lines (/) instead of filled out notes (●). Some teachers will prefer to use numerals or syllables and "figure" from these. Others will use the keyboard directly, and still others will employ lines on the chalkboard or on a transparency that indicate high and low in pitch and tonal duration. Some may tape the song and complete the notation later.

6. Have the class decide what the meter signature is. If the bar lines have not already been placed, they can be written before the heavily accented notes. Sometimes the song will need to be transposed to a more suitable key for the voices. The key signature will be determined, as will note values. Stems, flags, beams, and dots will be added wherever necessary.

7. Autoharp or piano chords can be added as desired.

8. The children can now evaluate their song. Does it reflect the meaning of the words suitably? Does it communicate the mood desired? Can the song be improved? Is it notated correctly?

9. If the song is of good quality, it should be saved by placing it in a class book. If it is in a key in which children can play recorder-type instruments, reproduce it on a duplicating machine so that the children may use notation at home in playing the song for their parents.

The goal of this group work is to develop the ability of individuals to compose music—for each child to write songs with the same ease as children paint pictures.

When children write their own music, they are personally concerned

with melody, form, tempo, dynamics, and correct notation. They a
further concerned with tension and release, repetition and contrast, rang
and how the tones move. Creating songs is a superior means of acquirin
music concepts.

Analyzing Melodies

When children analyze melodies, they should seek answers to such que
tions as:

How do tones move? (scalewise, stepwise, repeated tones)
What is the phrase arrangement?
What is the type of tonal organization? (major, minor, modal, pentatoni
tone row, ethnic scale, etc.)
What is the range?
Is there evidence of tension and release? If so, how is this achieved?
Is there evidence of a climax? If so, how is this achieved?
Are there other significant aspects? (such as rhythm patterns, tone patterr
dynamics, sequence).

Some Activities With Songs

There are numerous activities possible with songs. Among them are:

1. Move in time with the beat by motions such as clapping, swinging, tappin
   rocking, skipping, and jumping.
2. Walk on the beat while standing in place or moving in a circle formatio
3. Walk to the beat anywhere in the room, but with directions given su
   as "Do not touch or bump anyone," and "Walk in the same gener
   direction."
4. While walking to the beat of the song, do things such as clapping, slowi
   down, and speeding up.
5. Clap the rhythm of the melody.
6. Clap the rhythm of the melody while walking the beat.
7. Clap the beat while stepping the melody. (The song should be very sl
   and simple.)
8. Think the melody and clap it while stepping the beat.
9. Sing the first phrase; do "inner hearing" with phrase two; sing phrase thr
   do "inner hearing" with phrase four, except for singing the last pitch
   the song. Try this while walking the beat.
10. Establish the pitch and tempo. Clap the beat, think the song with "inn
    hearing," then sing only the final word.
11. The teacher or student leaders turn the singing on and off; the childr
    try to keep the rhythm steady so that they can come in at the same pla
    in the song.

12. The children stand in a circle. As they sing an object is passed from hand to hand on the beat. Next, it is passed on the first word of each phrase. (Maybe two objects can be used, one for the beat and one for the phrase.)

13. A one-measure rhythm pattern can be selected from the song, or created, to be sounded throughout the song as an ostinato while the children sing that song.

14. If the song is pentatonic, select a phrase from the song which a group can sing repeatedly while the rest of the class sings the song.

15. If the song is pentatonic, try it as a round.

16. If any two pentatonic songs are in the same meter and have the same number of measures, they can be sung at one time as "partner songs."

17. Have the children conduct the song by using the appropriate metrical beat pattern.

18. Act out pitch levels and/or the melodic contour with hands and arms.

19. Have the class analyze the melody in terms of scalewise and skipwise pitch movements.

20. Have the class identify any outstanding rhythm patterns and tonal patterns.

21. Determine whether the music swings in two's or three's.

Additional Suggestions for Lesson Plans

RHYTHM-RELATED EXPERIENCES

Rhythm pattern.

Select words or word-groups which occur in the text of a song or which reflect ideas associated with the song. By speaking them, discern their rhythm patterns. Select an appropriate percussion instrument and play one or more of the patterns throughout the song as an accompaniment.

Tonal memory.

To develop tonal memory in the "inner ear," the teacher or a child claps hands or plays a percussion instrument in the melody rhythm of a song that is familiar to the class. The game is to identify the song from hearing its rhythm. With very young children, ask them to choose between two or three known songs. Older children can vary the game by having each child in turn perform a different melody rhythm for the class to identify.

Combining melody rhythms.

Experiment with combining the melody rhythms of two songs. Example: "Are You Sleeping?" and "Row Your Boat," even though they are in different meters, ¾ and ⅝. Clap or play the rhythm of one melody at the same time as that of the other. At first teachers select well-known melodies having the same meters or combinable ones such as the above. Songs of different meters hav-

Tonal memory.
Rhythmic notation.

ing the same tempo for experimentation with
polymetrics are selected later.

Game: The children tap a steady beat while the
teacher plays or sings a short tune to the beat.
The tune can be one the children know, or it can
be improvised by the teacher. The game is for
the children to remember the tune and write it
in rhythmic notation. A third grade wrote this
teacher-improvised melody rhythm correctly:

Rhythm pattern.
Ostinato.

Ask children to devise a notated rhythm pattern
to use as an ostinato throughout a familiar song.
Let them evaluate its degree of success as they
listen to a few perform it with appropriate percussion instruments. Then ask them to clap it
while they sing the song. (They will be performing two rhythms at one time.) Two or three suggested ostinati might be combined and the result
evaluated by the class. The teacher should use a
tape recorder whenever this assists the evaluation.

Changing meter.

Experiment with well-known songs to find answers
to questions such as "What would it sound like if
¼ became ¢ in this song?" "If slow ⁶⁄₈ became
fast ⁶⁄₈?" "If ¾ became ³⁄₈?" "Can we change this
song from ¼ meter to ¾?" "How?"

Changing meter.

Experiment with writing a familiar song in a number of different meters, including some less common ones such as ⁵⁄₄ and ⁷⁄₈.

Changing note values and
meters, note reading.

Ask children to alter familiar songs of their choice
by changing note values and meters. Write them
on a transparency and have the class sing them as
a fun experience in note reading.

ABA form.
Improvising a dance.

This experience with form is for the primary level.
The song "Shoo Fly," commonly found in music
textbooks, is a good one to improvise a dance for,
and in doing so to enact ABA form. It might go
like this:

Shoo, fly, don't bother me,
Shoo, fly, don't bother me,
Shoo, fly, don't bother me,
For I belong to nobody.

(Walk in a circle to the
right as the class sings.)

I feel, I feel, I feel,
I feel like a morning star,
I feel, I feel, I feel,
I feel like a morning star.

*(Walk to the center of the
circle)*
*(Walk backwards from the center
to form the circle again.)*

Shoo, fly, don't bother me,
Shoo, fly, don't bother me,
Shoo, fly, don't bother me,
For I belong to nobody.

*(Walk in a circle to the right
as the singing continues.)*

The above dance is perhaps one of the most simple possible for the song. The teacher will ask questions that lead to the children's generalization, "When the music sounds the same again, we make the same motion," and the observations, "The song is different in the middle," and "If the song were drawn on the chalkboard, it might look like this."

$$\bigcirc \qquad \square \qquad \bigcirc$$

$$\text{(A)} \qquad \text{(B)} \qquad \text{(A)}$$

There are many other ways to emphasize ABA form such as this. For example, children could slap thighs for A and clap for B; they might draw something to represent A, and something different to represent B. The "game" is to show the difference between A and B in some interesting way. (There are many similar songs.)

Traditional dances.

Songs for specific dances can be useful when teaching those dances. Examples: "Weggis Song" for the schottische; "Buffalo Gals" for the polka, "Sweet Nightingale" (in *Singing With Children*) for the mazurka. The indexes of the music text books, books concerning dance, and some song collections will guide the teacher to song-dance relationships and the dance directions. These dances are generally for older children. Refer to pp. 121–123.

Ethnic dances.

Many songs and dances are closely related as they are taught and performed in conjunction with each other. Here is an example from the Maori people of New Zealand, "Me He Manu Rere."

ME HE MANU RERE

Contributed by Cheryl Lau

Me he ma - nu re - re a - hau e,
Kei te mo - e to ti - na - na,

Ku - a re - re ki to mo - e - nga,
Kei te o - ho te wai - ru - a,

Ki te a - whi to ti - na - na,
Kei te ho - tu te ma - na - wa,

E te tau ta - hu - ri mai.
E te tau ta - hu - ri mai.

VERSE 1

4 times

Me he manu rere ahau e, 1-4

3 Times

Kua rere ki to moenga, 5-8

Turn a full clockwise
circle in 6 steps

Ki te awhi to tinana, 9-12

E te tau tahuri mai. 13-16

VERSE 2

Kei te moe to tinana, 1-4

Fists move back and forth
6 times in time to music

right left
right left
right left

Kei te oho te wairua, 5-8

Kei te hotu te manawa, 9-12

E te tau tahuri mai. 13-16

*Me he manu rere ahau e,
Kua rere ki to moenga,
Ki te awhi to tinana,
E te tau tahuri mai.*

*Kei te moe to tinana,
Kei te oho te wairua
Kei te hotu te manawa,
E te tau tahuri mai.*

*Had I the wings of a bird,
To your side I would fly,
To hold you there and see you,
Please turn to me.*

*Though you are enchained,
Yet my spirit is free to roam,
My heart yearns for you,
Please turn to me.*

Action songs or chanted songs accompanied by simple steps and gestures are developed from the Maori term *waiata kori*, or dance song. The actions, which are completely complementary to the words and music, mirror and often intensify the meaning conveyed by the song. The song merits serious study, for it is a reflection of the modern Maori culture. It typifies the harmonious blending of the old and new; it embodies the music and poetry which is the soul of the race, and it expresses pride and hope for the Maori future.

PITCH DISCRIMINATION

Pitch.

Game: Children turn their backs to the teacher, identify the sound producer, and tell which pitch of two sounded is high or low. Later, ask them to

Vocal imitation.

High, low.

High, low.

High, low.

High, low.

match the pitch with their voices *if the pitch is in their normal singing range.*

Ask children to imitate vocally by singing, whistling, or other mouth sounds, the sounds of birds, animals, musical instruments, train whistles, auto horns, and other environmental sounds.

Game: The teacher of young children groups simple instruments or other pitch producers according to high and low in pitch. The children (one, two, or three at a time) experiment with them and compare their high and low sounds. Later the teacher mixes the sound producers and the children are asked to group them into those that produce high pitches and those that produce low pitches.

Have children relate high and low in pitch to relative high-low positions of the body and of objects. Reach high and low in relation to obvious high and low pitches. Use body movements, marks on a chalkboard, a glockenturm (a German bell-type instrument that is played vertically and shows visually the relationship of keyboard and staff), step bells, standard bell sets placed in vertical position with large bars down. Find or discover high-low in speaking voices, bars on resonator bells, and different sized drums. Work toward such generalizations as "the larger the sound producer, the lower the pitch."

Game: Use three pitches, middle C, the octave above, and the G in between. When the children hear the highest pitch, they place their hands over their heads; when they hear the middle pitch, they place their hands in front of them; when they hear middle C, they place their hands on their thighs (or hips, if standing). Having eyes closed at times will permit the teacher to find out if some are imitating others or if they are hearing the pitches. Another approach is to let the children freely dramatize the pitches to reflect high and low physically.

The teacher produces a pitched sound (on anything) in medium range, and repeats it at intervals so the children can remember it. They then explore the room to find objects that will produce (1) a lower sound, then (2) a higher sound. After this, "What can you do to change the kind of sound you made?"

*Rhythm of words
related to the minor
third interval, high,
low.*

Establish the rhythm of selected words. Then relate these to the minor third in a vocal range comfortable for the child.

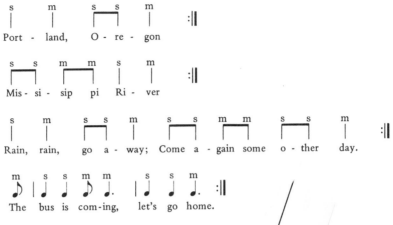

s	m	s	s	m	
Port -	land,	O -	re -	gon	:‖

| s | s | m | m | s | m | |
| Mis - | si - | sip | pi | Ri - | ver | :‖ |

| s | m | s | s | m | s | s | m | m | s | s | m | |
| Rain, | rain, | go | a - | way; | Come | a - | gain | some | o - | ther | day. | :‖ |

| m | s | s | m | m | s | s | m | |
| The | bus | is | com-ing, | | let's | go | home. | :‖ |

Melodic contour.

Use parts of exempla_____ _____iscover that pitches can move in three _____, up, down, or stay the same. Relate _____ _____ir to tension, climax, and release in mel _____ _____s. "I Love the Moun-tains" is an exa_____ _____e "Riddle Song" and "Jacob's Ladder" _____ _____ *With Children.* Some songs are obviou_____ _____ear in this than others, and the teacher _____ _____ the best examples.

Improvised question-and-answer.

Use tonal conve_____ _____n which the teacher sings questions, comme_____ directions to which the chil-dren improvise singing replies. They may use any pitch they like. Examples:

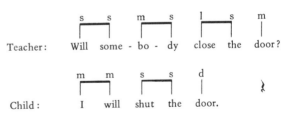

| | s | s | m | s | l | s | m | |
| Teacher: | Will | some - | bo - | dy | close | the | door? |

| | m | m | s | s | d | | |
| Child: | I | will | shut | the | door. | ⸯ |

Hand signs for so, mi.

Have children first clap hands on hearing *so* (5), and slap thighs upon hearing *mi* (3). The teacher sings various combinations of the two pitches; the children listen, then respond by singing and the above body responses. Later, have them hold palms together for *so* and hold palms down for *mi* (no clapping or slapping). Later, relate the tonal patterns sung to the *ti-ti tahs* and to the abbreviated notation:

"Children's chant"
5–3–6–5–3.

Use this tone pattern in many creative combinations. Show it on the staff as a picture of what is sung. Expand the activities used with *so-mi* to include *la* (6).

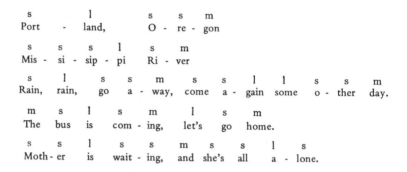

s	l		s	s	m
Port	- land,		O -	re -	gon

s	s	s	l	s	m
Mis -	si -	sip -	pi	Ri -	ver

s	l	s	s	m	s	s	l	l	s	s	m
Rain,	rain,	go	a -	way,	come	a -	gain	some	o -	ther	day.

m	s	l	s	m	l	s	m
The	bus	is	com -	ing,	let's	go	home.

s	s	l	s	s	m	s	s	l	s
Moth -	er	is	wait -	ing,	and	she's	all	a -	lone.

Hand sign for la.

Teach the hand sign for *la* and ask the children to sing with the three signs they now know (*so, mi,* and *la*). Game: The teacher makes hand signs for some sequence of the three pitches. The children watch, think silently what the pitches will sound like, then at the teacher's signal, sing what signs they observed, first in syllables, then with the *ti-ti ta's.*

Name songs.

Using bars CDE GA from a set of resonator bells, have each child play a tune representing the rhythm of his name.

A	G	E	C
Keith	By -	ing -	ton

or

C	E	D	C
Keith	By -	ing -	ton

Then sing the name with the words, syllables, letter names, and the *ti-ti ta's.*

Home tone.

The teacher sounds the chord sequence that centers the children's hearing on the home tone: I V$_7$ I, using Autoharp, guitar, or piano. The class may also sing the scale demanded by these chords, and the teacher will again center attention on the home tone (*do* or 1). Next the teacher plays on piano, bells, small wind instrument, or sings well-known melodies such as "Mary Had a Little Lamb," omitting *do* each time it appears. The class is to sing every *do* omitted by the teacher. Next, the teacher will sound the tune in a different key so that the class will have the experience of identifying and singing the home tone in other keys.

Ear training.

The teacher sings the child's name in pitches of the common pentatonic scale. The child answers by singing the same pitches in syllables or numbers.

Improvisation.

The teacher plays a repeated drone interval of a perfect fifth on the piano or low-pitched xylophone, metalophone, or cello. After listening to the drone, a child or small group experiments vocally, relating their improvised pitches to the drone. The mood may vary from an Indian dance to a lullaby.

Tonal memory.

The children know a familiar song. They sing it. The game takes place when the teacher gives a prearranged signal during the singing. When the teacher does this, the class does not sing, but continues to *think* the melody silently as it continues in their minds. When another signal is given, the children resume singing. Words, syllables, or numbers can be used. The teacher or a child hums a melody, or sings it with a neutral syllable such as "la" or "loo." The children then try to identify the melody. When it is identified, the entire class may sing it with the leader.

*Hand signs for re
and do.*

Teach these signs; then use scale tones 1,2,3, 5,6 for song-like drills and for the creation of tunes and songs by the children. Eventually show the pitches on the staff to explain, "This is what it looks like when it sounds that way."

Tonal memory.

After giving the pitch of 1 or *do* the teacher makes hand signs in silence. The children remember the signs and sing the signaled pitches. At first the teacher repeats the signs as the children sing, but later does not. (They are to develop memory of pitches without this repetition of signs.)

Improvising endings.

The teacher provides the first two measures of a four-measure phrase. Individual children improvise vocally the final two measures to complete it. Example:

So, mi, do.

Game: The teacher sings at random the pitches of scale tones 5, 3, 1 (*so, mi, do*). Children use hand signs to identify which of the three pitches is sung.

Fa.

The hand sign for scale tone 4 (*fa*) is taught. The teacher sings in syllables or numbers the pitches 1,2,3,4,5,6 in song-like drills. Children make hand signs to match the pitches sung. Later the teacher sings these pitches with *loo* or *la* (neutral syllables) and the children continue to identify the pitches by hand signs.

Tone patterns.

Game-drill: Children sing selected common tone patterns from chalkboard, transparency, magnetic board, or flash card, responding with numbers, syllables, or note names as the teacher requires.

Tone matching.

Game: The class is divided into two teams. Each has an interesting name the children invent. Corners of the room are the four bases of a baseball diamond. A score-keeper is appointed. At first the teacher uses scale tones 1–2–3–4–5 and later increases these to the complete major scale. Short tone patterns that always begin on 1 are played on an instrument. At first there are no skips, only scale lines and repeated tones. After careful listening, the one "at bat" reproduces what was played by singing each pitch accurately. If he or she does this successfully, this person advances to the next base. After three players strike out, the other team goes to bat. Score is kept on the chalkboard. The difficulty is increased as the players' skill grows. A variant of the game adds a flannel or magnetic board on which what was played is notated. Another variant asks that the children respond with syllables or numerals. Still another asks them to respond with hand signs.

Pitches.

Employ the following scale patterns in improvised drills, using a pointer, or hand signs, or notation. The children are to sing in response to the teacher's directions. The major objective is to become familiar with common scale patterns.

$$5 \quad 4 \quad 3 \quad 2 \quad 1$$
$$3 \quad 2 \quad 1 \quad 7_1 \quad 6_1$$
$$6 \quad 5 \quad 4 \quad 3 \quad 2 \quad 1 \quad 7_1 \quad 6_1$$
$$1' \quad 7 \quad 6 \quad 5 \quad 4 \quad 3 \quad 2 \quad 1$$

Pentatonic scale.

Create song-like drills with scale tones 5_1 6_1 1 2 3

5 6. The children can respond with syllables, hand signs, numbers, and the *ti-ti ta's.*

NOTATION OF PITCH

Tonality.

Examine known songs and analyze the melodies to find and notate pitches which form the scales upon which these songs are constructed. They may be major, minor, pentatonic, or modal scales. Assist the students to discover that the final pitch of a song is a fairly reliable clue to the first step of the scale. Example: "Wayfaring Stranger," p. 358. Some students may decide that the scale is D minor while others may find a pentatonic scale with D as the tonic (tonal center).

*Note values and
composing.*

Select a simple poem of four phrases to be set to music. Give the children the first phrase with the pitches written in even note values. The words are placed under the staff. The class changes note values to add rhythmic interest to this first phrase. Then the teacher assigns groups to compose the melody for the other three phrases. The class evaluates the results and suggests changes if these seem necessary.

Modulating melodies.

Challenge the class to learn to read examples of modulating melodies with syllables, numbers, and hand signs. Example:

| d | r | m | f | s | l | s | | d | t | l | t | d | d | | s | f | m | r | | d | r | d |

Atonal melodies.

The teacher writes an example of an atonal melody on chalkboard or transparency. The class is challenged to sing it, using the *fixed do* system in which middle C is always *do.*

SCALES AND THE TONAL CENTER

Scale.

Write the major scale vertically on the chalkboard in numbers or syllables. Game: The class or child sings the pitches to which the teacher points. Make it very easy at first, then increase the difficulty as the children master the relation of the pitches to their position within the scale.

Home tone.

In emphasizing the tonal center or home tone, the teacher sings or plays a melody, but stops before it is complete. The children are to sing the home tone or make up an ending that concludes with the home tone, depending upon what point in the melody the teacher ceases singing or playing.

Major and minor.

Plan so that children experience major and minor tonalities through familiar songs. For example, first sing "Merrily We Roll Along" in a major key, with a chorded accompaniment. Then sing it in minor, again with a chorded accompaniment. Ask the class to describe the differences, and ask them which suits the spirit of the song best. Do the same with "Old Aunt Rhody" ("The Old Grey Goose").

Relative minor.

Analyze "The Erie Canal" to find out why there can be major and minor sections in a song with the key signature unchanged. What kind of minor scale is used? (relative) What are the two relative keys? (F major and D minor) Notate, compare, sing and play these scales. Use the keyboard to see how the two keys are related and can use the same key signature. Try playing the following major and relative minor scales on the bells or piano by ear: C major and A minor; G major and E minor.

Key signatures.

Explore the reasons for key signatures. Play familiar songs with arbitrarily changed key signatures. What is the result? Why are key signatures used by composers? This study can relate to scales.

Pentatonic scale.

Relate the common pentatonic scale to the black keys of keyboard instruments. Then transpose this scale pattern of whole steps and minor thirds to keys that we think of as C, F, and G. Compare the pentatonic scale pattern to the major scale pattern in those keys. After this, find the form of pentatonic scale that reminds us of the natural minor: major scale steps 6–1–2–3–5–6. Use these scales to compose pentatonic songs and tunes. Listen to a recording of pentatonic music such as Bartók's *An Evening in the Village* (Adventures in Music 5, v 2).

Relative minor.

Write major scales in a two-octave range. Find the relative minor scale in each of these and enclose them with bar lines.

Parallel minor.

Parallel scales have the same first pitch (tonic). Write and compare C major and C minor; G major and G minor; F major and F minor. Help the students conclude that these scales, unlike the relative scales, need different key signatures. Ask the students to form their own definitions of relative and parallel scales.

Minor chords.

Relate major and minor scales to major and minor chords by singing and playing the first, third, and fifth steps of each scale. Find parallel and relative chords on the Autoharp. The 15-chord instrument can sound D major and D minor; G major and G minor; F major and D minor; C major and A minor; Bb major and G minor.

Relative minor.

Examine "We Three Kings of Orient Are." Decide whether relative keys or parallel keys are present, and justify your decision.

Parallel minor.

Listen to Bizet's *Farandole* from L'Arlesienne Suite No. 2, AM 6 v. 1. Try to determine whether there are relative or parallel keys present.

Parallel minor.

Sing "Streets of Laredo," p. 320, in major as written except the last verse; sing that in minor. Determine whether you have sung in parallel or relative keys; notate the scales.

Natural minor.

Find the natural minor scale pattern by beginning the scale on *la* or 6 of the major scale in any given key signature. Draw its pattern to show where the whole and half steps are. Relate the scale to songs in this tonality—the Aeolian mode. Compare the natural minor scale pattern with the major scale pattern. Have children play the two scales on the bells or small wind instruments. Have them compose melodies in this minor tonality.

Whole-tone scale.

Notate "Lovely Evening" in a whole-tone scale and sing it from notation.

Invented scales.

Have the children invent their own original scales. These might have as few as four steps or as many as twelve. Ask them to write melodies based on these scales. Use them with familiar songs to discover what happens when a song is played in a new scale setting.

Multiple concepts.

When older children analyze melodies, they should seek answers to questions such as: How do tones move? (scalewise, stepwise, repeated notes) What is the phrase arrangement? What is the tonal arrangement? (major, minor, pentatonic, modal, whole tone, tone row, ethnic scale, etc.) What is the range for singing? Is there evidence of tension and release? If so, how is this achieved? Is there evidence of unity and variety? If so, how is this achieved? Is there a climax? If so, how did the composer achieve it? Are there other significant aspects such as rhythm patterns, intervals, meter, tone patterns, dynamics, sequence?

EXPLORATORY ACTIVITIES

1. Make a collection of songs that can be taught in ways that give the out-of-tune singers pleasurable participation and experiences that lead to their eventual singing in tune.
2. The black keys of the piano form a pentatonic scale. Compose a song or tune on the black keys. Add a bagpipe (open-fifth) bass for an accompaniment.
3. Investigate ways other than numerals, syllables, and note names to help identify scale tones. The American shapenote system is one. Another is an idea of the late W. Otto Miessner which he stated in an article, "The Art of Tonal Thinking," *Music Educators Journal,* January 1962.
4. Learn to identify songs that are in minor keys from the notation of the song. If the song's final note can be identified as scale tone six in the *major* scale derived from the key signature, then the song is in minor, and this note is the name of the minor key in which it is written.
5. A fifth-grade boy asks, "Why are there two flats in the key of B♭ major?" Ask him to answer his own question by using the bells. Clues: Remember the half steps between scale tones 3 and 4, and 7 and 8; build the scale beginning on B♭.
6. Listen to Mary Helen Richards' *Threshold to Music* Teacher Training Recording and identify more activities teachers use to attain their objectives.

References for singing will be found at the end of Chapter 13.

Part-Singing

13

Part-singing is a pleasurable activity that relates to the study of harmony and polyphony. It is a necessity for boys whose voices are beginning to change. Furthermore, every singer enjoys the aesthetic and social values of good part singing.

Traditionally, two-part-singing is emphasized for ten-year-olds and three-part-singing is introduced and worked with for eleven-year-olds. There are types of preparatory singing in the primary grades that include chants (vocal ostinati) and simple rounds, canons, and descants.

Dialogue Songs

Among the several theories about progressing toward comprehension of the vertical aspects of music (hearing more than one part at a time) is one that begins with the dialogue song, in which children are divided into two groups which take turns singing the sections. While this is not part-singing in the harmonic sense, it is assumed that the singers will become accustomed to being assigned to groups which are responsible for singing

297

their respective parts at the proper time in relation to the other parts. An example of a dialogue song for intermediate grades is "The Keeper."

THE KEEPER

Old English
Dialogue Song

Unknown

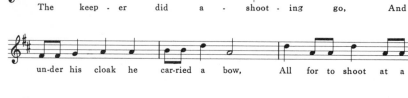

The keep-er did a-shoot-ing go, And

un-der his cloak he car-ried a bow, All for to shoot at a

mer-ry lit-tle doe, A-mong the leaves so__ green, O!

Jack-ie boy!   Sing ye well!   Hey down,

Mas-ter!   Ve-ry well!   Ho down,

Der-ry der-ry down, A-mong the leaves so__ green, O! To my

A-mong the leaves so__ green, O!

hey, down, down!   Hey down,

To my ho, down, down!   Ho down,

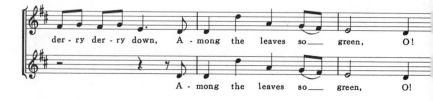

der-ry der-ry down, A-mong the leaves so__ green, O!

A-mong the leaves so__ green, O!

Rounds and Canons   The singing of rounds and canons [1] is believed to be a step toward the comprehension of harmony. Whether this opinion can be justified depends upon how such songs are taught. If children are taught to sing them in a manner that leads them to out-shout other parts, or to put their hands over their ears so that they cannot hear the other parts, then no real part-singing is taking place. If, on the other hand, they are taught in a manner that leads the singers to hear how the other parts join with theirs, then the experience can justifiably be called a form of part-singing. The teaching procedure may be outlined as follows:

1. The children learn the melody well.
2. The children learn to hear the harmony upon which the melody is based. The teacher chords this harmony on the Autoharp or piano, or uses a recording that provides a clear and simple harmonization. The children are told how many times they are to sing the song.
3. The hearing of the new part (second entrance) of the round is accomplished by the teacher singing or playing this part while the class is softly singing the first part and is listening to how the parts join together to make interesting music.
4. Some children join with the teacher on the new part. Listening to all the parts and how they join together in the harmonic setting is stressed. Balance of the parts so that all singers can hear all of the parts is essential.
5. If the round is of more than two parts, the new parts are added in the same general manner as above.
6. Rounds can be ended in three different ways: each part can finish separately, all parts can end on a chord together (each part stopping wherever it may be in the round), and each part can sustain the final note of that part until all parts are finished.

A tape recorder can focus attention on listening to both parts and how they relate vertically, as well as on tone quality and balance.

Rounds and canons are emphasized in fourth and fifth grades and are used less frequently in the primary grades because many of the children are not of sufficient musical maturity to be able to sing them well and to hear with understanding what they are doing. It is possible, however, for first-grade children to sing canons like "Old Texas" because they are *echo-type* songs.

Frequently sung rounds include "Are You Sleeping?", "Three Blind Mice," Little Tom Tinker," "Row Your Boat," "Scotland's Burning," "Sweetly Sings the Donkey," "Kookaburra," and "The Canoe Song."

[1] Rounds and canons are similar. A round repeats (goes back to the beginning) whereas a canon does not. A round is a "circle canon" that is in unison; every performer sings the same part, but at different times. Canons may be more complex than rounds, with entrances at different pitch intervals.

OLD TEXAS

Cano

I'm goin' to leave ___ ol'___ Tex - as now ___ They've got no

use ___ for the long-horn cow. ___

I'm goin' to leave ___ ol'___ Tex - as now ___

— They've got no use ___ for the long-horn cow.

ROUND OF THANKS

Traditional   Four-part roun

For health and strength and dai - ly food we

give Thee thanks, O Lord!

PRAY GOD BLESS

Four-part roun

Pray God bless all friends here, A

mer - ry mer - ry Christ - mas and a hap - py New Year.

**Composing
Chants**

Chants have been defined as recurring vocal patterns or figures. These added parts have value as creative and part-singing activities as well as being music that some immature singers can sing in tune. Easy chants can be sung in the primary grades.

Initial experiences in writing simple chants may be gained through the use of well-known songs that can be accompanied by only one chord such as "Row Your Boat," "Are You Sleeping?" and "Little Tom Tinker." The first tone to be used would be the chord root. Using this tone, invent a rhythm pattern that contrasts with the melody. The regular recurrence of this rhythmic pattern is sung on the pitch of the chord root (i.e., the home tone, "1," or "do"). For example, in the case of "Row Your Boat" the patterns that can be composed to be sung in conjunction with the melody are myriad. A few of them are:

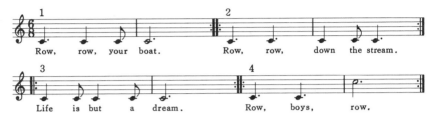

Percussion instruments are frequently used to accentuate the rhythm of a chant, and melody instruments are sometimes of aid in keeping some children on pitch. For dramatic effect those children singing the chant often begin about four measures before the melody begins, thus adding an *introduction* to the song. They also may continue for a few measures after the melody is finished, thus adding a *coda.* "Row Your Boat" may be sung as a melody with an added chant. When sung as a two-part round, addition of the chant results in a form of three-part singing, and when extended to be a four-part round, the chant adds a fifth part. With such simple song material, three- and four-part singing of this type can be done in fourth grade. Furthermore, the chant itself can be extended so that still more parts result.

For example, the above chants are pitched on "1" (C) of the tonic chord. The chanters can be divided into two groups with one group singing on scale tone 3 at the same time the other sings on 1. When this is learned, the chanters can be divided further into three groups singing on scale tones 1, 3, and 5 respectively. This is an example of vocal chording done in the rhythm of a chant. The melody adds a part. If the chant now consists of three parts and the round is sung in four parts, a seven-part song results. The teacher is, of course, limited in the number of possible parts by the musical maturity and size of the group. However, the possibilities present in this simple music are surprising. Chording instruments can be a companion activity to this type of part singing.

Thus far we have been concerned with the one-note chant. There are other possibilities. For example, "Are You Sleeping?" could have chants as follows:

"Little Tom Tinker" could have these:

Some Chant Patterns for

I-Chord Harmonization	V₇-Chord Harmonization
5 5 5	5 5 5
5 6 5	5 6 5
5 3 5	5 2 5,5 4 5
3 5 3	2 5 2,4 5 4
1 3 5,5 3 1	5 4 2,2 4 5
1 8,8 1	5₁5,5 5₁
8 5 8	2 5 2,7 5 7
8 7 6 5	7 7 6 5,7 6 5 5
8 5 6 7	5 5 6 7,7 6 5 5
8 5 6 5	7 5 6 5,2 5 6 5
8 7 6 5,5 6 7 8	5 4 3 2

Multiple chants (two or more different ones) could conceivably be employed in the same song. However, if too many different words are sung at one time, the meaning is lost and the effect ceases to be very musical. Experimenting by substituting neutral syllables or melody instruments may be worthwhile.

When chants are sung with two-chord songs, the initial experiences are usually with scale tone 5 because that tone is common to two chords, I and V₇. This is the only tone of the scale on which it is possible to create a one-tone chant in such songs. Such rhythmic chants for "Three Blind Mice" might be:

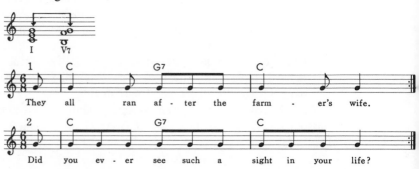

Children often alter the final repetition of such chants in order that the last pitch sung will be the home tone.

Another commonly used chant is one based on the scale tones 5 and 6. Scale tone 6 is a member of neither the I nor the V₇ chord yet it has the unusual quality of not interfering with the harmony as long as it is placed on an unaccented part of the measure. This kind of a chant for "Looby Loo" could be:

This 5–6–5 pattern works very well with songs like "Old Texas," "Ten Little Indians" and "Skip to My Lou"; children can invent many rhythmic variants of it.

LOOBY LOO

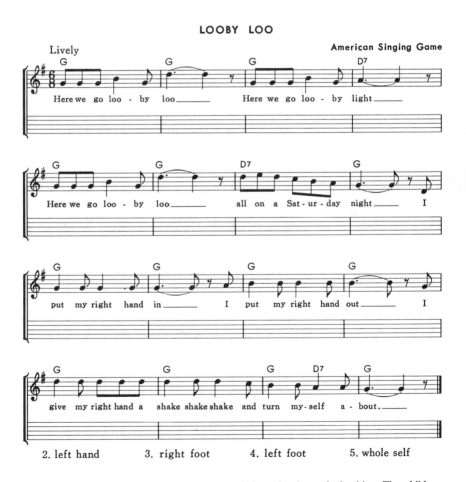

2. left hand   3. right foot   4. left foot   5. whole self

This song describes an old American custom before the days of plumbing. The children are taking a bath in a washtub near the kitchen stove which burned wood or coal. They are testing the temperature of the water before getting into the tub.

Although all good chants are essentially simple, slightly more comple chants can be written for songs like "Looby Loo." One way to procee with writing such a chant is to analyze the harmony of "Looby Loo" an chart it to find what this harmony demands of a four-measure-long chan Looking at the song, we find that it consists of four four-measure phrase: The problem is to find what chords harmonize each of the measures, an view this in a vertical fashion to find how to write a chant that will fit thi harmonic arrangement. We find:

measure	1	2	3	4 (*of each phrase*)
phrase 1......	G	G	G	D$_7$
phrase 2......	G	G	D$_7$	G
phrase 3......	G	G	G	G
phrase 4......	G	G	GD$_7$	G
	G	G	G&D$_7$	G&D$_7$

Looking down the columns it can be seen that a chant for "Looby Loo" must be written in the following harmonic scheme: the first measure o the chant requires a pattern related to the G chord (I); the second measur requires a pattern related to the G chord; the third and fourth measure require patterns related to *both* G and D$_7$ (V$_7$) chords. This means tha during measures three and four, the chant is restricted to patterns such a those made up of scale tone 5, or scale tones 5 and 6—simple patterns tha sound well with *either* chord I or V$_7$.

The following chart is included for those who wish to pursue mor

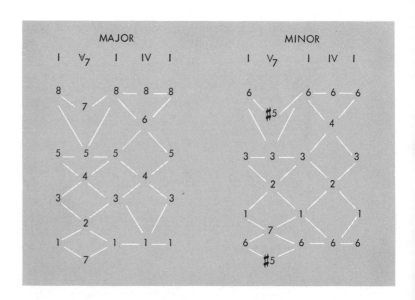

fully the writing of chants and other added parts to songs. It endeavors to picture some of the simple movements of tones possible during common chord changes. It will assist in the writing of descants as well as chants.

Chants may become monotonous because of their constant repetition. Therefore it is desirable that they be omitted from sections of some songs. Chants for three-chord songs are necessarily more complex, since they are based upon the tones of three chords rather than two.

Counter-melodies and Descants

Singing countermelodies and descants constitutes another of the many approaches. A countermelody is an added melodic part, usually lower than the original melody, which often *imitates* it and often moves in *contrary motion* to it. Ideally, a descant is a melody in its own right although written to accompany another melody. In practice, the descant is subordinate to the melody. It is usually higher in pitch than the melody; a small group of children sing it while the majority of the children sing the melody. The reason for this is that high pitches sound relatively louder than low pitches when they are combined in part-singing; therefore a small group on a high part balances with a larger group on a low part. When teachers understand the relation between countermelodies or descants, the chords and the original melodies, they can guide children to compose

DOWN IN THE VALLEY

American Folksong
Aranged by R. E. N.

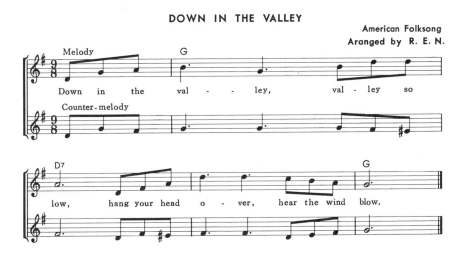

them. The first example is a countermelody to "Down in the Valley." In this case it is of such melodic nature in its own right that it is easier to sing than the real melody. Eight-year-olds can sing this simple polyphony.

A beautiful traditional-type descant, higher than the melody, and therefore to be sung by a small group, is one composed by Ewald Nolte to "Silent Night." It is intended for sixth grade.

SILENT NIGHT

Joseph Mohr

Franz Gruber
Descant by Ewald Nolte

From Beattie, Wolverton, Wilson, and Hinga, *The American Singer, Combined Grades.*
Used by permission of American Book Company.

Ideally, countermelodies and descants should be learned in integral relation to the original melody, because when they are learned as separate songs and then combined, many children fail to hear the harmonic relationship of the two parts. The melody should be well learned first of all, and a feeling for the harmony should be established with guitar, Autoharp, or piano.

The elementary school chorus may learn a descant or countermelody to be sung while the rest of the children sing a melody; and these may be combined in an assembly program. Likewise, children who are musically advanced may prepare descants out of school to be used in class with the melody sung by the other children. Another use for this type of added part is with certain melody instruments—from Song Flutes, Melody Flutes, recorders, and bells to violins and flutes. If done with discretion, employing a melody instrument is a way of strengthening either or both parts.

Partner Songs   Some songs having identical harmonization can be sung simultaneously. A major value of this is recreational, because the attempt is **fun.** However, this has value in learning to sing in parts if it is taught in the same general manner suggested for rounds, remembering that the children should hear both parts as they sing, and that aesthetic values should not be forgotten. "Three Blind Mice," "Row Your Boat," "Are You Sleeping," and "The Farmer in the Dell" can be combined with each other. Other combinations are "Ten Little Indians" and "Skip to My Lou"; the choruses of "Blue-Tail Fly" and "Shoo Fly"; "Solomon Levi" and "A Spanish Cavalier"; "Darling Nellie Gray" and "When You and I Were Young, Maggie"; "Goodnight Ladies" and "When the Saints Come Marching In"; "Keep the Home Fires Burning" and "There's a Long, Long Trail"; "Humoresque" and "Old Folks at Home"; and "Ring the Banjo" and "The Girl I Left Behind Me." Frederick Beckman has developed this idea in his two collections, *Partner Songs* and *More Partner Songs,* published by Ginn and Company. They can be used in intermediate grades.

Children should be guided to answer the question, "Why do these songs sound acceptable when they are sung at the same time?" The answer should be found by conducting experiments. "Let's try 'America' and 'The Star-Spangled Banner' to find out how they sound together." "What happened?" "Why don't they sound well in certain places?" "Let's write those notes on the board to see what they are and how they combine." "How many different aspects of music must be the same when two songs can be combined?" "Let's try to list them." Older children may be able to make a generalization that when melodies have the same meter, tempo, and harmonic arrangement, they can be combined. An example of combining songs is the following, in which "Lone Star Trail" and "Leaving Old Texas" are arranged to "fit together."

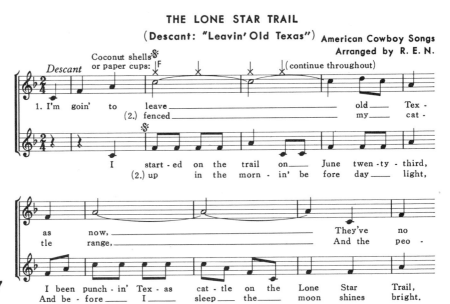

THE LONE STAR TRAIL
(Descant: "Leavin' Old Texas") American Cowboy Songs
Arranged by R. E. N.

From *This Is Music*, Book V, by William R. Sur, Robert E. Nye, William R. Fisher, and Mary R. Tolbert, Copyright © 1967 and 1962 by Allyn and Bacon, Inc. Used by permission

Harmonic Endings

This simple and effective way to develop a feeling for harmony may be initiated in third grade, where two-part harmonic endings may be used, and expanded in the fourth grade to three-part endings. In this activity teachers add a part or parts to the final note or notes of a song. For example, "Three Blind Mice" ends with scale tones 3 2 1. The children would be told to sing or hum those tones softly while they listen to the teacher [1] sing the words on scale tones 3 2 3. Next, the children who believe they can sing the new part will join with the teacher while the others continue singing the melody. It has been the experience of many teachers that some children may have never been conscious of their ability to hear two different pitches at one time in this fashion. These children may ask to sing such a harmonic ending again and again in order that they may fully enjoy what is to them a new comprehension of beauty.

This idea can be expanded as follows:

[1] A woman teacher is referred to here because the female voice has the same pitch as the unchanged child voice. A man teacher would probably play the new part on an instrument to avoid using his octave-lower voice.

Harmonic endings can be easily created by teachers and children. It is recommended that these be taught first by rote, since the aim at this juncture is to develop harmonic feeling. Notation can then be used to show how the already experienced harmony looks. Eventually this can lead to an understanding and purposeful use of the notation of part-singing. This activity develops a helpful background for later improvising of parts ("barbershop harmony"), and for singing in thirds and sixths.

Chord Roots

Chord roots constitute one of the easiest parts to add to a song because of the harmonic strength of the root, which is the foundation tone of each chord. Although this activity is primarily of intermediate grade level, it is possible for some younger children to take part in it. The songs employed are those that are best harmonized by only two or three chords. The following example can be harmonized by G and D_7 (I and V_7). First, the melody is learned; then the harmony is experienced by chording an accompaniment or from a recorded accompaniment; finally, the chord roots are added. The words can be sung in melody rhythm on the pitch of the chord root. Numerals, note names, or syllables are sometimes sung on the pitch indicated.

It seems undeniable that singing chord roots stresses the concept of chord change, especially since chord change is the essence of harmony. The singing or playing of melodies to which children "find" the roots by ear is another aspect of this study of harmony. It requires harmonic thinking without the aid of notation. Because this thin texture of melody and chord root is not always aesthetically satisfying, success with the activity quickly prompts the addition of more parts in order that a richer texture will make the harmony more complete.

To provide for individual differences and to support the new chord root part, some children can play this part on bells, piano, and small winds. The viola and cello can provide a bass effect. Let us assume that the children are going to build a score for the singing and playing of "Put Your Little Foot," a score that will reveal their ideas about rhythm and harmony as well as about melody. The teacher has placed the melody on the chalkboard and has also written the two chords that accompany this song. The children's first task is to find where in the song each of the chords is needed, if it is to be sounded on the piano or Autoharp to accompany the song. Since they have been taught that the note that receives the heavy accent or accents is ordinarily a tone of the required chord, they have an important clue on which to work. They know that the first beat of the measure in every meter signature is the most heavily accented beat, and that in 3/4 meter there is only one primary accent (the first beat) in each measure. (In 4/4 meter there are two—a primary accent on the first beat and a secondary accent on the third beat.) The children find that in the first three measures of "Put Your Little Foot" the note on the first beat is B. Looking at the chords, they notice that B is a member of the tones of the G (I) chord, but not of the D_7 (V_7) chord.

VARSOVIENNE
(Put Your Little Foot)

Traditional

Put your lit - tle foot, put your lit - tle foot, put your

Chord root

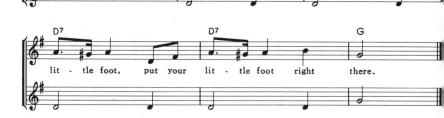

lit - tle foot right there, Put your lit - tle foot, put your

lit - tle foot, put your lit - tle foot right there.

Therefore, the chord needed for those three measures (or at least at the beginning of them) is the G chord. The note at the beginning of the fourth measure is A. The children find A to be a member of the D_7 chord; therefore this is the chord needed in the fourth measure. They proceed in this manner to the end of the song, then "try out" their harmony with the melody to see if it is correct. In some songs, the note D may be on the first beat of a measure. In this case, the children will decide by listening which of the chords is the right one to use. They can also tell by analyzing all the notes of any measure to find to which chord most of the notes belong. This is an important clue whenever students are determining chords for songs for which chords are not designated.

Now that the children have found the chords, they may write these on a staff below the melody, later creating a more interesting piano part derived from these chords. If one knows the chord, he or she knows the note that is the chord root, because the note G is the root of the G (I) chord and the note D is the root of the D_7 (V_7) chord. These notes are placed on a staff below the other music already written. Next, the children may invent rhythm patterns for the song, which they will play on suitable percussion instruments. There will be continuous experimenting which will involve singing and playing of parts, a use and understanding of harmony, and different ways of presenting the melody. The beginning of the score may look like this:

Put Your Little Foot

To add to this simple melody, harmony, and rhythm, children may create more parts in the form of chants and simple countermelodies:

The opportunities for creative experiences are many in this approach to music. Creating and experimenting with such a score can provide a basic experience for understanding harmony. Singing chord roots contributes markedly to the further comprehension of harmony because they form the foundation tones of the harmonic structure that supports the melody. Since comprehending chord roots comes from understanding the chords (and chording) on the piano and Autoharp, it stimulates the addition of other harmonic parts.

Learning to Hear Chord Changes

The experience with chord roots is basically an experience in sensing and identifying chord changes. Teachers plan similar experiences with chording on the piano and Autoharp. They contrive situations in which the sounding chord is "wrong," and the children are to notice this and want it corrected. The wrong and right chords are played; the children choose the one that "fits" the melody best. The experience commonly includes the teacher's selecting a familiar two-chord song (I and V₇ or I and IV) and playing the tonic chord all the way through, or until the children show in some way that the harmonic accompaniment should be corrected. The children are motivated to search for the best sounding chord. The measures of some songs have alternate harmonizations. Teachers let the children select the Autoharp or piano chords which sound the best to them; they continue to help them be conscious of chord sounds and chord changes. After children have learned to play the Autoharp, they can let them improvise accompaniments to songs of simple harmonization "by ear"— listening to find when the melody demands a chord change, then choosing the chord that sounds best. With two-chord songs the children's problem is a simple one of deciding which of two chords should be used. When skill in this has been developed, teachers select three-chord songs for them to work with. Some children can become expert in chord selection on the Autoharp and develop extreme sensitivity to chord changes when their teachers have planned experiences which help them to develop this responsiveness to harmony.

The particular chords at the end of phrases form *cadences*. These pertain to a feeling of momentary or permanent conclusion. Children might analyze cadences, classify them accordingly, and apply them in their own compositions.

Thirds and Sixths

An approach older from the standpoint of general use than singing chord roots is the employment of thirds and sixths. As in other approaches to harmony, children are assumed to know the melody very well, and to have heard the song on a recording or accompanied by the Autoharp or piano in a manner that helps them comprehend the integral relation of the melody and harmony. The singing of thirds was introduced in the section on harmonic endings. This use of thirds can be expanded to include parts of songs and eventually entire songs, providing the melodies accommodate this. For example, "London Bridge" can be sung in thirds except for near the end, where a sixth is necessary.

LONDON BRIDGE

English Game Song

312

Lon - don Bridge is fall - ing down, fall - ing down, fall - ing down,

Lon - don Bridge is fall - ing down, My Fair La - dy.

The music textbooks include songs that rely heavily on thirds to introduce part-singing. A song that can be sung in its entirety in thirds is the well-known "Polly Wolly Doodle."

POLLY WOLLY DOODLE

American Song

Oh, I went down South for to see my Sal, Sing - ing

Pol - ly Wol - ly Doo-dle all the day; My___ Sal, she is a___

spunk - y gal, Sing - ing Pol - ly Wol - ly Doo-dle all the day.

Chorus

Fare thee well, fare thee well, fare thee well my fair - y fay, For I'm

goin' to Loo - si - an - a for to see my Su - sy - an - na, Sing ing

Pol - ly Wol - ly Doo - dle all the day.

An interval that sounds similar to the third is the sixth, which is the inversion of the third. After children have become accustomed to singing in parallel thirds, they can easily learn to sing in parallel sixths. Any song that can be sung in thirds can be sung in sixths. "Polly Wolly Doodle" illustrates this. However, when the interval is changed in this way the key must often change also to accommodate the voice range.

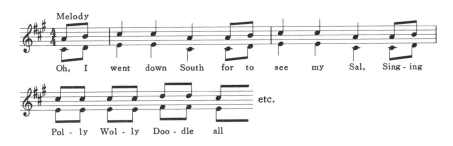

Melody

Oh, I went down South for to see my Sal, Sing - ing

etc.

Pol - ly Wol - ly Doo - dle all

Songs such as "Lightly Row," "Goodbye My Lover, Goodbye," "Yankee Doodle," "Hand Me Down My Walking Cane," "To Puerto Rico" (page 176), "Catch a Falling Star," and the refrain of "Marching to Peoria" can be used to advantage in approaching part-singing through the use of thirds and sixths.

There are older methods of teaching part-singing which include drilling on each part, then putting them together. Today the emphasis is upon helping children to hear a new part in relation to the melody and the harmony so that they hear all of the music. This principle is applicable no matter what type of part-singing is being done, whether it be round, descant, or traditional two- and three-part singing. The general outline of progress in part-singing in grades four, five, and six is as follows:

1. The learning of the melody.

2. The comprehension of the harmony (chord structure) that accompanies the melody by use of Autoharp, piano, or guitar chording, or a suitable recording.

3. The introduction of the new part in a manner that permits the children to hear the integral relation of the two parts. (Children hum the melody or sing it softly while the teacher sings or plays the new part.) Harmony must be *heard* before it is *made*.

4. The singing of the new part by those children who are ready for part-singing, always working for a balance in volume that permits the hearing of both parts by all of the children.

5. Introducing a third part by repeating Steps 3 and 4, adding the new part to the two parts previously learned.

6. When children have learned to feel secure in part-singing activities, then the sight-reading of part songs can be an interesting and challenging activity. When this skill is developed, Steps 1, 2, and 3 are eliminated. Since sight singing is a complicated skill, neutral syllables instead of words are generally used at first so that the children can concentrate on the notation. The words are added when children feel secure on the parts.

In general, the voices of fifth- and sixth-grade children are unchanged and have approximately the same range, with the exception of boys in the first stage of the voice change whose ranges have dropped approximately a fourth. Technically, it is incorrect to call these immature voices "soprano" or "alto." It is more accurate to abandon these adult terms and to call the children's voice parts "high," "low," and "middle," rather than "first soprano," "alto," and "second soprano." It is the aim of the teacher that every child sing each of these parts, changing from one to another according to the directions of the moment or by being assigned them in different songs.

In the fifth grade books will be found songs that stress parallel thirds. Following songs in thirds will be those that include both thirds and sixths, then some fourths and fifths. Every teacher of the older children should know the sequence of songs through which part-singing skills are expected to be learned in the particular books available in the school and suggestions in the teacher's book must be studied carefully. Some two-part songs are included in the fourth-grade books in preparation for the emphasis on harmony in the fifth grade.

An interesting creative approach to singing thirds and sixths is one in which children compose songs confined within four pitches of the major scale, 3, 4, 5, and 6. After such a song has been composed and learned, a parallel third part can be added below. When this new part is transposed one octave higher, parallel sixths result. Try this with "Sleep, Baby, Sleep."

SLEEP, BABY, SLEEP

Traditional Words
Arranged

The male teacher is at some disadvantage in teaching part-singing, since his voice sounds one octave lower than the child voice. Therefore, it is necessary for him to use some melody instrument instead of his voice when he wishes to illustrate part-singing of unchanged voices. His voice is excellent, however, in the singing of chord roots. There is seldom a changed voice among sixth-grade children, but in case there should be, the singing of special parts, such as chord roots by the male teacher along with the boy, will help the child adjust to his temporarily unique situation.

Improvising Harmony Parts

The improvising of harmony parts has often been overlooked as one practical approach to part-singing. "Barber-shopping" or "singing harmony by ear" has a definite carry-over into the natural musical expression of boys and girls when they are on field trips or picnics, at camp and at home. The writers know of an elementary school where the improvising of parts by children's volunteer neighborhood quartets was an activity of importance, even affecting school and community programs. A list of songs that have had use in this activity includes "Home on the Range," "Down by the Old Mill Stream," "There's a Long, Long Trail," "Moonlight and Roses," "Let the Rest of the World Go By," "Eyes of Texas" (I've Been Working on the Railroad"), "Red River Valley," "Oh My Darling Clementine," "A Bicycle Built for Two." This activity is usually most effective at sixth-grade level, where it develops into three-part singing, although some fifth grades can do well with it.

Vocal Chording

An example of one type of vocal chording was mentioned on page 30? in connection with I-chord songs. Usually, chording of the vocal type consists of the same tones that are often used for piano chording in the treble clef. The children may be divided into four groups, with one assigned the melody and the other three assigned the three chord tones. This activity would logically begin with one-chord melodies and progress to three-chord melodies. It may start in a simple way in third or fourth grade. It is sometimes emphasized in fifth and sixth grades as an approach to three-part singing. The ease with which children can learn to chord vocally will be determined by their ability to hear harmony; their ability to learn harmony will be favorably influenced by successful experiences in instrumental chording and by guided listening activities that aid the hearing of chord changes. A chord root part can be added if the range is appropriate.

The chords to be sung can be arranged in several positions. This chart illustrates chord positions that are sometimes used as exercises to introduce children to this activity. Although numbers or syllables may be used to introduce this work, humming or the neutral syllable "loo" is used in performance. The words of the song are sung on the chord tones in the same rhythm as the melody.

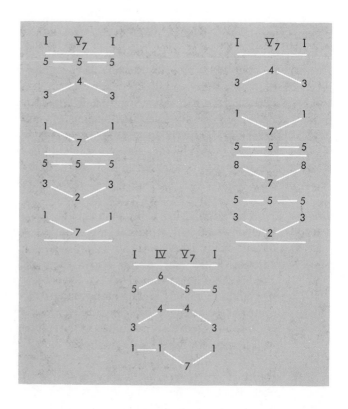

The following excerpts from "Silent Night" illustrate this activity:

**The Elementary
School Chorus**

Among the special interest groups in the elementary school are the orchestra, band, and chorus. The instrumental groups are generally the responsibility of special music teachers but the chorus is frequently taught either by the music teacher or by a classroom teacher. Although some schools have a primary grades chorus which sings unison songs, the usual chorus is composed of fifth and sixth graders. Today's teachers are fortunate in having an improved selection of song materials to use, some of which are listed at the end of this chapter. Not only do the series books include chants, descants, and countermelodies in addition to the standard types of two- and three-part songs, but there are valuable supplementary materials. There is no standard seating arrangement for elementary choruses. However, it is best to have the lowest and highest parts seated so that each can hear the other well. In this way the group is able to keep more accurately on pitch. In chorus work which has a goal of public performance, the children are more or less permanently assigned to one of the parts (high, middle, or low).

Activities for Lesson Plans

RELATING MELODY AND HARMONY

Canon.

The teacher creates simple canons and writes them in numbers or syllables for the class to sing. There will be two parts. Later, some of these should be notated and sung from notation. Examples:

1 1 2 3 4 5 – 5 4 3 2 1 –
    1 1 2 3 4 5 – 5 4 3 2 1 –

*Hearing two pitches
at once.*

One half of the class sustains one pitch, *do* or *1*, while the other half sings other pitches as indicated by the teacher's pointing to scale degrees written in numbers or syllables on the chalkboard, or by the teacher's use of hand signs. Later, both *do* and *so,* and *la* and *mi* can be used as alternating sustained pitches.

Write the major scale vertically in numbers or syllables. Divide the class into two groups, left hand and right hand. Each group sings to the corresponding hand of the teacher as he or she points with it. The teacher points to scale degrees that will produce interesting two-pitch combinations. It is good to start with a unison and experiment from there. Later on, do the same with scales other than the major. For older, experienced children, this activity can progress until both groups are singing moving parts, indicated by two-hand signs given by the teacher or an advanced student. From this they can proceed to a chart or chalkboard with notation.

Round.

Write all or part of a traditional round with all parts fully notated on the chalkboard, or prepare this on a transparency. Children are asked to sing rounds and to listen to them, but they seldom see them notated in complete form so that they can obtain a visual image of what a round is. First, the class should learn to sing the round. This one can be sung in from two to four parts; a new group enters two measures after the preceding group. Then after studying the score, questions such as the following can be asked. "What is the harmonic plan of this round?" (a two-measure phrase in which C and G_7 share the first measure with two beats each, while C harmonizes the second measure.) "Analyze this round vertically to be sure that this harmonic plan is really in operation." (The notes, viewed vertically, can be made into chords and played on bells or piano to show that harmonic plan is consistent—that the C and G_7 chords are really there.) Older children can be given manuscript paper and asked to write a round, using this same plan. Next, other rounds are studied and their harmonic plans revealed. Then rounds with other specified harmonic plans can be written by the children.

Examples for study:

Let's Sing a Round, Bowmar Records.
Round and Round, Franson YPR 431 (ages 6–10).
 From round to canon to fugue.
Franck: *Violin Sonata,* last movement (a beautiful example)

Descant, counter-melody, and round.

Sing and play songs that have descants and counter-melodies. Ask the children to describe the difference between rounds and added parts of these types. Page 229 in *Singing With Children* lists songs with descants; also see indexes of music textbooks. A counter-melody is a melody composed to be sung or played with another melody. Of the songs listed in *Singing With Children,* the following contain what could be termed counter-melodies: "Mystic Number" (first half), "Streets of Laredo," "Ash Grove," and "O Give Me the Hills."

Polyphony.

Sousa: *Semper Fidelis,* AM 3 v 1. Have children explore this march to discover the different melodies and how Sousa combines them.

Texture.

Ask questions to help children develop a vocabulary of terms descriptive of texture such as light, heavy, thick, thin. Use recordings in which children can easily compare a thick texture with a thin texture. Compare the combining of melodic lines in polyphony with threads in weaving tapestry. Examples of contrasting textures:

Saint-Saëns: "The Swan" from *Carnival of the Animals,* AM 3 v 2 (homophonic texture)
Ligeti: "Atmospheres" from *Space Odyssy,* Columbia MS 6733
Bach: *Little Fugue in G Minor,* AM 6 v 1; BOL 86

HARMONIC PART-SINGING

Improvising harmony.

Present the class with the task of improvising parts for "Streets of Laredo," using only scale tones 3, 4, and 5. This song has been selected because it is harmonized by only two chords, I and V_7. Scale tones 3 and 5 are members of the I-chord and scale tones 4 and 5 are members of the V_7-chord. In this particular song the chords alternate regularly; this makes it easy to think in terms of choices of chord tones the singers select to improvise their simple harmony parts. The class selects the pitches it wants for each of the measures of the song (which is either on the chalkboard or on a transparency), and writes them on the chalkboard. The class next sings the two parts (the melody and the new part) together until it performs it well and is satisfied with the added part. Next, the class adds another new part by writing it the interval of a third lower. Now it has two new parts in parallel thirds. It then sings the three parts. The children evaluate the result and try to analyze what made it possible.

STREETS OF LAREDO

Cowboy Song

| Wrapped | in ·white | lin - en | as | cold | as | the | clay. |
| Shot | in the | breast and | I | know | I | must | die." |

3. *"It was once in the saddle I used to go dashing,*
Once in the saddle I used to go gay;
First down to Rosie's and then to the card-house;
Got shot in the breast and I'm dying today."

4. *"Get sixteen gamblers to handle my coffin,*
Let six jolly cowboys come sing me a song,
Take me to the graveyard and lay the sod o'er me,
For I'm a young cowboy, I know I've done wrong."

5. *"Oh, beat the drums slowly and play the fife lowly,*
Play the dead march as they carry me along,
Put bunches of roses all over my coffin,
Roses to deaden the clods as they fall."

6. *(Repeat Verse 1.)*

Chord root parts.

Words of songs can be sung on the pitches of the chord roots—the "1" of a chord in root position (1 3 5). The letter names of the Autoharp chord designations placed above the song notation tell the reader the pitch to be sung or played.

Improvising part singing.

Explore harmonizing parts "by ear," using songs such as "Goodbye, My Lover, Goodbye," "Good Night Ladies," "Kum Ba Yah," "Michael, Row the Boat Ashore," and "Sally Go Round." Others in *Singing With Children* are "Daisy Bell," "Golden Slippers," "Mary and Martha," "Hush, Little Baby," and "Sidewalks of New York."

Singing parallel thirds "by ear."

There are some songs and parts of songs that can be sung and played in parallel thirds. *This is one of the easiest approaches to part singing.* Among these songs are "Hot Cross Buns," "Sally Go Round," "Polly Wolly Doodle," and "San Sereni." The last one is in *Singing With Children*. First review the melody thoroughly, with a strong harmonic accompaniment on Autoharp, piano, ukulele, or guitar. Often times the teacher says to part of the class "Start singing the song on this pitch," and gives them the pitch that results in a third interval from the melody. Because the harmony has been well absorbed, automatic adjustments will take place in the new part, and the class may surprise itself by singing the song at once in two parts. The two parts should then be revealed on the chalkboard or transparency in order that the children see the related parts—"see what it looks like when it sounds that way." The interval of a third should be identified by sight and by sound. On the staff it is either line-line or space-space. In subsequent lessons the teacher can help children formulate the following ideas: (1) melody with harmonic accompaniment is *homophonic* music; (2) the interval of a third in this instance is a vertical or harmonic interval as compared to the horizontal or melodic interval that appears in melodies; (3) both types of intervals might be found in a two-part song.

Examples:
Harmonic intervals:
thirds and sixths.

Tchaikovsky: *Italian Caprice* (a prominent theme is in thirds)

Mendelssohn: *Symphony No. 4*, First Movement (theme two has a two-part melody in thirds)

Charpentier: "On Muleback" from *Impressions of Italy,* AM 5 v 1 (theme three has a two-part melody in thirds and sixths)

Dissonance.

Experiment with singing as a round a known song that is not a round, having active harmonic changes of irregular nature. It should be a song that when sung this way will result in obvious dissonances (disagreeable sounds). Perform it this way, tape it, and let the class hear it. Ask the children to analyze the reasons for the dissonances, to try to define dissonance, and to evaluate their performance that exemplified it. Since dissonance is one of the characteristics of contemporary music, children should have some experience with it and know what it is.

Nonharmonic music.

Before asking young children to comprehend chord changes that are characteristic of harmonic music, they should have experienced a great deal of music in which there are no chord changes. This includes short tonal fragments and calls, pentatonic music, I-chord songs, and unaccompanied melodies that do not suggest harmonic changes. One chord played on the Autoharp suffices to accompany such music. Examples include "Old MacDonald" and "The Farmer in the Dell." More I-chord songs are listed in the Autoharp Accompaniments Index under the heading "Exemplary Songs," *Singing With Children,* p. 228.

Bitonality.

The class sings a familiar song such as "Twinkle, Twinkle, Little Star" while the teacher plays the accompaniment on the piano in another key. This could be done on the Autoharp if the instrument is amplified. In any event, the result should be taped and played back to the class for evaluation. Listen to recorded examples of bitonality and evaluate them.

References for Singing

Articles and Books

GARY, CHARLES L., ed., *The Study of Music in the Elementary School: A Conceptual Approach.* Reston, Va.: Music Educators National Conference, 1967, pp. 51–65. Helpful in writing lesson plans; choral compositions, pp. 162–63.

INGRAM, MEDELINE, and WILLIAM C. RICE, *Vocal Techniques for Children and Youth.* Nashville, Tenn.: Abingdon Press.

NORDHOLM, HARRIET, *Singing in the Elementary School.* Englewood Cliffs, N.J.: Prentice-Hall, Inc., 1966.

SLAUGHTER, C. H., "Those Dissonant Boys," *Music Educators Journal,* February–March 1966, pp. 110–12. Sociological factors relating to boys' disinterest in music.

TUFTS, NANCY P., *The Children's Choir,* Vol. 2. Philadelphia, Pa.: The children's choir, the boy choir, the handbell choir.

Songs for Children

BACON, DENISE, *Let's Sing Together: Songs for 3, 4, and 5 Year Olds.* Oceanside, N.Y.: Boosey & Hawkes, Inc., 1971.

BAILEY, CHARITY, *Sing a Song with Charity Bailey.* New York: Plymouth Music Company.

ERDEI, PETER, and KATALIN KOMLES, *150 American Folk Songs to Sing, Read and Play.* Oceanside, N.Y.: Boosey & Hawkes, Inc., 1974.

KERSEY, ROBERT, *Just Five.* Westminster, Md.: The Westminster Press. Pentatonic songs.

———. *Just Five Plus Two.* Westminster, Md.: The Westminster Press. *Fa* and *ti* are added.

LANDECK, BEATRICE, *Songs to Grow On; More Songs to Grow On.* New York: Marks and Sloane. Recorded by Folkways Records.

SCOTT, RICHARD, *Clap, Tap, and Sing Choral Method.* Minneapolis, Minn.: Handy-Folio Music Company. For grades 2–5. Beginning with rhythm, this 48-page book takes children through sight-singing to part-singing. All songs are playable on small wind instruments.

SEEGER, RUTH CRAWFORD, *American Folk Songs for Children; Animal Folk Songs for Children; American Folk Songs for Christmas.* New York: Doubleday and Company, Inc.

Part-Singing

BACON, DENISE, *46 Two-Part American Folk Songs.* Oceanside, N.Y.: Boosey & Hawkes, 1974.

BECKMAN, FREDERICK, *Partner Songs; More Partner Songs.* New York: Ginn and Company. Combinable songs for grades 5–7.

BELL, LESLIE, *The Festival Song Book One*. Melville, N.Y.: Belwin-Mills 11746. For unaccompanied voices.

BURKART, ARNOLD E., *Bicinia Americana Vol. 1*. Muncie, Ind.: Keeping Up With Music Education, 1976.

COOPER, IRVIN, *Songs for Pre-Teentime*. New York: Carl Fischer, Inc. For grades 6–7.

EHRET, WALTER, *The Youthful Chorister*. New York: Marks Music Corp. SA.

GEARHART, LIVINGSTON, *A Christmas Singing Bee*. Delaware Water Gap, Pa.: Shawnee Press.

JUREY, EDWARD B., *Mills First Chorus Album*. Melville, N.Y.: Belwin-Mills.

KENT, WILLYS PECK, *A Book of Descants*. New York: Vantage Press. For grades 5–8.

KRONE, BEATRICE, and MAX KRONE, *Our First Songs to Sing with Descants* (for upper primary); *Very Easy Descants; Songs to Sing with Descants; Descants for Christmas; Our Third Book of Descants; From Descants to Trios; Descants and Rounds for Special Days*. Park Ridge, Ill.: Neil A. Kjos Music Company.

SCOTT, RICHARD, *Sevenfold Choral Method*. Minneapolis, Minn.: Handy-Folio Music Company. For grades 5–7.

**General
Collections**

ADES, HAWLEY, *One for the Melody*. Delaware Water Gap, Pa.: Shawnee Press. 26 unison songs by classic composers, with a story about each composer.

DALLIN, LEON, and LYNN DALLIN, *Heritage Songster*. Dubuque, Iowa: Wm. C. Brown Company Publishers. Traditional songs Americans sing.

HAYNES, MARGARET S., and RICHARD A. COOLIDGE, *Owls, Pussy Cats, Cabbages, and Kings*. Dubuque, Iowa: Kendall-Hunt, Publishing Co., 1973. Composed modal songs and serial piano pieces. (1973)

LEISY, JAMES, *The Good Times Songbook*. Nashville and New York: Abingdon Press, 1974. For informal singing.

NYE, ROBERT E., VERNICE T. NYE, NEVA AUBIN, and GEORGE KYME: *Singing With Children (2nd ed.)*. Belmont, Calif.: Wadsworth Publishing Co., 1970. Selected songs for teaching music to elementary school children.

TOBITT, JANET E., *The Ditty Bag*. Pleasantville, N.Y.: P.O. Box 97.

Recordings for Singing

BOWMAR RECORDS, INC., 622 Rodier Drive, Glendale, California 91201. *Bowmar Records Catalog*. Lists approximately 20 albums for singing, including three for children "with special needs."

CAPITOL RECORDS DISTRIBUTING CORPORATION, 1750 North Vine St., Hollywood, California 90019. *Music For Children* Album. English children demonstrate rhythm and melody through the methods of Carl Orff on an Angel Recording.

CHILDRENS MUSIC CENTER, 5373 West Pico Blvd., Los Angeles, California 90019.

The Best Records and Books for the School Curriculum Catalog. Lists selected recordings for school use.

CLASSROOM MATERIALS CO., 93 Myrtle Drive, Great Neck, New York 11020.
Johnny Can Sing Too. (K-3) Vol. 1, 2. For discovering singing voices and helping them develop.
You Too Can Sing! (4–6) For children with singing problems.
Classroom Sing Along (4–6) To aid the teacher in teaching songs.

FOLKWAYS RECORDS, 701 Seventh Ave., New York, N.Y. 10036.
You'll Sing a Song and I'll Sing a Song (Ella Jenkins) FC 7664
See the Folkways Catalog for many more.

FRANSON CORPORATION, 225 Park Ave. South, New York 10003. Children's Record Guild and Young People's Records.
Albums: *Let's Sing* (1–5)
          Folk Songs (1–5)
          Songs to Sing (1–4) activity songs

RCA VICTOR EDUCATIONAL SALES, 155 E. 24th Street, New York, N.Y. 10010.
RCA Victor Basic Record Library for Elementary Schools: *The Singing Program.* One album each for primary grades, fourth, fifth, and sixth grades.
RCA Victor Educational and Library Record Catalog. Issued annually.

STANLEY BOWMAR CO., INC., Valhalla, New York.
Records, Tapes, and Instructional Materials for the Classroom Catalog. Lists many records for singing activities.

The Sight and Sound of Music: Shawnee Press, Delaware Water Gap, Pa. 18327.
A vocal sight reading course for third and fourth grades. Books, recordings, projections, teaching aids, and lesson plans are provided.

Learning Music
by Playing Pitched
Instruments

Since developing music concepts by playing instruments has been considered in various settings in previous chapters, the reader has already given consideration to this activity as an integral part of a balanced music program. Musical instruments have been viewed as extensions of the body, as interpreters of actions and stories, as means of experimenting in sound for both aesthetic and scientific reasons, as aids in singing, as accompaniments to singing and dancing, and as means of learning to read notation and to acquire music knowledges and skills. This chapter will expand upon playing instruments as a skill as well as a means of expanding music concepts.

The variety of possible instrumental experiences in the general music class can accommodate all the types of individual differences resulting from physical development in normal children that affect the manipulation of instruments, as well as variations in physical coordination resulting from deviant growth patterns or disease, and degrees of musical ability. For some children, manipulating an instrument is an important physical release, while for others it is an intellectual challenge. For those unable to sing well it is an opportunity to succeed in another area of music.

Melody Instruments

Children are characteristically interested in mechanical things. Making music by playing an instrument, no matter how simple the instrument, attracts them. It follows that if teachers guide this interest along the lines of learning both the skills of playing and the understanding of the elements of music, it can yield great benefits.

When melody instruments are employed to invent introductions, codas, interludes, and to play tone patterns, concepts of melody and form are being expanded. The concept of *interval* can be made clear by seeing intervals on keyboard instruments, by seeing and feeling them on blowing-type (small wind) instruments, and by comparing what is seen, felt, and heard with written intervals on the staff. The key signature is relatively unimpressive to the singer, but of undeniable significance to the player of pitched instruments. Note reading becomes clearly practical and functional when the player must relate notation to the keyboard or to fingerings on a wind instrument. Instruments are also useful in studying aspects of music such as scale line, chord line, legato, staccato, and a host of others related to analysis and performance. Flute-type instruments lend atmosphere to American Indian music; the individually plucked strings of the psaltery, Autoharp, guitar, and ukulele can produce imitation Oriental melodies; and the marimba contributes in an authentic manner to Latin American music. Children can use melody instruments to compose melodies. They are easy to play; they can be taught by the classroom teacher. Their use combines auditory, tactile, and visual perception to build music concepts. Some children will be more interested in trying to match tones with their voices when they produce pitches themselves on a melody instrument. Furthermore, the more experienced and gifted children can have additional musical experiences with instruments.

Water Glasses and Bottles

Some teachers use water glasses and bottles as introductory experiences to keyboard instruments such as bells, xylophone, and piano. There are tuned glasses that can be used without water, obtainable from various sources on order, even from some variety stores. Other teachers employ glasses with water, knowing that this probably means some spilling and evaporation, both of which necessitate retuning because of the change in water levels. Some use bottles with water, often corked or capped to keep retuning at a minimum.

One of the first listening activities for young children is experimenting with sounds made with metal, wood, glass, and stone. These early experiences lead to experiments with water glasses and bottles. By striking glasses and bottles when they are empty and when they contain water, children can make certain scientific observations. They discover that the pitch and tone quality are affected by size and thickness. They may also discover that decreasing the amount of water raises the pitch and increasing the amount of water lowers the pitch—except in some glasses and bottles that will not tune lower no matter how much water is added. They may also discover that striking glasses or bottles with soft objects such as felt-covered mallets produces soft tones. Let the children generalize from their experimentation that: The more water one pours into a glass or bottle, the lower the pitch is. The lowest pitch is made by filling glasses and bottles full of water. The highest pitch is produced when a glass or bottle is empty. The best tone quality is produced when a soft mallet strikes the glass as if pulling the sound out, not hitting it in.

After experimenting with glasses and bottles, children and teacher may decide that bottles are superior because if one can seal them, the pitch will remain stable. However, the most important element of comparison should be the beauty of the sound, which could be determined by the quality of the glass. Paint or paper strips can be placed on them to show the water level that produces the desired pitch. Numeral names, note names, or syllable names can be painted on or written on paper stickers. Some teachers put vegetable dyes or other coloring in the water to add interest. Placing glasses on a thick cloth will result in a better tone.

Interest in playing melodies on bottles may prompt the teacher or the children to make or obtain a rack from which to suspend the bottles. When this is done, each bottle is suspended by two loops of string, one on each side of the bottle neck, to help it to hang with more stability.

The first experience in playing songs on glasses or bottles is generally with only three pitches: 3–2–1 (mi-re-do). However, it is good to compose a song with only one pitch, that of 1 (do); then a song with scale tones 1 and 2; and finally, a song with tones 1, 2, and 3, arriving at the three-pitch stage in a logical way. Known songs in the three-tone category are "Hot Cross Buns" and "Merrily We Roll Along." After this, the next step is to use four- and five-tone melodies. Teachers often devise their own three-, four-, and five-tone songs as examples, then encourage the children to compose others with scale-tones 1–2–3–4–5. After this experience has been digested, more scale tones are added until melodies are created on all eight pitches of the major scale. A pentatonic tonal organization can be used also, beginning with songs based on scale tones 5–3, then 5–6–3, then 1–2–3–5–6. It is advantageous to transfer skills acquired on glasses and bottles to bells and xylophones; they provide a good introduction to the piano keyboard. Some teachers prefer to go directly to them rather than introduce them by means of experimental glasses and bottles.

Bells and Xylophones   When children have had opportunities to explore the bells for themselves, they can make a number of discoveries:

Long bars sound low pitches.
Short bars sound high pitches.
The arrangement of white keys and black keys is the same as that of the piano except that the piano has more keys.

To play a scale going up, one plays from left to right.

To play a scale going down, one plays from right to left.

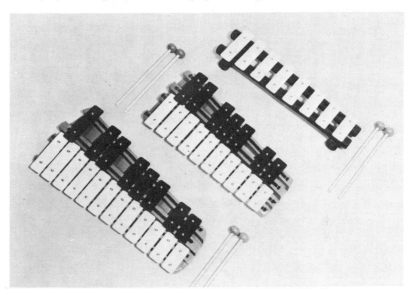

PERIPOLE INC., Brown Mills, N.J. 08015

Penguin Song Bells

A five-note (pentatonic) scale can be played on the black keys.

White keys played from C to C sound the C major scale.

If a standard bell set can be stood on end, with large bars down, and held against the chalkboard or chart paper, staff lines can be drawn from the bars to relate the keyboard to the staff.

To produce the best tone, one strikes the middle of the bar and draws the tone out rather than hitting it in.

The same sequence of pitches is used to initiate playing the bells as was described for glasses and bottles. *Resonator* bells are made of individual tone bars that can be taken from the carrying case if desired. For example, if children are to compose tunes with only three or four pitches, those particular bars can be removed from the set, placed in order, and played apart from the other bars to prevent possible confusion of young children when they would try to play those bars in keyboard position among all the other bars.

Before children understand music notation, teachers guide them to play by ear and by numeral notation.[1] The scale-tone numbers can be written

[1] A well-known book that introduces numeral notation in kindergarten and first grade is *Timothy's Tunes* by Adeline McCall (Boston Music Company). The *Psaltery Book* by Satis Coleman (John Day Company) is another. *Fun with the Melody-bells* by Rj Staples (Follett) further expands the use of numeral notation.

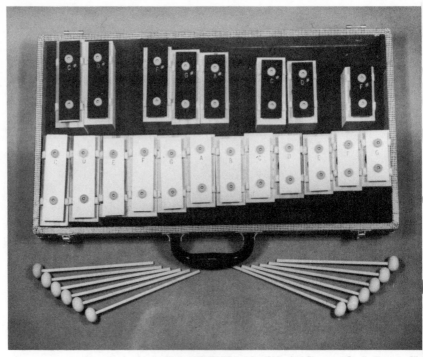

B. F. KITCHING CO., INC., 505 Shawmut St., LaGrange, Ill.

Resonator Bells

on the white metal keys with black crayon, or they can be placed on tag-board in back of the bells. Numeral notation could appear as follows. Notice that the "fast notes" are circled.

Hot Cross Buns	*Mary Had A Little Lamb*
3 2 1 – 3 2 1–	3212 333– 222– 333–
⟨1111⟩ ⟨2222⟩ 3 2 1–	3212 3333 2232 1——

five-note tune	six-note tune
Jingle Bells	*Are You Sleeping?*
333– 333– 3512 3——	1 2 3 1 1 2 3 1 3 4 5–3 4 5–
4444 433⟨333⟩223 2–5–	⟨5654⟩3 1 ⟨5654⟩3 1 1 5₁1–1 5₁1–
333– 333– 3512 3——	
4444 433⟨335⟩542 1——	

Use C major or G major to avoid black keys. Use F major to introduce one black key (B♭). *Hot Cross Buns* and *Mary Had a Little Lamb* can be played on the group of three black keys. Some teachers prefer to introduce the piano keyboard in this way to overcome possible hesitation about the black keys later. With guidance and careful listening, young children can play songs or parts of songs in keys such as F and G major where one black key is necessary. The general procedure at first is to learn a song well by rote before attempting to play it (*listen, sing,* then *play*).

Although children may begin playing songs with the aid of numerals, they are soon looking at notation the teacher has prepared for them that includes the numerals written beneath (or above) the note they represent. Later, teachers prepare notation in which the numerals appear only with the beginning note of each measure, then only with the beginning note of each phrase, and finally they are abandoned altogether because the children have made the transition from numerals to the notes on the staff.

The bells have many uses. If a classroom teacher has difficulty with his or her singing voice, the instrument can be used to teach rote songs. Difficult tonal patterns in songs can be isolated and studied by means of the bells. They are often employed to establish the pitch of songs by sounding the keynote, playing tones of the tonic chord (I), then playing the starting pitch. Special sound effects such as chimes, church bells, and sleigh bells

THE DRUNKEN SAILOR

Dorian mode

English Folksong

2. *Into the longboat till he gets sober*
   Into the longboat till he gets sober
   Into the longboat till he gets sober
   Early in the morning

Bells accompaniment:

| d | a | d | a | c | g | c | g |

| d | a | d | a | c | g | a | a :|

can be produced to enhance songs. Children can play simple parts of songs involving a single tone up to an entire scale, and they can play complete songs. Introductions, codas, and interludes—all created on the bells—can be added. Older children can write descants and other added parts to songs and play them on the bells. Bells can assist part singing.

The "suggestions to the teacher" in one of the music series states that if children had access to keyboard instruments, many of the problems in teaching understanding of pitch differences, of the interval relationship of tones, and of music notation generally would be minimized. The reason is that the keyboard constitutes a highly significant *audiovisual* tool for learning. Children enjoy "picking out tunes" and in doing so on the bells or piano they *see* and *feel* and *hear* the interval relationships of tones. This can lead to a genuine comprehension of the meaning of the notes on the staff—a comprehension frequently lacking in children whose musical experiences have been confined to a singing approach. In every elementary classroom there should be a music corner that includes bells and easy music to play on them. Some teachers have a "song of the week" which children learn to play before school, after school, and during the school day. When played with a padded mallet or a pencil with a rubber eraser, this soft-toned instrument seldom disturbs other classroom activities.

The *xylophone* is similar to the bells, but made of wood instead of metal. *Xylo* is the Greek word for wood. Because its wood strips do not vibrate as long as the metal bars of the bells, it has a more percussive quality. A more attractive xylophone is the *marimba,* which has resonators, usually metal tubes, beneath the wood strips. German music educators use the term xylophone, but prefer the terms *glockenspiel* or *metallophone* to bells. The metallophone is lower pitched than the glockenspiel.

Other forms of bells are the step bells, which are made in the form of

EDUCATIONAL MUSIC BUREAU, 1834 Ridge Ave., Evanston, Ill. 60201

Xylophone

stair steps illustrating the ascending and descending pitches of the scale, and the *glockenturm,* a German instrument which is played vertically and reveals visually the relationship of keyboard and staff.

The Piano As a Melody Instrument

The piano can be used by children in connection with songs in the same informal ways the percussion instruments and bells are used. Like the bells, the keyboard provides an audiovisual tool. The piano can be used as an instrument of percussion, melody, harmony, and in any combination of these. It is therefore a superior means by which to gain concepts in music study.

Classroom teachers do not need to be pianists to teach music through keyboard experience. They need only to be introduced to it so that they can proceed in the same way the children do. In the beginning a child can play a tone that sounds "one" when the clock strikes "one" in *Hickory Dickory Dock,* as he or she may have done earlier on the bells. In a song that has words of importance on one or two tones, children may play these at the time they occur in the melody. The same little three-note melodies played on glasses, bottles, and bells can be played on the piano keyboard. As time goes on, four- and five-finger patterns can be used in an incidental way in both ascending and descending forms. Here are some examples of such usage:

One Finger	The child plays repeated single tones such as the beginning of *Jingle Bells.* A tone-matching game can be played by striking a pitch that is within his voice range, then trying to match it vocally.
Two Fingers	The child plays repeated motives in songs and can also match tones, playing as well as singing such scale tones as 5 and 3 ("so" and "mi").
Three Fingers	The scale tones 3 2 1 can be played whenever the words "three blind mice" occur in the song of that name. The tonal pattern 1 2 3 1 can be played with the words "Are you sleeping?" in the song of that name.
Four Fingers	Scale tones 4 4 3 3 2 2 1 in *Twinkle, Twinkle, Little Star* can be played when the following words appear: "How I wonder what you are," and "Twinkle, twinkle all the night." Scale tones 5 5 4 4 3 3 2 can be played along with the words, "Up above the world so high," and "Like a diamond in the sky."
Five Fingers	Scale tones 5 43 21 are used at the end of *Row Your Boat* with the words, "Life is but a dream," and the scale tones 5 443 2 1 are used with the words "Ten little Indian boys" at the end of that song. Songs requiring only five fingers can easily be played. Such songs are listed near the beginning of this chapter.
Scales	Many songs are based on scales and parts of scales that can be played on the keyboard.

333

A natural outgrowth of such piano-song relationships is the composing of little songs within the limitations of three, four, and five scale tones—songs that children can both sing and play. Eventually this activity will lead to the use of more scale tones in song composition.

Another simple use of the piano is the playing of the notes according to the chord names to provide an easy added part to songs. Example: play F with the F chord, G and with the G chord, and so on. Still more for children to do with the keyboard instruments include playing the rhythm of children's names with one tone or a series of tones; playing tones that illustrate the concepts of high and low pitch; playing short tone patterns for tone-matching purposes or to add interest to songs; playing octave intervals in songs that emphasize this interval; playing other intervals in songs that feature them; playing different note values and rhythm patterns for children to respond to; playing entire characteristic phrases such as the beginning of "The Caisson Song," and playing ostinatos.

Playing the bells, a small instrument, logically comes before playing the piano, a very large instrument. Whatever is done on the bells, however, applies directly to the piano.

Electric organs are used in schools. These vary in size from small two-octave instruments to the type people purchase for home use. The larger ones can be played without disturbing others by use of earphones through which only the player can hear what is being sounded.

M. HOHNER, INC., Hicksville, N.Y. 11802

Organa 12

Such instruments provide an additional type of tone quality for the classroom. The large ones have stops which produce a number of different tone qualities. Certain experiences in dynamics can be studied with the organ, and its sustained and accurate pitch is an advantage. The older (non-electric) reed organ often has a pleasant tone that blends well with voices.

Small Winds As Melody Instruments   Experts in this field recommend that young children have individual experience with the six-hole tin whistle or fife before using instruments such as the Song Flute, Tonette, Flutophone, and Melody Flute. This early beginning would be experimental and without the use of notation. Simple familiar songs could be found on it, and children would naturally make up their own tunes by playing it. Playing small winds by notation would then be introduced at the third or fourth grade level, with the Melody Flute following these. Its superior tone is similar to that of the real flute. The *recorder* is popular in the intermediate grades. Its period of greatest popularity was between the fifteenth and eighteenth centuries. In recent years there has been a strong revival of interest in it because: (1) it is an adult instrument played by adults with pleasure; (2) there is a substantial amount of excellent solo and ensemble music available to play on it, including music by "name" composers of both the past and the present; (3) it is easily blown, although more difficult than the Song Flute, Tonette, Flutophone, and Melody Flute; and (4) it is comparatively inexpensive.

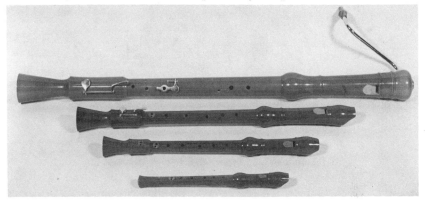

RHYTHM BAND, INC., Forth Worth, Texas 76101

A Family of Recorders

Acceptance of the recorder for upper elementary and junior high school use has been speeded by reductions in price to a low figure when purchased by schools in quantity. The range of the soprano instrument permits sounding middle C as the lowest pitch and continuing upward as high as the normal vocal range. The soprano is widely used because it is built in the key of C, thus having immediate use in playing the music children sing directly from series books; also, it costs less than the larger recorders. Helpful information can be obtained from companies and music dealers that specialize in the recorder, such as Hargail Music, Inc., 28 W. 38th St., New York, N.Y. 10018, a company that imports recorders and sells recorder music.[2]

The baroque recorder is preferred to the German, despite the somewhat

[2] Hargail offers teachers complimentary copies of *New Hargail Recorder Curriculum for Teachers* and *The Recorder in Our Schools*.

easier fingering of the latter, because of better pitch accuracy. The bes¹ recorders are made of wood, and the best of these are higher priced. Dol·metch and Schott are respected names among recorder manufacturers Acceptable plastic instruments are available from firms such as Empiro Music Company, 3216 44th Avenue S.W., Seattle, Washington 98116 and Trophy Music Company, 1278 West 9th Street, Cleveland, Ohio 44113 Plastic models are less expensive and usually more practical for elementary school use.

Now let us discuss some problems involved with the other small winds.

CONN CORPORATION, Oak Brook, Ill. 6052¹
Song Flute

NORLAND MUSIC, INC., 7373 Cicero St., Lincolnwood, Ill
Tonette

TROPHY PRODUCTS CO., 1278 W. 9th St., Cleveland, Ohio 4411³
Flutophone

These instruments have a range of a ninth:

The Tonette can be tuned by adjusting the mouthpiece. Advantages o¹ tuning are offset by the fact that the plastic material wears when the mouth·piece is pulled in and out frequently, and that the teacher must be sure tha¹ all Tonettes are tuned alike when they are played by a group. After a mouthpiece has become worn, it can be kept from falling out by placing a thin strip of paper between the mouthpiece and the body of the instru·ment where they join. Some teachers use tape to hold the parts together The Song Flute cannot be tuned. This disadvantage is offset by having all instruments in the same pitch, and by the assurance that no mouthpiec¹ will fall out. Both the Song Flute and the Tonette are constructed so tha¹ children's fingers fall naturally in place on the finger-holes, which are set in a curved line, while the Flutophone has finger-holes that are set in a straight-line.

The sound of these instruments is essentially soft, as is necessary for classroom use. Because all three instruments are limited to the range previously mentioned, their most common use is in connection with songs within the range of the ninth beginning on middle C. A ninth is the interval of an octave plus one whole-step. Two frequently used instruments having a larger range—each of about two octaves beginning on middle C— are the Symphonette and the Melody Flute. These are somewhat more difficult to play than those of smaller range and, in the opinion of the authors, should seldom be used below fifth grade. Of all these simple instruments, the one with the most pleasing tone is the Melody Flute. All except the Melody Flute finger like the saxophone, the flute, and the upper register of the clarinet. The Melody Flute's fingering is one finger removed from that of the standard instruments. This does not bother children who later change to a real flute, clarinet, or saxophone which, for example, fingers G with three fingers while the Melody Flute fingering for the same note requires only two fingers.

MELODY FLUTE COMPANY, Laurel, Md.

Melody Flute

There are music supervisors who object to the use of these instruments in the classroom. Their major objections are: (1) the children enjoy them so much that unless a teacher knows how to control the situation they may be overemphasized to the neglect of other aspects of the music program— particularly singing; (2) when they are played out of tune their use constitutes a poor musical experience. It follows, then, that the teacher who uses the instruments must avoid these pitfalls.

Out-of-tune playing need not occur. A convention of music educators was startled by the perfection of pitch and the beauty of tone exhibited on the Flutophone by primary level children under the direction of a classroom teacher. When the musicians asked her how she had achieved this result, she replied that she had instructed the children in blowing through soda straws into glasses of water before she had given them the instruments to play. The children blew bubbles in the water at her direction, starting and stopping them at her signal, and they had taken the straws home with them to continue such exercises. Other teachers have agreed that breath control is the "secret" in gaining mastery of pitch and tone quality with these little instruments. Some have used exercises employed by teachers of wind band instruments, such as having children hold sheets of thin paper on a wall with their exhaled breath for increasing lengths of time. Others have profited from suggestions of vocal music supervisors who learned certain breath control exercises in their voice training. The teaching procedure described below in connection with the *Modern Musical Fun* book includes another approach to the problem of playing in tune that should be considered in the serious study of the small winds.

If teachers can learn to teach these instruments properly, they will find that they can teach listening, note-reading, sight-singing, part-singing, and composition as well as playing.

After the teacher decides to use the instruments, the first task is to choose the one best suited to the group. If possible, the children should participate in the choice by experimenting with several of them. Of course, when two or more children blow the same instrument the teacher should have available a sterilizing agent.[3] The teacher should learn to play the chosen instrument well before attempting to teach the class how to play it. Skill on any of them is easy to acquire, so this is not an obstacle.

A good beginning book for elementary classroom use should contain many well-known songs to sing and play, including some to sing and play in parts. A book that fills these requirements is *Modern Musical Fun,* distributed by Lyons, 520 Riverview Ave., Elkhart, Ind. 46514. Its subtitle is "For Singing and Playing with the Tonette." This implies that the playing should supplement the singing—not dominate it or obstruct it.

The following teaching procedure is implied by the subtitle. The standard procedure in teaching any of the small winds is to begin with the notes B, A, and G on the staff. On page two of this book we find the first fingering to be learned by the children, the note B on the middle line of the staff. Before attempting to play this note the children should first *hear* the pitch and *sing* it. The teacher plays the note several times while the class listens to the pitch and to the tone quality. Then the teacher sings the pitch. The class sings the pitch—singing the note name B, for the children are going to learn the note names in a purposeful setting. There may follow more answering back and forth from the teacher to the class and from the class to the teacher (class sings B until everyone has matched the pitch vocally and has really "absorbed" it). Thus, when the children finally play B on their instruments, they will tend to match the pitch they have heard to the extent of adjusting their lips and mouths automatically to produce it with some accuracy. Next, this book presents the note A, and we recommend that it be taught in the same manner that B was taught. Following the presentation of B and A is a little song constructed on these two pitches. Here the teacher asks the children to sing B and A again. When this is accomplished (i.e., when the children have matched tones again and remember each pitch distinctly), they are asked to sing the song "On Tip Toe" using the note names. This done, they next sing the song with the words. Then they play the song on the instruments. Thus the children have had, first, meaningful experiences in listening (tone matching), then

---

[3] A variety of disinfectants is available at drug stores. One should be selected that will not affect plastics adversely.

in sight-singing, and finally in playing the instruments. Some of them will be concentrating on notation for the first time in their lives.

On page three the note G should be learned in the same manner that B and A were learned. The children then sight-sing the next song, "A Safety Song," which employs the three pitches. They sing them first with the note names, then with the words. Lastly, they play the song. These same three notes can now be played in songs that emphasize the three-note pattern: "Hot Cross Buns," "Old MacDonald," "Trampin'," and "Yankee Doodle."

FINGERING
(For Small Winds Such as Tonette, Song Flute, and Flutophone)

	D	C	B	B♭	A	G	F♯	F	E	D	C
Thumb	○	●	●	●	●	●	●	●	●	●	●
Left Hand	○	○	●	●	●	●	●	●	●	●	●
	○	○	○	○	●	●	●	●	●	●	●
	○	○	○	●	○	●	●	●	●	●	●
Right Hand	○	○	○	○	○	○	○	●	●	●	●
	○	○	○	○	○	○	●	○	●	●	●
	○	○	○	○	○	○	○	○	○	●	●

At the bottom of page three there is a song called "Melody." Words can be invented by the children when they have learned to sing it with note names and to play it. It can be sung one line at a time and as a rudimentary duet introducing part-singing. It is then played a line at a time and as a duet. To aid the part-singing, some instruments can remain on each part when the class sings.

Proceeding from this very simple introduction with the above method, B♭, F♯, and the other tones of the C scale are learned. Keen listening for proper pitch, sight-singing, music notation study, and part-singing are combined in this type of instrumental experience. Appropriate songs to play can be found in the music books, and listening and singing based on the instrumental activity can be continued from this source of material.

The Melodica, which uses metal reeds like the harmonica, is a small wind instrument built in the form of a keyboard. Some teachers use it to play melodies to substitute for singing or to guard against over-use of their singing voices. A mouthpiece attachment permits the child to see the keyboard when he plays it to better understand intervals, note patterns, chords, and scalewise melodies. The instrument sounds chords as well as melodies.

M. HOHNER, INC.

Melodica

M. HOHNER, INC., Hicksville, N.Y. 11802

Melodica Piano

Teaching With Melody Instruments

Matching pitch.

The use of individual resonator bars by children in relation to songs gives a helpful indication of pitch. Also, a game can be played in which each child plays his or her melody note each time it appears in the song. A pitch is *real* when held in the hand and struck with a mallet. There are many variations of this game. For example, "I Love the Mountains," a song used in elementary middle and upper grades can be used with six resonator bars, F, G, A, B♭, C, and D, given to as many children. When their pitch is on the first beat of any measure, they play their resonator bar on that beat. Obviously, this can be done with other songs.

Low-high.

Relate low and high (vertical relationship of objects) with the keyboard left and right.

Experiment in composition.

Have individual young children select any four resonator bells. Arrange them in scale order and make up tunes on them.

Composition on black keys.

Let children create pentatonic tunes and songs on keyboard black keys or on resonator bars representing a pentatonic scale on other keys.

Scale.

Build the major scale concept (and later on, other scales) by means of children's playing them on keyboard instruments: bells, xylophone, Melodica, piano. Have them analyze scale patterns by examining the keyboard.

Tonal relationships.

Have a large chart of the keyboard at the front of the room so that it can be used to answer questions and solve musical problems.

Ear training with bells.

The teacher plays a few consecutive scale tones on the bells; a child is asked to come to the bells and reproduce the pitches. A child can make up a short tune, then ask another to play what was heard. If this is done correctly, that child has the privilege of making up a tune and calling on another classmate to remember it and play it. If a child cannot remember the tune, another is called on. The class listens and judges. (This needs to be a game, not "pressure.") The teacher asks a child to play an easy, well-known song. At first the teacher will give the starting pitch. Later, as the game grows more demanding, the child will have to find that pitch. Later, older children can "take dictation" from the teacher's playing the bells. The teacher will give the name of the first note and the key in which the dictation will be given. Then the children will write the pitches they hear on the staff in notation, either individually on paper or collectively with a flannel or magnetic board. The chalk board could be used by a number of children, each working alone.

Adding simple parts.

A simple bell or piano part can be added to songs by asking the player to sound only the note that is the first one in each measure. While technically any song can be used for this, songs that have each measure harmonized with one chord are obviously good. The Danish song "Han Skal Leve," sometimes titled "Birthday Song," is one. Parts of some songs, such as "Weggis Song," are good to use. Songs with melody-lines that suggest scale patterns are also appropriate. The following are in *Singing With Children:* "Carrousel," "Clap Hands With Me," "Blow the Winds Southerly," "The Donkey," "Streets of Laredo."

Transposition.

Help older children develop comprehension of this concept by playing a familiar song in several keys on a melody instrument. Ask the class what they think you did. Then ask the children to find easy tunes by ear, beginning on pitches selected by the teacher.

Key signature.

This puzzle game relates to both ear training and tonal memory. The children will find that transposition demands different key signatures, which is another puzzle relating to the scale in which the song was played.

*Improvising
(pentatonic).*

Make up a melody with the right hand on the piano black keys. Then make up an accompaniment with the left hand on black keys.

Composing.

Create a melody or song from playing on a xylophone or bell set. Notate it and perform it for a friend.

Improvising with bells or xylophone.

Choose a child to improvise a free accompaniment to a pentatonic song. Have him or her experiment with accompaniments that use only two notes, only three notes, and so on until all five notes of the pentatonic scale are utilized.

Tonal memory.

A game to be played by two recorder players is one in which the first player performs a short series of pitches to be imitated by the second player.

Tonal memory.

Have individual children find on the black keys of the piano or bells pentatonic melodies they know such as "Goodby, Old Paint," "Grandma Grunts," "The Riddle Song," "Nobody Knows the Trouble I've Seen," "Night Herding Song," "Old MacDonald," "All Night, All Day," "Get on Board," "Auld Lang Syne," "Land of the Silver Birch," "The Campbells Are Coming," and "Swing Low, Sweet Chariot."

Bitonality.

Play a well-known song such as "Hot Cross Buns," using two keyboard instruments, each in a different key. "Farmer in the Dell" and "Mary Had a Little Lamb" are other candidates. Have the class judge the effect of hearing two keys at once. The effect can be altered somewhat by the tone qualities of the instruments used.

Exploration and practice.

Provide for individual practice and experimentation on the keyboard by using a small classroom organ with head sets so that only the player hears the sound.

Less common intervals.

For advanced children. Arrange for students to discover by means of the keyboard the two kinds of seconds, thirds, sixths, and sevenths (major or minor, or large or small). What might an *augmented* interval be? (Expand a major interval by another half step.) What might a *diminished* interval be? (Contract a minor interval by another half step.) Use the keyboard, then notation to answer these questions so that the students see, hear, and feel these intervals. A question by a student, "Why are fourths, fifths, and octaves called *perfect* intervals?" is difficult to answer. The subject is not important at the elementary level, but any child's question is important to him. Technically, a perfect interval is one in which each tone of the interval appears in a major scale in which the other is *do* or *1*. This is true of fourths, fifths, and octaves, thus these are the "perfect" intervals.

*Transposing
instruments.*

When older children examine a band or orchestra score that they borrow from the instrumental music teacher, they will find that the music is written in a number of different keys. They may find that some instruments are built in different keys. By experimenting with notes on instruments and comparing the resulting pitch with the piano or bells, they can discover that when B♭ instruments play written C, the pitch is B♭, and when E♭ instruments play C, the pitch sounded in E♭. The teacher could plan a discrepant event by asking children who play instruments to all play the same song from a music textbook. This would be one way to discover which instruments are transposing instruments and which are not.

Harmony Instruments

*Exploring
Combinations
of Pitches*

Among the first experiences children have with harmony in the class-room are the accompaniments of songs they have learned as monophonic (unaccompanied) melodies. From this, the thinnest of textures, they are transported into a different world of sound by accompaniments played by the teacher on Autoharp, guitar, piano or by means of recordings. This is usually homophonic music (melody with accompaniment). Many different textures can be produced in accompaniments, and children should be guided to discern what types they are. Thin, thick, heavy, and light are simple descriptive terms for textures, but there should be a good many other adjectives in use as time goes by. As soon as they are able, children should be helped to find how music is organized to produce these various effects. An interesting question to ask when using the piano is, "What would happen if the melody (in the treble clef) and the harmony (in the bass clef) were inverted?" and then proceed to find out by experimenting. Older children can find chords in chordline (disjunct) melodies and relate these to chords they can build on the bells and piano, or play on the Autoharp to accompany these melodies.

Some teachers make it possible for children to experiment with combining all sorts of pitches and sounds, both as isolated "chords" and as a series of sound effects.

The approach of Carl Orff includes the addition of instrumental *ostinati* (recurring melodic fragments) to pentatonic melodies to provide a polyphonic texture. Accompaniments to melodies may begin with a *bourdon* (open fifth in most instances) in the bass. From this can develop "moving bourdons" produced by alternating the two tones; both growing from this and adding to it are the repeated tonal fragments, the ostinati. It is assumed that within these limitations children can create music that is truly children's music, rather than music which is basically too adult and too harmonically complex for children to comprehend fully.

Lit - tle Miss Muf - fet   sat   on   a   tuf - fet,   etc

Accompanying bourdons and ostinati possible with the above melody:

Carl Orff designed keyboard mallet instruments on which these bourdons and ostinati are played. They are as follows:

soprano glockenspiel	sounds two octaves higher than written
alto glockenspiel	sounds one octave higher than written
soprano metallophone	sounds one octave higher than written
soprano xylophone	sounds one octave higher than written
alto metallophone	sounds as written
alto xylophone	sounds as written
bass metallophone	sounds one octave lower when written in the treble clef
bass xylophone	sounds one octave lower when written in the treble clef

The increasing popularity of the Orff approach and of these fine quality instruments has led to their manufacture both in Europe and in the United States, to imitations of them, and currently to their availability from nearly all the suppliers of percussion instruments and Autoharps. Sonor and Studio 49 are respected European manufacturers. See *Sources of Classroom Instruments* at the end of this chapter.

The Autoharp   The Autoharp is an instrument of ancient lineage which has come to be popular in elementary and junior high schools, and is used by folk singers. The model most in favor today has fifteen push-button bars with felts that prevent the vibration of strings other than those that sound the chord tones desired. The 21-chord model is growing in popularity.

Although some children in primary grades are able to play the instrument satisfactorily, it is not until the fourth grade that most children can do so. In early primary grades teachers often press the bars while children strum the strings. It is believed that guiding children to listen carefully to Autoharp chording assists the development of a feeling for harmony, which is part of the preparation for part-singing. It is a substitute for the piano in situations where no piano is available. Hearing chord changes and playing the correct chord at the proper time are valuable for ear-training purposes, and teachers should emphasize these as listening experiences in

OSCAR SCHMIDT-INTERNATIONAL, INC., and
MUSIC EDUCATION GROUP, Union, N.J. 07083

Autoharp

OSCAR SCHMIDT-INTERNATIONAL, INC., and
MUSIC EDUCATION GROUP, Union, N.J. 07083

their efforts to develop children's musicianship. The act of chording is a
rhythmic response. A child who is yet unable to sing beautifully may be
able to make as beautiful music on the Autoharp as anyone else; thus success
on this instrument can help children feel a sense of accomplishment. Chord-

ing on the Autoharp is an effective way to stimulate interest in the study of chords on the piano and on the staff. Another use of the Autoharp is to establish the tempo and key of a song by playing introductory chords in the desired rhythm.

The Autoharp is placed on a desk or table, with the corner between the two straight ends of the instrument pointing somewhat toward the player. Fingers of the left hand press firmly on the appropriate chord bar while the right hand strokes the full range of the strings from left to right with a pick. Sometimes the player may choose to stroke the strings on the left side of the bridge to produce a deeper-toned effect. *Finger forms* are important, and the player needs to analyze the chord progressions he is to play, then plan the most simple and efficient way to place the correct finger on the bar. In most of the music suggested for Autoharp chording there will be no more than three chords, the tonic (I), the dominant seventh (V_7), and the subdominant (IV). The finger form for these chords in the keys of C major, G major, F major, D minor, and A minor is as follows:

	IV	V_7	I
left hand			
	ring finger	middle finger	index finger

Try this finger form in the above keys, and find the straight position and the triangular position of the fingers in this basic finger form.

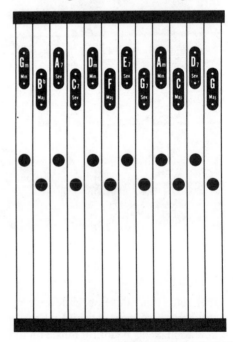

MUSIC EDUCATION GROUP, Union, N.J. 07083

Autoharp, 21-Chord Model

The strings are stroked with a pick held in the right hand, unless the player is left handed. The loud tone produced with a plastic pick is needed for most classroom singing, while the soft tone produced with a felt pick is best for solo and small ensemble singing. Picks are made in different shapes and sizes. Some are worn on fingers while others are held between thumb and index finger. Plastic fasteners from bread wrappers are used as substitutes, and men often use their fingernails instead of a pick.

When teaching children to play the Autoharp, it is the usual practice to begin with songs that require only one chord to accompany, proceeding to those requiring two chords, then to songs in which three chords are necessary. It is desirable to play part of the time by rote to be sure that the children are *hearing* the chord changes, not simply pushing buttons mechanically. Such songs follow:

	key:
One-chord songs:	
"Row Your Boat," "Little Tom Tinker"	C major
"Are You Sleeping?" "Farmer in the Dell," "For Health and Strength"	F major
"Canoe Song"	D minor
"Zum Gali Gali"	G minor
Two-chord songs:	*key:*
"Mary Had a Little Lamb," "Sandy Land," "Looby Loo,"	G major
"London Bridge," "Ten Little Indians," "Hush Little Baby," "Polly Wolly Doodle"	F major
"Old Smoky," "Oats, Peas, Beans, and Barley," "Little Red Caboose"	C major
"Down in the Valley," "Long Ago," "Bow Belinda," "Shoo Fly," "Susie Little Susie"	F major
"Nobody Home"	G minor
"Lovely Evening" (I-IV)	F major
"Wayfaring Stranger"	D minor
Three-chord songs:	*key:*
"Silent Night," Brahms' "Lullaby," "Marines' Hymn"	C major
"My Bonnie," "Jingle Bells," "Camptown Races," "Old Brass Wagon"	G major
"Red River Valley," "Twinkle Twinkle, Little Star," "This Old Man," "Hickory Dickory Dock," "Home on the Range"	F major
"Go Down, Moses"	A minor
"Old King Cole"	D minor

Since some two- and three-chord songs are not written in these common keys, using the Autoharp to accompany them requires *transposing* them into keys that will make it possbile to play such songs on the instrument. This involves placing the fingers in the finger form of the key nearest to the original key of the song and following the I, V$_7$, and IV designations, or their equivalent in letter names. The teacher should be certain that the range of pitches in the new key is suitable for children's voices. The 15-bar model permits playing in B♭ and D major also.

A problem in the use of Autoharps is tuning them.[4] There is no universally accepted method. Ordinarily, one tunes to a piano that is in proper pitch, although a pitch pipe can be used. The strings sounding the C major chord may be tuned first (all the C's, E's, and G's), then the strings of the G$_7$ chord (all B's, D's, and F's—the G's having been tuned as part of the C chord), and next the F major chord (all A's—the F's and C's having been tuned as pitches belonging to the other chords). These three chords should then be played slowly to hear whether any of the strings need further adjusting. After this, the other strings may be tuned as individual tones of the

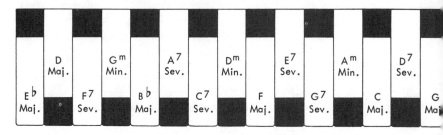

Autoharp Bridge (15-bar Model)

chromatic scale (all the half-steps). Then every chord of the instrument is played slowly to determine possible need for further tuning. A child can play the pitches on the piano while the teacher adjusts the strings. As a general rule, the teacher must do the adjusting of the strings. The only cases the authors know where strings have been broken are those in which elementary school children tighten strings to the breaking point because they think they hear the pitch to which they are tuning one octave higher than it sounds. To keep the instrument in tune and to protect it, it should be kept either in the case it comes in or on a covered shelf, out of the sunlight and away from sources of heat, cold, or dampness. When the instrument is subject to changes in temperature, the expansion and contraction of the strings causes changes in their tension, hence changes in pitch.

Some European music educators do not look with favor on chording instruments such as the Autoharp at the primary level, claiming that children do not possess sufficient harmonic sense at this age to profit from it. However, many American educators believe that chording instruments can provide a valuable listening experience for this age group. Young children can learn to recognize the I-chord as the "home" chord, the V$_7$-chord as the "away-from-home" chord, and the IV-chord as the "longing-for-home" or "leaning" chord. They can identify them by appropriate motions: the "home" chord with folded arms, the "away-from-home" chord with outstretched arms, and the "leaning" chord by raising both arms to the left or to the right. Children can create other interpretations of the characteristic sound of each of these chords, and create their own related body responses.

---

[4] The new Autoharps remain in tune much longer than the earlier models.

Types of Autoharp accompaniments Like any other musical instrument, the Autoharp should be played with good taste, and there should be logical reasons for the particular style of the accompaniment played. The mood of the song indicates whether the player uses a slow relaxed stroke (as for lullabies and quiet songs), or a strong fast stroke (as for marches and rhythmic songs). For some waltzes, an um-pah-pah style is called for. This can be made by strumming the first beat of each measure with low-pitched strings and the other two beats with highpitched strings. A deeper, richer effect is obtained by playing on the left side of the bridge. This brings out the sound of the lower strings and omits a few of the highest pitches. The player can make an appropriate accompaniment for some Spanish-type music by chording in the rhythm of ♩. ♪♩ ♩ . A bagpipe or bourdon effect is made by holding down two bars at the same time; G major and G minor, D₇ and D minor, and A₇ and A minor. This effect is useful for pentatonic music, for some Scottish music, and for folksongs based upon the open fifth of the bagpipe or musette. Individual strings can be plucked to simulate Oriental-type music. A zither or tamburitza effect that characterizes some Eastern European folk music can be produced by two players on the same instrument. One player presses the bars while the other strokes the strings rapidly with wooden mallets. A metal bar or object placed across the strings will produce a steel guitar effect. Minor seventh chords can be sounded when two instruments are used. For example, G minor and B♭ major chords played simultaneously will sound the G minor seventh chord. A minor plus C major will sound the A minor seventh chord, and D minor plus F major sounds the D minor seventh chord. For songs of slow tempo, a skilled player can produce both the melody and the harmony. To obtain this effect, a chord is played for each tone of the melody, and the player strums the strings only as far as the melody pitch. A harp effect is obtained by reversing the usual stroke, the player beginning the stroke with the high strings and moving the pick toward the low strings.

A valuable teacher's guide to the Autoharp is *Teaching Music With the Autoharp,* Music Education Group, Union, N.J. 07083. The book includes advanced techniques for playing the instrument.

Ukulele and Guitar

If the desirability of chording experiences on the Autoharp has gained wide acceptance, it follows that there should be similar values in other chording instruments such as the ukulele and guitar. The ukulele has supporters from the fourth grade on, and chording on the guitar is done by some children who are ten and eleven years old.

Standard tuning on the ukulele was once G-C-E-A from low to high strings. In recent years a preference for tuning the instrument one whole step higher, to A-D-F♯-B, has developed. Thus, the ukulele beginner

finds two tunings in current use. Notice that if the teacher employs both tunings, the fingering for the common chords in G major and F major become the same, as does that for D major and C major.

Most ukuleles are made of wood, and need the same protection against dropping, cold, heat, and sun that the Autoharp needs. Extreme dampness, dryness, or temperature changes will change the tuning and could crack the body of the instrument. Children need to be informed about how to strum the instrument or they may break strings by pulling them.

Experts in ukulele playing state that while the baritone ukulele is superior in tone quality and many teachers prefer it to the soprano (standard) instrument, the soprano is best for elementary school children in terms of student hand size; it is easier for children to play. It is easily retuned in C. when this is desirable for a whole-step lower singing range, and it costs

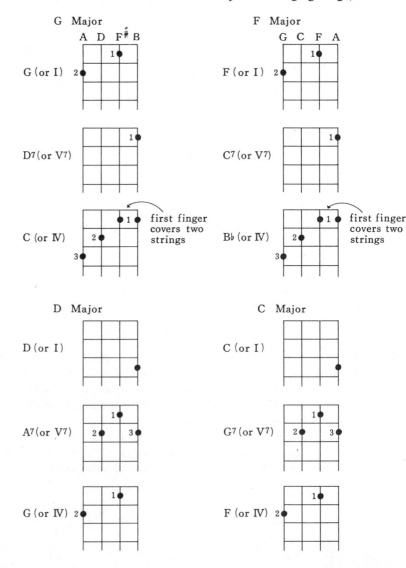

less than the baritone. Wood is preferred to plastic. Some teachers introduce the ukulele in a way that relates to the guitar and string bass. The following describes this approach, which begins with the D tuning of the soprano ukulele: A D F♯ B.

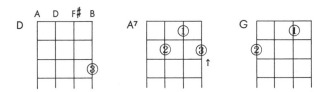

With these three primary chords one can play many folk songs.

When left-handed children play the soprano ukulele, the tuning should be changed to B F♯ A D or A E C G so that when the fingerboard is held in the right hand, the left-handers will be able to use the tablature written for right-handers.

The baritone, which is becoming a popular instrument for adults, is tuned a 5th below the soprano ukulele. Its first string, however, is an octave and a 5th below the soprano's first string, making its strings the same as the top four strings of the standard guitar.

Baritone Tuning:

(guitar strings)

This makes it a good instrument for beginners who may want to transfer to a standard guitar later on. The chords will be formed in the same way but will sound in different keys.

If one is using both instruments simultaneously, it is possible to stagger the teaching of these fingerings, permitting the advantage of being able to practice together. A system one teacher [5] devised to teach seven fingerings on each instrument makes possible playing all primary chords in two keys in common plus one extra key for each. Directly below these are the added fingerings for the other two strings on the guitar.

These seven fingerings are the easiest for the beginner to play. They comprise the primary triads of the keys of D, G, and C major for the ukulele, and G, C, and F major for the baritone ukulele.

Guitar chords that are easiest for the older child to play are those to follow. They are not easily learned.

The lower four guitar strings are the same as those on the string bass. The chord-roots are plucked with the index finger on the string bass. Since the bass does not have frets, small thin strips of masking tape can be used to mark the half steps for inexperienced players.

[5] Erma Kleehammer, University of Calgary, Alberta, Canada.

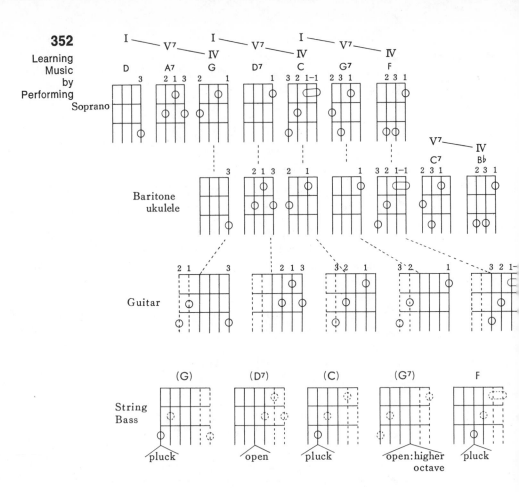

Some of the more common minor chords for the ukulele, baritone and guitar are:

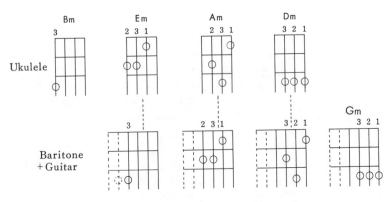

Piano Chording

Since the 1 3 5 note pattern becomes a familiar one to children, being used both in their songs and in the procedure that enables the class to have a feeling for the key before singing, this is a logical note combination to use in the initial teaching of chording. This 1 3 5 chord (a major *triad* in *root position*) is also a basic concept in the study of music theory.

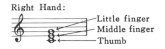

Should a child be unable to exert equal pressure through these three fingers or in any way be unable to control them at first, the playing of the chord may be accomplished by using any combination of fingers of both hands or by playing only the two highest notes of a three-note chord. The teacher may help the child to play the chord in a steady walking tempo and as this playing of the chord on the beat continues, have the class sing "Row, row, row your boat." The discovery by the child that an accompaniment can be provided for a well-known song in this way is thrilling. There are few songs that can be accompanied in their entirety by the lone 1 3 5 chord. Some were listed earlier in this chapter.

Songs that rightfully require two chords (I and V₇) but that might be usable as one-chord songs include "Old MacDonald," "Farmer in the Dell," "Three Blind Mice," "Goodbye Old Paint," "Swing Low, Sweet Chariot," "Taps," and "Shortnin' Bread."

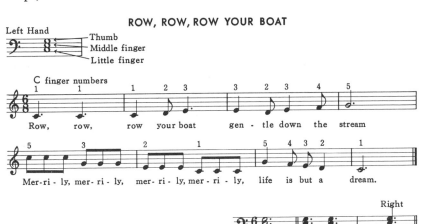

ROW, ROW, ROW YOUR BOAT

Summary of possibilities:

Play the melody with the right hand.
Play the melody with the left hand.

353

Play the chord with the left hand.

Play the chord with the right hand.

Play the chord with both hands.

Play the melody with the right hand and the chord with the left hand.

Play the melody with the left hand (in bass clef) and the chord with the right hand (in treble clef).

Play the chord in other forms, such as one note at a time.

How often the chord is sounded depends on how the individual feels about the song. One child may play a chord on every beat. Another may choose to sound the chord every other beat. Still another child may alter the steady pattern of chord-sounding by a pause at the end of a phrase. Children should be free to be as individually creative as possible in this simple way.

When a child has learned how to build 1 3 5 chords on different pitches such as C, F, G, and has learned to recognize the distinctive sound of the major chord, the 1 3 5 chord in minor may be easily taught. A child can soon learn that the minor chord has its own characteristic sound and that major and minor chords can be built at will. Experience will expand the child's concept of the difference in sound between major and minor. The mechanical difference between major and minor 1 3 5 chords is merely that the middle finger, which plays scale tone 3, is placed one half-step lower in minor than in major. Few commonly known songs can be accompanied by the lone minor 1 3 5 chord, but children can compose such songs easily. An example follows:

SLAVE SONG

Piano chording:

Suggested rhythmic responses:

Drum pattern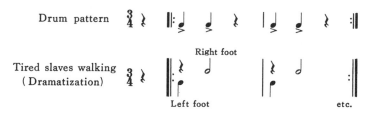

Tired slaves walking
(Dramatization)

Singing and playing:

A piano part invented later which can be sung as a chant:

Two hands

The children discovered that their song could be sung as a round.

A song of Israeli origin that can be accompanied by the G-minor chord is "Zum Gali Gali."

If children have used the Autoharp with songs requiring two or more different chords, the addition of the V_7 chord to permit improvising a piano accompaniment to many familiar songs is relatively easy. A simple form of the chord change from I to V_7 and back to I is as follows:

Left hand   Right hand

Using the hand position for the 1 3 5 *chord as a starting point,* the following directions apply in *all* major keys:

> *right hand:*   The little finger remains on the same key. The fourth finger is placed one half-step higher than the third finger was. The thumb is placed one half-step lower than before.
>
> *left hand:*   The thumb remains on the same key. The index finger is placed one half-step higher than the middle finger was. The little finger is placed one half-step lower than before.

Many songs can be harmonized with the I and V_7 chords. Some of the most familiar were listed earlier for Autoharp chording.

Since most songs in minor keys are based on a scale in which the seventh tone is raised one half-step, practically all minor I-V_7 chord songs will have the V_7 chord played exactly the same as it is played in the major keys of the same name, i.e., the V_7 chord in G minor is the same chord as in G

CLEMENTINE

Piano chords:

major. Thus, the only difference in chording would be in the I chord, which in minor would have its third (the middle note) one half-step lower than in the major chord. It is a simple matter, then, to play "Nobody Home" in G minor: [6]

NOBODY HOME

Three-Part Round

Piano chording:

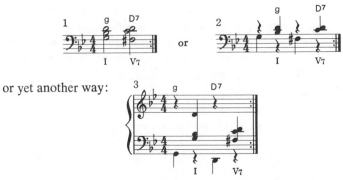

or yet another way:

[6] Some musicians abbreviate G minor by writing "g," and G major by "G."

Suggestion: Try making up an introduction using the style of Example 3. Also, improvise an ending for this round. Add suitable percussion instruments and hand clapping.

Other interesting songs in minor that use these same chords are the French carol "Pat-a-pan" and the English carol, "Dame, Get Up." Percussion instruments go well with "Pat-a-pan."

The hand position for the IV chord is easier than the hand position for the V_7 chord. The "rule" for the change from I to IV is as follows:

left hand: The little finger remains on the same key. The index finger is placed one half-step higher than the middle finger was. The thumb moves up one whole step.

right hand: The thumb remains on the same key. The middle finger is placed one half-step higher than before. The little finger moves up one whole step.

The round "Christmas Bells" provides a good introduction to this chord change. Use the above chords as marked.

The familiar round "Lovely Evening" and the cowboy song "The Railroad Corral" (*This Is Music: Book 6*) are other examples of songs that require only the I and IV chords for their harmonization.

CHRISTMAS BELLS

The IV chord in minor is played by lowering the highest of the three tones of the major IV chord one half-step. An American folk song that can be harmonized with only I and IV chords is "Wayfaring Stranger":

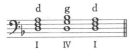

WAYFARING STRANGER

stran-ger____ a - trav'- ling through ____ this world of woe;____ but there's no sick - ness, toil nor dan- ger____ in that bright world____ to which I go.____ I'm go - ing there____ to see my mo-ther,____ I'm go - ing there____ no more to roam, ____ I'm just a - go - ing o - ver Jor - dan, ____ I'm just a - go - ing o - ver home.

Examples of the many songs in major keys easily chorded with I, IV, and V₇ chords are "The Caisson Song," "Oh Susanna," "He's a Jolly Good Fellow," "The First Noel," "Night Herding Song," "Eyes of Texas (I've Been Working on the Railroad)," "All Through the Night," "Sing Your Way Home," "Deck the Halls," "Happy Birthday to You," "Old Oaken Bucket," "Auld Lang Syne," "Annie Laurie," "Old Folks at Home," "Reuben and Rachel," "Santa Lucia," and "The Muffin Man." Others were listed earlier for Autoharp chording.

CINDY

Appalachian Mountains Song

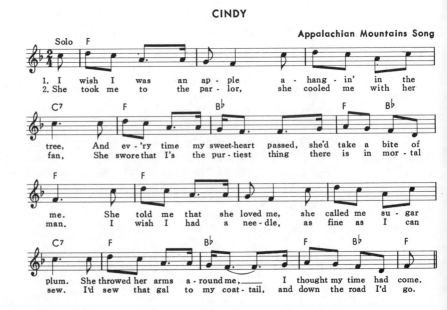

1. I wish I was an ap - ple a - hang - in' in the tree, And ev - 'ry time my sweet-heart passed, she'd take a bite of me. She told me that she loved me, she called me su - gar plum. She throwed her arms a - round me, ____ I thought my time had come.

2. She took me to the par - lor, she cooled me with her fan, She swore that I's the pur - tiest thing there is in mor - tal man. I wish I had a nee - dle, as fine as I can sew. I'd sew that gal to my coat - tail, and down the road I'd go.

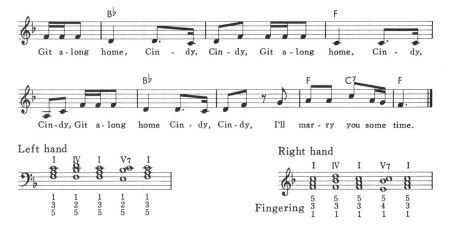

This use of the piano in the classroom can result in a teacher's learning to play comparatively well. Should any teacher desire to hasten this learning process, there are beginning piano books that employ and expand the method of chording used in this chapter.

Teachers should use the sustaining pedal of the piano sparingly. A common fault of piano players is overuse of this pedal, which results in a blur of tones rather than in the clarity and distinctness children need to hear.

If one can chord with I, IV, and V_7 chords in major keys, it is not difficult to chord in minor keys with I, IV, and V_7. Incidentally, minor keys are not as important as major keys as far as common usage in the United States is concerned. While peoples of Eastern Europe find in minor tonality a natural expression, the people of the United States lean rather heavily toward the major tonality. American children should be able to identify minor and major and to enjoy hearing the changes from minor to major and vice versa in songs such as "We Three Kings of Orient Are," "When Johnny Comes Marching Home," and "Minka."

Children sometimes ask the question, "From where do the V_7 and IV chords come, and why are our fingers in the positions they are on the keyboard?"

A 1 3 5 chord can be built on every step of the scale. We could chord by using only 1 3 5 chords, but it would be very awkward to do, and it would not sound well. What we are trying to do with our chord positions at the piano is to move our fingers as little as possible. It is something like being "intelligently lazy"—which in this case is also being efficient. Here are the I, IV, and V chords in the 1 3 5 position in the C-major scale:

These can also be called C, F, and G, because they have two names, one being the Roman numeral that corresponds to the Arabic number name of the scale tone on which the chord is built, and the other being the letter name of the note that is "1" when the chord is in the 1 3 5 (root) position. Here is the V_7 chord in root position:

We are still in the key of C major. Compare the V_7 with the V above. This chord is called V_7 because a note has been added that is seven lines and spaces above G. The notes from the bottom to the top in this chord are G, B, D, and F, or 1 3 5 7. It is V_7 because G is the fifth step of the scale of C, and we are using that key in this illustration.

The following illustration shows where we obtain the simple three-finger hand position for chording:

By rearranging the G 1 3 5 7 chord into another *position,* and by omitting the note D, which is the one we can most easily eliminate without injuring the sound of the chord, we can keep the hand in the same place as in playing the I chord and move only the fingers.

The IV chord that we use in piano chording is another position of original 1 3 5 arrangement of the notes:

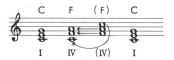

Common chord positions are:

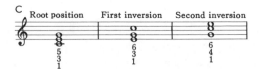

The first inversion is called 6–3 because if one counts from the lowest note to the highest, numbering the lowest note "1", the *interval* is found to be that of a *sixth.* Counting in similar manner, from the lowest note to the middle one, reveals that this interval is a *third,* hence this is a 6–3 chord. The origin of the name of the 6–4 chord can be counted out in the same way. The two intervals here are a sixth and a *fourth,* hence the name 6–4 chord. See "The Blacksmith," to find how these chords appear in a melody line.

THE BLACKSMITH

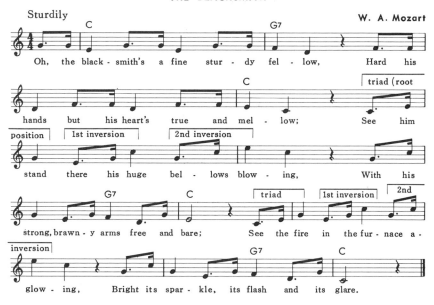

2. *Blow the fire, stir the coals, heaping more on,*
Till the iron is aglow, let it roar on!
As the smith high his hammer keeps swinging,
Fiery sparks fall in showers all around;
And the sledge on the anvil keeps ringing,
Giving out its loud clanging sound.

These inversions appear in the melody of many songs. For elementary school children, the names of the inversions are not particularly vital; the important factor is the comprehension that the same notes in these different positions form the same chord. Compare these horizontal chords with the vertical chords in piano chording, and plan similar experiences for children. Try using the chords indicated in the melody for accompanying those measures. Another song to use is "My Home's in Montana." The children's generalization resulting from a series of such experiments could be, "When tones of specific chords appear in melodies, those chords form a suitable accompaniment." Other possible generalizations might include, "A chord is a vertical arrangement of three or more tones," and "When there are changes in a melody, there are usually changes in the harmony."

A triad or root position chord is a 1–3–5 tonal structure; another third is added to form a seventh chord, a 1–3–5–7 arrangement of tones. The relation of the I and V_7 chords to the major scale is as follows:

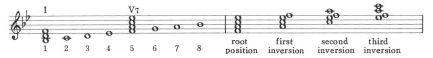

Seventh chords, or parts of them, are commonly found in melody lines. Find some in "The Blacksmith," "The Lone Star Trail," and "Down in the Valley." Children should rediscover that the I-chord yields a feeling of stability, whereas the V_7-chord is restless and seems to demand change (resolution). The IV-chord has the same pattern of inversions as the I-chord; its only difference is that it is constructed on the fourth degree of the scale while the I-chord is built on the first degree.

For studying chords in vertical position, some three-part songs in fifth- and sixth-grade series books are helpful. One of these is "Jarabe," in which *passing tones* and *nonchord* tones can be discovered and in which contrary motion can be reviewed.

JARABE

Melody and words from *Spanish-American Folksongs*, collected by Eleanore Hague; published by the American Folklore Society, Inc. Used by permission. Found in *This Is Music, Book V*, by William R. Sur, Robert E. Nye, William R. Fisher, and Mary R. Tolbert. Copyright © 1967 and 1962 by Allyn and Bacon, Inc. Used by permission.

The attention of older children can be drawn to songs in which there are key changes in order to solve the problem of how a composer *modulates* (changes) from one key to another. Two such songs are "The Erie Canal," and "We Three Kings of Orient Are," in which both major and minor tonalities occur. Relationships between the minor scales on which the songs are based and the minor chords used to accompany them can be examined, then compared with the relationships between major scales and major melodies. If there is sufficient interest, some questions might be, "What happens when triads are built on every degree of the major scale?" "What would happen if we build triads on every degree of the minor scale?" "Do you find any unusual chords?" "What might they be?" "How would you write them?" The harmonizations of "Ma Belle Bimba" and "We Wish You a Merry Christmas" require both major and minor chords; older children can create their own harmonizations, making aesthetic judgments as to which chords are the most pleasing.

The piano keyboard is a testing ground and experimental arena for hearing, seeing, and playing the chords extracted from songs and for trying out new harmonizations.

Chording with Bells

The "piano chords" can be played on resonator bells effectively. Teachers use these individual tone bars in many ways. The bars can be distributed among numbers of children, each having a bar and a mallet with which to strike it. In the key of C, for example, all children who hold bells marked C, E or G, will sound them when the C-major chord is needed, and when the F-major chord is required in the harmonization of the song, all children holding bars that sound F, A, and C will strike them. Of course, they must be struck at the same instant, and this demands the close attention of the players. To produce an interesting shimmering effect, the player needs two mallets, striking the bell in rapid alternation. Playing chords in this manner with appropriate songs can make truly beautiful music. Motivating a fourth, fifth, or sixth-grade class to harmonize a song in this way can initiate a study of chords and their relation to the staff and key signature.

Hand bells can be used also, and the Melodica was mentioned earlier as an instrument on which one can play both melody and harmony.

The Singing Classroom Orchestra

When children have learned to play small wind instruments, to chord on the piano and Autoharp, and to play the bells and percussion instruments, the possibility of the singing classroom orchestra presents itself. When the teacher finds a melody line in the range of the wind instruments with the chords named, there are opportunities for combining various instruments with voices, or alternating instruments and voices. Here is a creative activity developing musical discrimination—the children and the teacher will orchestrate the song according to their own judgment. Children can also have experiences in conducting such orchestras. Songs that are not found in books at hand can be presented by means of a projector or can be drawn on large (two by three feet) sheets of heavy paper or light cardboard and placed where all can see. Music can be quickly drawn on such paper. A staff liner with chalk is used to mark the staff. These chalk lines are drawn over with black crayon, freehand. When two-part songs are written, the melody part may be in black crayon while the harmony part is in another color for easier reading. Examples follow:

Theme from NINTH SYMPHONY

The Theme from the Ninth Symphony is an example of the very simple beginning music a classroom orchestra uses. Ordinarily, themes from the great symphonies are not applicable to this type of work. This particular theme, however, has the simplicity of folk music. It can be extended to include more of the original melody than appears here. An interesting and thrilling event after words have been set to it and the song is learned, is the teacher's playing a recording of a section of the last movement of the Ninth Symphony. The children will be fascinated listeners to "their song" and will be interested in what Beethoven does with it. Appreciation may be at an extremely high level at this point. The key of C was chosen because it is easiest for the playing of the instruments. The key of F is preferable as soon as the fingering of B♭ is learned, because it places the singing voice in a better range.

"Come, Ye Thankful People, Come" is more difficult and represents a later experience in the development of the classroom orchestra.

COME, YE THANKFUL PEOPLE, COME

While some classroom teachers will be able to write their own classroom orchestra arrangements and make their own charts, others may not be able to do so. In these cases the music specialist becomes the helper, the arranger, and perhaps the chart-maker who assists the room teacher.

Instrumental music activities in the general music program constitute not an end in themselves but an important aid in the teaching of better listening, singing, musical discrimination, creativity, part-singing, and note-reading, and serve as an introduction to simple music theory concepts, all in a setting that children enjoy, understand, and know to be purposeful.

Teaching With Harmony Instruments

HARMONY

I, V$_7$, IV chords.

These chords are the *tonic, dominant seventh,* and *subdominant,* respectively. The teacher plays the chords slowly and repetitively on the Autoharp, piano, or guitar. The children are asked to describe, identify, and compare the chords in some inventive way. When this has been done, an identification game can be played. For example, some children have identified the I-chord as the "at home chord," and the V$_7$-chord as the "away from home chord." They sometimes identify the IV-chord as the "leaning chord" or the "yearning for home chord." The chords can be identified by arm motions. V$_7$ may be arms up; I may be arms down; IV may be arms at an angle or out in front.

Major, minor chords.
Improvising harmony.

Adding to the above activity, children can identify major and minor chords by palms up for major and palms down for minor. The teacher plays on the piano, or loudly on an Autoharp, a slowly changing succession of chords. The class will listen carefully to the chords and hum pitches to "fit" the harmony the teacher is playing.

Autoharp chording.

Recordings: *Tuning the Autoharp,* Rhythm Band, Inc., Fort Worth, Texas
Tuning Your Autoharp, Oscar Schmidt—International, Union, N.J.

Chord.

Many children think of a chord as a triad of three notes, and they are correct. However, their concept of chord can be expanded by asking them to write on the grand staff the pitches of the C major chord as they are shown and sounded on the Autoharp. Ask them which chord tones are repeated at octave intervals, how this might affect their definition of "chord," and how this might relate to their future compositions. Have them try to play the Autoharp chord on the piano. How many hands will it require? Can the chord be extended to more pitches than are on the Autoharp?

Chording accompaniments.

Arrange for children to create their own Autoharp, piano, or ukulele accompaniments for easy two and three-chord songs. The songs are to have no chord designations to help the learners. The problem is to decide which chords to use. The solution can be done in groups, with reports being made back to the total group. The eye must be used to study the melody line for chord clues, and the ear must be used to test whether or not the chord "sounds right." The class may discover that some songs can be harmonized in several different ways.

Tone clusters.

Another technique in contemporary composition is use of the tone cluster, a multiple pitch sound used by composers such as Charles Ives and Henry Cowell. To make a tone cluster, place the entire palm or forearm on the piano keys. (They can be made in other ways, too.) Young children use tone clusters to imitate the sound of a large animal walking.

Quintal and quartal chords.

Traditional chords are constructed of thirds when in root position. Some chords used in contemporary music are constructed as a succession of perfect fourths—*quartal* chords, while others are constructed as a succession of perfect fifths—*quintal* chords. Have several children perform such chords at the piano. Discuss how they might be used in compositions and for sound effects.

Harmony.

Listen to three selected recorded compositions and compare the element of harmony found in each of them.

RELATING MELODY AND HARMONY

Composition over an ostinato.

Create a simple ostinato, then have individuals or small groups compose a melody over it. Teachers usually plan a pentatonic ostinato to begin with. Examples to learn from:
Pierné: *March of the Little Lead Soldiers,* BOL 54
McPhee: "Ostinatos" from *Tabuh Tabuhan,* Mercury MG 50103
Cowell: "Ostinato Pianissimo" on *Concert Percussion,* Time 8000

Relating chords to scales.

Dramatize the relation of chords to scales by forming a major scale of eight children standing before the class, each with a resonator bar representing the correctly-ordered notes of that scale from 1 through 8 (or 1'). The teacher asks children holding bars 1, 3, and 5 to step out in front of the scale and to play their tones together in tremulo style so that the chord can be sustained. "How can we make a minor chord?" "Can we make a minor chord based on scale step 2?" "How can we find the V_7 chord?" "Where are the notes belonging to the V_7 chord when we have only these eight pitches to work with?" "What does this look like in notation?" When notes are needed that are not in the eight scale tones, others from the class can be called upon, given the appropriate tone bar, and placed in keyboard position with the others. For example, a problem may be to act out the whole-tone scale. "What other bars will be necessary?" "What does it sound like?" "How can it be notated?"

Melodic improvisation based on chords.

Use written chord sequences as the basis for melodic improvisation. Begin with I IV I V_7 I sequence in familiar keys. One child can play the chords on Autoharp or piano while another improvises over the chords on bells, a small wind instrument, or with his singing voice.

$\frac{4}{4}$ F   B♭   F   C₇   F

References

GARY, CHARLES L., ed., *The Study of Music in the Elementary School: A Conceptual Approach.* Reston, Va.: Music Educators National Conference, 1967, pp. 67–81, harmony.

Autoharp Instruction   NYE, ROBERT E., and MEG PETERSON, *Teaching Music With the Autoharp.* Union, N.J. 07083: Music Education Group, 1973.

Guitar Instruction   EISENKRAMER, HENRY E., *Strum and Sing: Guitar in the Classroom.* Evanston, Ill.: Summy-Birchard Co., 1969.

Guitar Magic. Atlanta, Ga.: Educational Productions, Inc., 454 Armour Circle, N.E. 30324. An audiovisual method.

Mel Bay's Guitar Class Method. Kirkwood, Mo.: Mel Bay Publications, Inc., 107 W. Jefferson Ave. 63122.

SILVERMAN, JERRY, *Graded Guitar Method.* New York: The Big Three Music Corp., 1970.

TIMMERMAN, MAURINE, and CELESTE GRIFFITH, *Guitar in the Classroom.* Dubuque, Iowa: William C. Brown Company Publishers, 1971.

Multiple Instruments

BURAKOFF, GERALD, and LAWRENCE WHEELER, *Music Making in the Elementary School*, Hargail Music, Inc., New York, N.Y. 10018. Student's and Teacher's Editions. Uses recorder, voice, bells, and rhythm instruments.

CHEYETTE, IRVING, and ALBERT RENNA, *Songs to Sing with Recreational Instruments*, Theodore Presser Company, Philadelphia, Pa.

SLIND, LLOYD H., *Melody, Rhythm, and Harmony; More Melody, Rhythm, and Harmony*, Belwin-Mills, Melville, N.Y. 11746.

SNYDER, ALICE M., *Sing and Strum.* Belwin-Mills, Melville, N.Y. 11746.

VANDRE, CARL, *Adventures in Harmony, Rhythm, and Song*, Handy-Folio Music Company, Minneapolis, Minn.

WIEDINMEYER, CLEMENT, *Play-Sing-Chord Along*, Shawnee Press, Delaware Water Gap, Pa.

Melody Flute and Tonette Instruction

BECKMAN, FREDERICK, *Classroom Method for Melody Flute*, Melody Flute Company, Laurel, Maryland. Contains melodies but no words to sing; a very good piano accompaniment book is available.

BURGETT, ELAINE, et al., *Modern Musical Fun for Singing and Playing With the Tonette.* Elkhart, Ind.: Lyons, 530 Riverview Ave., 46514

Organ

Adventure in Keyboard, Lowrey Organ Company, Chicago, Ill. A ten-week program for elementary school students.

The Pointer System School Program, Pointer System, Inc., Winona, Minn. Includes instructional films.

Piano Books for Chording

Easy:

ECKSTEIN, MAXWELL, *Play It Now.* Carl Fisher.

FRISCH, FAY TEMPLETON, *The Play-Way to Music, Book Two.* Amsco Music Publications, Inc.

NEVIN, MARK, *Tunes You Like*, Books 1, 2, 3, 4. Schroeder and Gunther, Inc.

NEVIN, MARK, *Repertoire Album*, Book 1. Belwin, Inc.

STEINER, ERIC. *One, Four, Five.* Mills Music, Inc.; *Repertoire Album Book I*, Belwin, Inc.

Slightly more difficult:

BERMONT, GEORGES, *Play That Tune*, Books 1, 2, 3, 4. Musicord Publications.

115 Easy Piano Pieces and Folk Songs, Hansen Publications.

RICHTER, ADA, *Songs I Can Play.* M. Witmark and Sons.

STICKLES, WILLIAM, *Easy Hymns and Sacred Songs for the Piano.* Hansen Publications.

Recorder Instruction

BUCHTEL, FORREST, *Buchtel Recorder Method*, Book 1. Park Ridge, Ill.: Neil A. Kjos Music Company, 525 Busse Highway, 60068.

EARLE, FREDERICK, *Trophy Elementary Recorder Method, Baroque System.* Cleveland, Ohio: Trophy Music Co., 1278 W. 9th St. 44113.

LANAHAN, WALTER D., *Melody Method for the Recorder.* Laurel, Md.: Melody Flute Co.

NEWMAN, HAROLD, and GRACE NEWMAN, *Music Shall Live—Singing and*

Playing with the Recorder. New York City: Hargail Music Press, 28 W. 38th St. 10018.

Recorder Music Catalog. Melville, N.Y.: Belwin-Mills, 11746. Recorder music selected from many publishers.

RICHARDSON, ALLEN L., *The Breeze Easy One and All.* New York: Warner Brothers.

Sources of Classroom Instruments

CONTINENTAL MUSIC, Division of C. G. Conn, Ltd., 150 Aldredge Blvd., Atlanta, Ga. 30336.

B. F. KITCHING, 505 Shawmut St., LaGrange, Ill.

LYONS, 530 Riverview Ave., Elkhart, Ind. 46514.

MAGNAMUSIC-BATON, INC., 10370 Page Industrial Blvd., St. Louis, Mo. 63132.

MUSIC EDUCATION GROUP, Garden State Road, Union, N.J. 07083. Autoharp and all other instruments.

PERIPOLE, INC., P.O. Box 146, Lewiston Road, Browns Mills, N.J. 08015.

RHYTHM BAND, INC., P.O. Box 126, Fort Worth, Texas 76101.

SCIENTIFIC INDUSTRIES, INC., 823 S. Wabash Ave., Chicago: 60605. Song Bells and Tone Educator Bells.

WEXLER, 823 S. Wabash Ave., Chicago 60605.

ANALYZING MUSIC

Analysis

Analysis requires prior knowledge of music concepts, therefore it is the most advanced and sophisticated approach to music learning.

Analysis is a vital part of the approaches discussed in previous chapters. When children move to music, the teacher's questions help them in their rudimentary analyses of aspects of that music which suggest that they react physically, in other words, how tempo, dynamics, rhythmic details, melodic contour, and the form (repetition and contrast) dictate their movements. In this way children are helped to acquire expanding musical concepts to the point where they will have the ability to utilize these concepts as cognitive tools in the solution of musical problems and to acquire more knowledge. Musical performance is treated in the same manner; both the teacher's questions and the normal problems encountered in singing, playing, and conducting should develop a growing ability to analyze music performed and heard. When improvisation and composition form a pathway to music learning, all of the elements of music are utilized, and with experiences in

creating, in constructive criticizing, in performing, and in listening to both recorded examples and their own compositions, the children's capacity to analyze music expands. "Active involvement with the elements of compositional techniques . . . contributes to a more effective listening experience for students at all age levels." [1]

Music is a type of sound taking place in time. Various musical factors result in tension being built, then released. Because tension and release are found in both daily living and in music, people have claimed that music expresses feelings. It would be more accurate to say that music *sounds* the way people sometimes feel. Learning can be based upon how children feel in response to the music and how the teacher guides them in search for the causes of these feelings. Children may be guided to observe the relation of pitch to tension, climax, and release. This study is relatively complex because dynamics and other factors are contributing influences. Repetition of tone and rhythm patterns often builds tension to be relieved by a change in melody or rhythm. Sometimes tension and climax are brought about by successively higher pitches, and release accompanied by descending pitches. Duration of pitch—longer or shorter note values—can be another factor.

This chapter will reexamine concepts of tone quality and instrumentation, form, harmony and polyphony as musical tools to develop more advanced analysis skills, suggest some activities to further analysis, and list some recorded and other materials. The long-term goal of the reader should be to plan ways for children to acquire over the years a background of musical experiences that will enable them to answer questions such as those stated in the following guide.

Guides and Charts

**Guide for
Discussion-
Analysis**

What is the intent of the composer? How well does the music carry it out? How does the composer try to create interest?

What is the mood of the composition? How did the composer manage the musical elements in a way to achieve this effect?

If the composition illustrates a story or attempts to describe something, how does the composer utilize the elements of music to project these ideas?

How does the composer establish unity? (recurring phrases, melodic, rhythmic, or harmonic patterns)

How does the composer create contrast or variety?

Are aspects of tension and release present? (tempo, dynamics, pitch, instrumentation, harmony, polyphony, repetition)

Is a climax present? If so, how did the composer achieve it?

When preparing a lesson that includes listening, the teacher should study the music with analytical care. The following preparation charts may be of assistance.

[1] *Experiments in Music Creativity* (Reston, Va.: Music Educators National Conference, 1966), p. 61.

Teacher Preparation Chart
for Primary Level

General Plan to develop children's vocabulary of descriptive and musical terms. Plan questions to assist discovery of the outstanding aspects of the music to be studied. Do not expect to deal with all of the elements listed below in any piece of music; ordinarily one teaches for only those that are clearly discerned and fairly obvious. Questions should assist children to discover, verify, follow a sequence of events, and to examine music critically and analytically.

Musical Element	*Specific Concepts*	*Questions*
RHYTHM, TEMPO	the beat accent fast, slow, changing simple note values and rhythm patterns meter (ages 7, 8) syncopation	What is it like? (walking, clapping, skipping, jumping, an animal? heavy, light, big, little, fast, slow, what kind?)
DYNAMICS	degrees of loud and soft	
PITCH	high, low, same steps, skips (conjunct, dis- junct) shape of melody (contour) easy intervals sequence	Can you show with your hands how the melody, or this part of the melody goes?
HARMONY	major, minor restful, active traditional, contemporary, experimental	
TEXTURE	unison, accompanied, thick, thin	

FORM	phrase (same, different,
	  almost the same)
	ab, aba, round, rondo,
	  variation
	introduction, coda, interlude
		Can you show same and different by different movements?

TONALITY	tonal center (home tone)	
TONE QUALITIES	voices, instruments, or sound sources	
MOOD	See elements and specifics above; also see description and story.	How does it make you feel? What is there in the music that makes you feel that way? If the music describes something, how does the composer use musical elements to project this?

Teacher Preparation Chart
for Intermediate Level

General Continue to assist development of vocabulary. "What does this music communicate to you?" (mood, description, beauty, intellectual design, or . . .) "By what musical means does the composer accomplish this?"

By means of:

Musical Element	*Specific Concepts*
TEMPO	degrees of fast and slow
RHYTHM	beat, accent, meter note values, rhythm patterns syncopation characteristic rhythms and dances
PITCH	high, low, the contour ascending, descending conjunct, disjunct, note patterns, intervals major, minor, pentatonic melodies monophonic, homophonic, polyphonic modal, chromatic, whole-tone melodies composer's devices: sequence, diminution, augmentation, inversion, retrograde, retrograde inversion, octave displacement, thematic development 12-tone, atonal melodies
HARMONY	major, minor traditional, contemporary, experimental
DYNAMICS	degrees of loud and soft, climax and release
TONE QUALITIES	What kinds of sounds did the composer use or need to express his or her ideas? What instrument, instruments, vibrating object or device produced these sounds? Was it successful?
FORM	repetition and contrast of phrases (ab, aba) and of large sections (AB, ABA), rondo, variations unity and contrast as artistic principles introduction, coda, interlude fugue, sonata, overture, symphony, tone poem, concerto, duet, trio, quartet, quintet
TONALITY	tonic (home tone; key feelings), modal, atonal (absence of tonality)
TEXTURE	monophonic, homophonic, polyphonic, descriptive adjectives
STYLE	national, racial, composer's, historical periods and times.
OTHER	Consider possibilities for musical analysis through dance.

**Sample Student Answer Sheet
for Intermediate Level**

Directions: Listen to the music. Then fill in *only* the spaces to the right of the elements you identify; leave all others blank.

Musical Elements	*Comments and Analysis*

RHYTHM and TEMPO
    tempo and meter
    rhythm pattern
    other	

PITCH AND ARTICULATION
    contour
    legato-staccato
    conjunct-disjunct	

DYNAMICS degrees of loud and soft	

HARMONY
    major-minor
    traditional-contemporary
    other	

TEXTURE
    unison
    accompanied
    polyphonic
    other descriptive words	

TONALITY
    tonal center
    atonal (no center)
    other	

TONE QUALITIES sound sources, descriptive words	

FORM
    repetition-contrast, phrase, section
    introduction, coda, interlude
    other	

The primary purpose of the remainder of this chapter is to suggest a more in-depth study of some of the musical elements in order to continue to enrich and expand the experiences from which develops the learner's ability to listen to music with the understanding and comprehension that results in the capacity to analyze what is heard in terms of the elements comprising music.

From Tone Qualities to Instrumentation

When discussing tone qualities, the terms *tone color* and *timbre* (tam-bur) are often used. Tone color is a term borrowed from art; it implies that tone qualities are accomplished in music in the same general way the artist selects and combines colors in painting. Timbre is the French word for tone quality. Thus, tone quality, tone color, and timbre mean the same thing: the difference in sound between tones of the same pitch when produced by different instruments or voices. For example, the same pitch played on a violin, a trumpet, or a flute varies greatly in tone quality.

In music education of the past there was emphasis on identification of the sources of tone—the specific instrument or voice that produced it. Research has shown that very young children can learn to do such identification. The child's curiosity should be encouraged—what is there in the construction of a given instrument that produces its particular tone quality; how can the player of the instrument affect tone quality by his or her manner of playing; why are particular tone qualities selected by composers as the most suitable to enhance melodies and harmonies; what is the effect of range on tone quality; how does tone quality interrelate with melody, harmony, texture, and form to make music more attractive? If the study of tone quality can be based on the reasons for the employment of certain instruments in a composition, the mechanical construction and the method of playing them, then the identification of the instrument or combinations of instruments should become part of a logical scheme of things rather than the memorizing of isolated facts that may be soon forgotten.

When composers select certain instruments or voices to convey the meaning of a composition, one of the reasons may be to imitate a sound of nature. Children should decide why the clarinet, flute, and piccolo are often chosen to imitate a bird by comparing these tones with those of other instruments. It should be obvious why a composer would choose the tympani rather than a tambourine to imitate a clap of thunder. There are interesting psychological associations that man has acquired in listening experiences. When the French horn plays a certain type of melody, hunting may be brought to mind; when the oboe plays another type of melody, a pastoral scene, possibly with sheep and shepherd, is suggested. However, there is a vast amount of music that has no such associative meanings. When dealing with this, the study becomes one of discovery—why great composers select certain instruments to perform certain melodies, why these instruments suit these melodies better than other instruments, and how poorly some would sound if assigned the same melodies. Of course teachers know that once in a while children may disagree with great composers, yet when the children have logical reasons for their point of view, their judgment is to be respected. The Leonard Bernstein film, *What Does Orchestration Mean?* (McGraw-Hill Films, 1 hour, grades 5-up) deals with choosing "the right instruments at the right time in the right combination." Sometimes the sound of certain instruments and combinations of instruments can unite with melodies, harmonies, and textures to produce music suggestive of particular nations and localities. One example is music used on television and in films which is written to suggest the open spaces of the American West. This fascinating study requires ability to analyze, and it is complex for adults to manage. Therefore teachers must keep their expectations within the limits of the musical background of the class and not expect more than this. However, every student should acquire some appreciation for the great contribution tone qualities supply to satisfying the need for contrast and variety in music. In fact, the very first attraction to music may come from beautiful tones that infants hear; parents are wise to plan these experiences in music for very young children.

In the primary grades there is an emphasis on the function of percussion instruments to produce sound effects, and the children are helped to explore different types of tone qualities they can find by playing the instruments in experimental ways. This was discussed in Chapters 7 and 11. Classification of percussion instruments according to their tone qualities is part of the process of learning concepts relating to why and how certain sounds are produced by instruments and objects. This inquiry might not take place unless the teacher plans questions such as, "Does the woodblock sound the same as the rhythm sticks?" "Why do you suppose the sound is different?" "Look at each to see how it is made." "Yes, the woodblock is hollow; what difference might that make?" The ways of producing several different tone qualities on each instrument stress the importance of the method used to play them. For example, if a player uses two rapidly alternating mallets on a resonator bar, the continuous effect will be different from striking it once with one mallet; if three players each use two mallets in this way to produce a continuous-sounding chord, there will be a shimmering effect. From such beginnings, other instruments are introduced in relation to their sound and function. Several different ways of playing the Autoharp were presented in Chapter 14; children can find that playing on either side of the bridge yields a difference in tone quality. The enjoyment of beauty of tone is good in itself, and should be experienced often. Then there should come a time when attention is called to how this beauty is produced.

What Makes Sound?

For sound to occur, something must vibrate. Young children can experiment with a rubber band stretched across an open-top box. When they pluck it, they can see it quiver at a fast rate, and they can hear that this vibration makes a sound. Every time the rubber band moves back and forth, a sound-wave (cycle) is formed of molecules of air. The sound waves go through the air to reach our eardrums, causing them to vibrate. Nerves carry this sensation to the brain, and our stored experiences usually tell us what kind of a sound we are hearing. The children will find that if the rubber band is pulled out far, then let go, the vibration is wide and the sound is louder; if the band is pulled a short distance, the vibration is less and the sound is soft. Through further experimentation it will be found that the lowest pitch will be sounded when the entire band vibrates, and that higher pitches will be sounded when a finger is placed on the band to shorten the vibrating portion. Thus, children may be able to generalize that the length of a vibrating object influences its pitch; the longer, the lower; the shorter, the higher. It should also be discovered that a shorter length vibrates more rapidly than a longer length.

In some woodwind instruments—the flute and piccolo—the sound is produced by a vibrating column of air, while in others—the clarinet, oboe, and bassoon—the sound is initiated by a vibrating reed. By taking a bottle, and blowing across its open top, a sound can be made that comes from vibrating air. By pouring water into the bottle, children can discover that the longer the vibrating air column, the lower the pitch is; and the shorter the vibrating air column, the higher the pitch. To imitate the vibration of the double reed of the oboe and bassoon children can flatten one end of a soda straw, cut off the corners, and practice blowing into the straw through this flattened end. When brass instruments sound, the players' lips are the vibrating agent. Some children will be able to make a circular cup "mouthpiece" with their thumb and index finger, put their lips together on it and blow into it to produce a sound with their vibrating lips. They can watch large drumheads to see that striking them causes vibrations. They can examine a piano to discover that hammers strike the strings and cause them to vibrate. When string instruments are made to vibrate, the player either plucks the strings, as the children did the rubber band, or draws a bow across them. Perhaps the children can learn from a violinist that rosin is rubbed on the horse hair in the bow to increase the friction to make the strings vibrate. Perhaps they can answer the question, "Why is it that the player is never supposed to touch the horse hair of the bow?" (Because the oil in the skin transferred to the horse hair reduces the friction needed to make the string vibrate.) As this study continues with many different instruments, consideration should be given to the material the instrument is made of, the length of the instrument, the length of the vibrating section, and the existence of *resonating chambers,* such as those of the woodblock and the violin; all of these may affect tone quality. It might be noted that science tells us it should not matter what kind of material is used for instruments having vibrating air columns. However, many musicians continue to want recorders made of wood rather than of plastic, frequently arguing about the virtues of wood versus synthetic materials, while flute players now prefer metal instruments to the older wooden flute. Other topics of scientific or historical interest include the *vibrato* as it is used by instrumentalists and singers, the overtone series and its relation to tone quality, and the historical development of modern instruments; these can be investigated by older children. Some may be interested in the relation between the clavichord, harpsichord, and piano, in the relation of the viols and the modern string family, and in the evolution of the valve instruments.

There are teachers who plan experiences for children with such stress on qualities of sound and dynamics that they temporarily exclude melody. Children are encouraged to create new sounds with familiar instruments, such as placing materials of different types (pieces of metal, paper, felt pads) on piano and Autoharp wires, and combining these experimental tone qualities with percussion instruments like the gong and woodblock to create a background for a poem or choric reading. Some teachers challenge children to create new tone qualities by taking sounds from their environment, taping these, and arranging them in a suitable order. An example might be lunchroom sounds, in which a short piece would utilize the sound of feet, talking, trays being stacked, the bell, and so on. These could be varied by playing the tape at different speeds and retaping them. Another way might be to have children create a plan for using such sounds, then have the class imitate or reproduce them from an experimental score in the same general way that orchestra instruments imitate. Other ideas for children to work with could include sounds in the morning on the way to school, sounds of a shopping trip, sounds of the city, sounds of the country, and sounds of interesting tone qualities with no story.

Such an approach is used to involve children in the sounds of experimental composition. Electronic sounds are included, often using the assistance of a tape recorder; tone generators and mixers contribute to the many types of tone qualities composers use today.

Voices   Earlier in this book, an activity was recommended in which young children learned to listen to the speaking and singing voices of their unseen classmates to identify them in a game situation. Children will notice that some voices are higher or lower pitched than others, and that some are clearer in tone quality than others. They can generalize that all persons have a different, and perhaps unique, quality in their voices. While the voices of older children are best identified in terms of high, medium, and low, the terms for adult voices—soprano, alto, tenor, baritone and bass—can be introduced to them as degrees of high and low in the instance of women and men, respectively. Suitable recordings may be used to compare the qualities of each. If possible, the children should hear a soprano and an alto sing the same song in the same range, then discuss the difference in tone quality that will be revealed. The same can be done with a tenor and a bass. They will be interested when a man and a woman sing the same song an octave apart, and they should try to describe the tone quality in each of the above experiences. For eleven-year-olds these adult classifications may be subdivided further. For example, there are subdivisions of the soprano voice: *coloratura* (the highest), lyric, and dramatic. The *contralto* is a low alto, the lowest female voice. The male voice falls into three major classifications, tenor, baritone, and bass. The baritone is the middle range male voice. There are subdivisions of the male voices, but there is little need to enlarge upon this. Perhaps the essential knowledge consists of knowing the five major classifications and that each of these can be further subdivided. Each voice type has a characteristic tone quality.

The tone qualities of combinations of voices are studied by ten and eleven-year-olds. They should know the duet, trio, quartet, and quintet (and possibly the sextette, octette, and nonette), as well as the different types of choral groups—men's, women's, and mixed—and be able to recognize the sound of choral music, choruses singing sacred music, and choruses singing secular music. These small and large ensembles should be compared to instrumental groups; for example, children should be aware of similarities and differences between a vocal quartet of soprano, alto, tenor, and bass, and the string quartet of first violin, second violin, viola, and cello.

Recordings to illustrate voices are usually not found in the educational collections. Examples of arias from operas are often used. The following are a few examples:

"Bell Song" from *Lakmé* (Delibes)	Coloratura Soprano
"Queen of the Night Arias" from *The Magic Flute* (Mozart)	
Bachianas Brasilieras No. 5 (Villa-Lobos)	Lyric Soprano
"Depuis le jour" from *Louise* (Charpentier)	
"Habanera" from *Carmen* (Bizet)	Mezzo Soprano (Alto)
"Barcarolle" from *Tales of Hoffman* (Offenbach)	
"He Was Despised" from the *Messiah* (Handel)	Contralto
"Dido's Lament" from *Dido and Aeneas* (Purcell)	
"Song of India" from *Sadko* (Rimsky-Korsakov)	Tenor
"Celeste Aida" from *Aida* (Verdi)	
"Largo al factotum" from *Barber of Seville* (Rossini) (see *Making Music Your Own, Book 6,* recorded)	Baritone
"Toreador Song" from *Carmen* (Bizet)	Bass
"Mephisto's Serenade" from *Faust* (Gounod)	

The children should compare the different voices, verbalize about the tone qualities, and in the process expand their descriptive vocabularies. The teacher's role is to have the children explore, discover, identify, compare, evaluate, and describe tone qualities, telling them only what is necessary to help them learn for themselves.

Strings   The string family of the orchestra is made up of the violin, viola, 'cello, and double bass (string bass, bass viol). They are approximately the same shape except that the violin is the smallest, the viola somewhat larger, the 'cello so large that the player must sit in a chair and rest the instrument on the floor, and the double bass so very large that the player ordinarily stands up to play it. These instruments are called "the first family of the orchestra." Study of the seating plan of an orchestra will expain one reason why. Listening carefully to symphonic music will reveal that the strings are truly the backbone of the orchestra, with the brass, woodwinds, and percussion sections assisting by adding many contrasting tone qualities.

The string instruments produce a variety of tone qualities within their family. The violin, viola, and 'cello use *vibrato,* a slight varying of pitch produced by rapid movement of the left hand and forearm while pressing down on a string. The term *con sordino* means with a mute; when the mute is attached to the bridge, the device that supports the strings, the tone becomes smaller and more nasal. These instruments produce *harmonics,* higher pitches of reduced resonance with flute-like tones that occur when the player touches, but does not press down on a string, and bows very lightly on that string. When these instruments are played by plucking strings, this is called *pizzicato;* it produces still another tone quality. A short, fast stroke played in the middle of the bow with a slight bounce from the string is *spiccato* bowing. Double stops, the playing and bowing of two strings at once, gives another effect. The *tremulo* produces a rather tense impression; it is done by moving the bow back and forth a short distance at an extremely fast rate. A flute-like effect is made by *sur la touche,* a slight bowing over the finger board, and a glassy effect, *sul ponticello,* is made by bowing very close to the bridge. An unusual effect is the *col legno,* which means using the wood of the bow rather than the hair. The *glissando* is produced by playing scale passages with many tiny movements of the left hand to change the pitch in almost a sliding effect. The normal tone qualities of these instruments can be described in various ways. A beginning can be made with these:

violin:	The string instrument that most resembles the qualities of the human voice; great versatility in range of expression; extremely sensitive tone qualities.
viola:	a veiled and nasal quality; darker in color than the violin.
'cello:	the bass violin; a deep masculine voice of soulful quality.
double bass:	very low, heavy tone quality; it sounds one octave lower than the cello.

Children, older students, and adults should be asked to demonstrate these instruments. While films and recordings are helpful, nothing takes the place of a good, well-qualified, live performer.

The harp is another string instrument; the player is seated with the string section of the orchestra. It can be compared to the piano in some ways; it has a range of six octaves and a fifth. There are seven foot pedals, each of which can be pressed down two notches, each notch representing one halfstep. The harp makes splashing, cascading effects. The *glissando* is used frequently to produce these. Harmonics are sounded by placing the palm of the hand in the middle of the strings; this places the pitch one octave higher than normal, making possible a quality of mystery. A different effect is made by plucking strings close to the sounding board.

The keyboard instruments include the piano, harpsichord, and celesta. The tone qualities of the piano should be thoroughly explored; special experimental effects can be made. In the piano, felt hammers strike the strings; the harpsichord strings are made to vibrate by means of a plucking mechanism. The celesta is basically a percussion instrument. Its keyboard causes hammers to strike the steel bars of what approximates a type of glockenspiel (bell set). The tone is of unusual light quality; a famed celesta piece is "Dance of the Sugar Plum Fairy" from the *Nutcracker Suite* of Tchaikovsky. The harpsichord—older than the piano—was the favorite keyboard instrument at the time of Haydn and Mozart. Its tone quality is considerably lighter than the piano, and it has less expressive capability. The Young People's Record 411, *Said the Piano to the Harpsichord,* is informative, and it communicates to children.

Stringed instruments not part of the symphony orchestra include the guitar, banjo, ukulele, mandolin, lyre, zither, Autoharp, and others. These should be explored to identify the tone qualities they produce. There is excellent guitar literature, much of it from Spanish sources; children should know of Segovia and others who play the classical guitar. Bowmar 84 includes a guitar selection.

Examples of recordings portraying tone qualities of the symphony strings include:

Scheherazade Suite, Rimsky-Korsakov	violin cadenzas
Flight of the Bumblebee, Rimsky-Korsakov, Bowmar 53	violin
Eine kleine Nachtmusik, Mozart, Adventures in Music 4 v. 1	strings
The Wonderful Violin, Moore, Young People's Record 311	violin
Danse Macabre, Saint-Saëns, Bowmar 59	viola plays second theme
"The Swan," *Carnival of the Animals,* Saint-Saëns, Bowmar 59, Adventures in Music 3 v. 2	'cello
"Elephants," *Carnival of the Animals,* Saint-Saëns, Bowmar 51	double bass
"Jimbo's Lullaby," Debussy, Bowmar 51	double bass

Suggested films include:

Listening to Good Music: The String Quartet	Encyclopaedia Britannica Films
String Sounds	Churchill Films
The String Choir	Encyclopaedia Britannica Films
The String Trio	Coronet Instructional Films
The Trio	World Artists, Inc.

Woodwinds   The woodwind instruments not only blend well with the strings of the orchestra, but they add other interesting tone qualities which can be used in the performance of melodies or subsidiary parts that contribute to the effect the composer plans to achieve. It is of interest that the woodwinds in the concert band seem to substitute for the strings in the orchestra; for example in examining a concert band, one finds many clarinets instead of many violins.

The modern flute is a descendant of the recorder. It is a *transverse* flute, which means that one holds it at right angles to the mouth and blows across a hole in the side of it. The recorder is an end-blown flute. While it is said that the best recorders are made of wood, the modern flute is generally made of silver. Its tone quality varies with the range. Low pitches are relatively big and somewhat breathy, while higher tones become increasingly bright and penetrating with ascending pitches. An impressive flute solo at the beginning of a composition that emphasizes tone qualities is in Debussy's *Afternoon of a Faun,* followed by colorful effects on a harp. (Remember that a *faun* is a creature from rural Roman mythology, a man principally human, but with a goat's tail, pointed ears, short horns, and sometimes cloven feet.) Another favorite composition featuring flutes is Tchaikovsky's "Dance of the Toy Flutes," from the *Nutcracker* Suite, Bowmar 58. The piccolo is a small flute, half as long, and pitched one octave higher. It plays the highest pitches of any instrument in the woodwind family, and its tone quality is exceedingly brilliant and penetrating. A favorite piccolo solo is in Sousa's *Stars and Stripes Forever,* Bowmar 54. Others are found in the "Chinese Dance" from Tchaikovsky's *Nutcracker* Suite, Bowmar 59, and "Entrance of the Little Fauns" by Pierné, Bowmar 54.

The most commonly found clarinet is the B♭ instrument; some of the children who are studying this single reed instrument can demonstrate it. There is a family of clarinets, with the E♭ being smaller and higher in pitch, and the alto and bass being lower, as would be expected. There are other less common clarinets, including the clarinet in A and the double bass in B♭, the latter being an octave lower than the bass clarinet. The B♭ clarinet has three registers, each with a different tone quality. The lowest is rich and full-bodied, the middle is sometimes breathy and is the most difficult to make sound well; the highest is brilliant and versatile. This variety of tone qualities gives the clarinet a good deal of breadth of expression. Examples include Prokofiev's *Peter and the Wolf,* Saint-Saëns' "Cuckoo in the Deep Woods," from *Carnival of the Animals,* Bowmar 51, and the second movement of Rimsky-Korsakov's *Scheherazade* Suite. Clarinets are made of wood, ebonite, and occasionally of metal.

The saxophone is seldom used in orchestras, but it is widely used in bands and dance bands. There is a family of saxophones, including soprano, alto, tenor, baritone, and bass. The most commonly seen are in the following

order, alto, tenor, and baritone. These are in most school bands and in many dance bands. Although they have cane reeds like clarinets, they are made of metal. The tone quality of the instrument is such that it blends with woodwinds or brass instruments. This tone quality can be changed markedly by the player, thus can be sweet, raucous, or brusque as desired in certain types of jazz and dance music.

The oboe family includes all of the double reed instruments. The oboe is about the same size as the B♭ clarinet. The English horn is an alto oboe and the bassoon is the bass instrument of the family. The contra-bassoon is an octave lower than the ordinary bassoon. The oboe tone quality is often described as nasal, pastoral, oriental, and plaintive. *Peter and the Wolf* demonstrates the oboe tone quality, as does the second movement of Tchaikovsky's Symphony No. 4 and his "Puss in Boots and the White Cat," from the *Sleeping Beauty,* Adventures in Music 3 v. 1. The English horn has a pear-shaped bell which is one source of its melancholy tone quality. Examples of its sound appear in the "Largo" of Dvořák's *New World* Symphony, Sibelius' *Swan of Tuonela,* and "Puss in Boots and the White Cat," mentioned above. Children should discover how the bassoon is built, since the design permits it to have a great length of tube. (The contra-bassoon has over sixteen feet.) Besides serving as a bass instrument, its tone blends well with the French horn and enables it to play solo passages of distinction. While its tone quality is rather even except at extreme high and low ranges, it has a versatility which enables it to project plaintive, gruff, and humorous impressions. It can play over a wide range with both legato and staccato articulation. Examples are found in "In the Hall of the Mountain King," from *Peer Gynt* Suite, by Grieg, Adventures in Music 3 v. 2, and Bowmar 59; "Berceuse" from Stravinsky's *Firebird* Suite; the second movement of Tchaikovsky's Symphony No. 4; and in *Rondo for Bassoon and Orchestra,* Children's Record Guild 1009. The grandfather theme in *Peter and the Wolf* is played by a contra-bassoon.

Additional variety in the performance of woodwind instruments is attained by legato and staccato tonguing, as well as double, triple, and flutter tonguing. Double tonguing can be explained by letting out the breath with a series of repeated "t-t" tonguings; triple tonguing is a repeated "t-k-t." These are of particular importance in flute playing.

The film *Introducing the Woodwinds,* Indiana University, introduces the instruments of the woodwind quintet to children. These are flute (and piccolo), clarinet, oboe, bassoon, and French horn—the brass instrument that possesses a tone quality which blends with both the woodwinds and the brasses. *Wind Sounds,* Churchill Films, deals with woodwinds and brasses.

Brasses

Children can quickly find a major difference between a bugle and a trumpet, or cornet, in that the bugle lacks valves. They can then discern why the bugle can play only bugle calls whereas the other instruments can play both bugle calls and melodies. They should study the valve and its length of tubing to find what valves do to the length of the air column, and how much each valve lowers a pitch. They will see that the cornet is shorter than the trumpet, and they will hear that its tone quality is less brilliant. The player has a great deal to do with the sound of these instruments, producing tones of both coarse and pleasing qualities at will. The baritone is a larger instrument found in bands; the melophone is an instrument about the size of a French horn but which lacks the golden quality of the French horn tone; it is used for marching bands and for students who may later progress to the more difficult French horn. The tubing of the French horn should be examined to try to determine how long the instrument would be if it were a straight horn like the alphorn, a folk instrument from the Alps. Both tone quality and pitch are influenced by a practice called *stopping,* which is the insertion of the hand into the bell. Mutes made of metal, wood, or fiberboard change the tone qualities of the cornet, trumpet, French horn, and trombone. Both school band and dance band players of trumpet and trombone can demonstrate their several types of mutes in the classroom. While the cornet and trumpet have the most commanding tones, the French horn has the tone that blends with other instruments the best, although it can be bold and brassy when this is desired. The tones of these instruments can be varied by legato and staccato tonguing, double and triple tonguing, flutter tonguing, and the use of mutes. Four sizes of trombones are used in the symphony orchestra, the most common being the tenor. This instrument and an occasional bass trombone will be seen in school bands. The trombone and baritone have larger mouthpieces than those of the cornet, trumpet, and French horn; this results in a tone quality of less brilliance, but of more dignity and solemnity. Children will be interested in how the trombone's slide shortens or lengthens the air column in place of the valve mechanism. Because of the slide, trombones can produce a *portamento,* which is a gliding from one tone to another through all degrees of pitches. The lowest pitched instruments of the brass family are the tubas and sousaphones. The sousaphone is the instrument carried on the shoulder of its players in marching bands; its huge shiny bell makes an impressive appearance. New plastic materials are being used today in place of metal in order to reduce the weight the player must carry. The tuba player is seated in the orchestra and appears occasionally in the band. As expected, these bass instruments have the largest mouthpieces. As told in the children's recording, *Tubby the Tuba,* Decca Records, the tuba seldom plays melodies. Instead, it normally supports the band as the primary low bass instrument, and it assists the double basses of the orchestra. Its tone is deep and its execution somewhat ponderous.

Examples of brass instrument tone qualities include:

"Finale," *William Tell* Overture, Rossini, Adventures in   Trumpet
   Music 3 v. 1; Bowmar 76
"Changing of the Guard," *Carmen* Suite, Bizet, Adventures in Music 3 v. 2
The King's Trumpet, Children's Record Guild 5040

Peter and the Wolf, Prokofiev   French horn
"Nocturne," *Midsummer Night's Dream,* Mendelssohn
"Third Movement," Symphony No. 3, Brahms
"Prelude to Act 3," *Lohengrin,* Wagner   Trombone
Stars and Stripes Forever, Sousa, Adventures in Music
    4 v. 2; Bowmar 54
"Bydlo," *Pictures at an Exhibition,* Moussorgsky, Ad-   Tuba
    ventures in Music 2; Bowmar 82
"Departure," *Winter Holiday,* Prokofiev, Adventures
    in Music 2

Percussion

Example of percussion instrument tone qualities include:

Danse Macabre, Saint-Saëns
"Dagger Dance," *Natoma,* Herbert, Adventures in   Cymbals, Drums
    Music 3 v. 1
Semper Fidelis, Sousa, Adventures in Music 3 v. 2
"In the Hall of the Mountain King," *Per Gynt* Suite,   Drums, Timpani
    Grieg Adventures in Music 3 v. 2; Bowmar 59
"Tarantella," *Fantastic Toy Shop,* Rossini, Adventures   Tambourine
    in Music 3 v. 2; Bowmar 56
The Alligator and the Coon, Thomson, Adventures in   Xylophone
    Music 3 v. 2
Said the Piano to the Harpsichord, Young People's   Piano, Harpsi-
    Record 411   chord
Concert Percussion for Orchestra, Cage, Cowell, *et al.,*
    Time 58000
Music of Bali, Period SPL 1613

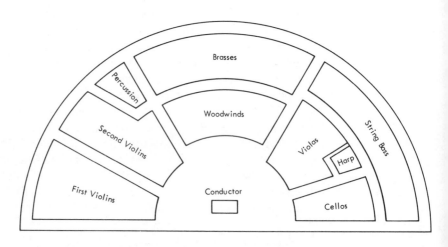

Films:
Percussion Group   Encyclopaedia Britannica Films
Percussion, Pulse of Music   Indiana University
Percussion Sounds   Churchill Films

Clarinets, trombones, cornets, saxophones, and other large instruments can be played by children in the intermediate grades. However, their tones are too powerful to blend with the light voices of children, thus they are ill-suited for inclusion in a classroom orchestra that is associated with the singing program. The authors of some of the music series books have nonetheless included some interesting uses for these instruments. These include instrumental solos, duets, descants, and true orchestrations of some of the songs. It appears that the best use for these orchestrations is in the playing of instrumental introductions and/or accompaniments for songs on special programs or for large vocal groups.

Lessons given on these instruments by the teacher of instrumental music should be scheduled in the special interest period when possible. The temporary withdrawal of some children from the classroom may be a disruption unless the teacher can make plans in accordance with it. Much of the irritation that sometimes comes when children leave the classroom for these lessons can be avoided if all teachers concerned have an opportunity to plan the instrumental music schedule cooperatively.

Teachers of general music in grades four, five, and six can encourage membership in band and orchestra classes. Preliminary steps toward this end can include bulletin board displays of instruments and instrumentalists; presenting recordings, films, and film srtips that illustrate instruments and families of instruments in ways that attract the interest of the age group; displaying attractive catalogues obtained from instrument manufacturers; displaying commercially produced charts of orchestra instruments; and making available to the children books that include pictures of children playing instruments. The general music teacher and the specialist in instrumental music should plan together times when the specialist can speak to the class and when he or she and children can demonstrate instruments. The sending of notices to parents and the planning for parent-teacher conferences about the selection, rental, or purchase of instruments should also be done by joint consideration of the general teacher and the specialist. A time should be decided upon when the specialist will bring instruments to the class and permit children to try them. (This will necessitate use of a germicide.) The specialist should explain to the class why certain children are suited to the playing of certain instruments, but not for others and should demonstrate the importance of finger size, length, and flexibility in playing the clarinet, for example, and the importance of being able to "buzz" the lips in playing the trumpet. Teeth formation should be revealed as important. For instance, a small overbite is preferable for small brass instruments while a large overbite is acceptable for bass and baritone. The instrumental teacher should avoid teaching fingering in a way that confuses "finger numbers" with scale-tone numbers. To say that A is played with the first and second fingers is correct, but to say that "A is two" is confusing to the child who is learning numeral names of scale tones. Both the general music teacher and the specialist can utilize instrumental scores in series books, and they can plan some of these correlated activities together. Singing in the instrumental class can assist in pitch accuracy on the instruments and in the growth of balanced musicianship. To sing, then play rote melodies demands and teaches musical skills. The instrumental score can at times be sung.

The child most likely to succeed in band and orchestra will be one who is sufficiently mature physically to play the instrument, who is generally musical, and who possesses reliability and perseverance.

Activities and Suggestions for Lesson Plans

FOR OLDER STUDENTS:

Tone qualities and note reading.
Examine an orchestra score. While the composition is played on a record player, follow a specific instrument part with the finger.

Music history.
Listen to a recording of instrumental music. Then design a record jacket that will include information about the history of the composition and facts about its composer.

Evaluation.
Listen to several recordings of the same composition and compare the conductors' interpretations and the performers' skills.

General Suggestions

Children can identify and compare the recorded tone qualities of the orchestra and band.

Study the many folk instruments and their tone qualities. One reference is Album L 24, *Folk Instruments of the World,* Follett Publishing Company, with an explanatory folder that includes drawings of the instruments.

Identify and compare the tone qualities and the make-up of various vocal and instrumental ensembles: duets, trios, quartets, quintets, sextets, etc.

Investigate the seating arrangement of a band. Draw it, and compare this plan with that of the orchestra.

Research the organ as a class of instruments. Listen to masterworks for the organ; describe the tone qualities of organs and compare them with other instruments.

When children examine a band or orchestra score they will find that instrument parts are written in different keys. They may find that some instruments are built in different keys. By experimenting with playing written notes on instruments and comparing the resulting pitch with the piano or bells, they can discover that when B♭ instruments play written C, the pitch is that of B♭, and when E♭ instruments play C, the pitch sounded is E♭. The teacher could plan a discrepant event by asking children who play instruments to all play the same song from a series book. This would be one way to discover which instruments are "transposing" instruments and which are not.

Plan for advanced older children to explore acoustics. Help them study resonance, harmonics, the overtone series, partials, and vibrato. Relate music and science.

Arrange to have children hear some electronic music. Have them discuss the tone qualities they hear, and try to determine the function of this music.

Children can compare the tone qualities and the instrumentation of the military band, the symphonic band, and the dance band.

Arrange for a group of children to create a dance based upon the various instruments heard in a colorful symphonic recording.

If possible, let children work with an *oscilloscope,* an electric machine which pictures the sound waves produced by tone qualities. Let them compare the wave forms of the flute, violin, and trumpet when they sound the same pitch.

Percussion Listen to a recording of a gamelan orchestra from Indonesia. Then create an imitation which will require a conductor to bring in different sections and to have other sections stop playing at times. Groups of children select, or are assigned percussion instruments of contrasting tone qualities. Each group will repeat a very short rhythm pattern as long as the conductor desires. For example, long-short-long could be one such pattern. A bell set or other melody instrument could be used to improvise a tune to sound along with various combinations of the groups. Have children evaluate the experiment.

AUDIO AND VISUAL MEDIA

Identifying classes of instruments.	*Third Movement of Symphony No. 4,* Tchaikovsky, BOL #71 (Bowmar Orchestral Library)
Specific instruments.	*King's Trumpet, The,* Franson Corporation, 225 Park Avenue South, New York, N.Y. 10003, Children's Record Guild (CRG) 5040 (ages 5–8)
	Licorice Stick: Story of the Clarinet, Franson, Young People's Record (YPR) 420 (ages 6–10)
	Guitar Music from the Courts of Spain (Romera) Mercury
	Pan the Piper, on Columbia CL 671
	Peter and the Wolf (Prokofiev), on Columbia CL 671
	Popular Classics for the Guitar (Bream), RCA Victor
	Rusty in Orchestraville, Capitol Records
	Said the Piano to the Harpsichord, Franson YPR 411
	Tubby the Tuba, Decca (ages 6–7)
	Wonderful Violin, The, Franson YPR 311 (ages 6–10)

Do You Know? by Virginia Kreuger. Individualized programed instruction for ages 5–10 via cassette and hard cover workbook with color photographs of child players and 10 wipe-off work pages. 12 instruments are identified. MuGin Publications, Box 36528, Los Angeles, Ca. 90036. $12.95.

Instruments of the orchestra.

Many manufacturers have albums under the title *Instruments of the Orchestra:* Capitol, Columbia, Decca, Vanguard, Victor, Bowmar, Wonderland, Keyboard.
Child's Introduction to the Orchestra, Golden Records
Orchestra and Its Instruments, The, Folkways
Symphony Orchestra, The, Decca

Films and filmstrips.

Churchill Films, 622 N. Robertson Blvd., Los Angeles, Calif. 90069: *What is Music?, Wind Sounds, String Sounds, Percussion Sounds, New Sounds in Music*
Instruments of the Symphony Orchestra (recordings with six filmstrips) Jam Handy, Prentice-Hall, Media, 150 White Plains Rd., Tarrytown, N.Y. 10591
Meet the Instruments (recordings with two filmstrips) Bowmar Records, 622 Rodier Drive, Glendale, Calif., 91201
Music for Young People Series, NET Films Service, Indiana University, Bloomington, Ind. 47401; *Introducing the Woodwinds, Percussion, Pulse of Music,* and more
Musical Books for Young People, a series of six filmstrips, Society for Visual Education, 1345 Diversey Pkwy., Chicago, Ill., 60614. Strings, brass, woodwinds, percussion, keyboard, and folk instruments. (ages 9–13)
Symphony Orchestra, The, Encyclopaedia Britannica Films, 425 N. Michigan Ave., Chicago, Ill., 60611. Traces growth of the symphony orchestra from string quartet to the modern orchestra. (ages 9–11)
We Make Music, Film Associates, 11559 Santa Monica Blvd., Los Angeles, Calif., 90025. *The Violin, The Bassoon,* and more

References

COPLAND, AARON, *What to Listen for in Music* (rev. ed.). New York: Mentor Books, 1964, Chapter 7.

GARY, CHARLES L., ed., *The Study of Music in the Elementary School—A Conceptual Approach*. Reston, Va.: Music Educators National Conference, Washington, D.C., 1967. pp. 136–56.

WALTON, CHARLES, *Teaching Guide*. Camden, N.J.: RCA-Victor, (for Instruments of the Orchestra Recordings).

Pictures and Charts

Construction of the Grand Piano; Evolution of the Grand Piano, Baldwin Piano Company, Cincinnati, Ohio. Also pamphlet, Story of the Baldwin Piano.

Instruments of the Band and Orchestra, F. A. Owen Publishing Co. (publishers of *Instructor Magazine*). Pictures of children playing instruments.

Instruments of the Orchestra Charts, J. W. Pepper and Son, 1423 Vine Street, Philadelphia, Pa. 22 charts for use with RCA recordings.

Meet the Instruments, Bowmar Records, 622 Rodier Drive, Glendale, Calif. 91201. 25 laminated posters.

Musical Instrument Pictures, C. G. Conn, Ltd., 616 Enterprise Rd., Oak Brook, Ill. 60521

Musical Instruments, York Band Instrument Company, Grand Rapids, Michigan.

Range Chart for Band and Orchestra Instruments, C. G. Conn, Ltd., Oak Brook, Ill. 60521.

Recordings

BOWMAR ORCHESTRAL LIBRARY

Ensembles, Large and Small, Album 83. Includes Britten's *Young Person's Guide to the Orchestra,* a string quartet, percussion ensemble, brass ensemble, and chorale.

COLUMBIA RECORDS, 799 Seventh Ave., New York, N.Y.

Carnival of the Animals, Saint-Saëns, and *Young Person's Guide to the Orchestra,* Britten. ML 5768.

First Chair, ML 4629. Features bassoon, cello, clarinet, flute, French horn, oboe, trumpet, and violin. For upper elementary.

The Military Band, Col. 1056.

Peter and the Wolf, Tubby the Tuba, and *Pan the Piper,* all on CL 671.

FRANSON CORPORATION, 225 Park Avenue South, New York, N.Y. 10003. Children's Record Guild and Young People's Records.

Drummer Boy

Hunter's Horn, The

King's Trumpet, The

Licorice Stick (clarinet)

Little Brass Band

Mr. Grump and *The Dingle School Band*

Neighbor's Band

On Lemmer Lemmer Street (violin)

Rondo for Bassoon and Orchestra

Runaway Sheep (wind instruments)

Said the Piano to the Harpsichord

Strike up the Band

Wonderful Violin

MERCURY RECORD CORPORATION

The Composer and His Orchestra, Vol. 1. Howard Hanson tells how he uses
   instruments.

Guitar Music from the Courts of Spain, Caledonia Romera plays.

MUSIC EDUCATION RECORD CORPORATION, BOX 445, Englewood Cliffs, N.J.

The Complete Orchestra. 5 records, 33 instruments featured. Ages 10–adult.

RCA VICTOR

Popular Classics for Spanish Guitar, Julian Bream plays.

Form

Children can discover natural divisions of melodies in answer to the questions, "Is the tune the same now or is it different?" and "Is it different or
almost the same?" This division is the phrase. Phrases are often thought
of as being four measures in length, and while most songs seem to demonstrate this, phrases can be found that vary from two to eight measures and
even longer. The important concept is not their length as much as it is that
melodies can be divided into logical parts called phrases. This, of course,
is the generalization teachers want children to make. Sometimes two phrases
relate to each other in a special way; these two phrases are called a *period*.
They can be improvised in the classroom by the teacher singing the first
phrase and children taking turns improvising the second phrase; the teacher
sings a "question," and the child sings an "answering" phrase.

Sometimes an entire phrase or a part of the melody within a phrase is
found to be repeated on a different degree of the scale, either higher or
lower than the first appearance of the phrase or note pattern. This was
identified as the *sequence*.[2]

Identifying *same* or *different* is the key to understanding form. Young
children's experience with this is at first more physical than it is intellectual.
The teacher suggests that they move their bodies in relation to what they
hear in the music and "act out" the music to show when it is the same and
when it is different. In learning to recognize different phrases or larger
contrasting sections of music, children may change movements or steps,
reverse directions, and play different kinds of percussion instruments.
Phrase repetition and difference are found in the songs children sing and
in recorded music to which they listen. As in all aspects of teaching music,
teachers select *very clear examples* of the phrase or larger sections of music
when their objective is to help children distinguish "same" and "different."
Very young children can compare Bartók's *Bear Dance,* which consists
of repeated A sections separated by interludes, with Prokofiev's *Waltz on
Ice* (both in Adventures in Music 3 v 2) which has three different sections
in simple rondo form—ABACA. Their discoveries may include that music

[2] A recorded example of sequence in orchestral music is "The Hurdy-Gurdy"
from Carpenter's *Adventures in a Perambulator,* Adventures in Music 5 v 2.

is made of different tunes or parts; sometimes these are the same, sometimes they are different, and some music has more parts than other music. Teachers can use visual aids, such as hats, costumes, streamers, masks, dancers, and colors, to dramatize same and different parts of music. To emphasize this in phrases, one group of children can be asked to sing phrases that are alike and another group those that contrast—boys and girls, those with black hair and those with brown hair, those with rubber-soled shoes and those with leather-soled shoes, and so on. Children can sound finger cymbals to mark the ends of phrases; this gives them a purpose for listening carefully. Older children can classify phrases as being alike, different, and almost alike; they can study the notation of recorded music or familiar songs to form the generalization that when phrases look alike, they sound alike. Suggestions in the booklets that accompany the *Adventures in Music* Albums are helpful.

Children are sometimes guided to "act out" phrases in ways such as the following arm movements:

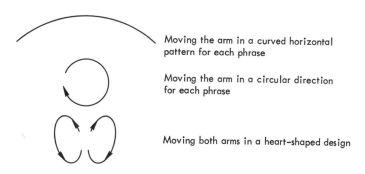

Moving the arm in a curved horizontal pattern for each phrase

Moving the arm in a circular direction for each phrase

Moving both arms in a heart-shaped design

Children do not always agree in their physical responses to a phrase, some feeling the phrase to be half the length that others may feel it to be. In certain songs it is interesting to note that adults are more apt to feel long phrases than are children, who often feel twice the number of phrases that the adults do. When this occurs, the children usually divide each long phrase into two shorter ones. In the opinion of the authors, this is not of particular importance, the real point being that children learn to sense that *music is divided into logical sections.* In view of individual differences in musical background, unanimity of response to phrase length cannot be expected. However, the simplicity of most of the songs makes for fairly obvious phrase lengths.

In some songs, recordings, and piano selections there are obviously contrasting sections of the music, each of which may be comprised of a number of phrases.

Teachers have learned that some older children are not greatly interested in phrases and some other structural aspects of music. While from an artistic point of view form is highly important because all works of art have form, and while scholars have written that understanding form is the most fundamental aspect of music learning, children of elementary-school age do not always find themselves in agreement with the scholars. These children are practical people, and they are not impressed unless they can understand the *function* of phenomena like form. The function of form seems to be to provide for two opposing concepts, *unity* and *contrast* or variety. Children who have acquired concepts of unity and contrast may find meaning in form. For example, when children are confronted with a phrase order such as *a a b a,* or *a b a c a,* and the teacher asks, "What is there in this tune that gives us a feeling of variety or contrast?" and "What is there that gives us a feeling of unity?" the function of form is made clear. Phrases *b* and *c* provide variety, and phrase *a* provides unity with its repetitions. Understanding this brings added meaning to the form of their own compositions. There are a number of interesting discoveries when they apply the principles of unity and contrast. Perhaps they will decide that the sequence serves both; it offers unity because it is a repetition, but it offers variety because the pitch is different.

Another generalization which concerns form is that melodies can be extended and altered by composers in various ways. By listening to music, making music, and creating music, children discover and use introductions, codas, and interludes. Introductions and codas are usually derived from melodies, but an interlude is often a contrasting section. Repetition is an obvious way to extend melodies. *Thematic development* is a term that describes what composers do with themes (tunes) they use in their larger compositions. When themes are developed they are extended or altered in many ways, including augmentation, diminution, canon, inversion, retrograde, and octave displacement. These are only a sampling of what composers do with the two themes in the middle (development) section of sonata-allegro form.

Before we leave forms *in* music, we should again refer to unity and variety. Aspects of form should be tested and analyzed by children in these terms. The various forms of melodic alteration sometimes contain both elements. For example, an inverted melody has a natural relation with the original melody; because of this there should be some degree of unity found in it. The children can discover that the rhythm remains the same, providing rhythmic unity. The inverted melody sounds different, however, so variety is also achieved by the inversion. Eventually children will discover that they must analyze unity and variety in terms of the elements of music. Unity may be attained by *repetition* of rhythm, melody, harmony, texture, tempo, dynamics, and tone quality. Variety may be attained by *changes* in rhythm, melody, harmony, texture, tempo, dynamics, and tone quality. When the form *of* music is understood, form can be added to the above list of musical elements. This infers that teachers' questions can be quite to the point. "How is unity achieved in this composition?" "Was there repetition of (any of the above elements of music)?" "How was contrast achieved?" "Was there a change in (any of the above elements of music)?" "How did it change?" In this way analytical listening is guided, and the function of these aspects of form is made clear to the learner. Form becomes a logical scheme of things.

Forms of Music

The songs in the series books have been identified as being made of phrases, some repeated note-for-note, some repeated with changes, and some contrasting and different. These are placed in an order that makes musical sense. Songs such as "At Pierrot's Door," (Au Claire de la Lune), "The Blue Bell of Scotland," "The Marines' Hymn," "O Susanna," and "Long, Long Ago," have clearly defined phrases, both repeated and contrasting. Most of the songs are printed with one phrase on each line of a page. When songs are not printed that way, commas, semicolons, and periods in the texts, or rests in the melody offer semireliable clues as to the length of phrases. Song forms presented earlier were one-part (unary) with a phrase arrangement of *a a;* two-part (binary) with a phrase arrangement of *a b* or *a a b b;* and three-part (ternary) with a phrase arrangement of *a b a* or *a a b a.* It was stated that there are many variants of these forms.

Examples of one-part songs are Bach's "Cradle Hymn," and the folk song "Whistle, Daughter, Whistle." Other commonly used examples include:

Two-Part Song Form	*Three-Part Song Form*
"Du, Du, Liegst Mir im Herzen"	"Cradle Song" (French folksong)
"Go Tell Aunt Rhody"	"Lightly Row" (includes sequence)
"Li'l 'Liza Jane"	"Rosa, Come and Go Dancing"
	(includes sequence)
"Shortnin' Bread"	"Shoo Fly" (includes sequence)
	"Twinkle, Twinkle, Little Star"
	"Drink To Me Only With Thine Eyes"

From the child's point of view, identifying phrases and larger sections in terms of letters of the alphabet is not very appealing or even as logical as some other ways. To dramatize phrase differences, some teachers find that freeing the children to draw the form in their own creative ways can attract interest and induce far more learning. For example, phrases *a b a* might be:

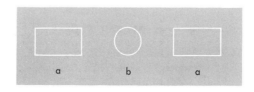

The sections of a rondo could be:

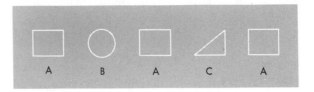

Another form might be drawn as:

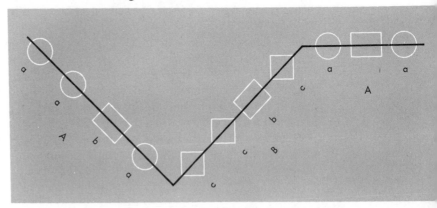

Using colors adds more interest because color highlights the contrasts. Some children will draw objects rather than the geometric designs illustrated here. The evaluative criterion is, "Does this drawing tell us clearly what the form is?" or "Does it show us all the parts in their true order?"

The A B A sectional form is common to many larger compositions. It is the same principle as the *a b a* phrase arrangement except that the concept is expanded into large sections instead of only several phrases.

Thematic development Thematic development as a means of extending melodic-rhythmic ideas can be studied by having older children explore the beginning of Beethoven's Fifth Symphony. "What different things did the composer do with his short idea?" "List them." (The first thing Beethoven did was to write a sequence.)

Two-part (Binary) Form

Ginastera: "Wheat Dance" from *Estancia,* AM 4 v 1
Handel: "Bourrée" and "Menuetto" from *Royal Fireworks
Music,* AM 3 v 2; BOL 62
Milhaud: "Copacabana" from *Saudades do Brazil,* AM 4 v 2

Respighi: "Danza" from *Brazilian Impressions,* AM 5 v 2
Bach: "Badinerie" from Suite No. 2 in B Minor, AM 3 v 1

Three-Part (Ternary) Form

Brahms: *Hungarian Dance No. 1 in C Minor,* AM 5 v 2
Debussy: *En Bateau,* BOL 53
Offenbach: "Barcarolle" from *Tales of Hoffman,* AM 3 v 1
Schumann: "Traumerei" from *Scenes of Childhood,* AM 4 v 2; BOL 63
Stravinsky: "Berceuse" from *Firebird* Suite, AM 1
Tchaikovsky: "Trepak" from *Nutcracker* Suite, BOL 58
Vaughan Williams: *Fantasia on Greensleeves,* AM 6 v 2
Walton: "Waltz" from *Facade* Suite, AM 6 v 2

Compound Ternary Form   The compound ternary form is one in which each of the A B A sections may be a binary or ternary form within itself. It is found in classical minuets of Haydn and Mozart.

Bizet: "Minuetto" from *L'Arlésinne* Suite No. 1, AM 4 v 2
Haydn: "Menuetto" from Symphony No. 6 in G Major, BOL 63
Mozart: "Menuetto" from Divertimento No. 17 in D Major, AM 5 v 2
Mozart: "Minuet" from Symphony No. 40 in G Minor, BOL 62
Sousa: *Stars and Stripes Forever,* AM 4 v 2 BOL 60

Rondo   The principle of the rondo is a basic theme or section, A, which is alternated with two or more contrasting themes. Children sometimes compare its scheme with a sandwich. The shortest rondo is A B A C A. If one compares A to a slice of bread and B and C to different sandwich fillings, the result is a special kind of double-decker sandwich. Longer rondos may be A B A C A B A or A B A C A D A. The rondeau is similar; it is an extension of the latter example using a different contrasting section each time; only A repeats. A beginning concept of the rondo is acquired by young children in simple ways. This might begin with establishing a beat, then asking the class to say the name of the school ("Oak Ridge School") followed by the name of a child, then the name of the school followed by the name of another child, and so on. The teacher's questions will help the class to realize the scheme of what they are doing—what is the same and what is different. Next, the same rondo principle is done with percussion instruments and even with rows of objects in the room. From here the children apply the scheme to short melodies and soon they are composing rondos. To help them compose, the teacher may write the recurring section of a rondo on the chalkboard and assign groups of children (or individual children) to extend the composition according to the plan.

Rondo for Bassoon and Orchestra, Franson, YPR 1009 (ages 6–10)
Beethoven: "Scherzo" from Symphony No. 7, BOL 62
Dvořák: Slavonic Dance in C Minor, AM 4 v 2
Haydn: "Gypsy Rondo" from Trio in G Major, BOL 64 (A B A C A Coda)

Khachaturian: "Waltz" from *Masquerade* Suite, AM 4 v 2 (A B A Interlude
C A B A)

Mozart: "Romanze" from *Eine kleine Nachtmusik*, AM 4 v 1 (A B A C A
Coda)

Prokofiev: "Waltz on Ice" from *Winter Holiday*, AM 3 v 2

Smetana: "Dance of the Comedians" from *Bartered Bride*, AM 6 v 2; BOL
56

Tchaikovsky: "Waltz" from *Sleeping Beauty*, AM 4 v 1

Kodály: "Viennese Music Clock" from *Hâry János* Suite, AM 2 v 1; BOL
81

Variation Form   This form is an extension of the concept of altering
melodies. However, as learners' concepts of variation grow, they find,
that the music can be varied in terms of its melody, rhythm, harmony,
texture, tempo, dynamics, form, tone quality and its general style. This can
make listening to variations somewhat like a mystery which gradually
resolves itself as the listener detects which musical elements the composer
changes in order to create the variation. Generally there is a theme (melody), followed by the different treatments of it. Unity is provided by the
theme, which is always present in some form; variety is provided by the
changing of any of the musical elements. There are variations in which a
melody or chord progression is repeated over and over, with variety coming
from changes in the other elements.

Hot Cross Buns, Franson CRG 5005 (ages 5–8)

Guarnieri: *Brazilian Dance*, AM 6 v 2; BOL 55

Anderson: *The Girl I Left Behind Me*, AM 5 v 2

Copland: "Simple Gifts" from *Appalachian Spring*, BOL 65

Cailliet: *Variations on Pop! Goes the Weasel*, AM 4 v 1; BOL 65

Ives: *Variations on "America,"* Louisville Records [3]

Kraft: *Variations for Percussion Instruments*, BOL 83

Gould: *American Salute*, AM 5 v 1; BOL 65

Variation Form: Teaching   The Cailliet *Variations on Pop! Goes the
Weasel* can be useful as an example of how to help children learn the
principles of the form. Its sections are as follows:

Introduction and theme:	Can the children sense the meter? Can they tell if a full orchestra is playing? Can they hear whether or not one section of the orchestra predominates?
1. Fugue	In a fugue, the same melody is played at different times by different instruments at different pitch levels, but it gives the impression of a round because of the entries of these parts. Does it sound that way here?

---

[3] An analysis of Ives' *Variations on America* appears in the October, 1974, *Music
Educators Journal*, pp. 66–67. The recording referred to in the article is Columbia
MS-6161, *The Organ in America*.

What is the order of the entering instruments? (Six instruments are emphasized before the entire orchestra plays the tune.)

2. Minuet

What is the meter in this formal dance, the minuet? Hear two melodies played at once. Which instrument plays the melody and which plays another tune? Can *augmentation* (playing the melody in longer note values) be identified?

3. Adagio

What elements of the music produce the mood here, and what do you think this mood is? A new tune is introduced, a Jewish wedding song.

4. Music box

What is a music box? What instruments are used to sound like a music box? What did the composer do to make the "oomp pa pa" effect?

5. Jazz

What meter does the composer choose here? Listen to the trumpet with the "Wa Wa" mute. What do you think the player does with the mute to make this sound? How does the composer make the music sound like jazz? What happens to the melody this time? Now ask the children to define "variation form" in their own words. Ask them in how many ways a melody can be varied in a variation form.

Fugue
The fugue is a rather complex polyphonic form. A theme (subject) is introduced by two or more voices in turn, developed in what can be considered another section, then restated in the final part of the form. If children should describe a fugue after listening to it carefully, they might say that when one voice or instrument states a theme and then continues playing another melody while a second voice states the theme a fourth lower or a fifth higher, the beginning of a fugue has been created. The melody the first voice plays or sings when the second voice sounds the theme is called the "countersubject." This process may continue with the entrance of other voices, each beginning with the subject. This first section is called an *exposition*. It is followed by a free section consisting of statements of the subject, often in altered forms, and "episodes," something akin to interludes, based on tone patterns or rhythm patterns found in the subject and countersubject. Sometimes there is a *stretto* near the end, when the voices sound the subject in a way in which there is overlapping of the entrances. The subject is restated at the end to establish unity. Contemporary composers do not always plan their fugues in the traditional scheme described here.

The fugue may appear complicated by its description, and the teacher must use good judgment in knowing how far to expect a class of eleven-year-olds to proceed with it. Depending on the group, going into fine detail will be something only advanced children will find interesting. However, the entire class can detect the unique beginning and the texture of the fugue; even young children can do this.

Fugue	McBride: *Pumpkineater's Little Fugue*, BOL 65
	Thomson: *Fugue and Chorale on Yankee Doodle,* BOL 65
	Scarlatti: *Cat's Fugue,* Keyboard Junior Recordings
	Bach: Little Fugue in G Minor, BOL 86, AM 6 v 1
	Bizet: "Farandole" from *L'Arlésienne* Suite No. 2, AM 6 v 1

Sonata-Allegro Form   The sonata-allegro form is an expanded A B A form. Its plan is a statement of two different themes followed by a development of those themes as a contrasting section, then a restatement of the themes to provide unity. Sometimes one of the themes will be in a familiar song-form. The first theme is apt to be masculine and vigorous while the second theme may be feminine and lyrical, thus providing contrast. Often there are transitional passages between this first part of the form, the *exposition,* and the second part, the *development*. In the development section the themes and parts of themes are treated in many different ways, and the listener may identify inversion, rhythmic alteration, sequence, change of key, and many other techniques composers use in creating variety. The final section is the *recapitulation,* in which there is a restatement of the themes, often followed by a coda. This form is used as the first movement of a symphony, sonata, concerto, quartet and quintet, as well as appearing in some overtures and other forms.

Schubert: First Movement from Symphony No. 5, AM 5 v 1
Mozart: First Movement from Symphony No. 40, BOL 71
Prokofiev: *Classical* Symphony, BOL 73

The Suite   The suite has an interesting history which some advanced children may want to research. The suites we hear today are often dance suites in which a series of related dances constitute the composition, the ballet suite, the opera suite, and suites based on dramatic (stage) works. The dance suites are usually made up of dances of the sixteenth and seventeenth centuries, the allemand, courante, saraband, gigue, and a number of others. The suites based on stage works such as opera, ballet, and drama, are selections taken from music written for these works and arranged for concert performance. Still other suites are written on ideas such as philosophy, psychology, and geography.

Dance suites.	Bach: *English* Suites
	Handel: *Harpsichord* Suites
Ballet suites.	Tchaikovsky: *Nutcracker* Suite, BOL 58
	Stravinsky: *Petrouchka* Suite
	Ravel: *Daphnis and Chloe* Suite No. 2, BOL 86
	Rimsky-Korsakov: *Scheherazade* Suite, BOL 77

Based on stage works.   Grieg: *Peer Gynt* Suite, BOL 59

Walton: *Facade* Suite

Opera suites.   Bizet: *Carmen* Suite

Menotti: Suite from *Amahl and the Night Visitors,* BOL 58

Geographical suites.   Grofé: *Grand Canyon* Suite, BOL 61

Grofé: *Mississippi River* Suite, BOL 61

Tone Poem   The symphonic poem or tone poem is a work for symphony orchestra in which the form is dictated by a story, a description, or a character.

> Strauss: *Til Eulenspiegel and His Merry Pranks* (a lengthy work for older children)
>
> Moussorgsky: *Night on Bald Mountain,* BOL 81. This short tone poem is a favorite at Halloween time.
>
> Saint-Saëns: *Danse Macabre,* BOL 81. (Another Halloween favorite)

Opera, Oratorio, Cantata   These are large vocal works. The opera is a stage play in which the words are sung and in which the singers are accompanied by an orchestra. There may be duets, trios, quartets, sextets, and other ensembles, a chorus, and even a ballet. The *recitative* is a rather declamatory vocal style that attempts to imitate speech; an *aria* is a solo; an *arioso* is a style midway between the recitative and aria.

> Menotti: *Amahl and the Night Visitors* (can be used in its entirety at Christmas)
>
> Humperdinck: *Hansel and Gretel* (use selections from, and relate to the story)
>
> Bizet: *Carmen* (use selections from, and the story)
>
> Rossini: *William Tell Overture* (an opera overture to hear, and the story) BOL 76; AM 3 v 1
>
> Verdi: *Aida* (use selections from, and the story)
>
> Britten: *The Little Sweep* (can be used in entirety)
>
> Mozart: *The Magic Flute* (selections from, with simplified story)
>
> *Child's Introduction to Opera,* Childcraft Records, Album 38. (includes *Barber of Seville, Amahl and the Night Visitors,* and *Hansel and Gretel*)

Multiple Concepts

> Jurey: *Design in Music,* Bowmar Records (an album)
>   Contains the following:
>   Waltz: A B A form; Rondo: A B A C A; Theme and Five
>   Variations; Symphony in Miniature:
>   First Movement: Sonata-Allegro Form with the songs "Erie Canal" and "Red River Valley"
>   Second Movement: Song Form with "All Through the Night" and "All the Pretty Little Horses"
>   Third Movement: Scherzo Form with "Merrily We Roll Along" and "Good Night Ladies"

Fourth Movement: Rondo Form with more children's game songs
(transparencies for overhead projector containing themes of all compositions are available)

References

GARY, CHARLES L., ed., *The Study of Music in the Elementary School—A Conceptual Approach.* Reston, Va.: Music Educators National Conference,
1967. pp. 85–112. For teachers' lesson plans.

**Films and
Filmstrips**

Discovering Form in Music, BFA Educational Media, 2211 Michigan Avenue,
Santa Monica, Calif. 90404 (phrases and sections)

Forms of Music: Instrumental, Coronet Instructional Films, 65 E. South Water
St., Chicago, Ill. 60601 (sonata, concerto, symphony, and tone poem; for
advanced children)

Let's Discover the Design, EMC Corporation, St. Paul, Minn. 55101. (ages 10
and up)

Young People's Concert Series (Leonard Bernstein): *What Makes Music Symphonic? What Is a Concerto?; What Is Sonata Form?* McGraw-Hill Films,
1221 Avenue of the Americas, New York, N.Y. 10020. (60 min.) Ages
10–Adult. Also inquire at local Bell Telephone Office for possible free availability.

Harmony and Texture

The development of the harmonic sense follows the comprehension of
rhythm and melody. This is characteristic of western cultures. It is either
not as evident or is absent in other cultures, although the mass audio media
of our times is tending to produce a world music consisting of an amalgama-
tion of the contributions of all peoples. While Western music evolved to
emphasize harmony, music of Asia and Africa emphasized rhythmic and
melodic developments more complex than those of the West. In the ethnic
music of Asia and Africa, harmony is incidental to the interrelation of
rhythm and melody, although the octave, the fifth, and the fourth appear
vertically in much of it, as does some simple tonic-dominant harmony.

Polyphony is another word for counterpoint. Its earliest definition
had to do with point against point (note against note). For our purposes
we will regard it as a combining of melodic lines into a unified musical
fabric. In traditional Western music, polyphony operates in accordance
with certain harmonic principles. However, in some contemporary music it
operates with disregard of traditional common practice harmony. Thus,
there can be said to be two general types of polyphony, harmonic and
nonharmonic. According to traditional standards, harmonic polyphony
sounds well; it is consonant. Nonharmonic polyphony does not sound the
same; it is apt to be dissonant. The music of Johann Sebastian Bach is
polyphonic; it can be viewed as horizontal threads of melody moving along

together. At the same time, when this music is viewed vertically, chords and chord changes appear at certain places. We find it is a texture woven of threads moving in both vertical and horizontal ways. A common example of this combination of the horizontal and vertical aspects of music is the round. Teachers should occasionally write a round in full on the chalkboard, each entry written on a staff beneath the previous entry. Children can then see, as well as hear, how the polyphony fits together harmonically.

Texture refers to the number and general effect of the horizontal and vertical lines in music. Adjectives commonly used to describe texture include, heavy, light, open, thick, and thin. Texture can be thick or thin according to the number of parts employed, their pitches, and their tone qualities. A two-part round is of thin texture while three- and four-part rounds have correspondingly thicker textures. Low pitches can influence textures toward heaviness while high pitches can produce an opposite effect. When the parts are close together, the texture is correspondingly thicker; when they are far apart, an opposite effect can occur. The terms homophonic, monophonic, and polyphonic refer to classification of textures.

Children first learn melody, the monophonic (one-voice) horizontal line. It is believed they are able to sense next the moving of two or more melody lines together. This is reflected in the classroom in the use of canons, rounds, chants, ostinati, and descants that they can perform after they have learned to sing in tune or to play a melody instrument with a group. For most children the ability to hear and sing harmonically develops between the ages of nine and thirteen. In the elementary school this growing harmonic sense is reflected by an emphasis on part-singing for the ten and eleven-year-olds.

Among western nations there are differences in the degree of emphasis given to harmonic music by music educators. In the United States it has been emphasized throughout all levels of instruction to a greater degree than in most other nations. It is possible that young children like the sound of harmony even though most of them cannot hear it analytically and, on the other hand, harmony may be overused; it can confuse some children who are trying to comprehend and sing melodies. Research is needed to determine the suitability of harmonic music for young children. It seems logical that the young child should first be helped to comprehend rhythm and melody and that this should be done with as little interference from other elements as possible. Second, the child should be assisted in developing the ability to comprehend two or more melodic lines functioning at once and relating to each other. Third, this interaction of melodic lines should lead rather quickly into learning about harmony. It should also develop a certain independence in thinking and composing melodic lines, which may or may not be harmonically related. Thus, the child will be able to deal both with traditional harmony and with some of the music of today which avoids such harmony; the eleven-year-old should be helped to understand both types of music.

Some generalizations, conclusions, and findings for children to discover and develop in traditional harmony are:

Harmony is a vertical arrangement of pitches.

Tonality (key feeling) results when the harmony of a piece of music indicates a tonal center to which its other tones are attracted or related.

When two tones are on adjacent lines or spaces, they form the interval of a third.

Thirds (and other intervals) may be found vertically in harmonies and horizontally in melodies.

The tones of the dominant seventh chord (V_7) resolve naturally to the tonic chord; this fixes the tonality.

The tones of the subdominant (IV) chord resolve naturally to either the tonic chord or follow a progression to the dominant seventh chord followed by the tonic chord.

When at the end of a succession of chords in a phrase a feeling of repose is suggested, the chords which communicate this feeling comprise a cadence.[4]

The IV I cadence sounds like "Amen."

Contemporary Harmony

One possible approach to contemporary harmony would take place after the children have found that chords in traditional harmony are constructed in thirds. The teacher could ask, "What would happen if chords were built of fourths rather than thirds?" and let the children find out by their experimenting with fourths. Then the teacher might ask the same question about fifths, sevenths, and seconds. Another beginning could be in response to the question, "What kinds of chords are needed to harmonize a composition written in the whole-tone scale? Write one and be ready to tell the class about those chords."

Music of today is in a period of unlimited experimentation. It is described by some as involving deliberate violation of the traditional harmonic system of chords and chord resolutions by the employment of parallel chords, chords built with fourths, other arrangements leading to abandonment of former restrictions, and toward the absence of tonal centers. This does not mean that the music of the future is necessarily what the results of experimental composition seem to indicate, but it is likely that some of this will be a genuine part of it. It appears that music educators have the responsibility of helping children think musically in the two generally defined areas of traditional harmony and its opposite, and in the great area in between these two extremes. This area in between the extremes may be the most important when the future reveals itself in this time of rapid change.

In *tone row* composition tones of the row are combined as chords. In tonal polyphony the chords "happen" when horizontal lines of melody

---

[4] The cadence is the melodic and/or harmonic aspect of the phrase ending, which conveys the impression of momentary or full conclusion. The *perfect* cadence occurs normally at the end of a composition, when the keynote is sounded in the highest voice (harmonically as part of the tonic chord). When harmonized, either the dominant or subdominant chord precedes the final tonic chord. The *authentic* cadence is the result of a V-I chord sequence, and the *plagal* cadence is the result of a IV-I chord sequence. There are others: *mixed, imperfect,* and *deceptive.*

sound at one time. The pen of the less talented experimenter is likely to produce less artistic music; the more talented will use new harmonic resources with discretion and taste. The composers most likely to live in the history of music will do what the great ones have always done—find some way to integrate the new with the old in a pleasing way. In the elementary schools our duty is to expose children to all types of music, including the current experimentation. Experience with the tone row and its type of harmony can begin as early as the third grade. The fifth and sixth grades can sing a folk song in one key while chording it in another, record this bitonality on tape, play it back and evaluate the effect. They can also sing songs in parallel fourths and fifths for experimental purposes and evaluate them the same way. *Children like to experiment* and to evaluate what happens—and this seems to be one of the best times in history to do it. They can experiment with traditional harmony by finding different harmonizations for the same song. Improvisation can be done on the black keys while chording in the key of C major. Authentic recorded music of Africa and Asia can be listened to, studied, and its harmonic qualities can be examined and compared to Western harmony. In some of this music, harmony may be absent, in some it may be present but different from Western harmony, and in some the harmony may resemble that of the West.

Recordings useful in exploring contemporary harmony include:

Bartók: "Bear Dance" from *Hungarian Sketches* AM 3 v 2

Bartók: *Concerto for Orchestra.* Quartal harmony (chords built in fourths)

Milhaud: "Laranjeires: from *Saudades do Brazil,* AM 4 v 2 (dissonance, bitonality)

Milhaud: "Copacabana" from *Saudades do Brazil,* AM 4 v 2 (bitonality, dissonance)

Hindemith: *Mathis der Maler,* Columbia (harmony constructed of fourths and fifths)

Harris: *Folk-Song Symphony,* Vanguard (contemporary harmonizations of U.S. folksongs)

Honneger: "March from *King David,* Vanguard (polytonality: three keys at one time)

Ives: "Putnam's Camp" from *Three Places in New England,* BOL 75; Columbia; Mercury (bitonality; describes two bands playing in different keys). Also "Fourth of July," Columbia MS-6889 and *Variations on America,* Columbia MS-7269 and Victor LSC-2893.

Copland: "Circus Music" from *The Red Pony,* AM 3 v 1 (tone clusters, polytonality)

Webern: *The Complete Music,* Columbia K4L 232 (tone row music)

Sounds of New Music, Folkways FX 6160 (electronic music) tone clusters: see music of Charles Ives and Henry Cowell

Children's exploration of harmony and polyphony should deepen their insight into how melody and harmony interrelate. There is no better way to learn about music than to compose it. Although few children will be professional composers, every child can benefit from writing his or her own melody and harmony, regardless of how modest the level may be. Music paper should be standard equipment in the classroom.

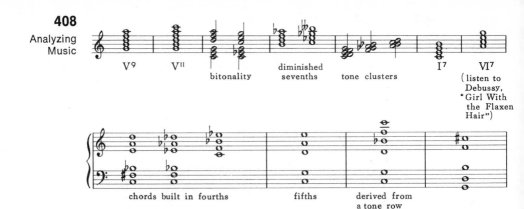

Electronic music is bringing about a reexamination of current definitions of harmony, polyphony, form, and other musical elements. In electronic music, the simultaneous sounding of two tone qualities, whether these have definite pitch or not, can be considered to be a type of harmony. Polyphony of electronic sounds may consist of simultaneous sounding of different streams or bands of sounds that produce a contrapuntal effect. When one finds that some of the recorded examples of "new" music listed in this book are from the 1950s and 1960s, the urgency of keeping abreast of this rapidly-moving thrust in music becomes evident. Some radio and television programs utilize electronic and other types of contemporary music. These can be tape recorded and brought into the classroom for analysis.

RECORDINGS RELATED TO HARMONY AND TEXTURE

Major and minor.
Moussorgsky: "Bydlo" from *Pictures at an Exhibition.* AM 2 v 1

Bizet: "Farandole" from *L'Arlésienne* Suite. AM 6 v 1 (also form)

Lecuona: "Andalucia" from *Suite Andalucia,* AM 4 v 1 (includes a canon)

Mozart: "Romanze" from *Eine kleine Nachtmusik,* AM 4 v 1

Charpentier: "Oh Muleback" from *Impressions of Italy,* AM 5 v 1

de Falla: "Spanish Dance" from *La Vida Breve,* AM 6 v 1

Common chords.
Brubeck: "Unsquare Dance" on *Time Further Out.* Columbia CS 8490

Mozart: "Romanze" from *Eine kleine Nachtmusik,* AM 4 v 1 (I, V_7, and IV chords can be heard and identified)

Ginastera: "Wheat Dance" from *Estancia,* AM 4 v 1

Milhaud: "Copacabana" from *Saudades do Brazil,* AM 4 v 2

Sousa: *Semper Fidelis,* AM 3 v 1. Have children explore this march to discover the melodies and how the composer combines them.

Saint-Saëns: "The Swan" from *Carnival of the Animals,* AM 3 v 2 (homophonic texture)

Ligeti: "Atmospheres" from *Space Odyssy,* Columbia MS 6733

Bach: Little Fugue in G Minor, AM 6 v 1; BOL 86

Britten: *Young Person's Guide to the Orchestra,* London 6671 (polyphony, theme and variations)

Benjamin, *Jamaican Rumba,* BOL 56 (homophony, polyphony)

FILMS

Elements of Composition (New York Wind Ensemble), NET Film Service, Bloomington, Ind. 47401 (melody, harmony, rhythm, and counterpoint)

Discovering Melody and Harmony, BFA Educational Media, 2211 Michigan Ave., Santa Monica, Calif. 90404 (Harmony is added to melody through use of descant and thirds and by playing instruments)

Harmony in Music, Coronet Instructional Films, Chicago, Ill. 60601 (introduces harmony and chords, ages 10–13)

Let's Get Together, EMC Corporation, St. Paul, Minn. 55101 (harmony, ages 10–adult)

Music, The Expressive Language, Sutherland Productions, 201 N. Occidental Blvd., Los Angeles, Calif. 90026 (rhythm, melody, harmony, reading music, for ages 9–11)

Music: Churchill Films, 662 N. Robertson Blvd., Los Angeles, Ca. 90069. From a popular series of music education films.

Two-Part Singing, Johnson Hunt Productions, Hollywood, Calif. 94105 (ages 9–11)

Refer to *Film Guide for Music Educators,* Music Educators National Conference.

Thematic Development

Familiar melodies comprise one successful approach to the study of symphonic music. When a song is well known by children, they thrill to its discovery in symphonic works and their interest in listening is stimulated. However, identifying the melody is only a first step. Because the essence of symphonic music is *thematic development,* the answer to the question, "What does the composer do with his or her tune?" can bring forth exciting explorations. How fully children are able to reply to the question will depend upon their stage of musical development. If they have a background of experience in composers' devices, they will identify many of them in their analyses of such compositions. Knowledge of variation form will assist such explorations.

A list of familiar melodies that appear in symphonic music follows.

Composer	Title	Song
ANDERSON	Irish Suite	"Irish Washerwoman," "Minstrel Boy," "Wearing of the Green," "The Girl I Left Behind Me"
BARLOW	The Winter's Passed	"Wayfaring Stranger," "Black Is the Color of My True Love's Hair"
BEETHOVEN	String Quartet Op. 59, No. 2	Russian hymn "Praise to God" (*This Is Music* Book 4)
	Symphony 8, Second Movement, Third Theme	"The Metronome" (Adventures in Music 6 v 1)
	Symphony 9, Fourth Movement	"United Nations Hymn" ("World Anthem") (*This Is Music* Book 6)
	Wellington's Victory	"For He's a Jolly Good Fellow"
BLOCH	America	"Yankee Doodle," "Old Folks at Home," "Hail Columbia"
BRAHMS	Academic Festival Overture	"Guadeamus Igitur" (student song often found in series books for grades 7–8) (Bowmar #76)
CAILLIET	Variations on Pop! Goes the Weasel	"Pop! Goes the Weasel" (Bowmar #65) (Adventures in Music 4 v 1)
CHOPIN	Fantasy Impromptu	"I'm Always Chasing Rainbows"
COPLAND	Appalachian Spring	"Simple Gifts" (Bowmar #75)
	Billy the Kid, Fourth Theme	"Goodbye, Old Paint"
	Lincoln Portrait	"Camptown Races," "Springfield Mountain"
	Rodeo	"Hoe-Down" (Adventures in Music 5 v 2) (Bowmar #55)
DOHNÁNY	Variations on a Nursery Tune (for older children)	"Twinkle, Twinkle, Little Star" (piano and orchestra)
DVOŘÁK	Symphony 5	"Swing Low, Sweet Chariot" (First Movement, Third Theme) "Going Home" (Second Movement, First Theme)
GOULD	American Salute	When Johnny Comes Marching Home" (Adventures in Music 5 v 1) (Bowmar #65)
	Cowboy Rhapsody	"Goodbye, Old Paint," "Home on the Range"
	Variations on When Johnny Comes Marching Home	"When Johnny Comes Marching Home"

Composer	Title	Song
GRAINGER	Londonderry Air	"Londonderry Air" (Adventures in Music 4 v 2)
GROFF	Death Valley Suite	"O Susanna" (Adventures in Music 4 v 1), "Old Folks at Home," "Old Black Joe"
GUION	Turkey in the Straw	"Old Zip Coon" (same tune)
HARRIS	Folk Song Symphony	"Irish Washerwoman," "Bury Me Not on the Lone Prairie," "Streets of Laredo," "Turkey in the Straw," "When Johnny Comes Marching Home."
HAYDN	"Emperor" Quartet in C Major	"Glorious Things of Thee Are Spoken" ("Austrian National Hymn") Appears in several of the music series.
HINDEMITH	Trauermusic (Funeral Music)	"Old Hundred" Both melody and harmony are manipulated.
HUMPERDINCK	Hansel and Gretel, Prelude to Act 1	"Prayer," "Song of the Gingerbread Children," "Partner, Come and Dance With Me"
IVES	Fifth Movement, Symphony No. 2	"Camptown Races," "Long, Long Ago," "Reveille"
KAY	Western Symphony	"Red River Valley," "The Girl I Left Behind Me," "Golden Slippers," "Jim Along Josie" (Vox Recording)
McBRIDE	Mexican Rhapsody Pumpkineaters Little Fugue	"Hat Dance," "Rancho Grande," "La Cucaracha" "Peter, Peter, Pumpkin Eater" (Bowmar #65)
McDONALD	Children's Symphony	"Farmer in the Dell," "Jingle Bells," (Adventures in Music 3 v 2) "London Bridge," "Baa, Baa, Black Sheep," "Oh, Dear, What Can the Matter Be?" "Little Bo Peep"

Composer	Title	Song
MAHLER	First Symphony, Third Movement	"Are You Sleeping?"
MOUSSORGSKY	Boris Godunov, Coronation Scene	"Praise to God" (*This Is Music* Book 4)
NELSON	Kentucky Mountain Portraits	"Cindy," "Skip to My Lou," "Paw Paw Patch"
QUILTER	A Children's Overture	"Girls and Boys Come Out to Play," "St. Paul's Steeple," "Dame Get Up and Bake Your Pies," "Over the Hills and Far Away," "The Frog and the Crow," "The Frog He Would A-Wooing Go," "Oranges and Lemons," "Baa Baa Black Sheep"
ROSSINI	William Tell Overture	"Lone Ranger Theme" (Bowmar #76) (Adventures in Music 3 v 1)
SIBELIUS	Finlandia	"Song of Peace" and other titles
SOWERBY	Irish Washerwoman	"Lane County Bachelor" and other titles
STRAVINSKY	Greeting Prelude	"Happy Birthday to You" (Columbia Record *Instrumental Miniatures*)
R. STRAUSS	Aus Italien	"Funiculi, Funicula"
THOMSON	"Cattle," from The Plow That Broke the Plains	"My Home's in Montana," "I Ride an Old Paint," "The Streets of Laredo" (Bowmar #65)
THOMSON	Fugue and Chorale on a Yankee Doodle Theme	"Yankee Doodle" (Bowmar #65)
TCHAIKOVSKY	1812 Overture Symphony 4, Fourth Movement	"Russian National Hymn" and other titles "The Birch Tree" (Adventures in Music 6 v 2)
VARDELL	Joe Clark Steps Out	"Old Joe Clark" (Mercury Recording)
VAUGHAN-WILLIAMS	Fantasia on Greensleeves	"What Child Is This?" ("Greensleeves") (Adventures in Music 6 v 2)

Tone qualities.	Cage, Cowell, Ussachevsky, *Sounds of New Music,* Folkways FX 6160. For stimulating sound exploration on piano and Autoharp.
	Kraft, *Theme and Variations for Percussion Quartet,* BOL #83
	The Science of Sound, Folkways FX 6007.
Legato, staccato.	Gretry, "Ballet Music" from *Cephale et Procris,* Tambourin, AM 2 v 1. Also useful for major, minor, and loud-soft concepts.
Melody (conjunct and disjunct).	Shostakovitch, "Petite Ballerina" from Ballet Suite No. 2, AM 2 v 1
	Bartók, "Jack-in-the-Box" from *Mikrokosmos* Suite No. 2, AM 2 v 1
	Schuller, "Twittering Machine" from *Seven Studies on Themes of Paul Klee,* AM 2 v 2. (12 tone music)
	Schubert, "First Movement" from Symphony No. 5, AM 5 v 1
Ostinato.	Cowell, *Ostinato Percussion,* Mainstream 5011.
	Kabalevsky, "Pantomime" from *The Comedians,* AM 1 v 1.
Improvisation.	Brubeck, *Dialogue for Jazz Combo and Orchestra,* Columbia CL 1466.
	Bernstein, "Improvisation I" from *Four Improvisations for Orchestra,* Columbia MS 6733
Changing and less common meters.	Brubeck, *Time Out* (²⁄₄, ³⁄₄, ⁴⁄₄, ⁴⁄₄ :‖) Columbia CL 1397
	———, *Time Further Out* (⁷⁄₄, ⁵⁄₄) Columbia CL 1690
	Tchaikovsky, "Second Movement" from Symphony No. 6 (⁵⁄₄ meter)
Intervals.	Bartók, "Second Movement" from *Concerto for Orchestra,* Pairs at Play (bassoons in 6ths, oboes in 3rds, clarinets in 7ths)
	Hanson, "Bells" from *For the First Time* on *The Composer and His Music,* Mercury MG 50357 (5ths)
Whole-tone scale.	Debussy, "Voiles" from *Preludes,* Book 1.
	Hanson, "Mists" from *For the First Time* on *The Composer and His Orchestra,* Vol. III, Mercury MG 50357

Twelve-tone music.

Schoenberg and others, piano music (Gould) Columbia ML 5336

Schoenberg and others, orchestral pieces, Columbia ML 5616

Stravinsky, Double Canon for String Quartet, Columbia MS 6272

Electronic music.

Mimaroglu, "Prelude XI" on *Electronic Music III* Turnabout VOX TV 34177. The sound of a rubber band on manipulated tape recorder.

Powell, *Electronic Setting,* Son Nova 1

Stockhausen, *Gesang der Jünglinge,* Deutsche Grammophon 138811

Ussachevsky, *Piece for Tape Recorder,* CRI 112

Varèse, *Poem Electronique,* Columbia ML 5478

Cage, Cowell, others, *Sounds of New Music,* Folkways FX 6160

Form.

Pinto, *Memories of Childhood,* BOL #68 (ABA, meter)

Vaughan-Williams, "March Past of the Kitchen Utensils" from *The Wasps,* AM 3 v 1 (phrase, repetition, contrast)

Menotti, "March of the Kings" from *Amahl and the Night Visitors,* AM 1 v 2 (rhythm pattern, form based on repetition and contrast of two melodies, coda)

McDonald, "Third Movement" from *Children's Symphony,* AM 2 v 1 (introduction, coda, contrast, interlude)

Delibes, "Swanhilde's Dream" from *Copelia,* AM 2 v 2

Prokofiev, "Waltz on Ice" from *Winter Holiday,* AM 3 v 2 (ABACA rondo)

Pinto, "Run, Run" from *Memories of Childhood,* BOL #68 (ABA sections, meters)

Haydn, "Andante" from Symphony No. 94, BOL #62 (theme and variations)

Sousa, *Stars and Stripes Forever,* AM 4 v 1

Mozart, Overture to *The Marriage of Figaro,* BOL #76 (overture)

El-Dabh, *Leilya and the Poet,* Columbia MS 6566 (form in tape processes)

Halloween Listening and Analyzing

Halloween provides an exceptionally promising time to analyze recorded music to determine how a composer employs the various musical elements to produce the effects desired. The following compositions are among those studied in relation to Halloween:

Berlioz	"Witches' Sabbath" from *Symphonie Fantastique*
Cowell	"Banshee" on *Sounds of New Music*, Folkways FX 6160
Dukas	*The Sorcerer's Apprentice*, BOL #59
Grieg	"In the Hall of the Mountain King," from *Peer Gynt* Suite, BOL #59
	March of the Dwarfs, BOL #52
Humperdinck	"Witches' Ride" from *Hansel and Gretel*
MacDowell	"Villain" from *Marionettes*, RCA Basic Library 45-5032
	"Witch," RCA Listening III
	"Witches' Dance," RCA Listening V
Moussorgsky	*Night on Bald Mountain*, BOL #82
Reinheld	*Dwarfs*, RCA Basic Library
	Gnomes, RCA Rhythm Album One
Saint-Saëns	*Danse Macabre*, BOL #59
Stravinsky	"Infernal Dance of the Kastchei" from *Firebird* Suite, BOL #69

Analyzing Ethnic and Intercultural Music

Black and Chicano music are of high importance today, and not only in communities that have large black and Chicano populations. As is true of all music, much can be learned from them. Many state departments of education, county and city school systems have compiled collections of Latin-American music that reflect the Spanish or Mexican-American cultures, one example being *Cancionero Alegre,* published by the Department of Public Instruction, State Capitol, Phoenix, Arizona. Probably because this music has long been considered to be a traditional part of Western culture, few sessions have been devoted to the teaching of it at the conferences and conventions of music educators.

The music of former Africans in many Latin-American nations has resulted in a merging of musical styles that has produced much popular music, folk music, and dance. The following are in large part of African origin:

country	*dance*
Argentina	Tango
Brazil	Samba, Maxixe
Cuba	Habañera, Rhumba, Congo, Danzon, Mambo, Cha-Cha
Haiti	Merengue (French and African influences)
Mexico	Huapango
Trinidad	Limbo

In addition to the above, the calypso, part of the popular music of Trinidad and the Bahamas, combines European melody and harmony with African rhythm. American composers who have utilized musical ideas from these sources include:

Benjamin   *Jamaican Rhumba*
Copland   *El Salon Mexico*
Gould   *Latin-American Symphonette*

Characteristics of black music from which all children can learn include the use of music in all phases of daily living, antiphony (call and response), use of pentatonic and gapped scales and flatted scale tones 3, 5, and 7, complex rhythms with syncopation and shifting meters, improvisation, alteration of melody, harmonies using I, IV, and V chords, story-telling in song, and performance techniques that include hand clapping, rhythmic movement, stamping, shouting, percussive vocal effects, ostinato effects, and falsetto singing. These elements of black or African music are found in blues, jazz riffs, and in rock and roll music. Negro folksongs are a vital element in American musical culture. They have been classified by John W. Work [5] under the following headings:

Call and response chant
Slow, sustained, long-phrase melody
Syncopated, segmented melody
Story-telling
Trial and tribulation
Faith and inspiration

Sessions in black music at conferences and conventions stress repeatedly that rhythm is the primary element in performing African-American music, thus *active physical movement* is a necessity.

One of the strong trends in music education is an interest in music of the world. While there have been songs from Western Europe and Latin America in music textbooks, Africa and Asia, where the majority of the people on the earth reside, have been poorly represented. Efforts are now being made to learn more about the indigenous music of all peoples. We become involved with generalizations such as:

1. The early history of the development of music in any country has a direct influence on the present and future types of music in that country.
2. The music of any country is undergoing more or less constant change.
3. The music of any country reflects the people's concerns in every aspect and area of life—social, esthetic, religious, political, and economic.
4. The music of most cultures has been altered and influenced by music from another or other cultures.
5. Folk songs in all societies undergo constant change which reflects the changes taking place in those societies; both words and melodies may change over the years (Example: Songs about "choo-choo" trains are not written today because the modern diesel engine does not make that sound.)

[5] John W. Work, *Negro Folk Songs and Spirituals* (New York: Bonanza Books, 1940).

6. The music of a particular culture has a distinctive style that differentiates it from all other cultures.
7. Every society has found a need for music, and has created its own types of music to serve its purposes.
8. The music, art, language, literature, architecture, recreation, food, clothing, and political and social customs of a people serve to bind them together into a national or cultural unit.

Music is sometimes considered solely as an art to be studied, and sometimes considered solely as an art that reflects humanity. This implied division is in many respects artificial, since music as an art is rooted in the lives of people. Both social studies and ethnomusicology demand that music be studied *in the context* of the society and times of which it is an expression. An example is the minuet, which became an official French court dance in 1650, and eventually became an expression of a courtly and aristocratic society. Its restraint and sophisticated artificiality reflected the patterned dignity and courtesies of the eighteenth-century ruling class. As this aristocratic society began to weaken, the minuet began to decline in importance as a dance, but became a movement in symphonies of Haydn and Mozart at a faster tempo, not danceable. This finally evolved to become the *scherzo* (literally joke) movement of Beethoven symphonies. Music is always communicating something, whether it is feelings of restraint or of freedom, a folk singer's reaction to the environment, aspects of a specific culture, or a sophisticated reflection of that culture by a professional composer.

Songs, dances, and instruments yield data about people's beliefs, values, and how they live or lived. Through the music of various people and times, children can discover *who they are,* and can find their places in the cultural stream that began in the past and will flow into the future. New songs explain the concerns of the present day, while old songs are a means of understanding the past and its influence on the present. The historian and the anthropologist find music an essential ingredient of a culture, society, or tribal organization; thus it is one of the essentials of a civilized state of being. Music is not necessary for mere physical survival, but it helps make survival worthwhile; it is a quality factor for living which indicates degrees of cultural sophistication.

The school music of Japanese children is similar to that of American children, while the original, authentic Japanese music occupies a minority position. The native Japanese music stems historically from Chinese culture, causing the Japanese children to find themselves amid two cultural streams of music. The excellent film, *Folk Songs of Japan,* useful for age eight and up, can be obtained from the nearest Japanese consulate (color, 29 min.). It portrays the beauty of the Japanese countryside while taking the listener through examples of all types of folk music including a contemporary popular song performed by young people at a ski resort. The combination of Japanese and American influences in this song encourages children's analyses of the music.

The Japanese haiku poem can be created, then set to music using a Japanese scale. Accompanying instruments can be added rather delicately, with gong, bells, woodblocks, finger cymbals, and a light rattle being appropriate in many cases. The poem includes a central idea, a suggested or inferred location, reference to seasons of the year, and seventeen syllables in three lines, although the latter is not always held to. An example might be:

The late poppy bloom
Withers in the cold.
Orange petals are falling.

Japanese scales (pentatonic scales with half-steps):

As children explore Asiatic music by means of television, recordings, films, and books, they will discover that concepts of music which differ from ours have a utility, charm, and worth of their own. Rhythm and melody, often accompanied by a simple drone, characterize the music of India. The scale and melodic structure is found in the *raga,* of which there are hundreds. Each of these has from five to seven pitches and one or two secondary pitches. The performer elaborates and improvises on the raga. Each raga has nonmusical implications which could be some feeling or emotion, a season, or a time of day. This music is horizontally conceived; there is no harmony as we know it—only the drone. Both melody and rhythm are more sophisticated than their counterparts in western music; our composers are being increasingly influenced by Indian concepts of melody and rhythm. The *tala* is the rhythmic structure, organized into a number of beats with recurring accents. Approximately thirty talas are in common use. Some are regular in meter, such as 4 + 4 + 4 + 4 beats, while others are irregular, such as the eleven-beat 7 + 2 + 2. The musician improvises rhythmically on the basis of the tala. Three popular instruments are the *sitar,* a many-stringed fretted instrument, the *tabla,* a double drum, and the *tamboura,* a long-necked unfretted instrument with drone strings.

The mixing of eastern and western music took place in the popular music field with the raga-rock concept. Arabic music is a worthy study, as is the *gamelan* music of Indonesia which influenced Debussy and other composers. Something to avoid is thinking of nonwestern music as stereotypes. It is infinitely varied. For example, there are many differences in the music of one section of a country like Nigeria from that of other sections; the same is true of China and almost every country. The music of Africa has been influenced by music of Asia, Arabia, and music of the West, with

Central Africa providing music more indigenous than other sections of that continent. American Indian and Hawaiian music are of special interest to people of the United States. American Indian music, generally speaking, utilizes steps smaller than our half-steps, uses a percussion accompaniment of drums, rasps, and rattles, employs the flute as a solo instrument, has no structured harmony, and has chant-like melodies which do not conform to the European scales. Original Hawaiian music has been practically destroyed by European musical influence, but researchers have managed to reconstruct some of it.

Native Hawaiian music was largely chant, centered about one pitch. Harmony was absent; the form was mainly of short repeated chants with instrumental interludes to provide contrast. The modern Hawaiian style resulted when missionary hymns and the Portuguese guitar were introduced. The guitar evolved to become the modern ukulele.

Recordings are a necessity when studying the music of the world, but listening to fascinating authentic music can have its problems when children are called upon to analyze it and to describe it. One problem is that of identifying the meter. The solution is a mathematical one; identify the two-beat and three-beat segments. While this can become a complex study, an easy introduction can begin with 5/4 meter, one that is used to some extent in the folk music of the West. Children accept this meter readily. While a few songs written in it are found in the music textbooks, a creative approach can be made by students composing their own percussion scores and songs in that meter. *The important principle is that the beats in this and the meters to follow are organized in groups of two's and three's.*

$$\tfrac{5}{4} = 3 \text{ plus } 2 \quad or \quad 2 \text{ plus } 3$$

Examples:

In Latin-American music we find occasional measures in fast 6/8 meter that are performed differently than those in traditional North American music. Traditional American music usually has this meter divided into two-beat measures. South of the border one finds a three-beat measure among the predominant two-beat measures.

Leonard Bernstein's "America" from *West Side Story* is an example:

In Eastern Europe, the Middle East, and Asia are found 7/8, 8/8, 9/8 and other meters. Measures in those meters can be divided by beat-count as follows:

$$
\begin{aligned}
7/8, \; 7/4 \; = \quad & 3 \text{ plus } 2 \text{ plus } 2 \\
& 2 \text{ plus } 2 \text{ plus } 3 \\
& 2 \text{ plus } 3 \text{ plus } 2 \\
8/8, \; 8/4 \; = \quad & 2 \text{ plus } 2 \text{ plus } 2 \text{ plus } 2 \\
& 3 \text{ plus } 3 \text{ plus } 2 \\
9/8, \; 9/4 \; = \quad & 2 \text{ plus } 2 \text{ plus } 2 \text{ plus } 3 \\
& 3 \text{ plus } 3 \text{ plus } 3
\end{aligned}
$$

Writing music in these rhythmic groupings can be a fascinating task.

Learning the Greek folk song *Gerakina,* in Chapter 7, will help one to become oriented to a less common meter. The tempo is fairly fast. When the song is learned, it will be found that counts 1, 4, and 6 mark the beats.

Another problem is identifying instruments. Because there are probably thousands of standard folk instruments, this becomes virtually impossible. Yet, the ear can classify the instruments heard so that class discussion about them can take place. The following classification has proved to be helpful:

string
    plucked
    struck
    bowed
    stroked
wind
    open hole (flute-type)
    single reed
    double reed
    brass
membrane (drum-type)
    pitched
    unpitched
percussion
    metal
    wood
    stone
    body sounds

Other headings to assist analysis are:

vocal sounds
rhythm
    regular beat
    flexible

pitch
  straight (true and unwavering)
  bent (swooping up or dropping down; unsteady)
melody, type of
harmony, if any
form (unity-contrast)

One can expect varying tonal (scale) organizations. Tempo and dynamics should be easily described. Acceptable tone qualities are different in various cultures.

The October, 1972 issue of the *Music Educators Journal* concerned music in world cultures. It contained nineteen articles on world musics, a glossary, a bibliography, discography, and filmography. It affords the reader greatly more than is possible to include in this textbook, so the authors refer to that publication for books, recordings, and films for use in this interesting area of emphasis.

The final Contemporary Music Project *Newsletter,* dated Spring, 1973, contains a recommended list of recordings of Asian and African music thought to be useful for teaching purposes. Those preceded by one asterisk are especially recommended; a second asterisk indicates that extensive notes are provided to help orient the listener.

JAPAN:

  Bell Ringing in Empty Sky, Solo Flute (Shakuhachi) music. Nonesuch 72025
  Music from the Kabuki. Nonesuch 72012
  Japanese Koto Classics. Nonesuch 72008
  Gagaku, Ancient Japanese Court Music. Everest 3322

SOUTHEAST ASIA:

  **Traditional Music of Thailand.* Institute of Ethnomusicology, UCLA, Los Angeles, 90046. Includes an excellent booklet by David Morten.
  Music from Cambodia. UNESCO Anthology, Bährenreiter 30L 2002
  Music from Vietnam I. UNESCO 30L 2022

INDONESIA:

  Golden Rain (Bali). Nonesuch 72028
  Gamelan Music of Bali. Lyrichord LLST 7179
  The Jasmine Isle (Java). Nonesuch 72031
  Gamelan Semar Pegulingan (*Gamelan of the Love God*) (Bali). Nonesuch H-72046
  Music for the Balinese Shadow Puppet Plays, Gender Wayang. Nonesuch H-72037

CHINA:

Shantung Folk Music and Traditional Instrument Pieces. Nonesuch
H-72051

AFRICA:

**Mbira Music of Rhodesia.* University of Washington Press, Seattle
The African Mbira. Nonesuch 72043
**Music of the Dan Territory.* Ocora, OCR 17
**Music of Central Africa (Musique centrafricaine).* Ocora, OCR 43
**Black Africa, Panorama of Instrumental Music (Afrique noire,
Panorame de la musique instrumentale).* BAM LD 409A
**Nigeria—Hausa Music I.* UNESCO 30L 2306

INDIA:

Sarangi, Voice of a Hundred Colors. Nonesuch 72030
**The Anthology of Indian Music, Vol. I.* World-Pacific WDS 26200
(three records and extensive notes)
Drums of North and South India. World Pacific WPS 21437
Indian Drums. Connoisseur Society CS 1466
West Meets East, Ravi Shankar and Yehudi Menuhin. Angel 36418
The Sound of Subbudlakshmi. World Pacific WPS 21440
The Music of India (South). Nonesuch 72003
**Ustad Ali Akbar Khan, Raga Chandranandan.* Connoisseur Society
Bhavalu/Impressions, South Indian Instrumental Music. Nonesuch
72019

PERSIA (IRAN), THE MIDDLE EAST:

The Persian Santur. Nonesuch 72039
The Living Tradition: Music from Iran. Argo ZFB 51
Music from Turkey. Living Tradition, Argo ZRG 561
Music from the Middle East (Syria, Iraq, Palestine). Living Tradi-
tion, Argo ZRG 532

TIBET:

**Anthology of Asian Music: Tibet.* AST 4005 (Anthology Record
Corp.), 135 West 41 St., N.Y. 10036

AFGHANISTAN:

Music of Afghanistan. UNESCO 30L 2003

In addition to the above, the educator can consider twelve long-playing records or cassettes produced by UNICEF. In them one hears native groups, soloists, and children performing music, songs, and dances of 48 different nations, 43 of them non-European.

Ethnic Music
After listening to a recording of some specific ethnic music, analyze it in terms of types of instruments and voices used, types of melody, harmony, rhythm, tone qualities and texture. Then compose music that has similar sounds.

The term "ethnic" should be applied to every person because all people have ethnic roots whether they be African, American Indian, Mexican Indian, Chinese, Irish, Spanish, Arabic, Irish, English, Polish, Swedish, "American," or Portuguese. Children can learn about their cultural origins through the music of their people's heriatge. Music can assist the understanding of other cultures and the commonalities and differences of mankind can be illustrated through the music of those cultures.

References for Music in African, Afro-American, and Other Cultures

AMOAKE, W. K., *African Songs and Rhythms for Children.* Mainz, W. Germany: B. Schott's Söhne, 1971. Belwin-Mills, Melville, N.Y. 11746, agent.

BALLARD, LOUIS W., "Put American Indian Music in the Classroom." *Music Educators Journal,* March 1970.

CURTISS, MARIE JOY, "India." *Music Educators Journal,* September 1969.

DEITZ, BETTY W., and MICHAEL OLATUNJI, *Musical Instruments of Africa.* New York: John Day, Inc., 1965. For grades 7–12.

FOX, SIDNEY, *The Origins and Development of Jazz.* Chicago: Follett Educational Corp., 1968.

INNISS, CARLETON, "A Practical Introduction to African Music." *Music Educators Journal,* February 1974.

MCNEIL, ALBERT J., "The Social Foundations of the Music of Black Americans," *Music Educators Journal,* February 1974. Includes a bibliography.

MALM, WILLIAM P., *Music Cultures of the Pacific, the Near East and Asia,* 2nd Ed. Englewood Cliffs, N.J.: Prentice-Hall, Inc., 1977.

Music Educators Journal, November 1971, Music and Black Culture Issue, October 1972, Music in World Cultures Issues. Includes glossary.

NKETIA, J. H. KWABENA, "Music Education in Africa and the West: We Can Learn from Each Other," *Music Educators Journal,* November, 1970.

PHILLIPS, ROMEO E., "Black Folk Music: Setting the Record Straight," *Music Educators Journal,* December 1973.

REEDER, BARBARA, "Afro Music: As Tough As a Mozart Quartet," *Music Educators Journal,* January 1970.

REEDER, BARBARA, and JAMES A. STANDIFER, *Source Book of African Materials for Music Educators*. Reston, Va.: Music Educators National Conference, 1972.

SOUTHERN, EILEEN, *The Music of Black Americans: A History*. New York: Norton, 1971.

WHITE, FLORENCE, and KAZUO AKIYAMA, *Children's Songs from Japan*. New York: Marks Music Corporation, 1965. Fifty songs that tell American Children how Japanese boys and girls live.

WHITING, HELEN, *Negro Art, Music and Rhyme*. Washington, D.C.: Associated Publishers, 1967.

WIANT, BLISS, *The Music of China*. Hong Kong: Chung Chi Publications, 1965.

WORK, JOHN W., *Jubilee*. New York: Holt, Rinehart & Winston, 1962.

Also see Music For Urban Education, Chapter 16.

References for American and Related Curricular Areas

COOPERATIVE RECREATION SERVICE, Delaware, Ohio. Source of inexpensive songbooks concerning states, nations, and peoples of the world.

ELLIOTT, RAYMOND, *Learning and Teaching Music*. Columbus, Ohio: Charles E. Merrill Books, Inc., 1966. Pages 269–359 relate to U.S. history in grades 5 and 6.

GLASS, PAUL, and LOUIS SINGER, *Songs and Stories of North American Indians; Songs and Stories of Afro-Americans: Songs of Forest and River Folks; Songs of Town and City Folk; Songs of Hill and Mountain Folk*. New York: Grosset & Dunlap, Inc.

HAUSMAN, RUTH L., *Hawaii: Music in Its History*. Rutland, Vt.: Charles E. Tuttle Co., 1968.

JAROLIMEK, JOHN, *Social Studies in Elementary Education*. New York: The Macmillan Company, 1971. Chapter 16, "Building World Understanding."

KARPELES, MAUD, ed., *Folk Songs of Europe*. London: Novello, 1956. Authentic folksongs edited for the International Folk Music Council.

KELLY, JOHN M., JR., *Folk Songs Hawaii Sings*. Rutland, Vt.: Charles E. Tuttle, 1963.

LANDECK, BEATRICE, *Echoes of Africa in Folk Songs of the Americas*. New York: Marks Music Corporation, 1973.

LOMAX, ALAN, *Folk Songs of North America*. New York: Doubleday & Company, 1960. Includes historical backgrounds.

LYONS, JOHN H., *Stories of Our American Patriotic Songs*. New York: Vanguard Press, Inc., 1942.

MICHAELIS, JOHN, *Social Studies for Children in a Democracy,* 5th ed. Englewood Cliffs, N.J.: Prentice-Hall, Inc., 1972. Music activities for social studies are described in pp. 384–91.

NETTL, BRUNO, *Folk and Traditional Music of the Western Continents*. Englewood Cliffs, N.J.: Prentice-Hall, Inc., 1968.

NYE, VERNICE T., ROBERT E. NYE, and H. VIRGINIA NYE, *Toward World Understanding With Song*. Belmont, Calif. 94002: Wadsworth Publishing Company, 1967. Social studies and music. Folkways Album FD 5720 is a companion recording available from Wadsworth.

PETERSON, FREDERICK A., *Ancient Mexico*. New York: G. P. Putnam's Sons, 1959. Chapter 9, "Song and Dance," describes ancient instruments.

SCHIMMERLING, H. A., *Memories of Czechoslovakia,* New York: Marks Music Corporation, 136 West 52 St., New York 10019. Insight into history and customs by means of songs. See catalog for other national song collections.

SEIDEMAN, LAURENCE I., "Teaching About the American Revolution Through Folk Songs," *Social Education,* November 1973, pp. 653–64.

SOOTIN, HARRY, *Science Experiments With Sound*. New York: Grosset & Dunlap, Inc.

SUR, WILLIAM R. et al., *This Is Music,* Book Five. Boston: Allyn & Bacon, Inc., 1967. Pages 18–161 reflect United States history in song.

Films and Filmstrips

Discovering the Music of Africa: Discovering American Indian Music; Discovering the Music of Japan; Discovering the Music of India; Discovering the Music of Latin America; Discovering the Music of the Middle East. BFA Educational Media, 2211 Michigan Avenue, Santa Monica, Calif. 90404.

Folk Songs in American History. Six Filmstrips and Six Records, WASP Filmstrips, Palmer Lane West, Pleasantville, N.Y. 1. Early Colony Days, 2. Revolutionary War, 3. Workers of America, 4. In Search of Gold, 5. The South, 6. Civil War.

Folk Songs of the Arab World. Bowmar, 622 Rodier Dr., Glendale, Calif., 91201. Also *Folk Songs of Israel.*

Man and His Music. Keyboard Publications, 1346 Chapel St., New Haven, Conn. 06511. Each of the following includes two filmstrips, a recording or cassette, and teacher guide. Some include student booklets: *Puerto Rico; Japan; China; Africa; Middle East; American Indian; Latin America; USSR.*

Music of Our Pacific Neighbors. Bowmar, 622 Rodier Dr., Glendale, California, 91201. Two color film strips, four recordings.

National Geographic Society, Washington, D.C. 20036. *The Music of the Ozarks; The Music of Spain; The Music of Tonga; The Music of Trinidad.* Includes background information.

Our American Heritage of Folk Music (social studies correlation). Twelve Filmstrips, Society for Visual Education, Inc., 1345 Diversey Parkway, Chicago, Ill. 60614. Group One: Songs of the Sea, Songs of the Cowboy, Songs of the Mountains, Songs of the Plains, Songs of the Railroad, Songs of the Civil War. Group Two: Songs of the American Revolution, Songs of the Old South, Songs of Pioneer Mid-America, Songs of the Western Frontier, Songs of the Mississippi Valley, Songs of the Old Southwest.

Composers and Musical Styles

Filmstrips with Recordings

Biographies of Great Composers, each 30 minutes: *Haydn, Mozart, Beethoven, Schubert, Verdi, Puccini,* Bowmar Records, Inc., 622 Rodier Dr., Glendale, Ca. 91201.

Famous Composers and Their Music: Chopin, Schuman, Mendelssohn, Tchaikovsky, Grieg, Brahms, Prentice-Hall Media, 150 White Plains Rd., Tarrytown, N.Y. 10591.

Great Composers and Their Music: Bach, Handel, Haydn, Mozart, Beethoven, Schubert, The Jam Handy Organization.

The Story of Handel's "Messiah," Society for Visual Education, Inc., 1345 Diversey Parkway, Chicago, Ill. 60614. 20 minutes.

The Story of Johann Sebastian Bach and His Christmas Oratorio, Society for Visual Education. 35 minutes.

The Story of the Nutcracker, Society for Visual Education. 32 minutes. Adapted from the Nutcracker legend and Tchaikovsky's musical score.

Tchaikovsky; Handy, Llewellyn, Ltd. P.O. Box 87, Madison, Miss. 39110.

Films

(Refer to *Film Guide for Music Educators,* by Donald J. Shetler, Music Educators National Conference, Reston, Va. 22091.)

The American Tradition (Copland, Harris, Thomson, Piston, Sessions, Ives), National Educational Television, Indiana University, Bloomington, Indiana 47401.

Electronic Music (Milton Babbitt), National Educational Television.

Music in Motion: The Enchanted Lake (Liadov), Musilog Corporation, P.O. Box 1199, Santa Barbara, California 93102. A pictorial interpretation of the music; impressionist music; a twelve-page manual accompanies the film. Similar films interpreting the music of 15 other composers are available.

Music of Williamsburg, Film Distribution Section, Colonial Williamsburg, Inc., Box C, Williamsburg, Virginia 23185. Depicts music's place in the everyday life of the Virginia colonists. Two versions, 29 minutes and 40 minutes.

The Peter Tchaikovsky Story, Walt Disney 16 mm Films, 350 South Buena Vista St., Burbank, California 91503. 30 minutes.

Young People's Concert Series: What Does Classical Music Mean?; What Is American Music?; What Is Impressionism?; Humor in Music; Folk Music in the Concert Hall; Jazz in the Concert Hall, McGraw-Hill Films, 1221 Avenue of the Americas, 10020/60 min. For ages 10–adult. Also *What Is Melody?; What Makes Music Symphonic?; What Does Music Mean?; Musical Atoms— A Study of Intervals?*

Miscellaneous Materials

Magazine: *Man and His Music.* Keyboard Publications, 1346 Chapel St., New Haven, Conn. 06511.

Magazine: *Pipeline.* Silver Burdett Co., Box 2000, 250 James St., Morristown, N.J. 07960. A monthly subscription series that uses today's popular music to help learn principles basic to all music. Recording, student newsletter, teacher guide.

426 Record series: *Learning to Listen to Music,* Records I–IV. Silver Burdett Co.

Charts and Pictures

Famous Composers, RCA-Victor Record Division, 155 East 24th St., New York, N.Y.

Great Composers, Willis Music Company, 124 East 4th Street, Cincinnati, Ohio.

Historical Panorama, Schmitt, Hall & McCreary Company, Park Ave. and 6th St., Minneapolis, Minn. Time line relates music and world history.

Music in Europe Map, Denoyer Geppert Company.

Portraits of Composers, Bowmar Educational Records. Two sets of 20 reproductions or folio of 20 sheets of portrait miniatures.

Portraits of Great Composers, Schmitt, Hall & McCreary Company.

Portraits of Great Composers, RCA-Victor Record Division.

427

FOR FURTHER STUDY

References
for Further Study

Elementary music education has become a multifaceted field that can no longer be fully accommodated by the standard music methods class. While the methods class is an essential beginning, the teacher who desires additional information finds it necessary to do individual study or to attend clinics, conferences, short sessions, or summer session classes to keep abreast of and to remain informed of the knowledge and theories of the times. Many of these areas of study require book-length treatment, and cannot be artificially compressed into chapters in a standard textbook. Because many students already have interest in special areas of elementary music education, and because they can study them as topics in the methods class, the authors have listed some of them, with selected references available at the time this book was written. Some references are to be found in listings in other chapters, and the book's index may also be of assistance.

The Music of the American Indian

American Indians (catalog). Los Angeles, Calif.: Children's Music Center, 5373 W. Pico Blvd., 90019, an annual catalog.

432

BALLARD, LOUIS W., "Put American Indian Music in the Classroom," *Music Educators Journal,* March 1970.

BUTTREE, JULIA M., *The Rhythm of the Red Man.* New York: A. S. Barnes & Co., 1973.

DENSMORE, FRANCIS, *The Study of Indian Music.* Washington, D.C.: Smithsonian Report, 1941. Reprinted by The Shorey Book Co., Seattle, Wash., 1966.

HOFFMAN, CHARLES, *American Indians Sing.* New York: John Day Company, Inc., 1967.

HUNT, W. BEN, *The Golden Book of Indian Crafts and Lore.* New York: Simon and Schuster, 1954.

PARTHUN, PAUL, "Tribal Music in North America," *Music Educators Journal,* January 1976, pp. 32–45.

The Indians Book. New York: Dover Publications, 1968, 184 Varick Street, 10014. A reprint of a song book.

film: Indian Musical Instruments, 1955, color, 13 min. University of Oklahoma, Norman. Demonstrates making and playing dance and hand drums, rawhide drums, beater, rattles, flutes, and the notched stick.

American Methods

CARABO CONE, MADELEINE, *A Learning Theory and Music Methods for Teachers of Elementary and Pre-School Children: A Sensory-Motor Approach to Music Learning.* Books I, II, III, IV, and corresponding teacher's manuals. New York: MCA Music, 445 Park Ave., 10022 or Belwin-Mills, Melville, N.Y. 11746.

DOOLIN, HOWARD A., *A New Introduction to Music.* Park Ridge, Ill.: General Words and Music Co., 525 Busse St. Also obtainable from Rhythm Band, Inc., 1212 E. Lancaster St., Fort Worth, Texas 76101. A complete music program in four levels designed for the classroom teacher, a purely American method, recently revised.

NASH, GRACE, *Music for Children:* Series 1, Series 2; *Recorder for Beginners,* 1965; *Rhythmic Speech Ensembles,* Series 3, 1966; *Verse and Movement,* 1967; *Teacher's Manual,* 1971; *Chamber Music for Tonebar Instruments and Recorder,* 1971; *Recorder Ensembles,* 1973; *Music in the Middle School,* Series 4, 1973. Scottsdale, Arizona: Nash Publications. *Creative Approaches to Child Development with Music, Language, and Movement Incorporating the Philosophies and Techniques of Orff, Kodály, and Laban.* New York: Alfred Publishing Co., 1974. A consolidation of European influences.

Dalcroze

DRIVER, ETHEL, *A Pathway to Dalcroze Eurhythmics.* New York: Thomas Nelson and Sons, 1963.

FINDLAY, ELSA, *Rhythm and Movement: Application of Dalcroze Eurhythmics.* Evanston, Ill.: Summy-Birchard, 1971.

GELL, HEATHER, *Music, Movement and the Young Child.* Sydney, Australia: Australian Publishing Co., 1969.

LANDIS, BETH, and POLLY CARDER, *The Eclectic Curriculum in American Music Education: Contributions of Dalcroze, Kodály, Orff.* Reston, Va.: Music Educators National Conference, 1972.

For further information contact Dr. Hilda Schuster, Director, Dalcroze School of Music, 161 E. 73rd Street, New York, New York 10021.

Music for Early Childhood

ANDRESS, BARBARA, et al., *Music in Early Childhood.* Reston, Va.: Music Educators National Conference, 1973.

ARONOFF, FRANCES W., *Music and Young Children.* New York: Holt, Rinehart & Winston, Inc., 1969. Contains a Dalcroze outline in an appendix.

Best Records and Books for Early Childhood (catalog). Los Angeles, Calif.: Children's Music Center, 5373 West Pico Blvd. 90019.

CHERRY, CLAIRE, *Creative Movement for the Developing Child* (rev. ed.). Belmont, Calif.: Fearon Publishers, 1971.

MAYNARD, OLGA, *Children and Dance and Music.* New York: Charles Scribner's Sons, 1968. Chapter One, "The Child at Home."

Music Educators Journal, March 1974. Early Childhood Issue.

NYE, VERNICE, *Music for Young Children.* Dubuque, Iowa: Wm. C. Brown Company Publishers, Inc., 1975.

Music for Exceptional Children

GASTON, THAYER, *Music in Therapy.* New York: The Macmillan Company, 1968.

GRAHAM, RICHARD M., comp., *Music for the Exceptional Child.* Reston, Va.: Music Educators National Conference, 1975.

JOHNSON, JANET M., and LINDA L. PHILLIPS, "Affecting the Behavior of Retarded Children with Music," *Music Educators Journal,* March 1971.

Music in Special Education. Reston, Va.: Music Educators National Conference, 1972.

NORDHOFF, PAUL, and CLIVE ROBBINS, *Music Therapy for Handicapped Children.* Blouvet, N.Y.: Rudolph Steiner Publications.

Electronic and Experimental Music

See references at end of Chapter 11.

Kodály

Basic References

Boosey & Hawkes, Oceanside, New York 11572, publish translations of Kodály's extensive series of books including *Bicinia Hungaria* I, II; *Let Us Sing Correctly; 101 Exercises in Intonation.* This company also publishes the following books written by Hungarians:

SZABO, HELGA, *The Kodály Concept of Music Education,* 1969.

SZÖNYI, ERZSÉBET, *Kodály's Principles in Practice,* 1973. The author is probably the leading Hungarian exponent of the method.

American Adaptations

BURKART, ARNOLD E., *Bicinia Americana: Two-Part Songs for American Schools Based on American Folk Materials.* Muncie, Ind.: Keeping Up With Music Education, 1975. Includes teaching notes for Kodály programs.

———, *Pentatonica Americana.* Muncie, Ind.: Keeping Up With Music Education, 1976. More two-part folksongs.

CHOKSY, LOIS, *The Kodály Method: Comprehensive Music Education from Infant to Adult.* Englewood Cliffs, N.J.: Prentice-Hall, Inc., 1974. An excellent source of information; includes 158 songs for teaching the method; describes the method and adapts it to American schools.

DANIEL, KATINKA S., *The Kodály Approach,* Workbooks 1, 2, 3. Belmont, Calif.: Fearson Publishers, 1973. Written by a former Hungarian music teacher for primary level.

LANDIS, BETH, and POLLY CARDER, *The Eclectic Curriculum in American Music Education: Contributions of Dalcroze, Kodály, and Orff.* Reston, Va.: Music Educators National Conference, 1972. An excellent source.

LEWIS, ADEN, *Listen, Look and Sing,* vols. 1–4. Morristown, N.J.: General Learning Corporation, Silver Burdett. Designed for use with *Making Music Your Own* textbooks.

WHEELER, LAWRENCE, and LOIS RAEBECK, *Orff and Kodály Adapted for the Elementary School.* Dubuque, Iowa: Wm. C. Brown Company Publishers, 1972.

ZEMKE, SR. LORNA, *Kodály 35 Lesson Plans and Folk Song Supplement.* Manitowoc, Wis.: Silver Lake College, 1974.

Denise Bacon
The Kodály Musical Training Institute, 525 Worcester St., Wellesley, Mass. 02181

BACON, DENISE, and others, "Controversy on Kodály," *Music Educators Journal,* September 1969, pp. 3–16.

BACON, DENISE, *Let's Sing Together!* Oceanside, N.Y.: Boosey & Hawkes, 1973. Songs for 3-, 4-, and 5-year-olds composed in accordance with the Kodály concept.

———, *46 Two-Part American Folk Songs.* Oceanside, N.Y.: Boosey & Hawkes, 1974. An acapella collection for elementary grades in accordance with the Kodály principles.

ERDEI, PETER, and KATALIN KOMLES, *150 American Folk Songs to Sing, Read, and Play.* Oceanside, N.Y.: Boosey & Hawkes, 1974.

Kodály for Beginning Levels. Wellesley, Mass.: The Institute. A two-volume curriculum textbook for teachers.

Mary Helen Richards
The Richards Institute of Music Education and Research, 149 Corte Madera Rd., Portola Valley, Calif. 94025

RICHARDS, MARY HELEN, *Threshold to Music.* Belmont, Calif.: Fearon Publishers, 94002, 1964. Charts and teacher's manual; *The Fourth Year,* 1967; *Teacher Training Record* (recording) 1966; *Teaching Music Through Songs, Hand Singing, and Inner Hearing,* 1966.

Language Arts Through Music. Portola Valley, Calif.: Richards Institute of Music Education and Research, 1971. Contact the Institute for information on other publications.

Periodical

Kodály Envoy, School of Music, Duquesne University, Pittsburgh, Pennsylvania 15219. The official journal of the Organization of American Kodály Educators, edited by Betsy Moll and Christine Kunko.

Orff

Basic References

Music for Children, vols. I–V, by Carl Orff and Gunild Keetman. Mainz, W. Germany: B. Schott's Söhne, 1950. American edition, adaptation by Doreen Hall and Arnold Walter; English edition, adaptation by Margaret Murray. Obtainable from several sources including Magnamusic Baton, 10370 Page Industrial Blvd., St. Louis, Mo., 63132, and Belwin-Mills, Melville, N. Y. 11746.

KEETMAN, GUNILD, *Elementaria.* Melville, N.Y.: Belwin-Mills, distributor for B. Schott's Söhne, Mainz, W. Germany. English translation by Margaret Murray, 1974. A guide for teachers.

KELLER, WILHELM, *Introduction to Music for Children.* Mainz, W. Germany: B. Schott's Söhne. Obtainable from Belwin-Mills, Melville, N.Y. 11746.

Music for Children record album, Capitol Records. English children perform.

Music for Children, film, Contemporary Films, 267 W. 25th St., New York, N.Y. 10001.

American Adaptations

BIRKENSHAW, LOIS, *Music for Fun, Music for Learning.* Toronto, Canada: Holt, Rinehart and Winston of Canada, Ltd. Obtainable from Magnamusic Baton, 10370 Page Industrial Blvd., St. Louis, Mo. 63132.

LANDIS, BETH, and POLLY CARDER, *The Eclectic Curriculum in American Music Education: Contributions of Dalcroze, Kodály, and Orff.* Reston, Va.: Music Educators National Conference, 1972.

NICHOLS, ELIZABETH, *Orff Instrument Source Books,* I, II. Morristown, N.J.: General Learning Corporation, Silver Burdett 07960. For use with *Making Music Your Own* textbooks.

RAMSETH, BETTY ANN, *Come Sing and Ring.* Minneapolis, Minn.: Augsburg Publishing House, 1972. Christmas songs with Orff instruments.

436

SALIBA, KONNIE KOONCE, *Sing About Sunshine*. Melville, N.Y.: Belwin-Mills, 1975. A song collection.

Tommy Thumb. New York: Oxford University Press, 1974. Ten unison songs for young singers with tuned and untuned percussion.

WHEELER, LAWRENCE, and LOIS RAEBECK, *Orff and Kodály Adapted for the Elementary School*. Dubuque, Iowa: Wm. C. Brown Company Publishers, 1972.

Miscellaneous

AMERICAN ORFF-SCHULWERK ASSOCIATION, P.O. Box 18495, Cleveland Heights, Ohio 44118.

Keeping Up With Orff-Schulwerk in the Classroom (periodical). Muncie, Ind.: 1220 Ridge Road, 47304.

Carl Orff's Music for Children and Related Supplementary Materials (catalog). Melville, N.Y.: Belwin-Mills Publishing Corporation, 11746.

Orff Newsetter. St. Louis, Mo.: Magnamusic-Baton, Inc., 10370 Page Industrial Blvd., 63132.

Music for Urban Education

JONES, BESSIE, and BESS LOMAX HAWES, *Step It Down*. New York: Harper & Row, Publishers, 1972. Games, plays, songs, and stories from the Afro-American heritage.

Music and Black Culture section, *Music Educators Journal*, November 1971. Contains "Selected Resources for Black Studies in Music."

Urban Education issue, *Music Educators Journal*, January 1970. Includes articles such as "General Music for the Black Ghetto Child," by Bennett Reimer; "Bibliography of Negro Music," and "Recommendations for Teacher Education Programs."

See "References for African, Afro-American, and Other Cultures" in Chapter 15.

Miscellaneous Topics

CHOATE, ROBERT A., ed., *Documentary Report of the Tanglewood Symposium*. Reston, Va. Music Educators National Conference, 1968.

"Contemporary Music Project," *Music Educators Journal*, May 1973.

GARY, CHARLES L., and BETH LANDIS, *The Comprehensive Music Program*. Reston, Va.: Music Educators National Conference, 1973.

Impact Project

Arts Impact: Curriculum for Change—A Summary Report. University Park, Pa.: The Arts IMPACT Evaluation Team, 1973.

WENNER, GENE C., et al., "IMPACT," *Music Educators Journal*, January 1973.

Suzuki Methods

KENDALL, JOHN D., *The Suzuki Violin Method in American Music Education.* Reston, Va.: Music Educators National Conference, 1966, 1973.

SUZUKI, SHINICHI, *Nurtured by Love.* Jerico, N.Y.: Exposition Press, 1967.

Books
for Elementary
School Children[1]

Appendix

Biographies   BURCH, GLADYS, and JOHN WOLCOTT, *Famous Composers For Young People.* New York: Dodd, Mead, 1939. $3.50. Gr. 4–9. Includes brief sketches of twenty of the world's greatest composers: Palestrina, Bach, Handel, Gluck, Haydn, Mozart, Beethoven, Schubert, Mendelssohn, Chopin, Schumann, Liszt, Wagner, Verdi, Foster, Brahms, Tchaikovsky, Grieg, MacDowell, Debussy.

BURCH, GLADYS, and JOHN WOLCOTT, *Modern Composers For Young People.* New York: Dodd, Mead, 1941. $3.50. Gr. 4–9. Brief biographies of twenty middle-nineteenth century composers. Moussorgsky, Dvořák, Rimsky-Korsakov, Humperdinck, Elgar, Delius, Strauss, Sibelius, Scriabin, Vaughan-Williams, Schoenberg, Ravel, Carpenter, de Falla, Respighi, Bartók, Stravinsky, Griffes, Prokofiev, Gershwin.

DEUCHER, SYBIL, *Edvard Grieg, Boy of the Northland.* New York: Dutton, 1946. $4.50. Gr. 3–7. This delightful story about Edvard Grieg will cause children to enjoy his music even more than they already do.

[1] Courtesy of the Oregon State Department of Education, Delmer Aebischer, Music Consultant.

————, *The Young Brahms.* New York: Dutton, 1949. $3.95. Gr. 3–7. An entertaining description of Brahms' life from age 6 to 16. Includes many of his compositions.

GOUGH, CATHERINE, *Boyhoods of Great Composers: Books I and II.* New York: Walck, 1960. $4 each. Gr. 4–6. Both books describe events in the lives of composers of interest to young people. Book I includes Handel, Mozart, Schubert, Mendelssohn, Grieg, Elgar. Book II includes Bach, Beethoven, Verdi, Chopin, Tchaikovsky, Vaughan-Williams. Incidents included are primarily anecdotal, having little to do with the importance of these men as composers.

MIRSKY, REBA PAEFF, *Beethoven.* Chicago: Follett, 1957. $3.50. Gr. 5–7. Beethoven's many struggles, disappointments and successes are emphasized in this book.

————, *Brahms.* Chicago: Follett, 1966. $4.98. Gr. 5–7. "A well-rounded picture of the composer's personality, his times, and his music." (McClurg. *Book News*).

————, *Haydn.* Chicago: Follett, 1963. $4.98. Gr. 5–up. The author describes Haydn's childhood and life as a court musician which climaxed with the composing of "The Creation."

————, *Mozart.* Chicago: Follett, 1960. $4.17. Gr. 4–6. "An entertaining account of Mozart's life and work, including excerpts from his letters." (American Library Assn.)

POSELL, ELSA Z., *American Composers.* Boston: Houghton Mifflin, 1963. $3.50. Gr. 4–up. An explanation of American music and twenty-eight brief stories of the musical background of composers, their personalities, manner of composing and style. Composers included are: Barber, Bernstein, Copland, Cowell, Creston, Dello Joio, Foss, Foster, Gershwin, Gould, Griffes, Grofé, Hanson, Harris, Hovhaness, Ives, Kay Lockwood, MacDowell, Mennin, Menotti, Moore, Piston, Porter, Riegger, Schumann, Sessions, Sousa, Still. (ALA)

————, *Russian Composers.* Boston: Houghton Mifflin, 1967. $3.50. Gr. 4–6. Biographcial sketches of 17 composers including Glinka, Khachaturian, Mashovskii, Moussorgsky, Prokofiev, Rachmaninoff, Rimsky-Korsakoff, Shostakovich, Stravinsky, Tchaikovsky and others.

SURGE, FRANK, *Singers of the Blues.* Minneapolis: Lerner, 1969. $3.95. Gr. 5–up. An introduction to "blues" for young readers, plus biographies of singers and photographs of each. Singers included are: Ma Rainey, Bessie Smith, Blind Lemon Jefferson, Leroy Carr, Rabbit Brown, Leadbelly, Blind Willy Johnson, Big Bill Broonsy, Billie Holiday, Lonnie Johnson, Big Joe Williams, Tommy McClennan, Furry Lewis, Lightnin' Hopkins, Muddy Waters, Sonny Terry, Brownie McGhee.

WHEELER, OPAL, Various titles listed below. New York: Dutton. Anecdotal incidents from composers' personal lives, written in story form with dialogue. The more recognizable works are included, also simple piano arrangements.
Adventures of Richard Wagner. 1960. $3.95. Gr. 3–7.
Frederick Chopin, Son of Poland. (2 books) *Early Years. Later Years.* 1948. $3.95. Gr. 3–7.
Handel at the Court of Kings. 1943. $3.95. Gr. 3–7.
Ludwig Beethoven and the Chiming Tower Bells. 1942. $4.70. Gr. 3–7.

Paganini, Master of Strings. 1950. $4.50. Gr. 3–7.
Peter Tchaikovsky. 1953. $3.95. Gr. 3–7.
Peter Tchaikovsky and the Nutcracker Ballet. 1959. $4.50. Gr. 3–7. (ALA)
Robert Schumann and Mascott Ziff. 1947. $3.95. Gr. 3–7.
Stephen Foster and His Little Dog Tray. 1941. $4.50. Gr. 3–7.

WHEELER, OPAL, and SYBIL DEUCHER, Various titles listed below. New York: Dutton. Same as preceding entry, with coauthor.
Edward MacDowell and His Cabin in the Pines. ND. $4.50. Gr. 4–8.
Franz Schubert and His Merry Friends. ND. $3.50. Gr. 4–7.
Joseph Haydn: The Merry Little Peasant. ND. $3.91. Gr. 4–7.
Mozart, the Wonder Boy. 1941. $3.95. Gr. 4–7.
Sebastian Bach: The Boy from Thuringia. 1937. $3.75. Gr. 4–7.

WICKER, IREENE, *Young Music Makers: Boyhoods of Famous Composers.* Indianapolis: Bobbs-Merrill, 1961. $3.95. Gr. 4–6. Stories with emphasis on musical talent and home life of Bach, Chopin, Gershwin, and others.

Folk Music   BERGER, DONALD P., *Folk Songs of Japanese Children.* Rutland, Vt.: Tuttle, 1968. $6.00. This book will be of value to teachers since it discusses the melody, rhythm, form, scale and meters used in Japanese folk music. A variety of song materials such as seasonal songs, lullabies, and play songs are included. Teacher oriented.

BERTAIL, INEZ, *Nursery Song Book.* New York: Lothrop, Lee & Shepard, 1947. $4.50. Gr. K–3. More than 150 nursery songs, with simple piano accompaniments. Directions for singing games are included.

BONI, MARGARET B., *Fireside Book of Folk Songs.* New York: Simon & Schuster, 1947. $6.95. Gr. 5–up. A collection of 147 favorite songs, including sea chanteys, cowboy songs, hymns, railroad songs, spirituals and Christmas carols. Easy piano accompaniments by Norman Lloyd. Information about each song and category of songs included.

CARMER, CARL, *America Sings: Stories and Songs of Our Country's Growing.* New York: Knopf, 1950. $6.19. Gr. 5–11. Stories of America's work songs and such legendary characters as Big Foot Wallace, Spadebeard and Philetus Bumpus. Music is included. Useful for social studies and folklore as well as music classes.

DIETZ, BETTY W., and MICHAEL BABATUNDE OLATUNJI, *Musical Instruments of Africa: Their Nature, Use and Place in the Life of a Deeply Musical People.* New York: John Day, 1965. $6.50. Gr. 4–6. Emphasizes the importance of music in the lives of native Africans. It pictures and describes the making of native instruments and their use in ritual and dance. Included are a list of records, an LP record of African music recorded in Africa, a glossary, and reading list. Useful for teachers.

DIETZ, BETTY W., and THOMAS CHOONBAI PARK, *Folk Songs of China, Japan, Korea.* New York: John Day, 1964. $4.97. Song materials plus explanatory notes, accompaniments and English translations. Pronunciation guide and many helps for teachers. Pencil drawings. Recording included.

FELTON, HAROLD W., *Cowboy Jamboree: Western Songs & Lore.* New York: Knopf, 1951. $3.94. A collection of 20 songs cowboys sing plus the legends and history concerning them.

FRASER, SIMON H., *Pooh Song Book*. New York: Dutton, 1961. $4.95. Gr. 1–4. Fifteen of Pooh's hums set to music; also fourteen poem songs from "When We Were Very Young"; plus a setting of the "King's Breakfast."

HOFFMANN, CHARLES, *American Indians Sing*. New York: John Day, 1967. $6.29. Gr. 3–6. How songs and lives of these people knit together, why and how they made music, why songs were so important to daily living. Last chapter deals with Indian music of today. Recording included. Useful to teachers and students.

HUGHES, LANGSTON, *Famous Negro Music Makers*. New York: Dodd, Mead, 1955. $3.00. Gr. 4–7. Biographies of seventeen outstanding Black music makers from folk singers to symphony conductors, and jazz musicians to church musicians. Artists included are: Fisk Jubilee Singers, James Bland, Bert Williams, Bill Robinson, Leadbelly, Jelly Roll Morton, Roland Hayes, William Grant Still, Bessie Smith, Duke Ellington, Ethel Waters, Louis Armstrong, Marian Anderson, Bennie Benjamin, Mahalia Jackson, Dean Dickson, Lena Horne. Photographs are excellent. Useful to teachers and students.

———, *First Book of Jazz*. New York: Franklin Watts, 1955. $3.75. Gr. 6–up. A history of jazz, as related to the life of Louis Armstrong. Begins with African drums and continues through work songs, jubilees, swing and bebop. Excellent record list included. Teachers and students.

JOHNS, ALTONA T., *Play Songs of the Deep South*. New York: Associated Publishers, 1944. $2.65. Gr. K–2. A collection of play songs which have been sung by black children in the south for many generations. Directions for rhythmic games are also included.

JOHNSON, JAMES WELDON, and ROSAMUND JOHNSON, *Lift Every Voice and Sing*. New York: Hawthorn, 1970. $4.95. Gr. 3–6. Book contains lyrics and simplified musical score for a song written by James Weldon Johnson. This song is sung with reverence by the Black race. Striking illustrations.

KELLY, JOHN M., *Folk Songs Hawaii Sings*. Rutland, Vt.: Tuttle, 1963. $4.95. Gr. 3–up. Supplies background on music of Asia and Polynesia plus song materials in native languages. Also contains pronunciation guide and English translations. Teacher oriented.

LANDECK, BEATRICE, *More Songs to Grow On*. New York: Morrow, 1954. $8.95. Gr. K–4. Folksongs with suggestions for dramatization and rhythm instrument accompaniment. Teacher oriented.

———, *Songs to Grow On*. New York: Morrow, 1950. $8.95. Gr. K–4. A collection of 60 American folksongs for children, including suggestions for activities. Musical arrangements are simple. Useful for teachers.

SACKETT, S. J., *Cowboys and the Songs They Sang*. Settings by Lionel Nowak. W. R. Scott, 1967. $5.95. Gr. 4–7. A "history of cowboy life and lore is woven around a selection of cowboy songs of the ranch and the range." (McClurg, Book News) Excellent western photographs.

SEEGER, RUTH CRAWFORD, *American Folk Songs for Children*. New York: Doubleday, 1948. $4.50. Gr. K–5. Ninety folksongs from various parts of the country to be sung and dramatized. Accompaniments are simple. Introductory chapters discuss value of folk music and the use of folk music with children. Useful for teachers.

———, *American Folk Songs for Christmas*. New York: Doubleday, 1953.

$5.70. Gr. K–5. A collection of 50 American folksongs about Christmas. Sources of songs and holiday celebration are included. Useful material for teachers.

————, *Animal Folksongs for Children.* New York: Doubleday, 1950. $3.50. Gr. 1–6. Forty American folksongs describing such animals as the cross-eyed gopher and the snake who baked a hoecake. Useful for teachers.

WHITING, HELEN ADELE, *Negro Art, Music, and Rhyme, Book II.* New York: Associated Publishers, 1967. $1.40. Gr. 2–3. A "reader" type book for primary children with Afro-American art, crafts, song, dance and rhyme. Attractive illustrations.

YURCHENCO, HENRIETTA, *Fiesta of Folk Songs from Spain and Latin America.* New York: Putnam's 1967. $3.96. Gr. 2–6. "Here are 34 folksongs—singing games and dances, songs for Christmas, and songs about people, animals and nature." (Booklist) Teacher oriented.

See also *Stories*, p. 286.

History and Origin of Music

BRITTEN, BENJAMIN, and IMOGEN HOLST, *Wonderful World of Music.* New York: Doubleday, 1968. $3.95. Gr. 5–up. Magnificently illustrated book concerning the historical development of music and the related arts; ancient to modern cultures are included.

CRAIG, JEAN, *Story of Musical Notes.* Minneapolis: Lerner Publications, 1962. $2.75. Gr. 4–7. This book presents the history of musical notation. It contains excellent examples of each method of music writing.

DAVIS, MARILYN K., and ARNOLD BROIDO, *Music Dictionary.* New York: Doubleday, 1956. $4.25. Gr. 5–7. An illustrated music dictionary containing over 800 definitions of words, terms, and instruments. Pages are large, definitions concise and illustrations are black and white sketches interesting for children.

GREENE, CARLA, *I Want to Be a Musician.* Chicago: Children's Press, 1962. $2.75. Gr. K–3. An excellent history showing the development of musical instruments and rhythm. Includes cavemen beating on logs, shepherd horns, reeds, a short explanation of counting and a description of present day instruments.

HUGHES, LANGSTON, *First Book of Rhythms.* New York: Franklin Watts, 1954. $2.95. Gr. 3–5. A delightful way to introduce children to the rhythms all around them. Includes rhythms of nature, rhythm in sounds, in design, and in movement, and serves as excellent motivation for a study of rhythm.

LERNER, SHARON, *Places of Musical Fame.* Minneapolis: Lerner Publications, 1962. $2.75. Gr. 4–7. A description of famous music halls such as Carnegie Hall, Lincoln Center, La Scala, Covent Garden, and many others.

NORMAN, GERTRUDE, *The First Book of Music.* New York: Franklin Watts, 1955. $2.95. Gr. 4–6. An introduction to the elements of music (rhythm, melody, and harmony), together with the development of music from past to present. Brief biographies of composers and explanation of the instruments are also included.

SELIGMANN, JEAN, and JULIET DANZIGER, *Meaning of Music: A Young Listener's Guide.* Waco, Texas: World, 1966. $4.95. Gr. 5–9. An introduction to the elements of music (rhythm, melody, harmony, tempo), the families of instruments of famous composers. Photographs and line drawings.

SPENCER, CORNELIA, *How Art and Music Speak to Us*. New York: John Day, 1963. $3.95. Gr. 5–up. Awakens children to the fact that man has expressed his deepest feelings and thoughts through the arts. A beautifully written book deserving of a place on the library shelf.

SURPLUS, ROBERT W., *Alphabet of Music*. Minneapolis: Lerner Publications, 1962. $2.75. Gr. 4–7. The elements of music are presented in an interesting manner for young children. An excellent guide to building awareness of what music is all about.

————, *Story of Musical Organizations*. Minneapolis: Lerner Publications, 1962. $2.75. Gr. 4–7. A history of musical performance organizations including bands, orchestras, choirs, chamber music groups, dance bands and combos. The music they play is also discussed.

Instruments

BALET, JAN B., *What Makes an Orchestra*. New York: Walck, 1951. $4.75. Gr. 4–6. An introduction to each instrument of the orchestra, what it looks like, how it is played, what "color" it adds to the ensemble.

BUNCHE, JANE, *An Introduction to the Instruments of the Orchestra*. Racine Wisc.: Golden Press, 1962. $2.79. Gr. 3–up. An illustrated story of musical instruments from early drums to the modern orchestra.

COLLIER, JAMES, *Which Musical Instrument Shall I Play?* New York: Norton, 1969. $3.93. Gr. 4–6. Intended as an aid to children in selecting the instruments they wish to play. The reader is guided through the families of instruments and informed of their characteristics and method of playing. Electrically amplified instruments are also discussed. Photographs are excellent. Interesting shots of hand positions are included.

COMMINS, DOROTHY BERLINER, *All About the Symphony Orchestra and What it Plays*. New York: Random House, 1961. $2.95. Gr. 5–9. A story of the symphony orchestra discussing the individual instruments, the conductor, and the music played. Contains sketches of 46 composers. Drawings by Warren Chappell, also photographs.

CRAIG, JEAN, *Heart of the Orchestra*. Minneapolis: Lerner Publications, 1962. $2.75. Gr. 4–7. The story of the violin, viola, cello, bass violin, and early string instruments; their role in the orchestra; similarities and differences; and how they are played.

————, *Woodwinds*. Minneapolis: Lerner Publications, 1962. $2.75. Gr. 4–7. A delightful introduction to members of the woodwind family. Attractive illustrations and little known facts concerning the instruments are also presented.

DAVIS, LIONEL, and EDITH DAVIS, *Keyboard Instruments*. Minneapolis: Lerner Publications, 1962. $2.75. Gr. 4–7. The development and history of the piano, harpsichord and other keyboard instruments. The "why" and "how" of the keyboard.

GILMORE, LEE, *Folk Instruments*. Minneapolis: Lerner Publications, 1962. $2.75. Gr. 4–7. Ten folk instruments of today are presented to children in an interesting fashion including history and how they are made and played. Instruments include the square dance fiddle, accordion, harmonica, Jew's harp and bagpipes.

HUNTINGTON, HARRIET E., *Tune Up: The Instruments of the Orchestra and Their Players*. New York: Doubleday, 1942. $3.25. Gr. 5–8. Photographs illustrate how shapes of instruments and handling by players combine to produce intricate sounds.

KETTLEKAMP, LARRY, *Drums, Rattles and Bells*. Morrow, 1960. $3.56. Gr. 4–6. The development of percussion instruments presented in an interesting fashion; includes illustrations and directions for making instruments such as waterglass carillon, drums and rattles.

————, *Flutes, Whistles and Reeds*. Morrow, 1962. $3.56. Gr. 4–7. The importance of wnid instruments in the orchestra, their history, and directions for easy to make pipes and whistles.

————, *Horns*. New York: Morrow, 1964. $3.56. Gr. 4–7. How animal horns, shells, and tusks contributed to the development of today's horn family.

————, *Singing Strings*. New York: Morrow, 1958. $3.56. Gr. 4–7. Instruction for constructing simple stringed instruments, as well as a discussion and illustrations of the various instruments: guitar, violin family, harp and piano.

LACY, MARION, *Picture Book of Musical Instruments*. New York: Lothrop, Lee and Shepard, 1942. $3.95. Gr. 3–7. Concise pen and ink drawings show how instruments have been used, past and present.

LEVINE, JACK, and TAKERU LIJIMA, *Understanding Musical Instruments—How To Select Your Musical Instrument*. New York: Frederick Warne, Inc., 1971. $3.95. Gr. 6–9. Two music teachers describe the different orchestral instruments, as well as some not found in the orchestra, and tell how each one is played. A useful list of recordings that feature the individual instruments is included. Illustrations show each instrument and the way it is held. A good reference book for both students and teachers.

POSELL, ELSA, *This Is An Orchestra*. Boston: Houghton Mifflin, 1950. $2.90. Gr. 4–6. Excellent photographs and descriptions of the instruments of the orchestra, plus helps for choosing and purchasing an instrument. Famous instrument makers, habits of practice, and suggestions for building a home record collection.

RICHARDSON, ALLEN L., *Tooters, Tweeters, Strings & Beaters*. New York: Grosset & Dunlap, 1964. $2.50. Gr. 1–4. An instrument book for young readers consisting of poetic jingles concerning each instrument of the orchestra; also includes guessing games.

SLOANE, ERIC, *The Sound of Bells*. New York: Doubleday, 1966. $2.75. Gr. 4–7. Descriptions of many kinds of bells and how they were used throughout the history of our country, including the Liberty Bell. Describes the ringing of the bells on Independence Day and encourages the return of this custom.

SMITH, PETER, *The First Book of the Orchestra*. New York: Franklin Watts, 1962. $2.95. Gr. 4–6. The four families of instruments are illustrated and described; includes a list of recorded listening suggestions.

SURPLUS, ROBERT W., *Beat of the Drum*. Minneapolis: Lerner Publications, 1962. $2.75. Gr. 4–7. The drum—from tree stump to modern drums of the symphony orchestra. Other percussion instruments are also presented.

————, *Follow the Leader*. Minneapolis: Lerner Publications, 1962. $2.75. Gr. 4–7. The story of conducting and its development through the years. Special emphasis is given the conductor, program planning, and musical scores.

TETZLAFF, DANIEL B., *Shining Brass*. Minneapolis: Lerner Publications, 1962.

$2.75. Gr. 4–7. The story of brass instruments with attention given to size, shape and appearance.

WEIL, LISL, *Things That Go Bang*. New York: McGraw-Hill, 1969. $4.50. Gr. 3–6. Many things go bang! A glimpse into the percussion world—from the gong to the xylophone. Includes suggestions for making instruments and music for a "kitchen combo."

Opera   BULLA, CLYDE R., *The Ring and the Fire, Stories from Wagner's Nibelung Operas*. New York: Crowell, 1962. $4.95. Gr. 5–up. A brief biography of Richard Wagner's life accompanies his stories of "The Rhinegold," "Valkyrie," "Siegfried," and "The Dusk of the Gods." Musical themes are included. Illustrated with woodcuts.

————, *Stories of Favorite Operas*. New York: Thomas Y. Crowell, 1964. $4.95. Gr. 4–6. Twenty-three opera stories with notes on composers and performances. Included are: "Marriage of Figaro," "Don Giovanni," "The Magic Flute," "Barber of Seville," "Lucia di Lammermoor," "Tannhauser," "Lohengrin," "Tristan and Isolde," "Mastersingers of Nuremberg," "Parsifal," "Rigoletto," "Il Trovatore," "Aida," "Faust," "Carmen," "Manon," "Cavalleria Rusticana," 'I Pagliacci," "La Boheme," "Tosca," "Madame Butterfly," "Der Rosenkavalier."

COLETTE, *The Boy and The Magic*. Translated by Christopher Fry. New York: Putnam's 1964. $4.00. Gr. K–up. An adapted version fo Collette's libretto for Ravel's opera.

CROZIER, ERIC, *The Magic Flute: Mozart's Opera & How It Was Written*. New York: Walck, 1965. $4.00. Gr. 4–6. Imaginary letters to his sister tell how Mozart's opera was written.

GIBSON, ENID, *The Golden Cockerel: Three Stories of Magic and Witchcraft from Russian Opera*. New York: Walck, 1963. $4.00. Gr. 4–6. Brief notes on the music as well as the stories of Glinka's "Ruslan and Ludmila," Prokofiev's "Love for Three Oranges," and Rimsky-Korsakov's "Golden Cockerel."

GRIMM, WILLIAM, *Hansel and Gretel*. New York: Knopf, 1944. $3.84. Gr. 3–5. Story of Humperdinck's opera—the poor woodcutter's children lost in the forest and their encounter with the witch. Illustrations by Warren Chappell contribute much to the book. Easy arrangements of selections are included.

HOSIER, JOHN, *Sorcerer's Apprentice and Other Stories*. New York: Walck, 1961. $4.00. Gr. 4–6. Information about composers and stories of "Lieutenant Kije," "Háry Janós," "Till Owlglass," "William Tell."

JOHNSTON, JOHANNA, *Story of the Barber of Seville*. New York: Putnam's, 1966. $3.95. Gr. 3–6. Story of Rossini's famous comic opera concerning Figaro, a clever barber. Delightful illustrations by Susan Perl.

MONTRESOR, BENI, *Cinderella*. New York: Knopf, 1965. $3.74. Gr. 2–4. Story and illustrations from Metropolitan Opera production of Rossini's opera in which Cinderella is transformed into a beautiful bride. A more sophisticated version of the usual story.

MORETON, JOHN, *The Love for Three Oranges*. New York: Putnam's, 1966. $3.64. Gr. 2–6. The delightful story of Prokofiev's fairy-tale opera, written especially for children. The illustrations add humor to this book.

ORGEL, DORIS, *The Story of Lohengrin: The Knight of the Swan*. New York:

Putnam's, 1966. $3.95. Gr. 3–6. This opera appeals to children and has been retold in a simplified version by Doris Orgel. Based upon the opera by Richard Wagner.

SPENDER, STEPHEN, *The Magic Flute*. New York: Putnam's 1966. $3.86. Gr. 2–up. The story of Mozart's opera, retold by Stephen Spender and illustrated by Beni Montresor.

UPDIKE, JOHN, *The Ring*. New York: Knopf, 1964. $4.79. Gr. 4–7. The story of "Siegfried" including musical themes and illustrations.

Sound and Music

ALEXENBERG, MELVIN L., *Sound Science*. Englewood Cliffs, N.J.: Prentice-Hall, 1968. $4.75. Gr. K–3. An imaginary "gloop" character helps children through a series of experiments which demonstrates the "how" of sound and variances in pitch and volume.

ANDERSON, DOROTHY, *Junior Science Books Series*. Champaign, Ill.: Garrard, 1962. $2.39. Gr. 2–5. Simple experiments illustrate how sound is made and travels; how musical instruments create sound; even how a grasshopper sings.

BAER, MARION, *Sound: An Experiment Book*. New York: Holiday, 1952. $3.50. Gr. 4–6. Tells how to make high and low tones; how to transmit sound from one place to another; how to bounce sound using things around the house.

BRANLEY, FRANKLYN M., *High Sounds, Low Sounds*. New York: Thomas Y. Crowell, 1967. $3.50. Gr. 2–5. Experiments using spoons, strings, straws help the young reader understand sound.

FREEMAN, IRA M., *All About Sound and Ultrasonics*. New York: Random House, 1961. $2.50. Gr. 5–6. Science of sound including excellent illustrations and experiments.

HAWKINSON, JOHN, and MARTHA F. FAULHABER, *Rhythms, Music and Instruments To Make*. Chicago: Whitman, 1965. $3.50. Gr. 3–6. How to make more advanced wind, string, and percussion instruments. Experimenting with pentatonic scale, rhythm and melody on various instruments.

HAWKINSON, JOHN, and MARTHA FAULHABER, *Music and Instruments For Children To Make*. Chicago: Whitman, 1969. $3.50. Gr. K–3. How to experiment with rhythm and sound and create rhythm instruments. Illustrated.

KRISHEF, ROBERT K., *Playback: The Story of Recording Devices*. Minneapolis: Lerner, 1962. $2.75. Gr. 4–7. A history of recording devices from Thomas Edison's first phongoraph to the record player of today.

LOWRY, L. F., *Sounds Are High, Sounds Are Low*. New York: Holt, Rinehart & Winston, 1969. $1.50. Gr. 2–4. "I Wonder Why" series. This is a popular series of science books for elementary children. Series includes 24 books.

———, *Sounds Are For Listening*. New York: Holt, Rinehart & Winston, ND. $1.50. Gr. 2–4. "I Wonder Why" series.

MANDELL, MURIEL, and ROBERT E. WOOD, *Make Your Own Musical Instruments*. New York: Sterling, 1959. $3.99. Gr. 3–8. Use of easy to find articles such as bottle tops, cigar boxes, hose, rubber bands, and strings to make more than 100 musical instruments. Illustrations are helpful.

OLNEY, ROSS R., *Sound All Around. How Hi-fi and Stereo Work*. Englewood Cliffs, N.J.: Prentice-Hall, 1967. $3.75. Gr. 4–7. What hi-fi is all about; tells function of each basic part, such as amplifier, tuner, record player, tape recorder and speakers. A glossary of terms is included.

PINE, TILLIE S., *Sounds All Around*. New York: McGraw-Hill, 1958. $2.50. Gr. 2–5. Uses bottles, straws and the singing voice to show how sounds are made and varied.

SPIER, PETER, *Gobble, Growl, Grunt*. New York: Doubleday, 1971. $4.95. Gr. K–2. Easy fiction. Unpaged, illustrated. A Junior Literary Guild Book. Pictures of animals, birds and fish with dynamic printing of sounds they make provide material for exploring voice sounds in vocal range with different degrees of dynamics.

Stories

ABISCH, ROZ, *Twas in the Moon in Wintertime*. Englewood Cliffs, N.J.: Prentice-Hall, 1969. $4.95. Gr. 3–6. This song is the Indian story of the birth of Christ and comes from the Huron Indians. Illustrated with woodcut type pictures.

ADAMS, ADRIENNE, *Bring the Torch, Jeanette Isabelle*. New York: Scribner's 1963. $3.25. Gr. 2–6. A picture book illustrating the old French carol telling of the villagers going with torch light to the creche.

BROWNE, C. A., *The Story of Our National Ballads*. Revised by Willard Heaps. New York: Thomas Y. Crowell Co., 1960. $5.00. Gr. 6–9. Each song discussed has found a place in the hearts of Americans. There are twenty-one chapters. Songs of the Civil War, the Spanish American War, World War I and World War II are included.

CHAPPELL, WARREN, *The Nutcracker* (adapted). New York: Knopf, 1959. $3.74. Gr. K–3. An illustrated version of the story of the Nutcracker. Lots of color. Includes familiar themes from the Tchaikovsky ballet.

DAVIS, KATHERINE, *The Little Drummer Boy*. New York: Macmillan, 1968. $3.95. Gr. K–3. A handsome picture book containing the lyrics of the song about the nativity and the drummer boy. This song was originally called "Carol of the Drum."

EMBERLEY, BARBARA, *One Wide River to Cross*. Englewood Cliffs, N.J.: Prentice-Hall, 1969. $3.95. Gr. K–3. Woodcuts illustrate the song story of Noah's ark and the animals coming two by two.

FREEMAN, LYDIA, *Pet of the Met*. New York: Viking, 1953. $3.95. Gr. K–3. Easy fiction. 63 pages illustrated. A delightful illustrated story about a family of mice who live in the Metropolitan Opera House and are harassed by an evil cat who lives there too. The cat comes under the spell of "The Magic Flute" and the story ends happily. Provides an excellent introduction to Mozart's "The Magic Flute."

KARASZ, ILONKA, *Twleve Days of Christmas*. New York: Harper, 1949. $4.95. Gr. 1–5. "A thing of beauty and a joy forever. . . . The color is soft and rich and on the last two pages is the music for the song. Here are art and music and an old tradition for young and old all between the covers of one book." (Saturday Review)

KEY, FRANCIS SCOTT, *Star Spangled Banner*. New York: Thomas Y. Crowell, 1966. $3.75. Gr. 4–up. How our national anthem happened to be written. All stanzas of the song are included and colorfully illustrated.

LANGSTAFF, JOHN, *Frog Went A-Courtin'*. New York: Harcourt Brace Jovanovich, 1955. $3.99. Gr. K–3. (Caldecott Medal in 1956.) A picture book version of the favorite old ballad "Frog Went A Courtin'." Vivid colors.

LYONS, JOHN HENRY, *Stories of Our American Patriotic Songs*. New York: Vanguard, 1942. $3.95. Gr. 4–9. When, why and by whom ten American patriotic songs were written. Songs included are: "Star Spangled Banner," "Yankee Doodle," "Hail, Columbia," "America," "Columbia, The Gem of the Ocean," "Dixie," "Maryland, My Maryland," "Battle Cry of Freedom," 'Battle Hymn of the Republic," "America, the Beautiful."

MENOTTI, GIAN-CARLO, *Amahl and the Night Visitors.* New York: Whittlesey, 1962. $3.75. Gr. 3–up. The story of the Christmas opera as adapted by Frances Frost. Can be used with the recordings of the opera.

MILLER, NATALIE, *Story of the Star Spangled Banner.* Chicago: Childrens Press, 1965. $3.00. Gr. 2–5. How a poem became a national anthem during a battle.

MONTGOMERY, ELIZABETH RIDER, *The Story Behind Popular Songs.* New York: Dodd, Mead, 1966. $3.75. Gr. 7–9. Sketches of popular composers and their lyricists from 1851–1943 and stories of how some of their songs came to be written. (Junior High School Library Catalogue)

PATERSON, A. B., *Waltzing Matilda.* New York: Holt, Rniehart & Winston, 1972. Gr. 3–6. Delightful book containing lyrics to the song, although they vary somewhat from the version we sing in the United States. Children will enjoy beautiful illustrations by Desmond Digby. Received the "Picture Book of the Year" award in Australia, where it was originally published.

PAULI, HERTHA, *Silent Night.* New York: Knopf, 1943. $3.64. Gr. 3–7. The story of this famous Christmas carol, written in a small Austrian village, and why it remained a mystery for so many years.

PROKOFIEV, SERGE, *Peter and the Wolf.* Edited by Warren Chappell. New York: Knopf, 1940. $3.84. Gr. 4–6. Delightful picture version of the Russian fairy tale about the boy and the wolf. Musical themes are included.

QUACKENBUSH, ROBERT, *Old MacDonald Had a Farm.* Philadelphia: Lippincott, 1972. $4.82. Gr. 1–4. Delightful book illustrating each verse of this old cumulative folksong. History and music of song are also included.

ROUNDS, GLEN, *The Boll Weevil.* Gold Gate Junior Books, Los Angeles, Calif.: 1967. $3.95. Gr. 3–5. The Boll Weevil is first printed as a story with appealing illustrations and then as a song made famous by Carl Sandburg.

SCHACKBURG, RICHARD, *Yankee Doodle.* Englewood Cliffs, N.J.: Prentice-Hall, 1965. $3.75. Gr. 1–7. Woodcuts in red, white and blue by Edward Emberley illustrate this song. Notes on the text are added by the author.

SCOTT, JOHN ANTHONY, *The Ballad of America.* New York: Grosset & Dunlap, 1967. $5.95. Gr. 6–up. A history of the United States in song and story. Stories, words, and music of more than 125 songs.

SPIER, PETER. *Erie Canal.* New York: Doubleday, 1970. $4.50. Gr. 4–8. Another book about a folksong that is interesting beyond description. This artist is outstanding.

———, *The Fox Went Out on a Chilly Night.* New York: Doubleday, 1961. $3.50. Gr. 1–5. A delightfully illustrated book about the adventures of a a fox on a chilly night. This old folksong is printed at the end of the book. Illustrations are detailed beyond description.

———, *London Bridge is Falling Down.* New York: Doubleday, 1967. $3.95. Gr. K–2. "For the child who enjoys big pictures filled with small details, this version of the familiar verses should be a small treasure." (Saturday Review) A picture book with scenes of 18th century London. Musical score is included.

**Alphabetical Listing of Composers in *Adventures in Music*
for Elementary Schools (RCA)**

Anderson: Irish Suite—"The Girl I Left Behind Me," GR. 5, Vol. 2
Arnold: English Dances—
　Allegro Non Troppo, GR. 2, Vol. 2
　Grazioso, GR. 1, Vol. 2
Bach:
　Cantata No. 147—Jesu, Joy of Man's Desiring, GR. 5, Vol. 1
　Little Fugue in G Minor (Arr. by L. Cailliet), GR. 6, Vol. 1
　Suite No. 2—Badinerie, GR. 3, Vol. 1
　Suite No. 2—Rondeau, GR. 2, Vol. 2
　Suite No. 3—Gigue, GR. 1, Vol. 1
Bartók:
　Hungarian Sketches—"Bear Dance," GR. 3, Vol. 2
　Hungarian Sketches—"Evening in the Village," GR. 5, Vol. 2
　Mikrokosmos Suite No. 2—"From the Diary of a Fly," GR. 1, Vol. 2
　Mikrokosmos Suite No. 2—"Jack-in-the-Box," GR. 2, Vol. 1
450 **Beethoven:** Symphony No. 8—Second Movement, GR. 6, Vol. 1

Berlioz: The Damnation of Faust—Ballet of the Sylphs, GR. 1, Vol. 1

Bizet:
   Arlésienne Suite No. 1, *L'*—Minuetto, GR. 4, Vol. 2
   Arlésienne Suite No. 2, *L'*—Farandole, GR. 6, Vol. 1
   Carmen—"Changing of the Guard," GR. 3, Vol. 2
   Carmen—"The Dragoons of Alcala," GR. 2, Vol. 2
   Children's Games—"The Ball"; "Cradle Song"; "Leap Frog," GR. 1, Vol. 1

Borodin: *On the Steppes of Central Asia,* GR. 6, Vol. 1

Brahms: *Hungarian Dance* No. 1, GR. 5, Vol. 2

Cailliet: "Pop! Goes the Weasel"—Variations, GR. 4, Vol. 1

Carpenter: *Adventures in a Perambulator*—"The Hurdy-Gurdy," GR. 5, Vol. 2

Chabrier:
   España Rapsodie, GR. 5, Vol. 1
   Marche Joyeuse, GR. 4, Vol. 1

Charpentier: *Impressions of Italy*—"On Muleback," GR. 5, Vol. 1

Cimarosa: *Cimarosiana*—Non Troppo Mosso, GR. 2, Vol. 2

Coates: London Suite—"Knightsbridge March," GR. 5, Vol. 2

Copland:
   Billy the Kid Ballet Suite—"Street in a Frontier Town," GR. 6, Vol. 1
   The Red Pony Suite—"Circus Music," GR. 3, Vol. 1
   The Red Pony Suite—"Dream March," GR. 2, Vol. 2
   Rodeo—"Hoe-Down," GR. 5, Vol. 2

Corelli-Pinelli: Suite for Strings—Sarabande, GR. 6, Vol. 2

Debussy:
   Children's Corner Suite—"The Snow is Dancing," GR. 3, Vol. 1
   La Mer—"Play of the Waves," GR. 6, Vol. 2

Delibes:
   Coppelia—"Waltz of the Doll," GR. 1, Vol. 1
   Coppelia—"Swanhilde's Waltz," GR. 2, Vol. 2
   The King Is Amused—"Lesquercarde," GR. 1, Vol. 2

Dvořák: Slavonic Dance No. 7, GR. 4, Vol. 2

Elgar:
   Wand of Youth Suite No. 1—"Fairies and Giants," GR. 3, Vol. 1
   Wand of Youth Suite No. 1—"Sun Dance," GR. 2, Vol. 2
   Wand of Youth Suite No. 2—"Fountain Dance," GR. 2, Vol. 1

Falla: *La Vida Breve*—Spanish Dance No. 1, GR. 6, Vol. 1

Fauré: *Dolly*—Berceuse, GR. 2, Vol. 1

German: *Henry VIII* Suite—"Morris Dance," GR. 1, Vol. 2

Ginastera: *Estancia*—"Wheat Dance," GR. 4, Vol. 1

Glière: *The Red Poppy*—"Russian Sailors' Dance," GR. 6, Vol. 2

Gluck:
   Armide Ballet Suite—Musette, GR. 2, Vol. 2
   Iphigenie in Aulis—"Air Gai," GR. 1, Vol. 1

Gottschalk-Kay: *Cakewalk* Ballet Suite—"Grand Walkaround," GR. 5, Vol. 1

Gould: *American Salute,* GR. 5, Vol. 1

Gounod: *Faust* Ballet Suite—Waltz No. 1, GR. 3, Vol. 1

Grainger: "Londonderry Air," GR. 4, Vol. 2

Gretry:
Cephale et Procris—Gigue (Arr. by Mottl), GR. 1, Vol. 1
Cephale et Procris—Tambourin (Arr. by Mottl), GR 2, Vol. 1

Grieg:
Lyric Suite—"Norwegian Rustic March," GR. 4, Vol. 1
Peer Gynt Suite No. 1—"Anitra's Dance," GR. 1, Vol. 2
Peer Gynt Suite No. 1—"In the Hall of the Mountain King," GR. 3, Vol. 2

Griffes: *The White Peacock,* GR. 6, Vol. 1

Grofé: *Death Valley* Suite—"Desert Water Hole," GR. 4, Vol. 1

Guarnieri: Brazilian Dance, GR. 6, Vol. 2

Handel:
Royal Fireworks Music—Bourrée, Minuetto No. 2, GR. 3, Vol. 2
Water Music—Hornpipe, GR. 2, Vol. 1

Hanson:
For the First Time—"Bells," GR. 1, Vol. 2
Merry Mount Suite—"Children's Dance," GR. 3, Vol. 1

Herbert:
Babes in Toyland—"March of the Toys," GR. 2, Vol. 1
Natoma—"Dagger Dance," GR. 3, Vol. 1

Holst: *The Perfect Fool*—"Spirit of the Earth," GR. 6, Vol. 2

Howe: "Sand," GR. 2, Vol. 2

Humperdinck: *Hansel and Gretel*—Prelude, GR. 5, Vol. 2

Ibert:
Divertissement—"Parada," GR. 1, Vol. 1
Histories No. 2—"The Little White Donkey," GR. 2, Vol. 1

Kabalevsky:
The Comedians—March, "Comedians Galop," GR. 3, Vol. 1
The Comedians—"Pantomime," GR. 1, Vol. 1
The Comedians—Waltz, GR. 1, Vol. 2

Khachaturian:
Gayne Ballet Suite—"Dance of the Rose Maidens," GR. 1, Vol. 2
Masquerade Suite—Waltz, GR. 4, Vol. 2

Kodály:
Háry Janós Suite—"Entrance of the Emperor and His Court," GR. 4, Vol. 2
Háry Janós Suite—"Viennese Musical Clock," GR. 2, Vol. 1

Lecuona: *Suite Andalucia*—"Andalucia," GR. 4, Vol. 1

Liadov: Eight Russian Folk Songs—Berceuse, GR. 1, Vol. 2

Lully: Ballet Suite—March, GR. 3, Vol. 2

MacDowell: *Second (Indian) Suite*—"In Wartime," GR. 5, Vol. 1

Massenet: *Le Cid*—"Aragonaise," GR. 1, Vol. 1

McBride:
Pumpkin Eater's Little Fugue, GR. 2, Vol. 2
Punch and the Judy—"Pony Express," GR. 1, Vol. 2

McDonald:
Children's Symphony (1st Movement)—*"London Bridge," "Baa, Baa Black Sheep,"* GR. 3, Vol. 2
Children's Symphony (3rd Movement)—*"Farmer In The Dell," "Jingle Bells,"* GR. 2, Vol. 1

Menotti:
  Amahl and the Night Visitors—"March of the Kings," GR. 1, Vol. 2
  Amahl and the Night Visitors—"Shepherds' Dance," GR. 4, Vol. 2

Meyerbeer: *Les Patineurs*—Waltz, GR. 2, Vol. 1

Milhaud:
  Saudades do Brazil—"Copacabana," GR. 4, Vol. 2
  Saudades do Brazil—"Laranjeiras," GR. 2, Vol. 1
  Suite Provencale—"Modere No. 1," GR. 1, Vol. 2

Moore: *Farm Journal*—"Harvest Song," GR. 1, Vol. 2

Moussorgsky:
  Pictures at an Exhibition—"Ballet of the Unhatched Chicks" (Orchestrated by Ravel), GR. 1, Vol. 1
  Pictures at an Exhibition—"Bydlo" (Orchestrated by Ravel), GR. 2, Vol. 1
  Pictures at an Exhibition—"Promenade" (Orchestrated by Ravel), GR. 1, Vol. 2

Mozart:
  Divertimento No. 17—Menuetto No. 1, GR. 5, Vol. 2
  Eine kleine Nachtmusik—Romanze, GR. 4, Vol. 1
  The Little Nothings, No. 8, GR. 1, Vol. 2

Offenbach: *The Tales of Hoffmann*—Barcarolle, GR. 3, Vol. 1

Pierné: *Cydalise* Suits No. 1—"Entrance of the Little Fauns," GR. 2, Vol. 2

Prokofiev:
  Children's Suite—"Waltz on the Ice," GR. 3, Vol. 2
  Lieutenant Kije—Troika, GR. 2, Vol. 2
  Summer Day Suite—March, GR. 1, Vol. 1
  Winter Holiday—"Departure," GR. 2, Vol. 1

Ravel:
  Mother Goose Suite—"The Conversations of Beauty and the Beast," GR. 5, Vol. 1
  Mother Goose Suite— "Laideronnette, Empress of the Pagodas," GR. 4, Vol. 2

Respighi:
  The Birds—Prelude, GR. 2, Vol. 2
  Brazilian Impressions—Danza, GR. 5, Vol. 2
  Pines of Rome—"Pines of the Villa Borghese," GR. 4, Vol. 1

Rimsky-Korsakov:
  Le Coq d'Or Suite—"Bridal Procession," GR. 4, Vol. 1
  The Snow Maiden—"Dance of the Buffoons," GR. 2, Vol. 2

Rossini: *William Tell* Overture—Finale, GR. 3, Vol. 1

Rossini-Britten:
  Matinees Musicales—Waltz, GR. 1, Vol. 2
  Soirees Musicales—Bolero, GR. 2, Vol. 2
  Soirees Musicales—March, GR. 1, Vol. 1

Rossini-Respighi:
  The Fantastic Toyshop—Can-Can, GR. 2, Vol. 1
  The Fantastic Toyshop—Tarantella, GR. 3, Vol. 2

Saint-Saëns:
  Carnival of the Animals—"The Elephant," GR. 1, Vol. 2
  Carnival of the Animals—"The Swan," GR. 3, Vol. 2

Scarlatti-Tommasini: *The Good-Humored Ladies*—Non Presto MA A Tempo Di Ballo, GR. 4, Vol. 2

Schubert: Symphony No. 5—First Movement, GR. 5, Vol. 1

Schuller: Seven Studies on Themes of Paul Klee—"The Twittering Machine," GR. 2, Vol. 2

Schumann: *Scenes from Childhood*—Traumerei, GR. 4, Vol. 2

Shostakovich:
Ballet Suite No. 1—"Petite Ballerina," GR. 2, Vol. 1
Ballet Suite No. 1—"Pizzicato Polka," GR. 1, Vol. 1

Sibelius: *Karelia* Suite—Alla Marcia, GR. 5, Vol. 1

Smetana: *The Bartered Bride*—"Dance of the Comedians," GR. 6, Vol. 2

Sousa:
Semper Fidelis, GR. 3, Vol. 2
Stars and Stripes Forever, GR. 4, Vol. 2

Strauss, R.: *Der Rosenkavalier*—Suite, GR. 6, Vol. 1

Stravinsky:
The Firebird Suite—Berceuse, GR. 1, Vol. 1
The Firebird Suite—"Infernal Dance of King Kastchei," GR. 5, Vol. 2
Petrouchka—"Russian Dance," GR. 1, Vol. 2

Taylor: *Through the Looking Glass*—"Garden of Live Flowers," GR. 3, Vol. 2

Tchiakovsky:
Nutcracker Suite—"Dance of the Sugar Plum Fairy," "Dance of the Reed Pipes," GR. 1, Vol. 2
The Sleeping Beauty—"Puss-in-Boots and the White Cat," GR. 3, Vol. 1
The Sleeping Beauty—Waltz, GR. 4, Vol. 1
Swan Lake—"Dance of the Little Swans," GR. 1, Vol. 1
Symphony No. 4—Fourth Movement, GR. 6, Vol. 2

Thomson:
Acadian Songs and Dances—"The Alligator and the 'Coon,' " GR. 3, Vol. 2
Acadian Songs and Dances—"Walking Song," GR. 1, Vol. 1

Vaughan-Williams:
Fantasia on "Greensleeves," GR. 6, Vol. 2
The Wasps—"March Past of the Kitchen Utensils," GR. 3, Vol. 1

Villa-Lobos: *Bachianas Brasileiras* No. 2—"The Little Train of the Caipira, GR. 3, Vol. 1

Wagner: *Lohengrin*—Prelude to Act III, GR. 6, Vol. 1

Walton: *Facade* Suite—Valse, GR. 6, Vol. 2

Webern: Five Movements for String Orchestra—Sehr Langsam, GR. 2, Vol. 2

Compositions in the

BOWMAR ORCHESTRAL LIBRARY

Appendix

Complete Listing of the Bowmar Orchestral Library, Series 1, 2, and 3

Series 1 ANIMALS AND CIRCUS (BOL #51)

CARNIVAL OF THE ANIMALS, Saint-Saëns. (Introduction, Royal March of the Lion, Hens and Cocks, Fleet Footed Animals, Turtles, The Elephant, Kangaroos, Aquarium, Long Eared Personages, Cuckoo in the Deep Woods, Aviary, Pianists, Fossils, The Swan, Finale)

CIRCUS POLKA, Stravinsky

UNDER THE BIG TOP, Donaldson. (Marching Band, Acrobats, Juggler, Merry-Go-Round, Elephants, Clowns, Camels, Tightrope Walker, Pony Trot, Marching Band.)

NATURE AND MAKE-BELIEVE (BOL #52)

MARCH OF THE DWARFS, Grieg

ONCE UPON A TIME SUITE, Donaldson. (Chicken Little, Three Billy Goats Gruff, Little Train, Hare and the Tortoise)

455 THE LARK SONG (*Scenes of Youth*), Tchaikovsky

LITTLE BIRD, Grieg

DANCE OF THE MOSQUITO, Liadov

FLIGHT OF THE BUMBLE BEE, Rimsky-Korsakov

SEASON FANTASIES, Donaldson. (Magic Piper, The Poet and his Lyre, The Anxious Leaf, The Snowmaiden)

TO THE RISING SUN (Fjord and Mountain, Norwegian Suite 2), Torjussen

CLAIRE DE LUNE, Debussy

PICTURES AND PATTERNS (BOL #53)

PIZZICATO (*Fantastic Toyshop*), Rossini-Respighi

MARCH-TRUMPET AND DRUM (*Jeux d'Enfants*), IMPROMPTU-THE TOP (*Jeux d'Enfants*), Bizet

POLKA (*Mlle. Angot* Suite), GAVOTTE (*Mlle. Angot* Suite), Lecocq

INTERMEZZO (*The Comedians*), Kabalevsky

GERMAN WALTZ-PAGANINI (*Carnaval*), Schumann-Glazounov

BALLET PETIT, Donaldson

MINUET, Mozart

A GROUND, Handel

CHOPIN (*Carnaval*), Schumann-Glazounov

VILLAGE DANCE, Liadov

EN BATEAU (In a Boat), Debussy

HARBOR VIGNETTES, Donaldson (Fog and Storm, Song of the Bell Buoy, Sailing)

MARCHES (BOL #54)

ENTRANCE OF THE LITTLE FAUNS, Pierné

MARCH, Prokofiev

POMP AND CIRCUMSTANCE #1, Elgar

HUNGARIAN MARCH (*Rakoczy*), Berlioz

COL. BOGEY MARCH, Alford

MARCH OF THE LITTLE LEAD SOLDIERS, Pierné

MARCH (*Love for Three Oranges*), Prokofiev

CORTEGE OF THE SARDAR (*Caucasian Sketches*), Ippolitov-Ivanov

MARCHE MILITAIRE, Schubert

STARS AND STRIPES FOREVER, Sousa

THE MARCH OF THE SIAMESE CHILDREN (*The King and I*), Rodgers

DANCES, PART I (BOL #55)

DANCE OF THE CAMORRISTI, Wolf-Ferrari

DANCA BRASILEIRA, Guarnieri

GAVOTTE, Kabalevsky

SLAVONIC DANCE #1, Dvořák

HOE-DOWN (Rodeo), Copland

FACADE SUITE, Walton (Polka, Country Dance, Popular Song)

HUNGARIAN DANCE #5, Brahms

SKATER'S WALTZES, Waldteufel

MAZURKA (*Masquerade* Suite), Khatchaturian

GALOP (*Masquerade* Suite), Khatchaturian

DANCES, PART II (BOL #56)

FOLK DANCES FROM SOMERSET (*English Folk Song* Suite), Vaughan-Williams

JAMAICAN RUMBA, Benjamin

BADINERIE, Corelli

DANCE OF THE COMEDIANS, Smetana

CAN CAN (*Mlle. Angot* Suite), Lecocq

GRAND WALTZ (*Mlle. Angot* Suite), Lecocq

TRISCH-TRASCH POLKA, Strauss

TARANTELLA (*Fantastic Toyshop*), WALTZ (*Fantastic Toyshop*), Rossini-Respighi

ESPAÑA WALTZES, Waldteufel

ARKANSAS TRAVELER, Guion

RUSSIAN DANCE (*Gayne* Suite #2), Khatchaturian

FAIRY TALES IN MUSIC (BOL #57)

CINDERELLA, Coates

SCHERZO (*Midsummer Night's Dream*), Mendelssohn

MOTHER GOOSE SUITE, Ravel (Pavane of the Sleeping Beauty, Hop o' My Thumb, Laideronette, Empress of the Pagodas, Beauty and the Beast, The Fairy Garden)

STORIES IN BALLET AND OPERA (BOL #58)

SUITE FROM AMAHL AND THE NIGHT VISITORS, Menotti (Introduction, March of the Three Kings, Dance of the Shepherds)

HANSEL AND GRETEL OVERTURE, Humperdinck

NUTCRACKER SUITE, Tchaikovsky (Overture Miniature, March, Dance of the Sugar-Plum Fairy, Trepak, Arabian Dance, Chinese Dance, Dance of the Toy Flutes, Waltz of the Flowers)

LEGENDS IN MUSIC (BOL #59)

DANSE MACABRE, Saint-Saëns

PEER GYNT SUITE #1, Grieg (Morning, Asa's Death, Anitra's Dance, In the Hall of the Mountain King)

SORCERER'S APPRENTICE, Dukas

PHAETON, Saint-Saëns

UNDER MANY FLAGS (BOL #60)

THE MOLDAU, Smetana

LAPLAND IDYLL (Fjord and Mountain, Norwegian Suite #2), Torjussen

FOLK SONG (Fjord and Mountain, Norwegian Suite #2), Torjussen

LONDONDERRY AIR, Grainger

FINLANDIA, Sibelius

LONDON SUITE, Coates (Covent Garden, Westminster, Knightsbridge March)

AMERICAN SCENES (BOL #61)

GRAND CANYON SUITE, Grofé (Sunrise, Painted Desert, On the Trail, Sunset, Cloudburst)

MISSISSIPPI SUITE, Grofé (Father of Waters, Huckleberry Finn, Old Creole Days, Mardi Gras)

Series 2

MASTERS IN MUSIC (BOL #62)

JESU, JOY OF MAN'S DESIRING, Bach

BOURRÉE FROM FIREWORKS MUSIC, Handel

VARIATIONS (from *Sunrise* Symphony), Hadyn

MINUET (from Symphony #40), Mozart

SCHERZO (from Seventh Symphony), Beethoven

WEDDING DAY AT TROLDHAUGEN, Grieg

RIDE OF THE VALKYRIES, Wagner

TRIUMPHAL MARCH (*Aïda*), Verdi

HUNGARIAN DANCE #6, Brahms

THIRD MOVEMENT, SYMPHONY #1, Mahler

CONCERT MATINEE (BOL #63)

CHILDREN'S CORNER SUITE, Debussy, (Doctor Gradus ad Parnassum, Jumbo's Lullaby, Serenade of the Doll, The Snow is Dancing, The Little Shepherd, Golliwog's Cakewalk)

SUITE FOR STRING ORCHESTRA, Corelli-Pinelli (Sarabande, Gigue, Badinerie)

MINUET (from *Surprise* Symphony), Haydn

ANVIL CHORUS, Verdi, (*Il Trovatore*)

NORWEGIAN DANCE IN A (#2), Grieg

TRAUMEREI, Schumann

MINIATURES IN MUSIC (BOL #64)

CHILDREN'S SYMPHONY, Zador

THE BEE, Schubert

GYPSY RONDO, Haydn

WILD HORSEMEN, Schumann

HAPPY FARMER, Schumann

LITTLE WINDMILLS, Couperin

ARIETTA, Leo

MUSIC BOX, Liadov

FUNERAL MARCH OF THE MARIONETTES, Gounod

DANCE OF THE MERRY DWARFS (*Happy Hypocrite*), Elwell

LITTLE TRAIN OF CAIPIRA, Villa-Lobos

MUSIC, USA (BOL #65)

SHAKER TUNE (*Appalachian Spring*), Copland

CATTLE & BLUES (*Plow that Broke the Plains*), Thompson

FUGUE AND CHORALE ON YANKEE DOODLE (*Tuesday in November*), Thomson

PUMPKIN EATERS LITTLE FUGUE, McBride

AMERICAN SALUTE, Gould

POP! GOES THE WEASEL, Cailliet

LAST MOVEMENT, SYMPHONY #2, Ives

ORIENTAL SCENES (BOL #66)

WOODCUTTER'S SONG, Koyama

THE EMPEROR'S NIGHTINGALE, Donaldson

SAKURA (folk tune), played by koto and bamboo flute

FANTASY IN MUSIC (BOL #67)

THREE BEARS, Coates

CINDERELLA, Prokofiev (Sewing Scene, Cinderella's Gavotte, Midnight Waltz, Fairy Godmother)

MOON LEGEND, Donaldson

SLEEPING BEAUTY WALTZ, Tchaikovsky

CLASSROOM CONCERT (BOL #68)

ALBUM FOR THE YOUNG, Tchaikovsky. (Morning Prayer, Winter Morning, Hobby Horse, Mamma, March of the Tin Soldiers, Sick Doll, Doll's Burial, New Doll, Waltz, Mazurka, Russian Song, Peasant Plays the Accordion, Folk Song, Polka, Italian Song, Old French Song, German Song, Neapolitan Dance Song, Song of the Lark, Hand-organ Man, Nurse's Tale, The Witch, Sweet Dreams, In Church)

OVER THE HILLS, Grainger

MEMORIES OF CHILDHOOD, Pinto (Run, Run; Ring Around the Rosie; March; Sleeping Time; Hobby Horse)

LET US RUN ACROSS THE HILL, Villa-Lobos

MY DAUGHTER LIDI, TEASING, GRASSHOPPER'S WEDDING, Bartók

DEVIL'S DANCE, Stravinsky

LITTLE GIRL IMPLORING HER MOTHER, Rebikov

Series 3 ## MUSIC OF THE DANCE: STRAVINSKY (BOL #69)

FIREBIRD SUITE (L'Oiseau de Feu) (Koschai's Enchanted Garden, Dance of the Firebird, Dance of the Princesses, Infernal Dance of Koschai, Magic Sleep of the Princess Tzarevna, Finale: Escape of Koschai's Captives.)

SACRIFICIAL DANCE from "The Rite of Spring" (*Le Sacre du Printemps*)

VILLAGE FESTIVAL from "The Fairy's Kiss" (Le Baiser de la Fée)

PALACE OF THE CHINESE EMPEROR from *The Nightingale* (*Le Rossignol*)

TANGO, WALTZ AND RAGTIME from *The Soldier's Tale* (*L'Histoire du Soldat*)

MUSIC OF THE SEA AND SKY (BOL #70)

CLOUDS (Nuages), Debussy

FESTIVALS (Fêtes), Debussy

MERCURY from *The Planets*, Holst

SEA PIECE WITH BIRDS, Thomson

OVERTURE TO "THE FLYING DUTCHMAN" (*Der fliegende Holländer*), Wagner

DIALOGUE OF THE WIND AND SEA from *The Sea* (*La Mer*), Debussy

SYMPHONIC MOVEMENTS, NO. 1 (BOL #71)

FIRST MOVEMENT, SYMPHONY No. 40, Mozart

SECOND MOVEMENT, SYMPHONY No. 8, Beethoven

THIRD MOVEMENT, SYMPHONY No. 4, Tchaikovsky

SECOND MOVEMENT, SYMPHONY No. 4, Schumann

THIRD MOVEMENT, SYMPHONY No. 3, Brahms

FOURTH MOVEMENT, SYMPHONY No. 3, Saint-Saëns

SYMPHONIC MOVEMENTS, No. 2 (BOL #72)

FIRST MOVEMENT, SYMPHONY No. 9 (*From the New World*), Dvořák

FIRST MOVEMENT, SYMPHONY No. 5, Beethoven

FIRST MOVEMENT (Boisterous Bourrée), A SIMPLE SYMPHONY, Britten

SECOND MOVEMENT, SYMPHONY No. 2, Hanson

FIRST MOVEMENT, SYMPHONY No. 2, Sibelius

SYMPHONIC STYLES (BOL #73)

SYMPHONY No. 99 (*Imperial*), Haydn (Adagio: Vivace Assai, Adagio, Minuetto, Vivace)

CLASSICAL SYMPHONY, Prokofiev (Allegro, Larghetto, Gavotte: Non troppo allegro, Molto vivace)

TWENTIETH CENTURY AMERICA (BOL #74)

EL SALON MEXICO, Copland

DANZON from *Fancy Free,* Bernstein

EXCERPTS, SYMPHONIC DANCES from *West Side Story,* Bernstein

AN AMERICAN IN PARIS, Gershwin

U.S. HISTORY IN MUSIC (BOL #75)

A LINCOLN PORTRAIT, Copland

CHESTER from NEW ENGLAND TRIPTYCH, Schumann

PUTNAM'S CAMP from *Three Places in New England,* Ives

INTERLUDE from FOLK SYMPHONY, Harris

MIDNIGHT RIDE OF PAUL REVERE from Selections from McGuffey's Readers, Phillips

OVERTURES (BOL #76)

OVERTURE TO "THE BAT" (*Die Fledermaus*), Strauss

ACADEMIC FESTIVAL OVERTURE, Brahms

OVERTURE TO "THE MARRIAGE OF FIGARO," Mozart

ROMAN CARNIVAL OVERTURE, Berlioz

OVERTURE TO "WILLIAM TELL," Rossini (Dawn, Storm, Calm, Finale)

SCHEHERAZADE BY RIMSKY-KORSAKOV (BOL #77)

The Sea and Sinbad's Ship, Tale of the Prince Kalendar, The Young Prince and the Princess, The Festival at Bagdad

MUSICAL KALEIDOSCOPE (BOL #78)

ON THE STEPPES OF CENTRAL ASIA, Borodin

IN THE VILLAGE FROM CAUCASIAN SKETCHES, Ippolitoff-Ivanov

EXCERPTS, POLOVTSIAN DANCES FROM "PRINCE IGOR," Borodin

RUSSIAN SAILORS' DANCE FROM "THE RED POPPY," Glière

L'ARLESIENNE SUITE No. 1, Bizet (Carillon, Minuet)

L'ARLESIENNE SUITE No. 2, Bizet (Farandole)

PRELUDE TO ACT 1, "CARMEN," Bizet

MARCH TO THE SCAFFOLD, from *Symphonie Fantastique,* Berlioz

MUSIC OF THE DRAMA: WAGNER (BOL #79)

"LOHENGRIN" (Overture to Act 1, Prelude to Act 3)

"THE TWILIGHT OF THE GODS" (*Die 'Götterdämmerung*) (Siegfried's Rhine Journey)

"THE MASTERSINGERS OF NUREMBERG" (*Die Meistersinger von Nürnberg*) (Prelude, Dance of the Apprentices and Entrance of the Mastersingers)

"TRISTAN AND ISOLDE" (Love Death)

PETROUCHKA BY STRAVINSKY (BOL #80)

COMPLETE BALLET SCORE WITH NARRATION

ROGUES IN MUSIC (BOL #81)

TILL EULENSPIELGEL, Strauss

LIEUTENANT KIJE, Prokofiev Birth of Kije, Troika

HÁRY JANÓS, Kodály (Viennese Musical Clock, Battle and Defeat of Napoleon, Intermezzo, Entrance of the Emperor)

MUSICAL PICTURES: MOUSSORGSKY (BOL #82)

PICTURES AT AN EXHIBITION (Promenade Theme, The Gnome, The Old Castle, Tuileries, Ox-Cart, Ballet of Chicks in Their Shells, Goldenberg and Schmuyle, The Market Place at Limoges, Catacombs, The Hut of Baga Yaga, The Gate of Kiev)

NIGHT ON BALD MOUNTAIN

ENSEMBLES, LARGE AND SMALL (BOL #83)

YOUNG PERSON'S GUIDE TO THE ORCHESTRA, Britten

CANZONA IN C MAJOR FOR BRASS ENSEMBLE AND ORGAN, Gabrieli

CHORALE: AWAKE, THOU WINTRY EARTH, Bach

FOURTH MOVEMENT, "TROUT" QUINTET, Schubert

THEME AND VARIATIONS FOR PERCUSSION QUARTET, Kraft

THEME AND VARIATIONS from SERENADE FOR WIND INSTRUMENTS, Mozart (K361)

462

For
Further
Study

CONCERTOS (BOL #84)

FIRST MOVEMENT, PIANO CONCERTO, Grieg

FOURTH MOVEMENT, PIANO CONCERTO No. 2, Brahms

THIRD MOVEMENT, VIOLIN CONCERTO, Mendelssohn

SECOND MOVEMENT, GUITAR CONCERTO, Castelnuovo-Tedesco

THIRD MOVEMENT, CONCERTO IN C FOR TWO TRUMPETS, Vivaldi

MUSICAL IMPRESSIONS: RESPIGHI (BOL #85)

PINES OF ROME (Pines of the Villa Borghese, Pines Near a Catacomb, Pines of the Appian Way)

FOUNTAINS OF ROME (The Fountain of Valle Giulia at Dawn, The Triton Fountain at Morning, The Trevi Fountain at Midday, The Villa Medici Fountain at Sunset)

THE BIRDS (Prelude)

FASHIONS IN MUSIC (BOL #86)

ROMEO AND JULIET (Fantasy-Overture), Tchaikovsky

LITTLE FUGUE IN G MINOR, Bach

SUITE No. 2 FROM "DAPHNIS AND CHLOË," Ravel

ROMANZE FROM A LITTLE NIGHT MUSIC (*Eine kleine Nachtmusik*), Mozart

PERIPETIA FROM FIVE PIECES FOR ORCHESTRA, Schoenberg

Publishers
of
Music Series

Appendix

ADDISON-WESLEY PUBLISHING COMPANY, Reading, Mass. 01867. *Comprehensive Musicianship through Classroom Music.*

ALLYN AND BACON, INC., Boston 02210. *This is Music for Today.*

AMERICAN BOOK COMPANY, New York 10003. *New Dimensions in Music.*

FOLLETT PUBLISHING COMPANY, Chicago 60607. *Discovering Music Together.*

GINN AND COMPANY, Boston 02117. *The Magic of Music.*

HOLT, RINEHART AND WINSTON, INC., New York 10017. *Exploring Music.*

MACMILLAN PUBLISHING CO., INC., New York 10022. *The Spectrum of Music.*

PRENTICE-HALL, INC., Englewood Cliffs, N.J. 07632. *Growing with Music.*

SILVER BURDETT COMPANY, Morristown, N.J. 07960. *Making Music Your Own* and *Silver Burdett Music.*

SUMMY-BIRCHARD, Evanston, Illinois 60204. *Birchard Music Series.*

Index of Songs

General Index